The Essential Series

What Is "Essential" About This Book?

What The Sams Publishing *Essential* series provides books that are "bare-bones," just the facts. The chapters are concise and have a task-oriented focus. This series is for readers who wonder How do I do this? and who want a straightforward answer without a lot of fluff.

Each book supplies the following:

- Direct and concise explanations of how to apply the language or product
- Simple, focused examples illustrating usage
- Specific answers to common questions:
    1. *What* is this particular topic?
    2. *Why* do I need to know the topic?
    3. *How* do I apply this information?

Why Read This "Essential" Book?

Why Most books written for beginners are full of fluff and superfluous material. Essential books are to-the-point. Although Essential books are written for people who are trying to learn a new product or language, the reader is assumed to be capable, just new to a particular subject. This series is for readers interested in learning a new subject in the quickest way possible and without any nonsense. Books in this series teach their topics in the fewest pages possible to convey the information effectively.

How The information is presented in the following manner:

What It's a new series by the industry leader, Sams Publishing, designed to give you the information you need in a clear, concise, and efficient style.

Why Because you demand a high-quality, easily referenced approach to the most difficult topics—delivered whenever new software is available.

How The Essential series focuses on the topics essential to your special interest—no cartoons, no cute diversions, just the no-nonsense approach you need to accomplish your goals.

Essential Visual C++™ 4

Mickey Williams

SAMS
PUBLISHING

201 West 103rd Street
Indianapolis, IN 46290

For Mom, the first programmer I ever knew.

Copyright © 1995 by Sams Publishing

FIRST EDITION

International Standard Book Number: 0-672-30787-1

Library of Congress Catalog Card Number: 95-74789

98 97 96 95   4 3 2 1

Interpretation of the printing code: the rightmost double-digit number is the year of the book's printing; the rightmost single-digit, the number of the book's printing. For example, a printing code of 95-1 shows that the first printing of the book occurred in 1995.

Composed in AGaramond and MCPdigital by Macmillan Computer Publishing

Printed in the United States of America

Publisher and President	*Richard K. Swadley*
Acquisitions Manager	*Greg Weigand*
Development Manager	*Dean Miller*
Managing Editor	*Cindy Morrow*
Marketing Manager	*Gregg Bushyeager*

Acquisitions Editor
Bradley L. Jones

Development Editor
Anthony Amico

Production Editor
Deborah Frisby

Copy Editors
Anne Barrett
Kris Simmons

Technical Reviewer
Greg Guntle

Editorial Coordinator
Bill Whitmer

Technical Edit Coordinator
Lynette Quinn

Formatter
Frank Sinclair

Editorial Assistants
Sharon Cox
Andi Richter
Rhonda Tinch-Mize

Cover Designer
Jay Corpus

Book Designer
Alyssa Yesh

Production Team Supervisor
Brad Chinn

Production
Mary Ann Abramson
Georgiana Briggs
Michael Brumitt
Terrie Deemer
Cheryl Dietsch
Louisa Klucznik
Ayanna Lacey
Paula Lowell
Kevin Laseau
Donna Martin
Casey Price
Brian-Kent Profitt

Overview

	Introduction	xxiii
PART I	**The Visual C++ Development System**	**1**
1	Introducing Visual C++ 4 Developer Studio	3
2	Exploring Developer Studio	11
3	Writing Simple C++ Programs	21
PART II	**The C++ Language**	**35**
4	C++ Basics	37
5	Control Structures and Classes	49
6	Arrays, Strings, and Polymorphism	63
7	Scope, Pointers, and Lifetime in C++	75
PART III	**The Microsoft Foundation Class (MFC) Library**	**89**
8	Object-Oriented Design and Virtual Functions	91
9	MFC Base Classes	103
10	Templates and the Standard Template Library	113
11	Collection Classes	125
12	Exception Handling and RTTI	133
PART IV	**The Windows Environment**	**141**
13	Using Visual C++ for Windows Programming	143
14	Messages and Event-Driven Programming	155
15	Menus	167
16	Dialog Boxes	177
PART V	**Control Classes**	**191**
17	Button Controls	193
18	Using Edit Controls	205
19	Using List-Box and Combo-Box Controls	217
20	Using Image Lists and Bitmaps	231
PART VI	**View Classes**	**241**
21	Tree Views	243
22	Up-Down, Progress, and Slider Controls	255
23	Control Bars	265
24	List View Controls	279

25 Document/View Architecture   291

26 Using Form Views   301

27 Multiple Views   311

28 Split Views   323

PART VII The Graphics Interface   **335**

29 Device Contexts   337

30 Using Pens   347

31 Brushes   359

32 Fonts   371

33 Icons   383

34 Cursors   391

PART VIII Miscellaneous Topics   **399**

35 Printing   401

36 Using Property Pages and Property Sheets   409

37 Rich Edit Controls   421

38 Subclassing and Superclassing Controls   433

39 Owner Drawn Controls   441

40 Using OLE Controls   453

41 Serialization   465

42 Serialization and Document/View   473

    Index   483

Contents

Introduction   **xxiii**

PART I   The Visual C++ Development System   **1**

1   **Introducing Visual C++ 4 Developer Studio**   **3**

What Is Visual C++ 4? 3
     The Visual C++ Environment 4
     MFC Libraries 5
     The Standard Template Library 6
Why Use Visual C++ 4? 6
How Is Visual C++ 4 Used? 7
     The Visual C++ Package 7
     Installing Visual C++ 7
     Using Developer Studio 9
     Integrating Developer Studio with Other Tools.......................9
     Building Applications with Developer Studio and Visual C++ 10
Summary 10

2   **Exploring Developer Studio**   **11**

What Is the Developer Studio Editor? 11
Why Use the Developer Studio Editor? 12
How Is the Developer Studio Editor Used? 12
     Editing a New Source File 12
     Saving a Source File 13
     Opening an Existing Source File 14
     Using Editor Commands 14
What Is InfoViewer? 15
Why Use InfoViewer? 15
How Is InfoViewer Used? 15
     Using Dockable Windows in Developer Studio 16
     Getting Context-Sensitive Help 16
     Searching for Help Using a Keyword 17
     Browsing Through the Contents Window 17
What Is AppWizard? 18
Why Use AppWizard? 18
How Is AppWizard Used? 18
     Compiling a Project 19
Summary 20

3   **Writing Simple C++ Programs**   **21**

What Is a Console Mode Program? 21
Why Write a Console Mode Program? 22

How Is a Simple Console Mode C++ Program Written? 22
  Components of a C++ Program 22
  Creating a Visual C++ Project 23
  Creating Your First C++ Source File 25
  Running Your First C++ Program 26
  The Basic Elements of a C++ Program 26
What Are Statements and Expressions? 27
Why Use Statements and Expressions? 28
How Are Statements and Expressions Used? 28
  Statements 28
  Declarations 28
  Assignment 29
  Other Common Expressions and Operators 29
  Relational Expressions and Operators 30
What Is an MFC Program? 31
Why Use an MFC Program? 31
How Is a Simple MFC Windows Program Written? 31
Summary 33

PART II The C++ Language   35

4   **C++ Basics**   37
What Are Variables? 37
Why Use Variables? 37
How Are Variables Used in C++? 38
  Understanding Type Safety 38
  Using Different Variable Types 40
  Variable Naming 41
  Assigning Values to Variables 43
What Are Functions? 43
Why Use Functions? 43
How Are Functions Used? 44
  Declaring Function Prototypes 44
  Defining Functions 45
  Calling Functions 46
  Using Function Return Values 47
Summary 48

5   **Control Structures and Classes**   49
What Is Execution Flow? 49
How Is Execution Flow Controlled? 50
  Selecting an Execution Path 50
  Executing Sequences in Your Program 54

What Are Data Structures? 56

Why Use Data Structures? 56

How Are Structures Used? 57

What Are Classes? 57

Why Are Classes Important? 58

How Are Classes Defined? 58

    Member Functions 58

    Constructors 60

    Destructors 60

    Summary 61

6   Arrays, Strings, and Polymorphism   63

What Are Arrays? 63

Why Use Arrays? 64

How Are Arrays Used? 64

    Declaring An Array 64

    Initializing Arrays 65

    Using Arrays 65

    Using Arrays as Function Parameters 66

What Are Character Strings? 68

How Are Character Strings Used? 68

    Using Character-Based String Functions 68

What Is the MFC *CString* Class? 70

Why Use the MFC *CString* Class? 70

How Is the MFC *CString* Class Used? 70

    Commonly Used *CString* Functions 70

What Is Polymorphism? 72

Summary 73

7   Scope, Pointers, and Lifetime in C++   75

What Is Scope? 75

Why Is Scope Important? 76

How Is Scope Used? 76

    Local Scope 76

    Function Prototype Scope 77

    Function Scope 77

    Class Scope 78

What Is Identifier Lifetime? 80

Why Is Identifier Lifetime Important? 80

How Is Identifier Lifetime Used? 80

    Static Lifetime 81

What Are Pointers? 82

Why Are Pointers Important? 82

How Are Pointers Used? 82
   The Indirection and Address Operators 83
   Using the Indirection Operator 83
  Summary 88

PART III The Microsoft Foundation Class (MFC) Library   89

8   **Object-Oriented Design and Virtual Functions**   **91**

What Is Object-Oriented Design? 91
Why Is Object-Oriented Design Useful? 92
How Is Object-Oriented Design Used? 92
   Describing Objects in a Class 93
   Organizing Classes and Objects 93
   Using Inheritance 95
   Using Pointers With Derived Classes 96
   Using a Pointer to a Base Class 97
   Using Virtual Functions 98
   Using Pure Virtual Functions 99
   Using Virtual Destructors 100
  Summary 102

9   **MFC Base Classes**   **103**

What Are MFC Base Classes? 103
   The *CObject* Base Class 104
   The *CWnd* Base Class 104
Why Use MFC Base Classes? 105
How Are the MFC Base Classes Used? 105
   Using *CObject* as a Base Class 105
   Using *CWnd* as a Base Class 110
  Summary 111

10   **Templates and the Standard Template Library**   **113**

What Are Templates? 113
Why Use Templates? 114
How Are Templates Used? 114
   A *CStack* Template Class 114
   Using Template Functions 117
What Is the Standard Template Library? 118
Why Use the Standard Template Library? 118
How Is the Standard Template Library Used? 119
   Using Containers 119
   Using Iterators 120
   Using Function Objects 121

Using the STL Algorithms 121
An STL Example 122
Summary 123

11   Collection Classes   125
What Are Collections? 125
Why Use Collections? 126
How Is the *CList* Collection Class Used? 127
How Is the *CArray* Collection Class Used? 128
How Is the *CMap* Collection Class Used? 130
Summary 131

12   Exception Handling and RTTI   133
What Is Run Time Type Information? 133
Why Use RTTI? 134
How Is RTTI Used? 134
What Is Exception Handling? 136
Why Use Exception Handling? 136
How Is Exception Handling Used? 137
Detecting Error Conditions 137
Using Exceptions to Detect Errors 137
Using Exceptions to Clean Up When Errors Are Detected 139
Detecting Errors During Construction 139
Summary 140

PART IV The Windows Environment   141

13   Using Visual C++ for Windows Programming   143
What Is a Visual C++ Windows Program? 143
Why Write a Windows Program Using Visual C++? 144
What Is the MFC Class Library? 145
Why Use the MFC Class Library? 145
How Is the MFC Class Library Used? 146
Examining the MFC Hello Program 147
Using Rectangles and the *CRect* Class 148
Using Device Contexts 148
What Is AppWizard? 149
Why Use AppWizard? 150
A Quick Overview of the Document/View Architecture 150
How Is AppWizard Used? 151
Using AppWizard to Create an SDI Application 151
How to Customize a Skeleton Program Built Using AppWizard 152
Summary 153

14 **Messages and Event-Driven Programming** **155**

What Are Messages? 155

Why Are Messages Used? 156

What Are Message Queues? 157

How Are Messages Handled? 157

Using a Traditional Windows Procedure 158

What Are the Different Types of Messages? 159

What Is ClassWizard? 160

Why Use ClassWizard to Handle Messages? 160

How Is ClassWizard Used to Handle Messages? 160

What Is a Message Map? 161

A Program to Test for Mouse Clicks 162

Messages Handled by MouseTst 162

Updating the *CMouseTstView* Class 162

Running MouseTst 165

Summary 165

15 **Menus** **167**

What Is a Menu? 167

Common User Interface Elements 168

Why Use a Menu? 168

How Are Menus Used? 169

Message Routing 169

Adding New Menu Items 170

Creating a Pop-Up Menu 173

Summary 176

16 **Dialog Boxes** **177**

What Is a Dialog Box? 177

Why Use Dialog Boxes? 178

Understanding Message Boxes 178

Using Dialog Boxes for Input 178

How Are Dialog Boxes Used? 179

Adding Message Boxes 179

Using the Bitwise *OR* Operator 181

Adding a Dialog Box 181

Adding a Control 185

Creating a Class for the Dialog Box 186

Adding a Message Handler for *WM_INITDIALOG* 187

Summary 189

PART V Control Classes — 191

17 Button Controls — 193
What Is a Button? — 193
Why Are Buttons Used? — 194
  What Are Pushbuttons? — 194
  What Are Radio Buttons? — 194
  What Are Checkboxes? — 194
  What Are Group Boxes? — 194
How Are Buttons Used? — 194
What Is a Dialog Box-Based Project? — 195
Why Use a Dialog Box-Based Project? — 195
How Is a Dialog Box-Based Project Created? — 195
  Adding Buttons to a Dialog Box — 196
  Using the Dialog Box Editor — 196
  Binding a Button Control to a *CButton* Object — 199
  Adding Button Events to a Dialog Box Class — 200
  Changing a Button's Label — 201
  Enabling and Disabling Buttons — 202
  Hiding a Button — 202
What Is Tab Order? — 203
Why Is Tab Order Used? — 203
How Is the Tab Order Set? — 204
Summary — 204

18 Using Edit Controls — 205
What Is an Edit Control? — 205
Why Use an Edit Control? — 206
How Is an Edit Control Used? — 206
  Building an SDI Test Project — 207
  Adding an Edit Control to a Dialog Box — 207
  Edit Control Properties — 208
  Attaching a *CEdit* Object to an Edit Control — 210
What Are DDV and DDX Routines? — 211
Why Are DDV and DDX Routines Used? — 212
How Are DDV and DDX Routines Used? — 212
  Associating a Control's Value with a Member Variable — 213
  Exchanging Edit-Control Information Using DDX Functions — 214
Summary — 215

19   Using List-Box and Combo-Box Controls   217

What Are List Boxes? 217

Why Use a List Box? 218

How Is a List Box Used? 218

    Adding a List Box to a Dialog Box 218

    List-Box Properties 219

    Using the *CListbox* Class 220

What Are Combo Boxes? 223

Why Use a Combo Box? 224

How Is a Combo Box Used? 224

    Combo-Box Properties 225

    Adding Items to a Combo Box 225

    Collecting Input from a Combo Box 226

    A Combo-Box Example 226

    Summary 229

20   Using Image Lists and Bitmaps   231

What Is a Bitmap? 231

Why Use a Bitmap? 232

How Is a Bitmap Used? 232

    Adding a Bitmap to a Project 232

    Loading and Displaying a Bitmap 233

What Is an Image List? 234

Why Use an Image List? 235

How Is an Image List Used? 235

    Creating an Image List 235

    Displaying an Image List Using the *CImageList::Draw* Function 238

    Displaying a Transparent Image 238

    Displaying an Overlapped Image 239

    Summary 240

PART VI View Classes   241

21   Tree Views   243

What Is a Tree View Control? 243

Why Use a Tree View Control? 244

How Are Tree View Controls Used? 244

    Using a Tree View Control as a View 245

    Adding Tree View Controls to Dialog Boxes 247

    Setting Tree View Control Properties 248

    Creating an Image List Control 249

    Modifying the Dialog Box Class 250

    Tree View Control Notifications 251

    Summary 254

22   Up-Down, Progress, and Slider Controls   255

What Are Up-Down Controls? 255
Why Use an Up-Down Control? 256
How Is an Up-Down Control Used? 256
   The Sample Program 256
   Adding an Up-Down Control to a Dialog Box 256
   Up-Down Control Properties 257
   Adding a Buddy Control 257
   Changing the Range of the Up-Down Control 258
What Are Slider Controls? 259
Why Use a Slider Control? 259
How Is a Slider Control Used? 259
   Slider Control Properties 260
What Are Progress Controls? 261
Why Use Progress Controls? 261
How Are Progress Controls Used? 261
   Using a Slider to Update a Progress Control 262
Summary 263

23   Control Bars   265

What Are Control Bars? 265
The CtrlBar Sample Program 266
What Are Status Bars? 266
Why Use Status Bars? 266
How Are Status Bars Used? 266
A Status Bar Example 268
What Are Dialog Bars? 270
Why Use Dialog Bars? 271
How Are Dialog Bars Used? 271
   Creating a Dockable Dialog Bar 271
   Adding a Dialog Bar Example to the CtrlBar Project 272
What Are Toolbars? 274
Why Use Toolbars? 274
How Are Toolbars Used? 274
   Creating the Bitmap Resource 275
   Creating a Toolbar Control 275
   Adding a Toolbar Example to the CtrlBar Project 275
Summary 277

24   List View Controls   279

What Is a List View Control? 279
Why Use a List View Control? 280
How Is a List View Control Used? 280
   List View Control Properties 280

Associating Image Lists with a List Control 282

Adding Items to a List View Control 282

Adding Column Information for the Report View 283

Changing the Current View for a List View Control 284

A List View Control Example 285

Summary 289

25   Document/View Architecture   291

What Is Document/View? 291

SDI and MDI Applications 292

Why Use Document/View? 293

How Is Document/View Used? 293

Using AppWizard 293

Using ClassWizard 295

What Are the Document/View Interfaces? 296

Why Use the Document/View Interfaces? 296

How Are the Document/View Interfaces Used? 297

Creating a Data Model 297

Initializing a Document's Contents 298

Getting the Document Pointer 299

Summary 300

26   Using Form Views   301

What Is a Form View? 301

What Are the Other Types of Views? 302

Why Use a Form View? 303

How Is a Form View Used? 303

Adding a Form View to the DVTest Project 303

Creating a Dialog Resource for a Form View 304

Adding a Form View Class to a Project 305

Using *CFormView* Instead of *CView* 306

Handling Events and Messages in the Form View Class 306

Handling *OnInitialUpdate* 308

Sizing a Form View to a Dialog Resource 308

Preventing a View Class from Being Resized 309

Summary 310

27   Multiple Views   311

What Are Multiple Views? 311

Why Use Multiple Views? 312

How Are Multiple Views Used? 312

Creating a New View 313

Modifying the *OnDraw* Function 314

Creating and Maintaining Multiple Document Templates 315
Adding Shared Resource 316
Adding Menu Items for New Views 318
Updating Multiple Views 319
Adding the *OnInitialUpdate* and *OnUpdate* Member Functions 320
Summary 322

28   Split Views   323

What Are Split Views? 323
Why Use Split Views? 324
How Are Split Views Used? 324
Creating a Scrolling, Dynamic Split View 325
Creating a Static Split View 329
Summary 333

PART VII The Graphics Interface   335

29   Device Contexts   337

What Are Device Contexts? 337
Types of Device Contexts 338
Why Use Device Contexts? 338
How Are Device Contexts Used? 339
Wizard Support for Device Contexts 339
Selecting an Object 340
Collecting Information 341
Setting Mapping Modes 341
Device Context Example 343
The DCTest Program 343
Summary 346

30   Using Pens   347

What Is a Pen? 347
Why Use a Pen? 348
How Are Pens Used? 348
Using Cosmetic Pens 349
Using Geometric Pens 349
Using Color with Pens 351
Using the *CPen* Class 351
Using Stock Pens 352
Drawing with Pens 353
A GDI Example Using Pens 354
Modifying the Mapping-Mode Dialog Box 354
Modifying the *CDCTestView* Class 355
Modifying the *CDCTestView* Member Functions 355
Summary 357

31   Brushes   359

What Are Brushes? 359

Why Use a Brush? 360

How Are Brushes Used? 360

    Hatch Styles for Brushes 361

    Using the *CBrush* Class 361

    Logical Brushes 362

    Using the Common Color Dialog Box 363

A GDI Example Using Brushes 364

    Changing the Mapping-Mode Dialog Box and

        CMapModeDlg Class 364

    Handling the *WM_CTLCOLOR* Message 366

    Updating the *CDCTestView* Class 367

    Changes to *CDCTestView* Member Functions 367

Summary 369

32   Fonts   371

What Are Fonts? 371

Why Use Fonts? 373

How Are Fonts Used? 373

    Font Attributes 373

    Creating a Font Using *CFont* 377

    Creating a Font Using a *LOGFONT* Structure 378

    Using the Common Font Dialog Box 378

Summary 381

33   Icons   383

What Is an Icon? 383

Why Use an Icon? 384

How Are Icons Used? 384

    Creating Icons Using the Image Editor 384

    Loading an Icon 385

    Changing a Program's Icon 386

    Retrieving Icons from Image Lists 386

    Displaying an Icon on a Button 386

Summary 389

34   Cursors   391

What Is a Cursor? 391

Why Use a Cursor? 392

How Is a Cursor Used? 392

    Creating a Cursor Resource 392

    Adding a Hotspot to a Cursor 393

    Changing a Cursor 393

Conditionally Changing a Cursor 394
Using the Standard Cursors 395
Changing the Cursor to the Hourglass 396
Clipping a Cursor 397
Summary 398

PART VIII Miscellaneous Topics   399

35   Printing   401

What Is Printing in a Windows Program? 401
Why Use the MFC Printing Support? 402
How Is the Printer in an MFC Program Used? 402
Understanding the MFC Printing Routines 403
Exploring the *CPrintInfo* Class 404
Using the *OnPreparePrinting* Function 404
Using the *OnBeginPrinting* Function 404
Using the *OnPrepareDC* Function 405
Using the *OnPrint* Function 405
Using the *OnEndPrinting* Function 405
A Printing Example 406
The *OnBeginPrinting* Function 406
The *OnEndPrinting* Function 407
The *OnPrint* Function 407
The *OnPrepareDC* Function 408
Summary 408

36   Using Property Pages and Property Sheets   409

What Are Property Pages and Property Sheets? 409
Why Use Property Pages and Property Sheets? 410
How Are Property Pages and Property Sheets Used? 411
Creating a *CPropertySheet* Object 411
Creating a Property Page 411
Calling the Property Sheet's *DoModal* Function 413
Exchanging Data with Property Sheets and Property Sheet Pages 413
The Cool Property Sheet Example 414
Creating the Dialog Resources 414
Creating the Property Sheet 417
Handling the Apply Button 418
Summary 419

37   Rich Edit Controls   421

What Is the Rich Edit Control? 421
What Is Rich Text Format (RTF)? 422

Why Use the Rich Edit Control? 422
How Is the Rich Text Control Used? 422
    Using the Rich Edit Document/View Classes 423
    Using the *CRichEditCtrl* Class 423
    Controlling Character Formatting 423
    Using the *dwMask* and *dwEffects* Flags 424
    Controlling Paragraph Formatting 425
A Rich Edit Control Example 427
    Creating a Format Dialog Box 427
    Creating the *CFormatDlg* Class 428
    Changes to the *CRichTextView* Class 429
Summary 431

38   Subclassing and Superclassing Controls   433

What Is Subclassing and Superclassing? 433
    About Subclassing 434
    About Superclassing 435
Why Use Subclassing? 435
How Is a Control Subclassed? 435
    Subclassing an Edit Control 436
    Using a Subclassed Edit Control 437
Summary 439

39   Owner-Drawn Controls   441

What Are Owner-Drawn Controls? 441
What Are Self-Drawn Controls? 442
Why Use Owner-Drawn Controls? 442
How Are Owner-Drawn Controls Used? 442
    Handling the *WM_DRAWITEM* Message 443
    Handling the *WM_MEASUREITEM* Message 444
    Handling the *WM_COMPAREITEM* Message 445
    Handling the *WM_DELETEITEM* Message 445
    An Owner-Drawn List Box 446
    Creating the *CListItem* Structure 447
    Adding Items to the List Box 447
    Handling the Owner-Drawn Messages 448
Summary 452

40   Using OLE Controls   453

What Is an OLE Control? 453
Why Use an OLE Control? 454

How Is an OLE Control Used? 454
    Using the Component Gallery 455
    Adding an OLE Control to the Dialog Editor 455
    Using ClassWizard to Configure an OLE Control 456
An Example Using an OLE Custom Control 457
    What Is a Grid Control? 457
    Why Use a Grid Control? 457
    Adding a Grid OCX to the Dialog Editor 458
    Adding a Grid Control to the Main Dialog Box 458
    Initializing the Grid Control 459
    Detecting Grid Control Events 460
    Recalculating the Grid Control Contents 462
Summary 463

41   Serialization   465
What Is Serialization? 465
Why Use Serialization? 466
How Is Serialization Used? 467
    The MFC Classes Used for Serialization 467
    Using the Insertion and Extraction Operators 468
    Using the Serialization Macros 469
    Overriding the *Serialize* Function 470
    Creating a Serialized Collection 471
Summary 472

42   Serialization and Document/View   473
What Is Document/View Serialization? 473
Why Use Document/View Serialization? 474
How Are Document/View Applications Serialized? 474
    Creating a New Document 475
    Tracking Modifications to a Document 475
    Storing a Document 475
    Closing a Document 476
    Loading a Document 477
A Document/View Serialization Example 478
Summary 482

Index   483

Acknowledgments

I owe a huge debt of thanks to a large number of people, without whom none of this would have been possible.

First of all, thanks to all the people at Sams Publishing, especially my acquisitions editor, Brad Jones, who was a constant source of inspiration and advice. Thanks also to Tony Amico, my development editor, who gave me great advice about the book's contents; to Anne Barrett and Kris Simmons, who did a fantastic job of editing my manuscript; and to Deborah Frisby, my production editor, who managed the final author review and made a final check of the manuscript. Finally, last but not least, thanks to Greg Guntle, who provided me with a great technical review and helped out during author review.

Thanks to all my co-workers at Ericsson who gave me great support and assistance, in no special order—Farnoosh Manouchehri, Bo Stenlund, James Woo, Roger Liu, Peter Claesson, Cuyler Buckwalter, and Cherif Gad. Special thanks to Paul Stephenson, who was a great source of information about exception handling and the Standard Template Library. Special thanks to Charls Grisham, Steve Edmonds, and Brad Hendricks, who always seemed to have an extra workstation available for me to use.

Thanks to Ed Dore, who ran the Visual C++ beta forum on CompuServe and answered all my questions. I'd also like to thank Bob O'Brien and all the folks at NuMega Technologies for their help.

Last, but certainly not least, thanks to my wife, René. A wonderful wife, mother, and friend, she is much more patient than any author, especially me, deserves.

About the Author

Mickey Williams is the author of *Develop A Professional Visual C++ Application in 21 Days,* from Sams Publishing. Williams is an engineering staff member at Ericsson, Inc., where he is responsible for developing software for Ericsson's Consono family of telecommunications products. Over the past twelve years, he has held marketing, research, support, and development positions. He is a member of the Association for Computer Machinery and the IEEE Computer Society. He can be reached on CompuServe at 75460,2102; on MSN at `MickeyWilliams`; or at `Mickey.Williams@ebu.ericsson.com`.

Introduction

This book is written for programmers, beginning or experienced, who want to develop programs using Visual C++ 4. This book is a no-nonsense guide to programming for Windows, using plenty of short, concise examples, without a lot of extraneous material or theory. In most cases, the examples are limited to about one page of source code per chapter. This allows you to cover a great deal of material easily, even if you're not an expert typist.

Overview

This book is divided into eight sections, each of which focuses on a different aspect of using Visual C++:

- Part I, "The Visual C++ Development System," is a short tour of the Visual C++ compiler and its associated tools.
- Part II, "The C++ Language," is an introduction to the C++ language that assumes no experience with C, C++, or other programming languages.
- Part III, "The Microsoft Foundation Class (MFC) Library," is a discussion of the class library included with Visual C++, as well as topics on object-oriented design.
- Part IV, "The Windows Environment," covers the basics of writing programs for Windows using the MFC Class Library.
- Part V, "Control Classes," introduces controls used in Windows programming, as well as the MFC classes used to interact with them.
- Part VI, "View Classes," discusses the Document/View architecture, as well as some advanced controls and user interface objects, such as tree view controls and control bars.
- Part VII, "The Graphics Interface," introduces the Windows Graphics Device Interface and how it is used to draw shapes and fill objects in Windows.
- Part VIII, "Miscellaneous Topics," includes important topics such as printing, using owner-drawn controls, and serialization.

What's New in VC 4.0?

Visual C++ 4.0 offers many new features and improvements over its predecessor, Visual C++ 2.0. A summary of the new features that are covered in this book are these:

- The compiler has improved support for the evolving ANSI C++ draft standard. Runtime type information and namespaces are now supported, and template support has been improved.

- The development system includes MFC 4.0, the latest version of the Microsoft Foundation Classes class library. The new version of the MFC class library includes new controls for programming Windows 95 controls.

- OLE controls can be added to dialog boxes and other windows with just a few mouse clicks, much like VBX controls were added in earlier versions of the compiler.

- The development environment is automatically integrated with other Visual tools installed on your computer, such as Microsoft Test or the Microsoft Developer Network (MSDN) Library.

- An improved online help system puts over 15,000 pages of documentation in easy reach, a mouse click away. The online help system can be configured to use the MSDN library if installed on your computer.

- A new project workspace window allows you to see three different views of your project. The classes used in a project can be displayed using the class view. The files included in a project can be displayed using the file view. Resources used by a project are displayed using the resource view.

What You'll Need

This book does not assume that you have any experience with the C or C++ programming languages, although some programming experience will be helpful. The first section of the book covers many basic parts of the C++ programming language, and other parts of the book discuss C++ language concepts as they are introduced.

To use the Visual C++ compiler, you'll need to use Windows 95 or Windows NT 3.51. You'll also need at least 16 megabytes of memory and at least ten megabytes of disk space, although some installation options require up to 170 megabytes of disk storage. Like most Windows programs, Visual C++ will benefit from adding more memory; most serious programmers use 32 megabytes of RAM or more.

That's all you'll need to get started. Now it's time to turn to Chapter 1 for an introduction to the Visual C++ development system.

PART I

The Visual C++ Development System

1 Introducing Visual C++ 4 Developer Studio

2 Exploring Developer Studio

3 Writing Simple C++ Programs

Introducing Visual C++ 4 Developer Studio

In this chapter, I discuss the basic features of the new Visual C++ compiler and how it is installed and used. I also discuss the tools supplied with the compiler, such as the Microsoft Foundation Classes (MFC) class library, InstallShield, and the Standard Template Library.

What Is Visual C++ 4?

Visual C++ 4 is the latest C++ compiler from Microsoft, continuing a long line of Microsoft tools for Windows development. The Visual C++ package contains not only a compiler, but also all the libraries, examples, and documentation you need to create applications for Windows 95 and Windows NT.

The Visual C++ Environment

The central part of the Visual C++ package is Developer Studio, the Integrated Development Environment (IDE) shown in Figure 1.1. Developer Studio is used to integrate the development tools and the Visual C++ compiler. You can create a Windows program, scan through an impressive amount of online help, and debug a program without leaving Developer Studio.

Figure 1.1.
Using Developer Studio to create a Windows program.

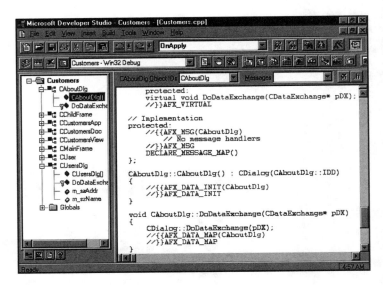

Developer Studio Tools

Once upon a time, Windows programmers used simple text editors and tools that were hosted on MS-DOS to create their Windows programs. Developing a program under those conditions was tedious and error-prone. Times have definitely changed; Developer Studio includes a number of tools that once you might have paid extra to purchase.

- An integrated editor offers drag-and-drop and syntax highlighting as two of its major features. You can configure the Developer Studio editor to emulate the keystroke commands used by two popular programmer's editors, Brief and Epsilon.

- A resource editor is used to create Windows resources, such as bitmaps, icons, dialog boxes, and menus.

- An integrated debugger enables you to run programs and check for errors. Because the debugger is part of Developer Studio, it's easy to find and correct bugs. If you find a programming error while debugging, you can correct the source code, recompile, and restart the debugger.

Developer Studio also features an online help system, which can be used to get context-sensitive help for all of the tools included in Developer Studio, as well as detailed help on the C++ language, the Windows programming interface, and the MFC class library.

Developer Studio Wizards

In addition to tools that are used for debugging, editing, and creating resources, Developer Studio includes three wizards that are used to simplify developing your Windows programs:

- AppWizard is used to create the basic outline of a Windows program. Three types of programs are supported by AppWizard: single document and multiple document applications based on the Document/View architecture and dialog box-based programs, in which a dialog box serves as the application's main window. Using AppWizard to create applications is covered beginning in Chapter 13, "Using Visual C++ for Windows Programming."

- ClassWizard is used to define the classes in a program created with AppWizard. Using ClassWizard, you can add classes to your project. You can also add functions that control how messages received by each class are handled. ClassWizard also helps manage controls that are contained in dialog boxes by enabling you to associate an MFC object or class member variable with each control.

- OLE ControlWizard is used to create the basic framework of an OLE control. An OLE control is a customized control that supports a defined set of interfaces and is used as a reusable component. OLE controls replace Visual Basic controls, or VBXs, that were used in 16-bit versions of Windows. Although the process involved in creating an OLE control is not covered in this book, OLE controls are used in Chapter 40, "Using OLE Controls."

MFC Libraries

Visual C++ 4 includes Version 4.0 of the Microsoft Foundation Classes (MFC), a class library that makes programming for Windows much easier. Most of the MFC classes fall into the following major categories:

- Application Architecture includes classes that help provide the basic plumbing for applications written using MFC.

- Dialog Boxes are derived from CDialog, a basic dialog box class. This category includes classes that handle the common dialog boxes that are included in Windows 95.

- Views are used in the Document/View architecture to represent the program's output. Classes that support scrolling, editing, and windows based on dialog boxes are included in this category.

- Controls are used to provide easy access to all of the controls offered by Windows 95 and Windows NT. Included in this category are classes that manage tree controls, list views, and combo boxes.

- Graphical Objects are used for creating the output in a Windows program. This category includes classes for pens, brushes, icons, and bitmaps.

- Exceptions are used to indicate that an unexpected event occurred during a program's execution.

- Collections is a special type of class used to contain objects from another class. Some of the collection classes offered in the MFC class library are template-based, which enables you to use them with almost any object.
- OLE classes are used to provide support for creating OLE-aware applications.
- Miscellaneous classes include classes for strings, rectangles, and WOSA (Windows Open System Architecture) services such as socket-based communication and MAPI (Messaging Application Programming Interface).

By using the MFC classes when writing your programs for Windows, you can take advantage of a large amount of source code that has been written for you. This enables you to concentrate on the important parts of your code, rather than worry about the details of Windows programming.

The Standard Template Library

A recent addition to the C++ draft standard is the Standard Template Library, called the STL. Unlike the MFC class library, which is used primarily for Windows programming, the STL is used for general purpose programming using templates.

The Visual C++ setup program does not copy the Stl to your hard disk. You can find the STL on the Visual C++ distribution CD in the \Stl directory. The STL is discussed in Chapter 10, "Templates and the Standard Template Library."

Why Use Visual C++ 4?

Why

Visual C++ and Developer Studio are a fully integrated environment that makes it very easy to create Windows programs. By using the tools and wizards provided as part of Developer Studio along with the MFC class library, you can create a program in just a few minutes.

Many of the programs used as examples in this book require less than one page of additional source code. However, these programs use the thousands of lines of source code that are part of the MFC class library. They also take advantage of AppWizard and ClassWizard, two of the Developer Studio tools that manage your project for you.

The Visual C++ compiler is also available on a subscription basis, enabling you to receive the latest upgrades and bug fixes as soon as they become available. If you need access to the latest in development tools, the Visual C++ subscription is the way to go. If you purchased the compiler with the subscription option, directions for activating your subscription are included in the Visual C++ package. If you did not buy the subscription option, an upgrade coupon is included in the compiler package.

How Is Visual C++ 4 Used?

Every chapter in this book has a section called "How…" that explains how the subject of that chapter is used. In this section, you install Visual C++ and see how the various parts of the Visual C++ system are used to create programs.

How

The Visual C++ Package

As with most compilers today, the Visual C++ compiler is shipped in a fairly small box containing a CD-ROM, a small manual to help you get started, and a registration card. Until recently, development systems for Windows were packaged in huge, environmentally unfriendly boxes that weighed 35 pounds or more. The bulky packaging was necessary to deliver the documentation and stacks of floppy disks required to develop programs for Windows.

Thanks to advances in PC hardware that mean almost every new PC has a CD-ROM drive, as well as advances in online help systems, a typical development system for Windows is shipped almost completely on CD. The only hard-copy documentation is usually a thin "Getting Started" booklet that is used primarily to keep the CD from rattling around inside the package.

Installing Visual C++

The first step toward using Visual C++ is to install it on your computer. As with all well-behaved programs written for Windows, Visual C++ is installed using a Windows-based setup program. The Visual C++ CD includes an AutoRun program, which is automatically launched when the CD is inserted into your CD-ROM drive. The AutoRun program creates a dialog box containing three choices:

- Install Visual C++ begins the installation process.
- Quick Tour takes you on a guided tour of Developer Studio.
- Browse CD Contents uses the Windows 95 Explorer to display the contents of the CD.

To launch the setup program, click the button labeled Install Visual C++.

Using the Setup Wizard

Most setup programs for applications written for Windows 95 use a setup wizard. A setup wizard is an easy-to-use tool that guides the user through the installation process. A setup wizard enables a user to navigate forward and backward through the setup process. The user can also ask for help or cancel the setup process at any time.

The opening screen for the Visual C++ setup wizard displays a welcome message and explains the setup process in general terms. This screen has no user options. It is only used to introduce the setup program.

Clicking the Next button displays the next screen, which is a software licensing agreement for the Visual C++ compiler. You must dismiss this screen by clicking either the Yes button or the No button. Clicking the No button stops the installation process, whereas clicking the Yes button enables the installation to continue.

The next screen collects user information. On this screen, you should enter your name, your company or organization's name, and the CD key that is located on the CD package or liner notes. This information will be displayed in the Developer Studio startup screen and in the About box.

The next screen presents a list of installation options. The option you select depends on the amount of free space on your hard disk, as well as the types of programs that will be developed using Visual C++. The installation options for Visual C++ are the following:

- `Typical` installs the most commonly used Developer Studio and Visual C++ components and leaves the remaining components on the CD. This option requires slightly more than 110 MB of disk space.

- `Minimum` installs only components that are absolutely required. This option requires approximately 70 MB of disk space.

- `CD-ROM` installs only Developer Studio to the hard disk and assumes that the Visual C++ CD is always available. The compiler and all libraries remain on the CD, enabling this installation to use only about 10 MB of disk storage.

- `Custom` enables you to pick the options to be installed on your hard disk. This option enables you to specify which components are immediately available on the hard disk and which items must be fetched from the CD. The best response time for Developer Studio and its tools is obtained by installing all components to the hard disk, which will take up about 250 MB of disk space.

The space requirements listed above might be different on your computer, depending on currently installed files and your operating system. If you don't remember exactly how much space is available on your hard drive, don't worry; this setup wizard displays the amount of space required for each option and the amount of free space available on the hard drive. If you select an option and find later that you need more components installed on the hard drive, you can add Visual C++ components at any time by running the setup program again.

After selecting the installation option, you use the next page to select the keyboard layout. There are two options: MSDEV style, which enables new keyboard functions introduced with this version of Developer Studio; and VC++ 2.0 style, which uses the keyboard functions from Visual C++ 2.0. In most cases, you should select the MSDEV option and click the Next button.

You use the next page to find out how the installation will proceed. To begin the installation, click the button labeled Next. The setup wizard copies the files needed for Visual C++, as indicated by the installation options that you selected earlier.

After all the files are copied to your hard disk, the setup wizard adds the Visual C++ group to your Program menu and adds icons for Developer Studio and other programs to the program group. This completes the installation process.

What's Not Installed

The Visual C++ CD includes a special version of InstallShield, a program used to create setup programs similar to the one used to set up Visual C++. To set up InstallShield, run its setup program, located in the \Ishield\Disk1 directory.

The Visual C++ CD includes the Standard Template Library, or STL, a set of algorithms and classes that are part of the ANSI C++ Draft Standard. The STL is located in the \Stl directory on the Visual C++ CD. There is no setup program, but installing and using the STL is discussed in Chapter 10.

Using Developer Studio

To start Developer Studio, click the Developer Studio icon located in the Visual C++ folder. To get to the Visual C++ folder, click the Start button on the taskbar and then select Programs. One of the items in the Programs folder is Visual C++. Figure 1.2 shows a start menu tree opened to the Microsoft Developer Studio icon.

Figure 1.2.
Starting Developer Studio from the Start button.

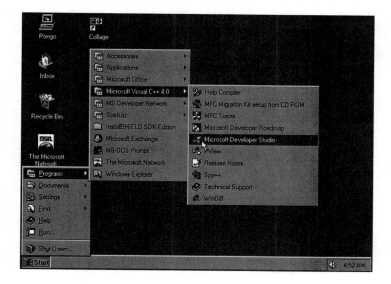

Integrating Developer Studio with Other Tools

If you have the latest versions of Microsoft FORTRAN Power Station, Visual Source Safe, or Visual Test, or if you are a member of the Microsoft Developer Network (MSDN), you can integrate those products into Developer Studio. For example, the Information Viewer can use a Microsoft Developer Network CD instead of Visual C++ Books Online when searching for help.

To use the Microsoft Developer Network CD in place of Books Online, select Open Information Title from the Developer Studio Help menu. You will see a dialog box that enables you to select the source used by the Information Viewer. Select Microsoft Development Library from the list box and close the dialog box.

Building Applications with Developer Studio and Visual C++

Building programs using Developer Studio and Visual C++ is the subject of the rest of this book. In general, the following steps are used to build a program using Visual C++:

1. Create a program skeleton using AppWizard.
2. Create the resources used by the program.
3. Add classes and message handling functions using ClassWizard.
4. Add the functionality required by your program. You actually have to write some code yourself for this part.
5. Compile and test your program, using the Visual C++ integrated debugger if needed.

Starting with Chapter 3, "Writing Simple C++ Programs," I discuss how programs are created using Visual C++. In the next chapter, you use some of Developer Studio's tools and wizards.

Summary

In this chapter, I introduced Developer Studio and Visual C++, as well as the main tools and wizards included in Developer Studio and the MFC class library. I also covered the steps required to install and start Visual C++.

Exploring Developer Studio

In this chapter, I present some of the most commonly used features of Visual C++ and Developer Studio: the online information viewer, AppWizard, and the sample code. I discuss each of these in turn, and you modify one of the sample code projects.

What Is the Developer Studio Editor?

What Developer Studio includes a sophisticated editor as one of its tools. The editor is integrated with the other parts of Developer Studio; files are edited in a Developer Studio child window.

You use the Developer Studio editor to edit C++ source files that will be compiled into Windows programs. The editor supplied with Developer Studio is similar to a word processor, but instead of having fancy text-formatting features, it has features that help make it easy to write source code. Well, maybe not easy, but that's something you'll tackle in the next 40 chapters.

Why Use the Developer Studio Editor?

Why

You can use almost any editor to write C++ source code, but there are several reasons to consider using the editor integrated with Developer Studio. The editor includes many features that are found in specialized programming editors.

- Automatic syntax highlighting shows keywords, comments, and other source code in different colors.
- Automatic "smart" indenting helps line up your code into easy-to-read columns.
- Emulation for keystrokes used by other editors helps if you are familiar with editors such as Brief and Epsilon.
- Integrated keyword help enables you to get help on any keyword, MFC class, or Windows function just by pressing F1.
- Drag-and-drop editing enables you to easily move text by dragging it with the mouse.
- Integration with the compiler's error output helps you step through the list of errors reported by the compiler and positions the cursor at every error. This enables you to make corrections easily without leaving Developer Studio.

How Is the Developer Studio Editor Used?

How

The easiest way to learn about the Developer Studio editor is to edit a file and run through a few common actions, such as creating a new source file, saving and loading files, and using a few keyboard commands.

Editing a New Source File

To edit a new source file, click the New Source File icon on the toolbar. The New Source File icon looks like a blank piece of paper with a yellow highlight in one corner. You can also open a new source file using the menu by following these steps:

1. Select New from the File menu. This displays the New dialog box, which enables you to create a new text file, project, or other type of file.
2. Select Text File from the New dialog box.

Each of the preceding methods creates an empty source file ready for editing. Type the source code from Listing 2.1 into the new file.

Listing 2.1. A minimal C++ program.

```cpp
// This is a comment
int main()
{
    return 0;
}
```

The source code in Listing 2.1 is a legal C++ program, although it doesn't actually do anything. As you typed the source code into the editor, the colors for some of the words should have changed color. This is called syntax highlighting, and it's one of the features of Developer Studio's editor. The first line in Listing 2.1 begins with //, which is used to mark the beginning of a single-line comment in a C++ program. By default, comments are colored green by the Developer Studio editor. In contrast, int and return are colored blue to indicate that they are C++ keywords.

Another editor feature is called *smart indenting*. This feature automatically arranges your text as you type, applying formatting rules to your text as each word or line is entered into the editor. For example, enter the source code from Listing 2.2 into the text editor. Press Return at the end of each line, but do not add any spaces or tabs. As each line is typed, the editor rearranges the text into a standard format for you.

Listing 2.2. A simple C++ class declaration.

```cpp
class CFoo
{
    int nFoo;
    int nBar;
public:
    CFoo();
}
```

The source code provided in this book follows the same formatting convention used by the Developer Studio editor. Although some coding styles might be more compact, this style is very easy to read.

Saving a Source File

To save the contents of the editor, click the Save icon on the toolbar. The Save icon looks like a small floppy disk. You can also press Ctrl+S or select Save from the File menu. When updating an existing source file, you don't see a dialog box, and no further action is needed on your part. The existing file is updated using the current contents of the editor. If you save a new file, you see the Save As dialog box, and you must choose a location and filename for the new source file. Save the contents of Listing 2.2 in the C:\ directory using the name CFoo.cpp. After saving the file, close CFoo.cpp by selecting Close from the File menu.

To save a file under a new name, select Save As from the File menu or press F12. Enter the new path and filename using the Save As dialog box described previously.

Opening an Existing Source File

To open an existing source file, click the Open icon on the toolbar. The Open icon looks like a folder that is partially open. You can also press Ctrl+O or select Open from the File menu. Any of these methods brings up the File Open dialog box.

To open the CFoo.cpp file for editing, pop up the File Open dialog box and navigate to the C:\ directory. Select the CFoo.cpp file and click the button labeled Open. The CFoo.cpp file is loaded into the editor.

Using Editor Commands

There is a large set of editing commands that are available from the keyboard. Although most editor commands are also available from the menu or toolbar, the following commands are frequently used from the keyboard:

- Undo, which reverses the previous editor action, is performed by pressing Ctrl+Z on the keyboard. The number of undo steps that can be performed is configurable in the Options dialog box.
- Redo, which is used to reverse an undo, is performed by pressing Ctrl+A.
- LineCut, which removes or "cuts" the current line and places it on the Clipboard, is performed by pressing Ctrl+Y.
- Cut removes any marked text from the editor and places in on the Clipboard. This command is performed by pressing Ctrl+X.
- Copy copies any marked text to the Clipboard but unlike the Cut command, doesn't remove the text from the editor. If no text is marked, the current line is copied. This command is performed by pressing Ctrl+C.
- Paste copies the Clipboard contents into the editor at the insertion point. This command is performed by pressing Ctrl+V.

This is only a small list of the available keyboard commands. To see a complete list, select Keyboard from the Help menu. A list of the current keyboard command bindings is displayed, as shown in Figure 2.1.

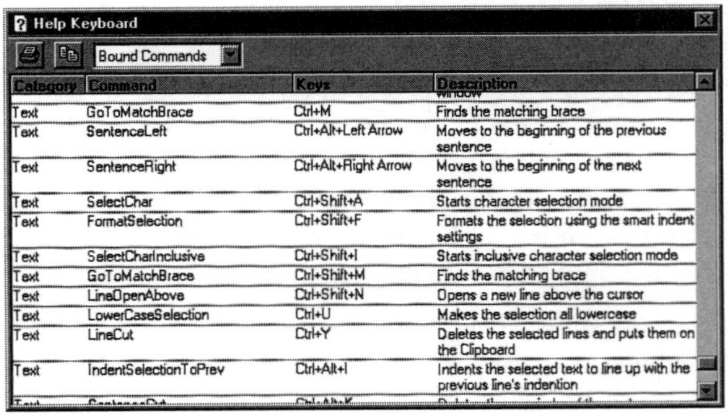

Figure 2.1.
An example of keyboard command bindings in Developer Studio.

What Is InfoViewer?

What

InfoViewer is the online help system integrated into Developer Studio. In previous versions of Visual C++, a stand-alone version of Books Online was used to provide help and online information. Books Online was a separate program and not a part of the development environment. Unlike earlier versions of Books Online, InfoViewer is also compatible with the Microsoft Developer Network CD, enabling you to search that database for information.

Usually, the indexes used by the InfoViewer are copied to your hard disk, and the actual database remains on the CD. This spares about 100 MB of hard disk space. If you would like to speed up InfoViewer, run Visual C++ setup again and install InfoViewer to the hard disk. Select a custom installation procedure and make sure you check the InfoViewer box.

Why Use InfoViewer?

Why

Because Visual C++ is not sold with a documentation set, InfoViewer is the only documentation that is included with the product. Although the online documentation is also available from Microsoft in book form, it costs you extra.

InfoViewer has several advantages over hard copy documentation.

- It is fully searchable. There's a saying, "You can't search dead wood," and it applies perfectly to the difference between hard copy documentation and Developer Studio's InfoViewer. Let's say you're having a problem with a list box control. In a few seconds, you can search the entire documentation set, including the MSDN library if you have it, and immediately begin looking up relevant information.

- You can add annotations. You can add Post-it notes to your hard-copy documentation too, but InfoViewer's annotations are guaranteed to stick to the page.

- You get context-sensitive help that brings up InfoViewer when you press the F1 key. When's the last time you pressed F1 and had a book fall off the bookshelf and open to the correct page?

- InfoViewer is completely integrated into Developer Studio. One of the tabs in the Project Workspace window displays the InfoViewer table of contents. The current topic is displayed in a Developer Studio child window.

- Last, but not least, you can always print out a hard copy when needed, and you don't even need a copying machine.

How Is InfoViewer Used?

How

You interact with the InfoViewer help system in two windows.

- The contents pane is displayed in the Project Workspace window.
- The information topic is an MDI child window.

Figure 2.2 shows both windows used by InfoViewer. In Figure 2.2, the Project Workspace window is docked against the left side of Developer Studio, and the InfoViewer window is an MDI child window.

Figure 2.2.
The Developer Studio InfoViewer with contents on the left and topics on the right.

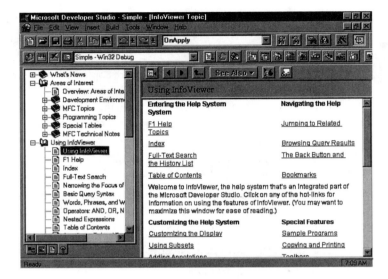

Using Dockable Windows in Developer Studio

Many of the views displayed by Developer Studio are dockable, which means they can be attached to the edge of the Developer Studio workspace where they remain until undocked. The Project Workspace window shown in Figure 2.1 is an example of a dockable view.

To "undock" a dockable window, double-click the window's edge. To dock a floating window, move it to the edge of the workspace. If it is a dockable window, it docks itself. If you want to move a dockable window close to the edge of a workspace without docking, press the Ctrl key on the keyboard when moving the window.

Getting Context-Sensitive Help

To get context-sensitive help from InfoViewer, press F1. You select a topic based on the current window and cursor position, and you see the InfoViewer window containing context-sensitive help. If you press F1 while editing a source file, help is provided for the word under the cursor. If there is more than one possible help topic, you see a list of choices.

Open a new document for editing, as described earlier in this chapter, and enter the source code provided in Listing 2.3. Don't worry about what it does; you're just playing with the help system for now.

Listing 2.3. Testing InfoViewer's context-sensitive help.

```
int main()
{
    return 0;
}
```

Every word in this example has a help topic. To get context-sensitive help, move the cursor to any word in Listing 2.3 and press the F1 key. The help topic is displayed in a dockable window next to your source code. To return the windows to their original sizes and hide the InfoViewer window, press Escape.

Searching for Help Using a Keyword

To search the InfoViewer keyword list, open the Search dialog box by selecting Search from the Help menu or by right-clicking in the InfoViewer window. The Search dialog box enables you to select a help topic by entering a keyword. The keyword list box scrolls as you make your entry, which is helpful when you're not quite sure how to spell a keyword.

The Search dialog box also enables you to create a query in order to find a topic. You can use a query to search the entire contents, a subset of the contents, or the results of the last query. The last option is useful when you're narrowing the scope of a search. You can apply the query to the entire contents of InfoViewer or to only the titles of each topic.

A query can be as simple as a single word, or it can be used to look for words that are adjacent or close to each other. You can use the AND, OR, NEAR, and NOT operators to create queries. For example, to find all of the topics where the words dialog and tab are close to each other, use the following query:

```
dialog NEAR tab
```

To look for topics where the word main is found but exclude any topics that contain the word WinMain, use the following query:

```
main not WinMain
```

Browsing Through the Contents Window

A third way to use InfoViewer is to browse through the contents pane in the Project Workspace window. The contents pane displays the titles for every available topic, arranged in an easy-to-use tree view.

When the InfoViewer contents tree is completely collapsed, the contents pane displays the titles for the top level of the available topics. The titles displayed at the top level are somewhat like the titles of a series of books; the icon even looks like a book. When the book icon is closed, there is a plus sign next to the book title, indicating that the book can be opened to display its contents. Clicking on the plus sign opens the book icon and expands the contents tree to display the contents of the open book. It also changes the plus sign to a minus, which you can click to close the book.

Every item displayed in the contents pane is either a book or a topic. A book displays an icon that looks like a book. Topics are represented by icons that look like a page of text. To display the selected topic, click the topic icon; the InfoViewer topic window opens.

What Is AppWizard?

What   AppWizard is a tool that generates an MFC project based on options that you select. AppWizard creates all of the source files required to make a skeleton project that serves as a starting point for your program. You can use AppWizard to create single-document, multiple-document, or dialog box-based applications.

Why Use AppWizard?

Why   AppWizard creates all of the source files required to build a skeleton Windows application. It also configures a project for you and enables you to specify the project directory. Although an AppWizard project is a skeleton of a future project, it uses the MFC class library to include the following functions:

- Automatic support for the common Windows 95 dialog boxes, including Print, File Open, and File Save As
- Dockable toolbars
- A status bar
- Optional MAPI, ODBC, and OLE support

After answering a few questions using AppWizard, you can compile and run the first version of your application in a few minutes.

How Is AppWizard Used?

How   To start AppWizard and create your first Windows program, follow these steps:

1. Select New from the File menu. A New dialog box is displayed.
2. Select Project Workspace and click the OK button. The New Project Workspace dialog box is displayed, as shown in Figure 2.3.
3. To create an MFC-based project, select MFC AppWizard as the project type. Enter Simple as the project name and click the Create button. This starts AppWizard.
4. The first AppWizard screen asks for a project type. AppWizard works similarly to the Developer Studio AppWizard, enabling you to move forward and backward using the Next and Back buttons. Select the radio button labeled Single Document and then click the Next button.

5. Move through all six AppWizard screens. Each screen enables you to change a different option about the Simple project. Although this example won't use any optional features, feel free to experiment with the options offered by AppWizard.

6. The last AppWizard screen presents a list of classes that is generated for the project. Click the button labeled Finish. AppWizard displays a summary of the project, listing the classes and features that you selected.

7. Click the OK button to start generating files required for the Simple project.

Figure 2.3.
The New Project Workspace dialog box.

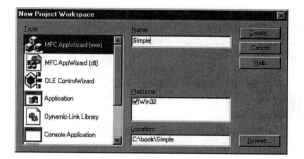

Compiling a Project

After you create the Simple project using AppWizard, the Simple project workspace opens. The Project Workspace window contains four tabs, each used to show a different view of the current project.

- The ClassView tab displays information about the C++ classes used in the Simple project. Don't worry if the information contained in this view seems strange right now. I discuss C++ classes in Chapter 5, "Control Structures and Classes."

- The ResourceView tab displays information about the resources used in the Simple project. All programs written for Windows have resources; beginning in Chapter 15, "Menus," you use this view to manage dialog boxes, bitmaps, and other resources.

- The FileView tab displays information about the files used for the Simple project. Even a small project such as Simple requires a large number of source files. In future chapters, I use each of these files; by the end of the book, you'll be familiar with all of them.

- The final view is the InfoView, which was discussed earlier in this chapter and is used for online information.

Compile the project by selecting Build Simple.exe from the Build menu. The Build window displays the progress of the build, which should look something like the following:

```
Compiling resources...
Compiling...
StdAfx.cpp
```

```
Compiling...
SimpleView.cpp
SimpleDoc.cpp
ChildFrm.cpp
MainFrm.cpp
Simple.cpp
Generating Code...
Linking...
Simple.exe - 0 error(s), 0 warning(s)
```

The last line displayed in the output window indicates that no errors or warnings were discovered. Congratulations; you have created a simple Windows program! To execute the Simple project, select Execute from the Build menu or press F5 on the keyboard. The most common way to launch a project from Developer Studio is to use the debugger. To start the debugger, click the Go button on the toolbar or press F5 on the keyboard.

Summary

In this chapter, I discussed the tools and wizards that are included in Developer Studio. You also used AppWizard to create a small project, which was then compiled and executed.

Writing Simple C++ Programs

Beginning with this chapter, you'll start learning some of the basic concepts of the C++ language. In this chapter, you build a simple console mode, or DOS program, as well as a simple Windows program, and some basic concepts of the C++ language are introduced, using the programs as examples.

What Is a Console Mode Program?

What Back before the days of graphical user interfaces (GUI), all programmers needed to worry about when their program interacted with the user was the keyboard. The user typed, and the program displayed. Although Windows has gone beyond this simple interface, there are still times when simplicity is the best answer. For this reason, Windows offers a console mode interface that looks much like the old DOS-type interface. A program using this interface gets a special window with a command line. It is not truly a Windows program, having only a line-in/line-out type of interface. It does not respond to mouse clicks or any other spontaneous actions by the person executing the program.

Why Write a Console Mode Program?

Why
Windows programming and Visual C++ can be intimidating, especially to someone new to the development environment. Writing a console mode program provides an easy way for the beginning programmer to build confidence. It is an easy way to demonstrate features of the C++ language without involving the complexities of the Windows operating system.

How Is a Simple Console Mode C++ Program Written?

How
As promised, in this chapter you actually start writing a few C++ programs. The classic way to start writing programs in any language is to create a program that displays `Hello World!` In Windows 95 or Windows NT, the simplest types of programs are console mode applications, so that's where we start.

Components of a C++ Program

Programs written using Visual C++ are *compiled*, meaning that a text file called the *source file* is translated into a stand-alone program that you can run outside the Visual C++ environment. Almost all C++ development systems compile executable programs. Some programming languages, such as some versions of BASIC, create programs that run only in the development environment. Some other languages—for example, Smalltalk—run in conjunction with a runtime library that assists the executing program.

In contrast, programs written using Visual C++ can be written and compiled into an executable program. That program can then be executed on any machine that has the Windows 95 or Windows NT operating system installed.

In most C++ development systems, a C++ program goes through several steps on its way to becoming an executable program.

1. You create one or more source files that contain the text of a C++ program.
2. You compile the program using a C++ compiler. This step could actually consist of several commands that are issued to compile the source files into intermediate files, also known as *object code* files.
3. The object code files are linked together using a tool called a *linker*.
4. You can now start the executable program.

These steps are shown in Figure 3.1. Until recently, most development systems required that you perform each of these steps either with separate products from the command line or with the aid of a tool that determined which files needed to be updated.

Figure 3.1.
The steps required to build a C++ program.

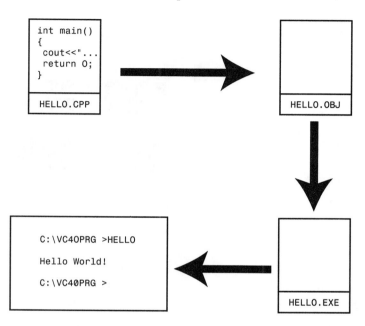

```
int main()
{
  cout<<"...
  return 0;
}
```
HELLO.CPP

HELLO.OBJ

```
C:\VC40PRG >HELLO

Hello World!

C:\VC40PRG >
```

HELLO.EXE

With modern tools such as Visual C++, building a program is much easier. The Visual C++ environment enables you to edit, compile, execute, and debug your programs inside the same environment. All the steps shown in Figure 3.1 are managed by the Visual C++ Integrated Development Environment (IDE), enabling you to concentrate on writing your program instead of managing lots of small details.

When you use Visual C++ for development, most of the work is managed as a *project*. Each project stores the information required to create a C++ program. Depending on the type and complexity of the program, the project might be as simple as two files or as complex as hundreds of files. The relationship between a project and a C++ program written using Visual C++ is shown in Figure 3.2.

Creating a Visual C++ Project

Before you actually start creating your first project, you should create a directory for your C++ programming work. For example, you might create a directory named C:\VC40PRG on your hard drive. Each sample program that you create can be located in its own subdirectory under C:\VC40PRG. This type of structure helps to keep your programs in a separate, easy-to-find area of your hard drive.

Figure 3.2.
The project contains the files required to build a program.

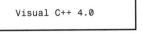

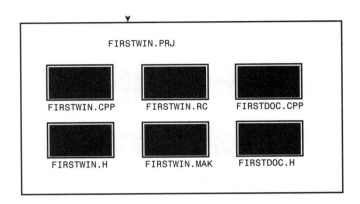

The first step in writing your first Visual C++ program is to create a project. Begin by selecting File|New from the Visual C++ main menu, and select Project Workspace from the New dialog box. When the New Project Workspace dialog box appears as shown in Figure 3.3, select Console Application as the Type. You must also specify a Name and a Location for your project. In Figure 3.3, the Name is Hello, and the Location is C:\VC40PRG\HELLO.

Figure 3.3.
The New Project dialog box.

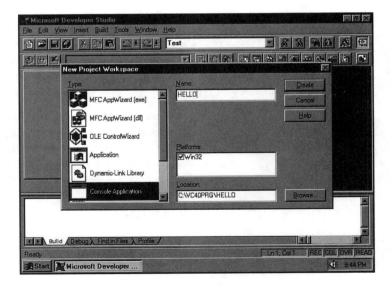

After you have selected the project type and the subdirectory, click the Create button to create the project. You will be presented with the Project Workspace. If not, select View|Project Workspace to see the files that were created for you. The Project Workspace enables you to add to the project any source files that you might have already created.

Creating Your First C++ Source File

The most important parts of any C++ program are the source files. To help keep the programs simple, all of the programs in this chapter consist of a single source file. Although the sample program provided in Listing 3.1 is very short, it has many of the elements present in all C++ programs.

Listing 3.1. A simple C++ console mode program.

```
#include <iostream.h>

int main()
{
    cout << "Hello World!" << endl;

    return 0;
}
```

Open a new source file document and type in the program exactly as shown in Listing 3.1. There are two ways to open a new source file for editing.

- Click the New Source File icon on the toolbar. This is the icon on the far left-hand side of the toolbar that looks like a blank page or empty piece of paper.
- Select File|New from the main menu. From the dialog box, choose Text File as the document type and click the OK button.

Note When using C++, remember that capitalization is important, but white space, such as the number of spaces before cout, is not significant from the compiler's point of view.

After you have entered the program in Listing 3.1, save the source file in your project's directory as HELLO.CPP. Add HELLO.CPP to the HELLO project by selecting Insert|Files into Project from the main menu. Select the HELLO.CPP source file and then click the Add button.

Compile and link the HELLO project by clicking the Build button on the toolbar. You can also build the project by selecting Build|Build HELLO.EXE from the main menu. A window displays information about your project as it is compiled and linked. If you entered Listing 3.1 correctly, the project is built with no errors, and the last line in the status window reads as follows:

```
HELLO.exe - 0 error(s), 0 warning(s)
```

If errors or warnings are displayed in the Build status window, there is probably an error in the source file. Check your source file again for missing semicolons, quotes, or braces.

Running Your First C++ Program

To run the HELLO program, open a DOS window and change the working directory to the project's directory. You'll see a subdirectory named DEBUG. The Visual C++ IDE puts all of the executable and intermediate files into this directory by default. Change to the DEBUG directory and execute the HELLO.EXE program by typing the following at the DOS prompt:

```
HELLO
```

The program loads and then displays Hello World! That's all there is to it.

All of the console mode or DOS programs used as examples in the first part of this book should be compiled and executed just like HELLO.EXE. You'll always create a project, add files to it, and then build the application. After the application is built, you then go out to DOS and execute the program.

The Basic Elements of a C++ Program

Let's take a look at the HELLO program because it has a lot in common with much larger C++ programs. The following first line of HELLO.CPP is a message to the compiler to include another file when compiling HELLO.CPP.

```
#include <iostream.h>
```

This #include statement tells the compiler to look for the file iostream.h and insert it into your source file. Actually, the #include statement is read by the preprocessor, a part of the compiler that scans the source file before the file is compiled. Statements read by the preprocessor are known as *preprocessor directives* because they aren't actually used by the compiler. Preprocessor directives always begin with a # in the first character position on any line in your source file. I'll cover more examples of preprocessor statements throughout the remainder of the book.

The next line of HELLO.CPP is the beginning of the main function. All C++ programs consist of one or more functions. The function named main is where the program begins executing, and all C++ programs must have a function named main. As you'll see later, you will usually not write a main function in a Windows program because one is provided for you in a library routine. However, for console mode applications, you'll need to create one, as follows:

```
int main()
```

This line defines a function named main that returns an integer value to the operating system when it has finished executing. The main function takes no parameters. The operating system uses the return value from main to determine if the program executed successfully. It's possible to return values that indicate success or failure to the operating system, as you'll see later in the discussion about the return statement.

The remaining four lines after int main() are the function body for main. A function body, also called a statement block, is always enclosed in a pair of curly braces, as follows:

```
int SomeFunction()
{
    //This is a statement block
    return 1;
}
```

I'll discuss functions in more detail in Chapter 4, "C++ Basics." For now, it's enough to know that statements inside the function body are executed whenever main is started, or *called*, by the operating system.

Inside the main function is a single statement. C++ statements are always terminated with a semicolon. This particular statement in HELLO.CPP displays a line of characters to the DOS window by using the iostream object cout. The iostream library is included with every C++ compiler, although it is not technically part of the C++ language definition. Using the iostream library, it is easy to perform simple input and output for your console mode program.

The iostream library uses the << symbol for output and the >> for input to and from iostreams. Think of a stream as a sequence of bytes, like a disk file, or the output to a printer or a character-mode screen. I'll discuss streams in detail in Chapter 41, "Serialization."

One simple rule of thumb is that when you see the << symbol, the value to the right of the symbol will be output to the IO object on the left. When you see the >> symbol, data from the IO object on the left is stored in a variable to the right.

The last line of the main function is a return statement. When a return statement is executed, the function *returns* or stops executing, and the caller of the function is passed the value provided after the return keyword. Because this return statement is inside main, the value 0 is passed back to the operating system. The return keyword can appear almost anywhere in a function. However, as a matter of style, most people prefer to have a single return statement in a function if possible.

What Are Statements and Expressions?

Statements and expressions are the elements defined by the C++ language that are converted into machine code by the compiler to build your C++ programs. This seems like a textbook-type definition, doesn't it? In reality, though, it is very hard to define exactly what they are. When talking about a building, we can say that it is made of bricks, boards, and other things; we can define the brick or board very easily. In the case of the C++ programming language, it is much more difficult. Here we are dealing with abstract concepts. The difference between a statement and expression is very subtle, as you will soon see. Although it appears to be confusing at first, the language will become understandable with practice. Eventually the C++ language will become as natural to you as your native language.

Why Use Statements and Expressions?

Why   Statements and expressions are a vital part of the C++ language and define what it is.

How Are Statements and Expressions Used?

How   Like the simple HELLO program, all C++ programs are made up of statements and expressions. Expressions and statements range from the simple statements that were shown in the HELLO program to very complex expressions that stretch across several lines.

Statements

All statements end with semicolons. In fact, the simplest statement is called the null statement, and it consists of only a single semicolon, as follows:

```
;
```

Don't laugh; there are times when the null statement is very useful. You'll see an example of its use later in Chapter 5, "Control Structures and Classes."

You use a statement to tell the compiler to perform some type of specific action. For example, in Listing 3.1, the following statement caused the characters Hello World! to be displayed on your screen.

```
cout << "Hello World!" << endl;
```

Declarations

A declaration is another type of statement. Declarations introduce a variable to the compiler. The following line is an example of a simple declaration:

```
int     myAge;
```

This tells the compiler that myAge is an integer. Declarations are covered in more detail in the next chapter, "C++ Basics."

Assignment

An assignment expression is used to assign a value to a variable using the assignment operator, =, as follows:

```
int     myAge;
myAge = 135;
```

Every expression has a value. The value of an assignment expression is the value of the assignment. This means that the following statement assigns the value 42 to the variables yourAge and myAge.

```
myAge = yourAge = 42;
```

The program in Listing 3.2 demonstrates how to assign a value to a variable.

Listing 3.2. A C++ program that assigns a value to a variable.

```
#include <iostream.h>

int main()
{
    int myAge;

    myAge = 42;
    cout << "Hello" << endl;
    cout << "My age is " << myAge << endl;

    return 0;
}
```

The assignment operator is just one example of the operators available in C++. More operators are discussed in the next section.

Other Common Expressions and Operators

The C++ language contains operators that you can use to write addition, subtraction, multiplication, and other expressions. Some common math operators are shown in Table 3.1.

Table 3.1. Some common math operators used in C++.

Operator	Description
+	Addition
-	Subtraction
/	Division
*	Multiplication

All math operators group from left to right. The multiplication and division operators have a higher precedence than the addition and subtraction operators. This means that the following expressions are equivalent:

```
a + 5 * 3
a + 15
```

You can use parentheses to force an expression to be evaluated in a preferred order. Note the grouping of the following expression:

```
(a + 5) * 3
```

This expression adds 5 to the value stored in a and then multiplies that value by 3. The math operators can also be combined with an assignment operator, as follows:

```
int myAge;
    myAge = 40 + 2;
```

The expression 40 + 2 has a value of 42. After that value is calculated, the value of the expression is stored in the myAge variable.

Relational Expressions and Operators

There are a number of operators in C++ that you use to compare the relationships between two values. These operators are known as the relational operators. The most common relational operators are shown in Table 3.2.

Table 3.2. Some common relational operators used in C++.

Operator	Description
<	Less than
<=	Less than or equal to
>	Greater than
>=	Greater than or equal to
==	Equality
!	Not
!=	Not equal

The value of an expression that uses one of the relational operators is either true or false. The values true and false can be stored in a variable called a Boolean variable or used in conditional statements, as in the following if statement:

```
if( myAge < 8 )
    cout << "Wow, that's young" << endl;
```

This if statement prints a message if the variable myAge is less than 8. The if statement is discussed in detail in Chapter 5. Listing 3.3 shows a program that demonstrates the greater-than relational operator.

Listing 3.3. A program that tests the value of input data with an `if` statement.

```cpp
#include <iostream.h>

int main()
{
    int myAge;

    cout << "Please enter my age ->";
    cin  >> myAge;

    cout << "My age is " << myAge << endl;

    if( myAge > 8 )
        cout << "Wow, that's old" << endl;

    return 0;
}
```

What Is an MFC Program?

When Microsoft developers programmed the Windows operating system, they used object-oriented techniques and created building blocks. Although a complete study of object-oriented programming is outside the scope of this book, we can make use of the *objects* that Microsoft created. An MFC program is one that does just that. The objects are available in the Microsoft Foundation Classes (MFC). Although the MFC program shown in a later section is functionally the same as the console mode program shown earlier in this chapter, it is the basis for a simplified method of programming for the Windows environment.

What

Why Use an MFC Program?

By using MFCs, you make your job of writing Windows programs a little easier (although it wouldn't appear so for this trivial example), and I guarantee that your program will grow as the Windows operating system changes.

Why

How Is a Simple MFC Windows Program Written?

A program that is the Windows equivalent to the console mode program shown in Listing 3.1 is a bit more complicated to write. Listing 3.4 is an example of a simple Windows program that has no menu and no dialog boxes. In fact, all it does is display `Hello World!` in the center of its *client area*, or main window.

How

Listing 3.4. A simple Windows program written using C++ and MFC.

```cpp
#include <afxwin.h>

// The CHelloApp class
class CHelloApp : public CWinApp
{
    public:
        BOOL InitInstance();
};

// The CHelloWnd class
class CHelloWnd : public CFrameWnd
{
    public:
        CHelloWnd();
    protected:
        afx_msg void OnPaint();
        DECLARE_MESSAGE_MAP()
};

// InitInstance - Returns TRUE if initialization is successful.
BOOL CHelloApp::InitInstance()
{
    m_pMainWnd = new CHelloWnd;
    if( m_pMainWnd != 0 )
    {
        m_pMainWnd->ShowWindow( m_nCmdShow );
        m_pMainWnd->UpdateWindow();
        return TRUE;
    }
    else
        return FALSE;
}

// Create a message map that handles one message - WM_PAINT
BEGIN_MESSAGE_MAP( CHelloWnd, CFrameWnd )
    ON_WM_PAINT()
END_MESSAGE_MAP()

CHelloWnd::CHelloWnd()
{
    Create( NULL, "Hello" );
}

// OnPaint - Handles the WM_PAINT message from Windows.
void CHelloWnd::OnPaint()
{
    CRect       rcClient;
    CPaintDC    dc( this );
    GetClientRect( rcClient );
    dc.DrawText( "Hello World!", -1, rcClient,
                 DT_SINGLELINE | DT_CENTER | DT_VCENTER );
}

// Create a single instance of the application.
CHelloApp   theApplication;
```

The simple Windows program provided in Listing 3.4 might seem large, but it's actually about half the size of a similar program written in C. Using the MFC class library enables you to leverage a large amount of source code that has already been written for you. There is a lot of strange-looking code in Listing 3.4, so don't try to understand it all right now.

To build the program, create an MFC Windows project. Begin by selecting File|New from the Visual C++ main menu; select Project Workspace from the New dialog box. In the New Project Workspace dialog box, select Application as the project type. You must also specify a Name and Location for your project, just as you did for the console mode program in Listing 3.1.

After the project has been created, open a new source file document and enter the contents of Listing 3.4 exactly as they are shown. Save the file as FIRSTWIN.CPP and add it to the project.

Set the linking options for the project by selecting Build|Settings from the main menu. On the tab marked General is an item labeled Microsoft Foundation Classes. It will have the value Not Using MFC. Change the selection to Using MFC in a Shared Dll (mfc40(d).dll). You can do this by clicking on the down arrow beside the Not Using MFC selection. This opens a box where you can then make the appropriate selection.

Build the project by clicking the Build button on the toolbar or by selecting Build|Build from the main menu.

Summary

In this chapter, you looked at some simple console mode programs and a single Windows-based program and learned some basic features of the C++ language.

PART II

The C++ Language

4 C++ Basics

5 Control Structures and Classes

6 Arrays, Strings, and Polymorphism

7 Scope, Pointers, and Lifetime in C++

C++ Basics

This chapter introduces some basic C++ concepts. You'll learn the fundamental data types that are available in a C++ program, as well as the C++ type system and type safety. You'll also cover functions and how they are declared, defined, and used.

What Are Variables?

What Computer programs are composed of instructions and data. Instructions tell the computer to do things, such as to add and subtract. Data is what the computer operates on, such as the numbers that are added and subtracted. In mature programs, the instructions don't change as the program executes (at least they're not supposed to). Data, on the other hand, can and usually does change or vary as the program executes. A variable is nothing more than the name used to point to a piece of this data.

Why Use Variables?

Why It would be a fairly worthless program indeed that had no data. The computer language would be more worthless if it provided no means to identify data. If a program is used to compute a payroll, the name of the employee being computed changes as the program scans through the staff. The variable in this case might be the area where the name of the employee is stored. By using the word EmployeeName to point to this area, we have a way to identify a piece of data to both the programmer and the compiler.

How Are Variables Used in C++?

How

The C++ language offers a number of fundamental data types. As in most other programming languages, these built-in types are used to store and calculate data used in your program. In later chapters, you use these fundamental types as a starting point for your own more complex data types.

C++ has a strong type system, which is used to make sure that your data variables are used consistently and correctly. This makes it easy for the compiler to detect errors in your program when it is compiled, rather than when it is executing. Before a variable is used in C++, it must first be declared and defined as follows:

```
int    myAge;
```

This line defines a variable named myAge as an integer. A declaration introduces the name myAge to the compiler and attaches a specific meaning to it. A definition like this also instructs the compiler to allocate memory and create the variable or other object. When the Visual C++ compiler reads the myAge definition, it will do the following:

- Set aside enough memory storage for an integer and use the name myAge to refer to it.
- Reserve the name myAge so that it isn't used by another variable. There are some exceptions to this rule, but I'll cover this in Chapter 7, "Scope, Pointers, and Lifetime in C++."
- Ensure that whenever myAge is used, it is used in a way that is consistent with the way an integer should be used.

It's possible to define several variables on a single line, although as a style issue, many people prefer to declare one variable per line. If you want to make your source file more compact, you can separate your variables by a comma, as follows:

```
int    myAge, yourAge, maximumAge;
```

This line defines three integer variables. Declaring all three variables on one line of code doesn't make your code execute any faster, but it can sometimes help make your source code more readable.

Understanding Type Safety

Some languages enable you to use variables without declaring them. This often leads to problems that are difficult to trace or fix. When using C++, you must declare all variables before they are used. This enables the compiler to catch most of the common errors in software programs. This capability to catch errors when the program is compiled is sometimes referred to as *type safety*.

You can think of type safety as a type of warranty that the compiler helps to enforce in your C++ program. For example, if you try to use an int when another type is expected, the compiler either complains or converts the variable into the expected type. If no conversion is possible, the compiler generates an error and you have to correct the problem before the program can be compiled.

For example, *floating-point values*, or numbers with a decimal point, are stored in float or double variables in C++ programs. These are the only two built-in (or fundamental) variable types that can store floating-point values. If you try to store a floating-point value in a variable declared as an int, the compiler complains. As an example, the console mode program provided in Listing 4.1 generates a compiler warning because a floating-point value will be truncated when stored in an int variable.

Listing 4.1. An example of a problem that can be caught by the compiler.

```
#include <iostream.h>

// This program will generate a compiler warning
int main()
{
    int     interestRate = 7.5; // Warning - some data may be lost
    cout << "The interest rate is " << interestRate << endl;
    return 0;
}
```

To see an example of a type mismatch that is caught by the compiler, create a console mode project with Listing 4.1 as the only source file, following the steps used in Chapter 3, "Writing Simple C++ Programs." The compiler flags line 6 with a warning; however, it still generates an executable program. If you run the program, you see that the interest rate is displayed as only 7 percent instead of displaying 7.5 as shown in the listing.

In order to get the program to compile with no warnings and run as expected, you need to change line 5, as shown in Listing 4.2.

Listing 4.2. A corrected version of the previous example.

```
#include <iostream.h>
// This program will compile properly.
int main()
{
    double     interestRate = 7.5;
    cout << "The interest rate is " << interestRate << endl;
    return 0;
}
```

Using Different Variable Types

So far, you've used `int` and `float` variables, two of the fundamental types available in C++. They're called fundamental types because they are the basic data types that are a part of the language definition. There is also a set of derived types that will be covered in the next few chapters. In addition, as you'll see later in Chapter 5, "Control Structures and Classes," you can define your own types that work just like the built-in types. The names of the built-in types used in C++ include the following:

- `bool` is a Boolean variable that can have the values `true` or `false`.

- `char` is a variable normally used for storing characters. In Visual C++, it can have any value from −128 to +127. If `char` is declared as `unsigned`, its range is from 0 to 255, and no negative values are allowed.

- A `short int` variable, sometimes just written as `short`, is similar to an `int`, but it can contain a smaller range of values. Think of it as a lightweight version of an `int` that can be used if data storage is a problem. A `short` variable can store any scalar (whole) value between −32768 and 32767. If a `short` is declared as `unsigned`, its range is from zero to 65535.

- `int` is an integer value used for storing whole numbers. When using Visual C++, an `int` is a 32-bit value so it can store any value from −2,147,483,648 to 2,147,483,647. If an `int` is declared as `unsigned`, its range is from zero to 4,294,967,295.

- A `long int`, sometimes just written as `long`, is a scalar variable like an `int`, only larger when using some compilers. In Visual C++, a `long int` can store the same values as an `int`.

- A `float` variable is the smallest variable type capable of storing floating-point values. It is often an approximation of the value that was originally stored. In Visual C++, a `float` stores up to six decimal digits.

- A `double` variable stores floating-point values just as a `float` does. However, the compiler stores the value with more precision, meaning that a more accurate value can be stored. A `double` can store up to 15 decimal digits.

- A `long double` has the same characteristics as a `double`. However, from the compiler's point of view, they are different types. The `long double` type is part of the C++ language, and on some machines and compilers, the difference between `double` and `long double` is that `long double` has greater precision.

Some of the variables in the preceding list can be declared as `unsigned`. When a variable is declared as `unsigned`, it can only store non-negative values. When a variable is declared as an `int`, it can store both negative and positive numbers. However, an `unsigned int` can store a much larger positive value than a plain old `int`.

An `unsigned int` can store a larger positive value because the computer has to use one bit of data in the memory location to handle the sign. This sign indicates whether the variable is positive or negative. Because using the sign bit reduces the number of bits that are available for storage, the maximum value for the variable is reduced by half. Figure 4.1 is an example of a variable that has been declared as int and another variable that has been declared as unsigned int.

Figure 4.1.
Most computers can use a sign bit to determine whether a variable is positive or negative.

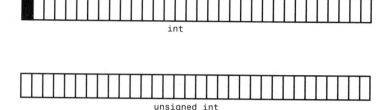

int

unsigned int

The fundamental variable types require different amounts of storage. As a rule of thumb, the char data type is large enough to contain all of the characters in the machine's native language, or eight bits. The int type is usually the "natural" variable size for the target machine, so int variable are 32 bits in Visual C++. Listing 4.3 uses the sizeof operator to display the number of bytes required to store each of the fundamental types.

Listing 4.3. Using sizeof to determine the amount of storage required for different fundamental types.

```
#include <iostream.h>

int main()
{
    cout << "Variable sizes, in bytes:" << endl;

    cout << "char       " << sizeof( char ) << endl;
    cout << "short      " << sizeof( short ) << endl;
    cout << "int        " << sizeof( int ) << endl;
    cout << "long       " << sizeof( long ) << endl;
    cout << "float      " << sizeof( float ) << endl;
    cout << "double     " << sizeof( double ) << endl;
    cout << "long double " << sizeof( long double ) << endl;

    return 0;
}
```

You can think of the sizeof operator as a function that is built into the language. It comes in handy later when you need to determine the size of more complicated data types.

Variable Naming

One important part of programming is the selection of names for your variables and other parts of your programs. The program listings you've seen so far have been very simple. As you become a more experienced user of Visual C++, you will need to establish some sort of naming convention for your identifiers.

When naming your variables, use names that are as long as necessary to indicate how the variable is used. A variable name in C++ is an example of an identifier. Identifiers in C++ are used to name variables and functions, among other things. In Visual C++, your identifiers can be up to 31 characters long and can include any combination of letters, numbers, and underscores, as long as the first character is a letter or underscore. Listing 4.4 is an example of several different variable declarations.

Listing 4.4. Some examples of good and bad variable names.

```
#include <iostream.h>

int main()
{
    // Good declarations
    int     nEmployees;       // Number of employees
    char    chMiddleInitial;  // A middle initial

    // Declarations that could be improved
    int     i, n, k;          // What are these vars used for ?
    float   temp;             // May not be enough information
    char    ch;               // Should have more information

    return 0;
}
```

When you declare variables in a Visual C++ program, case is significant for variable names, which means that cat and CAT are two different variables. However, you should not rely on capitalization alone to differentiate your variables. Instead, you should try to use descriptive names for your variables and establish some sort of naming convention for your identifiers.

No matter which technique you use for naming your variables, it's important to be consistent. For example, most of the sample programs and online help examples provided as part of Visual C++ use a naming convention known as Hungarian Notation, sometimes abbreviated as HN or just Hungarian for short.

When Hungarian is used properly, it's easy to tell the logical type of a variable at a glance without searching for its declaration. For example, most scalar variables like int, long, or short are prefixed with an n, so nAge, nYear, and nChapter are all of type int. Variables that are used to store characters are prefixed with ch, as in chEntry and chInitial. Most of the sample code available from Microsoft uses HN, which I'll also use for the remainder of the code listings in this book. Table 4.1 lists some common HN prefixes for the data types we have covered so far.

Table 4.1. Hungarian Notation prefixes for some fundamental data types.

Type	Prefix	Example
int	n	nMyAge
char	ch	chMenuSelection

Type	Prefix	Example
float	fl	flBalance
bool	b	bFinished

Assigning Values to Variables

As discussed in Chapter 3, you use the assignment operator to assign a value to a variable. The assignment operator is just an equals symbol used as follows:

```
nFoo = 42;
```

This line assigns the integer value 42 to nFoo.

If a floating point decimal value is assigned, it's assumed by the compiler to be a double, as was shown in Listing 4.2 or as follows:

```
dFoo = 42.4242;
```

Assignment to a variable of type char can be done in two ways. If you are actually storing a character value, you can assign the letter using single quotes as shown here:

```
chInitial = 'Z';
```

The compiler converts the letter value into a ASCII value and stores it in the char variable. Small integer values can also be stored in a char, and the assignment is done just like an int variable:

```
chReallyAnInt = 47;
```

What Are Functions?

A function is a block of computer instructions that is inside a computer program and that performs some task. If you buy a wagon, for example, you'll find that it comes with a full set of assembly instructions and has four identical wheels. Why should the instructions repeat the steps to assemble a wheel four times? It is much easier to describe the wheel assembly process once and indicate that you perform the process for each wheel. The wheel assembly instructions are a module (function) within the full set of assembly instructions (program) that are executed four times.

What

Why Use Functions?

Functions provide a way to break up a large program into more manageable parts. At the same time, functions make it possible to perform the same task at various points within the program without repeating the code.

Why

How Are Functions Used?

How
So far, the sample programs have been very simple, and each of them has had a single function, main. As discussed in Chapter 3, the main function is called by the operating system when your program runs. The operating system can use the return value from main, in this case 0, to determine if the program was executed correctly.

Complicated programs, such as word processors or spreadsheets, are too complex to be created inside a single function. For example, most programs use a number of functions from the standard C and C++ library. Listing 4.5 is an example of a short console mode program that uses some of the standard library functions to calculate raising a number to the third power and calculating a square root.

Listing 4.5. Using some of the math functions included in the standard library.

```
#include <iostream.h>
#include <math.h>

int main()
{
    double  dResult;
    dResult = pow( 2.0, 3.0 );
    cout << "Two cubed is " << dResult << endl;

    double dSquareRoot;
    dSquareRoot = sqrt( 225.0 );
    cout << "The square root of 225 is " << dSquareRoot << endl;

    return 0;
}
```

One of the great strengths of C++ is its rich set of library functions that you can use to make your programming life much easier. We use many of the standard library functions throughout the remainder of the book. A complete list of all of the available library functions is available in the Books On-Line help section that comes with the Microsoft Developer Studio.

Declaring Function Prototypes

Before you can use a function, you must declare it by supplying a function prototype to the compiler. Declaring a function is similar to declaring a variable. To declare a function, you specify the function's name, return value, and a list of any parameters that are passed to it, as shown here:

```
int  CalculateAge( int nYearBorn );
```

This line is a function prototype for the CalculateAge function, which takes a single integer as a parameter and returns an integer as its result. A function that returns no value is declared as returning the void type.

The traditional way to provide function prototypes is to place them in *header* files, which are named with an .h extension. Two examples of header files are iostream.h and math.h. These header files contain all of the prototypes and other declaration needed for iostreams and math functions to be compiled correctly.

Defining Functions

A function is defined the same way the main function is defined. All function definitions follow the same pattern; it's basically the function prototype with the function's body added to it. The function definition always consists of the following:

- The function's return value
- The function's name
- The function's parameter list
- The actual function body, enclosed in curly braces

Listing 4.6 provides a simple function that you can use to display a welcome message for a console mode application.

Listing 4.6. A function that displays a welcome message for a console mode program.

```
#include <iostream.h>

// Function prototype
void DisplayWelcomeMessage();

int main()
{
    // Call the display function
    DisplayWelcomeMessage();

    return 0;
}

void DisplayWelcomeMessage()
{
    cout << "Welcome to an Essential Visual C++ example\n"
         << "program. This example shows how to use a function\n"
         << "to display your welcome message."
         << endl;
}
```

Because this function accepts no parameters, there are no parameters listed, leaving only a pair of empty parentheses. Because the function doesn't return a value to the calling function, the return type is defined as void.

Calling Functions

In the C++ language, the act of transferring control to a function is known as *calling* the function. When a function is called, you supply a function name and a list of parameters, if any. The following steps take place when a function is called:

1. The compiler makes a note of the location that the function was called from and makes a copy of the parameter list, if any.
2. Any storage required for the function to execute is temporarily created.
3. The called function starts executing, using copies of the data that was supplied in the parameter list.
4. After the function has finished executing, control is returned to the calling function, and memory used by the function is released.

These steps are shown in Figure 4.2.

Figure 4.2.
Steps involved in calling a function.

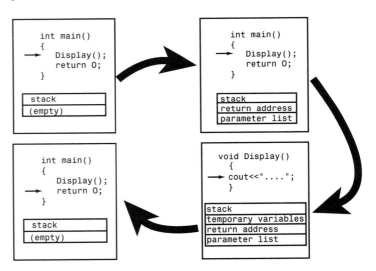

The requirement that you declare functions before using them is an extension of the C++ type system, which was discussed earlier in this chapter. Because function prototypes are required, the compiler can detect errors such as the one in Listing 4.7, where `DisplayWelcomeMessage` is called with the wrong parameter type. The Visual C++ compiler treats this as an error and does not compile it into a working program.

Listing 4.7. An attempt to call a function incorrectly will be caught by the compiler.

```cpp
#include <iostream.h>

void DisplayWelcomeMessage();

int main()
{
    // Attempt to call the display function with an integer
    // as a parameter.
    DisplayWelcomeMessage( 1456 );

    return 0;
}

void DisplayWelcomeMessage()
{
    cout << "Welcome to an Essential Visual C++ example\n"
         << "program. This example shows how to use a function\n"
         << "to display your welcome message."
         << endl;
}
```

Using Function Return Values

If a function supplies a return value, you can treat the return value as an expression. This means that you can assign the return value to a variable. Listing 4.8 uses a function to calculate and return the answer to "The Ultimate Question."

Listing 4.8. Storing a function's return value in a variable.

```cpp
#include <iostream.h>

int CalculateUltimateAnswer();

int main()
{
    int nAnswer;

    nAnswer = CalculateUltimateAnswer();
    cout << "The answer to the ultimate question is "
         << nAnswer << "." << endl;

    return 0;
}

int CalculateUltimateAnswer()
{
    // Normally we might perform some intensive calculations
    // here. But for now, let's just return an answer.
    return 42;
}
```

Summary

In this chapter, you learned about declaring, defining, and using the fundamental data types available in C++, as well as being introduced to how functions are defined and used.

Control Structures and Classes

In this chapter I present some of the ways that C++ programs are procedurally structured. The C++ language provides methods for selecting a choice from several alternatives, as well as methods for executing a series of statements multiple times. I also show you ways in which you can combine multiple variables so you can reference them collectively using one name.

What Is Execution Flow?

What The example programs that I've covered up until now all have executed in a straight line. That is, every line of code has been executed exactly once. In the real world, few programs are quite so simple.

Most programs exercise some sort of control over their execution flow. They perform different actions based on varying conditions as the execution progresses. Then, they repeat these actions until all their tasks are complete. For example, a Windows program may need to search for a certain record from a database or may take different actions depending on the messages that are sent to it.

How Is Execution Flow Controlled?

How There are two basic types of control statements in C++: *selection statements*, which are similar to choosing a fork in the road, and *sequence statements*, which determine how often a certain part of your program is executed.

Selecting an Execution Path

The first set of control statements to look at are the selection statements. If your program needs to take a particular action only if a certain condition is true, or if a user needs to make a choice from a list of possible items, these statements are for you.

All selection statements work by evaluating an expression, then taking an action based on the value of that expression.

Using the *if* Statement

The if statement allows one or more statements to be executed only if an expression inside the parentheses is true. If necessary, values inside the parentheses are converted into Boolean values, with zero being converted to false and all non-zero values converted to true.

Listing 5.1 provides a function that shows how the if statement is used. If the parameter passed to the function is greater than zero, the function returns a value of true.

Listing 5.1. A function that returns true if a positive number is passed to it.

```
#include <iostream.h>
#include <wtypes.h>        // Required for using FALSE, TRUE and BOOL

BOOL IsPositive( int nCheckValue );

int main()
{

    BOOL bPositive;
    bPositive = IsPositive( 42 );

    cout << "IsPositive returned " << bPositive << endl;

    return 0;
}

BOOL IsPositive( int nCheckValue )
{
    BOOL bReturn = FALSE;

    if( nCheckValue > 0 )
        bReturn = TRUE;

    return bReturn;
}
```

Using Compound Statements

The statement controlled by an `if` statement is executed only when the test condition is `true`. If more than one statement must be executed, group the statements together to form a compound statement. Compound statements are often called *blocks*, because they group statements into blocks of code.

A compound statement begins and ends with curly braces, just like a function body. All of the statements within a compound statement that follows an `if` statement are executed when the test condition is `true`, as shown in Listing 5.2.

Listing 5.2. Using a compound statement to group several statements together.

```
#include <iostream.h>
#include <wtypes.h>     //Required for using TRUE, FALSE or BOOL

int main()
{
    BOOL bShouldPrint = TRUE;

    if( bShouldPrint == TRUE )
    {
        cout << "A short demonstration of" << endl;
        cout << "a compound statement - also" << endl;
        cout << "known as a block." << endl;
    }
    return 0;
}
```

In Listing 5.2, the test for equality is made using ==, the quality operator. A common mistake is to use =, which is the assignment operator.

A standard code-formatting convention is to visually nest each conditional "level" of your source code by indenting statements, as was done in Listings 5.1 and 5.2. Indentation helps to make your code more readable, because it helps make the flow of control in your source code easy to see.

Using *else* With *if* Statements

You can couple an `else` statement with an `if` statement to create an either/or selection. When the expression tested by the `if` statement is `true`, the first statement (or block statement) is executed. When the expression is `false`, the statements grouped with the `else` statement are executed instead.

Listing 5.3 provides an example of a function that uses the `if` and `else` statements. This function always returns the larger of two parameters passed to it.

Listing 5.3. A function that uses the `if` and `else` statements.

```
#include <iostream.h>

int GetMax( int nFirst, int nLast );

int main()
{
    int nMaxValue;
    int nFirst = 27;
    int nLast  = 42;

    cout << "Testing "<< nFirst << " and " << nLast << endl;
    nMaxValue = GetMax( nFirst, nLast );
    cout << "The maximum value is " << nMaxValue << endl;

    return 0;
}

int GetMax( int nFirst, int nLast )
{
    int nReturn;

    if( nFirst > nLast )
        nReturn = nFirst;
    else
        nReturn = nLast;

    return nReturn;
}
```

Using the *switch* Statement

Sometimes you need to choose between more than just one or two alternatives. Let's say that you are implementing a simple menu function, with three choices. If you use the `if` statement, you might wind up with a function like the one shown in Listing 5.4.

Listing 5.4. A menu-selection function.

```
//
// Processes a selection from a character-based menu. If a
// valid selection is made, the proper functions are called,
// and true is returned. If an invalid selection is made,
// false is returned.
BOOL HandleMenuSelection( char chSelection )
{
    BOOL bValidSelection = TRUE;

    if( chSelection == 'F' )
        OpenNewFile();
    else if( chSelection == 'P' )
        PrintDocument();
    else if( chSelection == 'S' )
        SaveFile();
    else
```

```
        bValidSelection = FALSE;

    return bValidSelection;
}
```

This is already starting to look a little cluttered, but how bad would it look if you had a few more selections? What if you had 20 or 30? The solution is to use the `switch` statement. A `switch` statement evaluates an expression and then chooses from a list of choices, as shown in Listing 5.5.

Listing 5.5. Using the `switch` statement.

```
BOOL HandleMenuSelection( char chSelection )
{
    BOOL bValidSelection = TRUE;

    switch( chSelection )
    {
        case 'F':
            OpenNewFile();
            break;
        case 'P':
            PrintDocument();
            break;
        case 'S':
            SaveFile();
            break;

        default:
            bValidSelection = FALSE;
    }
    return bValidSelection;
}
```

As Listing 5.5 shows, the `switch` statement has several different parts. Here are the major features of a `switch` statement:

- The `switch()` expression. The expression contained inside the `switch` parentheses is evaluated and its value is used as the basis for making the selection.

- One or more case labels. Each `case` label includes a value. Every `case` label must be unique. If a `case` label's value matches the `switch()` expression, the statements after the `case` label are executed.

- One or more `break` statements. The `break` statement is used to stop execution inside a `switch` statement. A `break` statement is normally placed between every `case`. If a `break` statement is removed, statements in the next `case` are executed until a `break` is reached, or until no more statements remain inside the `switch`.

- A `default` label. The `default` label is selected when no `case` labels match the `switch()` expression.

Executing Sequences in Your Program

Another way to control the flow of execution in your program is to execute sequences, also known as loops or iterations. Popular uses for loops include waiting for user input, printing a certain number of reports, or reading input from a file until an End Of File (EOF) mark is detected. There are three different loop statements used in C++: the `for` loop, the `while` loop, and the `do-while` loop.

Using the *while* Loop

The `while` loop is used to execute a statement as long as a test expression evaluates as `true`. Listing 5.6 shows an example of a `while` loop.

Listing 5.6. A program that executes a `while` loop 10 times.

```
#include <iostream.h>

int main()
{
    int loopCounter = 0;

    cout << "About to enter the while loop" << endl;
    while( loopCounter < 10 )
    {
        cout << "This is loop number " << loopCounter << endl;
        loopCounter++;
    }
    cout << "The loop is finished" << endl;

    return 0;
}
```

In Listing 5.6, the compound statement following the `while` loop is executed as long as `loopCounter` is less than 10. Once `loopCounter` is equal to 10, the condition tested by `while` becomes `false`, and the next statement following the block controlled by `while` is executed. In this example, a compound statement is executed; however, a single statement can also be executed. It's also possible to control a null statement with a `while`, like this:

```
while( loopCounter < 10 );
```

Although the statement above is perfectly legal, it's almost certainly a mistake. How many lines are printed in the following `while` loop?

```
while( loopCounter < 10 );
{
    cout << "A new line" << endl;
    loopCounter++;
}
```

This loop displays only a single line to the screen. If you have problems with loops that don't seem to work, look for extra semicolons where they don't belong.

Using a *do-while* Loop

A relative of the while loop is the do-while loop. The do-while loop is used when a statement or series of statements has to be executed at least once. Listing 5.7 is an example of a do-while loop used to check an input character for 'Q'.

Listing 5.7. Using the do-while loop to test for user input in a console mode program.

```
#include <iostream.h>

int main()
{
    char ch;

    do{
        cout << "\nPress 'Q' to exit ->";
        cin >> ch;
        // Ignore input until a carriage return.
        cin.ignore( 120, '\n');
    }while( ch != 'Q' );

    cout << "Goodbye" << endl;

    return 0;
}
```

Using the *for* Loop

The for loop is often used in C++ programs to write a very compact loop statement. The for loop enables you to write loops in a more compact style than is possible using while loops. Listing 5.8 is equivalent to Listing 5.6, except that it has been rewritten using the for loop.

Listing 5.8. Using a for loop to print 10 lines to the screen.

```
#include <iostream.h>

int main()
{
    cout << "About to enter the while loop" << endl;

    for( int loopCounter = 0; loopCounter < 10; loopCounter++ )
        cout << "This is loop number " << loopCounter << endl;

    cout << "The loop is finished" << endl;

    return 0;
}
```

There are four components to every for statement:

```
for( expression1; expression2; expression3 )
    statement1
```

When the for loop begins, expression1 is executed. This is usually where you declare loop counters. As long as expression2 is true, the statement controlled by the loop is executed. After the controlled statement, statement1, has been performed, expression3 is executed. Loop counters are usually incremented in expression3.

In the example provided in Listing 5.8, I used loopCounter++ as a way to increment the value of loopCounter by one. If I had wanted to decrement the value, I could have used loopCounter--.

As a rule of thumb, if the loop is executed a fixed number of times, it's usually easier to use for instead of while. However, if you are waiting for an event to occur, or if the number of loops aren't easily predicted, it's better to use while.

What Are Data Structures?

What A *data structure* (or just a *structure*) is a data type that is an aggregate; that is, it contains other data types, which are grouped.

Why Use Data Structures?

Why Structures are commonly used when it makes sense to associate two or more data variables. An example is a payroll record, where the number of hours worked and the pay rate are combined in a structure, as shown in Figure 5.1.

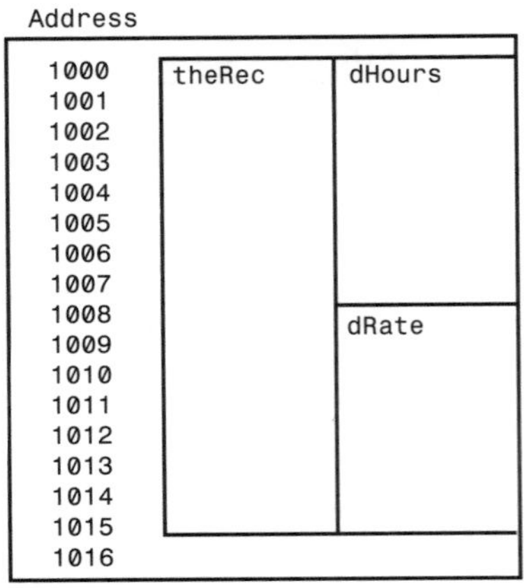

Figure 5.1.
Structures are made up of member variables.

```
struct TIME_REC
{
    double dHours
    double dRate;
};
TIME_REC    theREC;
```

Address		
1000	theRec	dHours
1001		
1002		
1003		
1004		
1005		
1006		
1007		
1008		dRate
1009		
1010		
1011		
1012		
1013		
1014		
1015		
1016		

How Are Structures Used?

Declaring a structure introduces a new type of variable into your program. Variables of this new type can be defined just like int, char, or float variables are defined. Listing 5.9 is an example of how a structure is typically used.

How

Listing 5.9. Using a structure to calculate a weekly salary.

```
#include <iostream.h>

struct  TIME_REC
{
    double    dHours;
    double    dRate;
};

int main()
{
    TIME_REC      payrollRecord;

    payrollRecord.dHours = 40.0;
    payrollRecord.dRate = 3.75;

    cout << "This week's payroll information:" << endl;
    cout << "Hours worked : " << payrollRecord.dHours << endl;
    cout << "Rate           :$" << payrollRecord.dRate  << endl;

    double dSalary = payrollRecord.dRate * payrollRecord.dHours;
    cout << "Salary          :$" << dSalary  << endl;

    return 0;
}
```

What Are Classes?

Classes are similar to structures; in fact, classes really are just structures with a different name. Classes have one feature that makes them very useful for object-oriented programming: Unless a member of a class is specifically declared as public, that member is generally not accessible from outside the class. This means that you can hide the implementation of methods behind the external interface.

What

You normally use classes to model objects in your program. Member functions, described in the next section, are used to access any data contained in the class. Direct access to any data members is normally either restricted, or not allowed.

Why Are Classes Important?

Why The implementation of classes is the most important part of object-oriented programming because it provides the mechanism to define the programming objects.

How Are Classes Defined?

How The definition of a class is similar to that of a structure, except that the keyword `class` is used instead of `struct`. Listing 5.10 provides a declaration for a `CWeeklyPayRecord` class. Prefixing the name of a class with a `C` is an MFC convention used for all classes provided in source code listings. MFC is the abbreviation for the Microsoft Foundation Class, which contains predefined class structures that can be used for building objects.

Listing 5.10. A declaration for a weekly pay record class.

```
class CWeeklyPayRecord
{
    public:
        void   HoursWorked( double dHours );
        void   PayRate( double dRate );
        double GetSalary();

    private:
        double m_dHours;
        double m_dRate;
};
```

The keywords `public` and `private` are used to grant or deny access to members of the class. Any members of the class declared after the `public` keyword can be accessed from outside the class, just as though they were members of a structure. Any members of the class declared after the `private` keyword are not accessible outside the class. Any number of `public` or `private` access specifiers can be present in a class declaration. The closest access specifier, reading from top to bottom, is the one that is currently controlling a declaration.

Member Functions

Classes and structures can contain member functions as well as data. However, as a style issue, member functions are almost always used with classes and almost never with structures. Because data members are usually public in a structure, member functions are rarely used.

Listing 5.11 is an example of the `CWeeklyPayRecord` class, with some typical member functions added.

Listing 5.11. A complete example using the CWeeklyPayRecord class.

```cpp
#include <iostream.h>

class CWeeklyPayRecord
{
    public:
        void    HoursWorked( double dHours );
        void    PayRate( double dRate );
        double GetSalary();
    private:
        double m_dHours;
        double m_dRate;
};
//
// main - Create a weekly salary object, and calculate this
//        week's salary.
//
int main()
{
    CWeeklyPayRecord      weeklyPay;

    weeklyPay.HoursWorked( 40.0 );
    weeklyPay.PayRate( 3.75 );

    cout << "This week's payroll information:" << endl;
    cout << "Salary        :$" << weeklyPay.GetSalary() << endl;

    return 0;
}
//
// Member functions for the CWeeklyPayRecord class
//
void    CWeeklyPayRecord::HoursWorked( double dHours )
{
    m_dHours = dHours;
}

void    CWeeklyPayRecord::PayRate( double dRate )
{
    m_dRate = dRate;
}

double CWeeklyPayRecord::GetSalary()
{
    return m_dHours * m_dRate;
}
```

Note that the member functions in Listing 5.11 are prefixed with CWeeklyPayRecord:: when they are defined. The names of all member functions are prefixed with their class names; this is the only way the compiler can determine to which class the function belongs. The only exception to this rule is a function that is defined inside the class declaration.

Constructors

A *constructor*, sometimes called a "ctor," is a special member function that is created when an object of the class is created. An object is created when it is defined, or when it is dynamically created, as I discuss in Chapter 7, "Scope, Pointers, and Lifetime in C++."

A constructor always has the same name as the class, and never has a return value, not even void. The purpose of the constructor is to place a newly created object into a known state. Typically, constructors may allocate system resources, clear or set variables, or perform some other type of initialization.

Destructors

A *destructor*, sometimes called a "dtor," is a special member function that is called as an object is destroyed. The destructor is declared as having no return type, and is never declared with a parameter list. The name of the destructor is the class name prefixed by a tilde (~) character. Listing 5.12 is a program containing a simple class that shows how a constructors and destructors are called.

Listing 5.12. An example showing how constructors and destructors are called.

```
#include <iostream.h>

class CSimple
{
    public:
        CSimple();
        ~CSimple();
};

CSimple::CSimple()
{
    cout << "A CSimple object is created." << endl;
}

CSimple::~CSimple()
{
    cout << "A CSimple object is destroyed." << endl;
}

int main()
{
    // A CSimple object is created here.
    CSimple    anObject;

    // A CSimple object is destroyed after the return statement.
    return 0;
}
```

It is not necessary to define a destructor unless there are specific tasks that must be performe to clean up after an object, such as releasing system resources that have may have bee allocated.

Summary

In this chapter I presented different methods that you can use to control the flow of control inside a C++ program, as well as some basic properties of classes and structures used in C++ programs.

Arrays, Strings, and Polymorphism

In this chapter, I present a derived data type, the array. I also discuss a special type of character array called a string, and I finish the chapter by introducing polymorphism.

> **Note** A derived type is created from one of the fundamental types discussed in Chapter 4, "C++ Basics." You also can make a derived type from a user-defined type, such as a `class`, `struct`, or `union`. An array is just one of the derived types; I discuss others throughout the remainder of this book.

What Are Arrays?

What Most programming languages have built-in array types, and C++ is no exception. Arrays are also commonly called *vectors* or *ranges*. An array is made up of several consecutive memory locations that have the same variable type, and are accessed using the same name.

Why Use Arrays?

Why   Arrays are one of the essential factors of computer programs. They enable you to refer to individual entries in a table of data items by using the same code and varying an index to the item.

How Are Arrays Used?

How   In order to access an element in the array, you must specify the array name and the element's index in the array. Figure 6.1 shows the layout of three arrays.

Figure 6.1.
*Arrays of int, float,
and char types.*

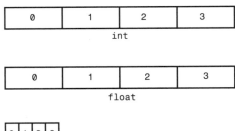

The total amount of space used by an array depends on three things:

- The number of elements in the array
- The size of each element
- The amount of "padding" required between each element, if any

Declaring An Array

The syntax you use to declare or define an array is straightforward. Declare the array just as you would a simple variable, except that you also specify the number of elements in the array in square brackets, like this:

```
int     arScores[9];
```

The line above declares arScores to be an array of integers containing nine elements. The letters ar are a Hungarian Notation prefix that indicates that the variable is an array. Other common Hungarian prefixes for arrays are rg (range) and v (vector).

One rule for your array definitions is that the compiler must be able to determine the size of the array when the program is compiled. In general, the size of the array cannot be another variable. The array definition below is not legal C++ code:

```
int     arraySize = 9;
int     arScores[arraySize];
```

I cover some exceptions to this rule in Chapter 7, "Scope, Pointers, and Lifetime in C++."

Initializing Arrays

When you define an array, the elements in the array can have any value. There is no guarantee that each element is initialized to zero—or any other value, for that matter. You can initialize arrays with starting values when you define them by using an initialization list, like this:

```
int    arScores[9] = { 0, 4, 5, 6, 7, 4, 3, 7, 12 };
```

The line above assigns the values from the list to elements in the array, beginning with the first element in the array. This is definitely much more convenient than trying to explicitly initialize the members of an array one by one.

The number of elements in the initialization list must be equal to or less than the number of elements in the array. If you try to outsmart the compiler by sneaking a few extra values into the list, the compiler will complain. If the array is larger than the number of values in the list, the extra array elements are initialized to zero. For example, the definition

```
int    arScores[9] = { 5, 4 };
```

initializes the first element of arScores with 5 and the second element with 4. The remaining elements are guaranteed to be initialized with zero.

It's possible to leave the size of an array undefined, and supply an initializer list. The compiler will create an array large enough to contain the values in the initializer list. For example,

```
int    arScores[] = { 7, 5, 2, 4, 5 };
```

defines arScores to be an array of int with five elements. The elements of the array are initialized with the values from the initializer list.

Using Arrays

An array element behaves just like a simple variable of the same type. For example, each element in an array of integers can be used just like any other integer. The only difference between an array and a simple variable is that an array element must have a specified index.

Unlike some languages, such as Pascal, the first element in an array is always referred to as "element zero." The last valid element in an array is always the array size minus one. This is a common source of errors in C++ programs. If an array has nine elements, the last element is element eight, not element nine. Listing 6.1 is a console mode program that uses a pair of arrays to track the score in a baseball game. Notice the for loop that is used to display the score. You will see that the loop begins with 0 and ends at 8, displaying the score for each inning up to and including the ninth.

Listing 6.1. Using arrays to track a baseball score.

```
#include <iostream.h>

int main()
```

continues

Listing 6.1. continued

```
{
    int arAwayScores[9] = { 1, 4, 0, 0, 1, 0, 1, 0, 1 };
    int arHomeScores[9] = { 0, 0, 2, 1, 0, 4, 1, 0, 1 };

    cout << "Inning by inning scores" << endl;

    // Display column headings for each inning and the total runs.
    cout << "Inning ";
    for( int nInning = 0; nInning < 9; nInning++ )
        cout << " " << nInning + 1;
    cout << " Total Runs" << endl;

    // Display the per-inning score for the away team.
    int cTotal = 0;
    cout << "Away    ";
    for( int nAwayInning = 0; nAwayInning < 9; nAwayInning++ )
    {
        cout << " " << arAwayScores[nAwayInning];
        cTotal += arAwayScores[nAwayInning];
    }
    cout << "         " << cTotal << endl;

    // Display the per-inning score for the home team.
    cTotal = 0;
    cout << "Home    ";
    for( int nHomeInning = 0; nHomeInning < 9; nHomeInning++ )
    {
        cout << " " << arHomeScores[nHomeInning];
        cTotal += arHomeScores[nHomeInning];
    }
    cout << "         " << cTotal << endl;

    return 0;
}
```

The total score for each team is accumulated using a new form of the assignment operator. The statement

```
cTotal += arHomeScores[nHomeInning];
```

tells the compiler to take the value stored in cTotal and then add the value stored in arHomeScores[nHomeInning] to it. There are also -=, *=, and /= operators that combine assignment with subtraction, multiplication, and division, respectively.

Using Arrays as Function Parameters

When an array is passed as a function parameter, the parameter can be declared as an array in either of two ways: the size of the array can be explicitly stated, or the array can be specified as having an unspecified size. Listing 6.2 gives examples of both declaration types.

Listing 6.2. Using arrays as parameters in function calls.

```cpp
#include <iostream.h>

void DisplayAwayScore( int arScores[9] );
void DisplayHomeScore( int arScores[] );

int main()
{
    int arAwayScores[9] = { 1, 4, 0, 0, 1, 0, 1, 0, 1 };
    int arHomeScores[9] = { 0, 0, 2, 1, 0, 4, 1, 0, 1 };

    cout << "Inning by inning scores" << endl;

    // Display column headings for each inning and the total runs.
    cout << "Inning ";
    for( int nInning = 0; nInning < 9; nInning++ )
        cout << " " << nInning + 1;
    cout << " Total Runs" << endl;

    // Display the per-inning score for the away team.
    DisplayAwayScore( arAwayScores );

    // Display the per-inning score for the home team.
    DisplayHomeScore( arHomeScores );

    return 0;
}

//
// Display the per-inning score for the home team.
void DisplayHomeScore( int arScores[] )
{
    int cTotal = 0;
    cout << "Home    ";
    for( int nInning = 0; nInning < 9; nInning++ )
    {
        cout << " " << arScores[nInning];
        cTotal += arScores[nInning];
    }
    cout << "         " << cTotal << endl;
}

// Display the per-inning score for the away team.
void DisplayAwayScore( int arScores[9] )
{
    int cTotal = 0;
    cout << "Away    ";
    for( int nInning = 0; nInning < 9; nInning++ )
    {
        cout << " " << arScores[nInning];
        cTotal += arScores[nInning];
    }
    cout << "         " << cTotal << endl;
}
```

What Are Character Strings?

What
In previous chapters, I have been using character strings without really explaining how they work. A *character string* is just an array of characters with a special null character at the end. Figure 6.2 shows how some simple strings look in memory.

Figure 6.2.
A string: a character array terminated with a null character.

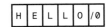

How Are Character Strings Used?

How
In this chapter, I present some simple ways to declare and define character strings. The easiest way to use a character string is as a string literal, like this:

```
cout << "Hello";
```

Look familiar? The string "Hello" is created and used by the compiler, and you don't need to worry about declarations or initializing the array—you can just use the string as is.

Another way to declare a character string is to declare an array of char with undefined size, and use an initializer, like this:

```
char    szHello[] = "Hello";
```

The prefix sz is a common Hungarian Notation identifier that means "a string that is terminated by zero." Because double quotes are used, the compiler knows that the character array should end with a zero. Here's an alternate, more error-prone declaration that has the same effect:

```
char    szHello[] = { 'H', 'e', 'l', 'l', 'o', '\0' };
```

Using Character-Based String Functions

The standard C++ library contains a number of functions that you can use to manipulate character-array based strings. There are functions to determine the length of a string; to add, or concatenate, two strings together; and to copy the contents from one string to another.

One problem with these functions is that you must make sure the string contained in a character array does not exceed the declared size of the array. If a large string is copied to a character array that is too small, the compiler overwrites variables stored in adjacent memory locations. This can lead to unpredictable results.

Determining the Length of a Character Array-Based String

To ensure that character array-based strings are handled correctly, one important piece of information is the size of the string. The standard C++ library includes the strlen function, which you can use to calculate the number of characters in a string, not including the null character.

To use strlen, pass the character array-based string to it as a parameter. The return value is the number of characters in the string. Listing 6.3 is an example that uses strlen.

Listing 6.3. Using strlen to calculate the length of a string.

```
#include <iostream.h>
#include <string.h>

int main()
{
    char szSlogan[] = "An example using the strlen function";

    int  nSloganLength = strlen( szSlogan );
    cout << "The length of this slogan is " << nSloganLength;

    return 0;
}
```

When programming for Windows, you should use a similar function named lstrlen. The lstrlen function is a part of the Windows standard library and requires less computing resources than strlen.

Copying a Character Array-Based String to a New Destination

The first step in copying the contents of a character array-based string to another destination is to make sure the destination is large enough to contain the copied string, including the null terminating character. Overrunning a destination when copying strings is one of the most common errors in C and C++ programs.

The standard C++ library function strcpy copies a character array-based string, including the null terminator, from one location to another. However, it does not test to make sure the destination is large enough to hold the string. Listing 6.4 shows how strcpy is typically used.

Listing 6.4. Using strcpy to copy character array-based strings.

```
#include <iostream.h>
#include <string.h>

int main()
{
    char szHelloWorld[] = "Hello World!";
    char szHello[80];

    strcpy( szHello, szHelloWorld );

    cout << szHello << endl;

    return 0;
}
```

In practice, it is not possible for a library function to have information about the size of the copy destination, so don't blame strcpy. Either exercise caution when dealing with character arrays, or use the CString class, as I describe in the next section.

What Is the MFC *CString* Class?

What

The MFC string class is the implementation of the string array object and its methods.

Why Use the MFC *CString* Class?

Why

It's not surprising that one of the most popular classes in the MFC class library is a string class. The CString class creates smart strings that you can easily add together, copy, and otherwise manipulate, without the worries that are involved when you use character arrays.

How Is the MFC *CString* Class Used?

How

Listing 6.5 shows some examples of how CString can be used.

Listing 6.5. Using the MFC CString class.

```
#include <afx.h>
#include <iostream.h>

int main()
{
    CString szAardvark("Aardvark");
    CString szZebra = "Zebra";

    if( szAardvark < szZebra )
        cout << "Aardvark comes before Zebra." << endl;

    szAardvark += " - king of beasts";
    cout << "szAardvark is now " << szAardvark << "." << endl;

    if( szZebra == "Zebra" )
        cout << "szZebra is equal to Zebra." << endl;

    cout << szAardvark << " and " << szZebra << "." << endl;

    return 0;
}
```

Commonly Used *CString* Functions

One of the great things about the CString class is the way a CString object behaves exactly like one of the fundamental types, like an integer. A CString object can be added, assigned, or copied just like an int. However, there are also a number of commonly used member functions that are defined for CString.

Calculating the Number of Characters in a *CString*

The CString class provides a GetLength member function that returns the number of characters stored in a CString object. This function is useful when storing CString objects, or when preparing for certain types of output. Listing 6.6 is an example of using GetLength.

Listing 6.6. Determining the number of characters in a CString object.

```
#include <afx.h>
#include <iostream.h>

int main()
{
    CString szInfo( "Testing the string length - " );
    int nInfoLength = szInfo.GetLength();

    cout << szInfo << " " << nInfoLength << " chars." << endl;

    return 0;
}
```

Searching Inside a *CString* Object for a Character

You can use the Find member function to search a CString object for a character or string of characters. This function is useful when you're searching through input strings for control characters. Listing 6.7 uses Find to search a CString object for a newline character.

Listing 6.7. Searching for a newline inside a CString object.

```
#include <afx.h>
#include <iostream.h>

int main()
{
    CString szTwoLines( "The string with\ntwo lines" );

    cout << szTwoLines << endl;

    // Search for the \n char and remove it.
    int nFirstReturn = szTwoLines.Find( '\n' );
    if( nFirstReturn != -1 )
    {
        szTwoLines.SetAt( nFirstReturn, ' ' );
        cout << "The new line has been removed." << endl;

        cout << szTwoLines;
    }
    return 0;
}
```

The SetAt member function is used to change the carriage return character into a space. You can use SetAt to change any character, as long as the new character is not the null character.

What Is Polymorphism?

What
Polymorphism is often used in object-oriented programming to refer to functions or operations that can be applied to many different types of objects. One aspect of polymorphism is the ability to use a function on several different objects, without needing a different function name for each object.

The C++ language allows a function name to be "overloaded"; that is, to have more than one definition. The compiler determines which particular function to call based on the parameter list. For example, the declarations below declare two different versions of the Print function:

```
void Print( char szName[] );
void Print( int nValue );
```

The compiler can decide which function to call based on the parameters passed to the function. Listing 6.8 shows how you can use overloaded functions.

Listing 6.8. Using overloaded functions.

```
#include <iostream.h>
#include <string.h>

void Print( char szName[] );
void Print( int  nValue );

int main()
{
    cout << "Calling Print with a string" << endl;
    Print( "Foo" );

    cout << "Calling Print with an int" << endl;
    Print( 42 );

    return 0;
}

void Print( char szName[] )
{
    int nLength = strlen( szName );
    cout << szName << " has " << nLength << " chars." << endl;
}

void Print( int  nValue )
{
    cout << "The answer is " << nValue << endl;
}
```

I use operator and function overloading throughout the rest of the book. The ability to have the compiler determine the proper function based on the parameter list is a useful feature of the C++ language.

Summary

In this chapter, I presented arrays, strings, and the MFC CString class, which makes string handling much safer and easier.

Scope, Pointers, and Lifetime in C++

This chapter discusses the scope and lifetime of variables. I also discuss pointers and addresses, as well as how to create objects dynamically.

What Is Scope?

What The scope of a variable refers to its visibility in a C++ program. An identifier used to name a variable or function has a specific scope when it is created, and this scope determines how and where that name can be used. If a variable is "in-scope" at a certain point in a program, it is visible and may be used in most circumstances. If it is "out of scope," it is not visible and your program will not be able to use that variable.

One simple type of scope is shown below. The following code is not legal because the variable myAge is used before it is declared.

```
myAge = 12;
int myAge;
```

Because the identifier myAge is not in the current scope, it cannot be assigned a value. This illustrates one simple property about visibility: it almost always runs "downward," beginning at the point where the variable is declared. There are also several different types of scope, ranging from very small to the very large.

Why Is Scope Important?

Why The scope of a variable or function determines how it is used. In many C++ programs, understanding how scope works can be a great help in designing a program that is more efficient, or when debugging a program that doesn't work.

In general, your program should use variables that have as small a scope as possible. The smaller the scope, the less likely it is that an identifier will be accidentally misused or subjected to side-effects. For example, it's always better to pass objects as parameters to a function, rather than relying on global variables. Using variables that are local to the function helps make the function more reusable and helps eliminate synchronization problems in a multithreaded environment such as Windows.

How Is Scope Used?

How The scope of an identifier comes into play whenever an identifier is declared. The types of scope available in a C++ program are these:

- Local scope
- Function prototype scope
- Function scope
- Class scope

I explain each of these types of scope in the following sections.

Local Scope

There are several types of local scope. The simplest example of local scope is a variable or other object that is declared outside of any functions, like this:

```
int foo;
int main()
{
    return 0;
}
```

In this example, the variable foo is in scope from the point of its declaration until the end of the source file. For this reason, this type of local scope is sometimes called *file scope*. All declarations that occur outside of class or function definitions have this type of scope.

Variables declared inside a function body have *local scope*. They are visible only within the function.

Another type of local scope is *block scope*, where a variable within a compound statement or other block is visible until the end of the block, as shown in Listing 7.1.

Listing 7.1. An example of local block scope.

```
#include <iostream.h>

int main()
{
    {
        int nMyAge = 42;

        cout << "My age is " << nMyAge << endl;
    }

    // nMyAge is not in scope here.

    return 0;
}
```

The variable nMyAge has block scope and can be used only between the curly braces. Variables declared inside conditional statements also have block scope.

Function Prototype Scope

Function prototype scope exists only inside a function prototype. It is extremely limited, and I mention it only for completeness. A variable with function prototype scope really is just a variable that is defined in a function prototype and that goes out of scope at the end of the prototype.

Function Scope

Function scope is rarely an issue. The idea behind function scope is to refer to labels that are declared within a function definition. The only time you would use a label is with the widely discouraged goto statement, as shown in Listing 7.2.

Listing 7.2. An example of function scope.

```
#include <iostream.h>

void LabelFunc();

int main()
```

continues

Listing 7.2. continued

```
{
    LabelFunc();
    return 0;
}

//
// LabelFunc() - a function with several goto labels.
//
void LabelFunc()
{
    int nAnswer = 42;

    goto AnswerLabel;

ReturnLabel:
    return;

AnswerLabel:
    cout << "The answer is " << nAnswer << endl;
    goto ReturnLabel;
}
```

None of the labels declared in LabelFunc function are visible outside the function. This means that the C++ language does not directly support jumping to a label outside the current function. It also means that you can reuse labels in different functions.

The goto statement works like a detour sign in your program. Program execution continues at the next statement after the label referred to in the goto statement. Using the goto statement is discouraged because it often leads to code that is not easy to read or maintain.

Class Scope

The name of a class, union, or structure member is tightly associated with the class, and has *class scope*. An identifier with class scope can be used within the class, union, or structure. If a class or variable name is used to qualify access to the identifier, it also is visible outside the class. For example, if a class is defined as follows, the variables m_myVar and m_myStaticVar are in scope for all of the CFoo member functions:

```
// class CFoo
class CFoo
{
public:
    CFoo();

    int     GetMyVar();
    int     GetStaticVar();

    int       m_myVar;
    static int m_myStaticVar;
};
int CFoo::m_myStaticVar;
```

Outside of the CFoo class, the variables can only be accessed through a CFoo object, as shown in Listing 7.3.

Listing 7.3. Some examples of using class scope.

```cpp
#include <iostream.h>

// class CFoo
class CFoo
{
public:
    CFoo();

    int     GetMyVar();
    int     GetStaticVar();

    int         m_myVar;
    static int m_myStaticVar;
};
int CFoo::m_myStaticVar = 0;

CFoo::CFoo()
{
    m_myVar = 0;
}
int CFoo::GetMyVar()
{
    return m_myVar;
}
int CFoo::GetStaticVar()
{
    return m_myStaticVar;
}

int main()
{
    CFoo aFoo;

    CFoo::m_myStaticVar = 1;
    aFoo.m_myVar = 42;

    cout << "m_myVar is " << aFoo.m_myVar << endl;
    cout << "m_myStaticVar is " << aFoo.m_myStaticVar << endl;

    return 0;
}
```

There is one exception to the rule that requires a member to be accessed with a variable name: a class member declared as *static* is shared by all objects of that class. Static members of a class exist even when no objects of a class have been created. To access a static class member without using a class object, prefix the class name to the member name, as done in Listing 7.3, to access CFoo::m_myStaticVar.

What Is Identifier Lifetime?

What   In a C++ program, every variable or object has a specific lifetime, which is separate from its visibility. It is possible for you to determine when a variable is created and when it is destroyed.

Why Is Identifier Lifetime Important?

Why   Lifetime can be an important issue when you design your program. Large objects can be costly to create and destroy. By understanding the lifetime of objects created in your programs, you can take advantage of features in the C++ language that help your programs run more efficiently.

How Is Identifier Lifetime Used?

How   A variable can be hidden by another variable with the same name that has a different scope. This means it's possible for a variable to be out of scope, and still exist. This often happens when a variable name is used in block or class scope, and hides another variable that uses the same name. Figure 7.1 shows how variables with the same name can exist in two different scopes.

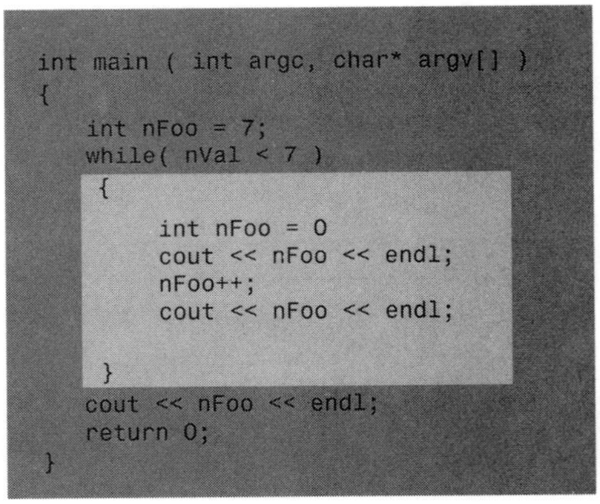

Figure 7.1.
*A new variable declared
in the current scope,
hiding another variable.*

```
int main ( int argc, char* argv[] )
{
    int nFoo = 7;
    while( nVal < 7 )
    {
        int nFoo = 0
        cout << nFoo << endl;
        nFoo++;
        cout << nFoo << endl;

    }
    cout << nFoo << endl;
    return 0;
}
```

Listing 7.4 shows how a variable can be out of scope but not yet destroyed.

Listing 7.4. A variable out of scope but not destroyed.

```
#include <iostream.h>

int main()
{
    int nMyAge = 52;
```

```
    cout << "My age is " << nMyAge << endl;

    // Create a new block with its own scope.
    {
        cout << "My age is still " << nMyAge << endl;

        int nMyAge = 42;

        cout << "My age is now " << nMyAge << endl;
    }

    cout << "My age is now " << nMyAge << endl;

    return 0;
}
```

Listing 7.4 also illustrates *name lookup*, which takes place when a variable name is encountered. The second nMyAge definition occurred inside a new block, so it "hides" the previous definition. When the end of the block is reached, the second definition goes out of scope, and the variable defined by the first definition is used again.

Static Lifetime

A variable declared as static in a function is created when the program starts, and is not destroyed until the program ends. This is useful when you want the variable or object to remember its value between function calls. Listing 7.5 is an example of a static object in a function.

Listing 7.5. A static object in a function, destroyed when the program ends.

```
#include <iostream.h>

void PrintMessage();

int main()
{
    for( int nMessage = 0; nMessage < 10; nMessage++ )
        PrintMessage();

    return 0;
}

void PrintMessage()
{
    static int nLines = 1;

    cout << "I have printed " << nLines << " lines." << endl;
    nLines++;
}
```

What Are Pointers?

What Pointers are important topics in C++ programming. A good understanding of the ways in which pointers are used will help you write programs that are more flexible and reliable. C++ relies very heavily on proper understanding and usage of pointers.

A pointer is nothing more than a numeric variable. This numeric variable is an *address* into memory where the actual data resides. Pointers must also follow the same rules that are applied to other variables. They must have unique names, and they must be declared before they can be used.

Every object or variable that is used in an application takes up a location or multiple locations in memory. This memory location is accessed via an address. Look at Figure 7.2.

Figure 7.2.
The text Hello *stored beginning at address 1000.*

1000	1001	1002	1003	1004	1005
H	e	l	l	o	

In this figure, the text *Hello* is stored in memory beginning at address 1000. Each character takes up a unique address space in memory. Pointers provide a method for holding and getting to these addresses in memory. Pointers make it easier to manipulate the data because they hold the address of another variable or data location.

Why Are Pointers Important?

Why Pointers give flexibility to C++ programs and enable the programs to grow dynamically. By using a pointer to a block of memory that is allocated at runtime, a program can be much more flexible than one that allocates all of its memory at once.

A pointer is also easier to store than a large structure or class object. Because a pointer just stores an address, it can easily be passed to a function. However, if an object is passed to a function, the object must be constructed, copied, and destroyed, which can be costly for large objects.

How Are Pointers Used?

How When using pointers and memory addresses, it often is useful to know the amount of memory required for each object pointed to. If you need to know the amount of storage required for a particular object or variable, you can use the sizeof operator, first introduced in Chapter 4, "C++ Basics." You can also use sizeof to determine the amount of storage required for your own classes and structures, as shown in Listing 7.6.

Listing 7.6. Using `sizeof` with class types.

```
#include <afx.h>
#include <iostream.h>

struct CStruct
{
    int     m_nAge;
    CString m_szName;
};

int main()
{
    int nSize = sizeof( CStruct );
    cout << "CStruct uses " << nSize << " bytes." << endl;

    return 0;
}
```

The Indirection and Address Operators

There are two operators that are used when working with addresses in a C++ program: the *address-of operator* (&) and the *indirection operator* (*). These operators are different from operators seen previously because they are *unary*, meaning that they work with only one operand.

The address-of operator, &, returns the address of a variable or object. This operator is associated with the object to its right, like this:

```
&myAge;
```

This line returns the address of the myAge variable.

The indirection operator, *, works like the address-of operator in reverse. It also is associated with the object to its right, and it takes an address and returns the object contained at that address. For example, the following line determines the address of the myAge variable, then uses the indirection operator to access the variable and give it a value of 42:

```
*(&myAge) = 42;
```

Using the Indirection Operator

You can use a pointer with the indirection operator to change the value of the other variable, as shown in Listing 7.7.

Listing 7.7. Using a pointer variable with the indirection operator.

```
#include <iostream.h>

int main()
{
    int  nVar;
    int* pVar;
```

continues

Listing 7.7. continued

```
        // Store a value in nVar, and display it. Also
        // display nVar's address.
        nVar = 5;
        cout << "nVar's value is " << nVar << "." << endl;
        cout << "nVar's address is " << &nVar << "." << endl;

        // Store the address of nVar in pointer pVar. Display
        // information about pVar and the address it points to.
        pVar = &nVar;
        cout << "pVar's value is " << pVar << "." << endl;
        cout << "*pVar's value is " << *pVar << "." << endl;

        // Change the value of the variable pointed to by pVar.
        *pVar = 7;
        cout << "nVar's value is " << nVar << "." << endl;
        cout << "pVar's value is " << pVar << "." << endl;
        cout << "*pVar's value is " << *pVar << "." << endl;

        return 0;
}
```

It's important to remember that the pointer does not contain a variable's value, only its address. The indirection operator enables you to refer to the value stored at the address instead of to the address itself.

As shown in Listing 7.7, a pointer variable is declared using the indirection operator, like this:

```
int*    pVar;  // declare a pointer to int
```

Note If you are in the habit of declaring several variables on one line, look out for pointer declarations. The indirection operator applies only to the object to its immediate right, not to the whole line. The declaration

```
int* pFoo, pBar;
```

declares and defines two variables: a pointer to an int named pFoo, and an int named pBar. The pBar variable is not a pointer. If you insist on declaring more than one pointer per line, use this style:

```
int *pFoo, *pBar;
```

Pointers are useful when you must change a parameter inside a function. Because parameters are always passed by value, the only way to change the value of a parameter inside a function is to send the address of the variable to the function, as is done in Listing 7.8.

Listing 7.8. Using a pointer and a function to change a variable's value.

```
#include <iostream.h>

void IncrementVar( int* pVar );

int main()
{
    int  nVar = 0;

    cout << "The value of nVar is now " << nVar << "." << endl;
    IncrementVar( &nVar );
    cout << "The value of nVar is now " << nVar << "." << endl;

    return 0;
}

void IncrementVar( int* nVar )
{
    *nVar += 1;
}
```

Figure 7.3 shows how the address is used to change the value of a variable outside the function.

Figure 7.3.
*Changing a variable's
address inside a
function.*

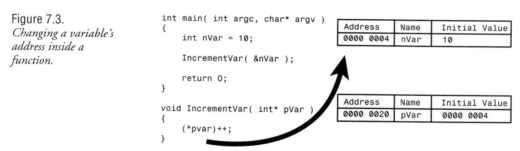

Another use for pointers is to keep a reference to memory that has been requested at runtime from the operating system. I discuss this in more detail later, in the section called "Using *new* and *delete* to Create Dynamic Objects."

References

In addition to using pointers to refer to other variables, the C++ language also has a derived type known as a *reference*. A reference is declared using the reference operator, &, which bears an uncanny resemblance to the address-of operator. Both operators use the same symbol; however, you use them in different contexts. The only time that & is used for a reference is in a declaration, like this:

```
int myAge;
int& myRef = myAge;
```

The code above defines a reference variable named myRef, which is a reference, or *alias,* for the myAge variable. The advantage of using a reference instead of a pointer variable is that no indirection operator is required. However, once defined, the reference variable cannot be bound to another variable. For example, the code such as that in Listing 7.9 often is misunderstood.

Listing 7.9. Using references to change the value of a variable.

```
#include <iostream.h>

int main()
{

    int nFoo = 5;
    int nBar = 10;

    // Define a reference to int that is an alias for nFoo.
    int& nRef = nFoo;

    // Display a table containing the variables.
    cout << "nFoo\tnBar\tnRef" << endl;
    cout << nFoo << "\t" << nBar << "\t" << nRef << endl;

    // Change the value of nFoo. nRef remains an alias for
    // nFoo, it does not become an alias for nBar.
    nRef = nBar;
    cout << nFoo << "\t" << nBar << "\t" << nRef << endl;

    return 0;
}
```

References are most commonly used when passing parameters to functions. It is often quite expensive in terms of computing resources to pass a class object as a function parameter. Using a pointer to pass a parameter is subject to errors, and affects the function's readability. However, if you use references as function parameters, you eliminate unnecessary copies, and you can use the parameter as if a copy were passed. To prevent the called function from changing the value of a reference variable, you can declare the parameter as const, like this:

```
void Print( const int& nFoo )
{
    nFoo = 12;  // error - not allowed to change const
    cout << "The value is " << nFoo << endl;
}
```

References to const objects often are used when large objects are passed to a function, because it can be expensive, in terms of computing resources, to generate a copy of a large object that is used only during a function call.

Using *new* and *delete* to Create Dynamic Objects

So far, I've talked about variables allocated as local objects that are created when a function or block is entered, and destroyed when the function or block is exited. Most programs that work in the real world use variables and objects that have a *dynamic lifetime,* meaning that they are explicitly created and explicitly destroyed.

In a C++ program, you can use the new and delete operators to allocate and destroy variables dynamically, as shown in Listing 7.10.

Listing 7.10. Using new and delete for fundamental types.

```
#include <iostream.h>

int main()
{
    int *pFoo = new int;

    *pFoo = 42;
    cout << "The answer is " << *pFoo << endl;

    delete pFoo;

    return 0;
}
```

Using *new[]* and *delete[]* to create arrays

You also can create arrays dynamically using new[], with the size of the array specified inside the square brackets. When you create an array using new[], you must use delete[] to release the memory allocated for the array. The size of the array is not specified when delete[] is used. Using delete[] is the only clue to the compiler indicating that the pointer is the beginning of an array of objects. Listing 7.11 is an example showing how to allocate and free a dynamic array.

Listing 7.11. Using new[] to create a dynamic array.

```
#include <iostream.h>

int main()
{
    int nMaxFoo = 12;
    int *arFoo = new int[nMaxFoo];

    for( int nFooIndex = 0; nFooIndex < nMaxFoo; nFooIndex++ )
    {
        arFoo[nFooIndex] = 42 + nFooIndex;
    }

    for( nFooIndex = 0; nFooIndex < nMaxFoo; nFooIndex++ )
    {
        cout << "The answer is " << arFoo[nFooIndex] << endl;
    }

    delete[] arFoo;

    return 0;
}
```

Note that in Listing 7.12, it's possible to use a variable to specify the size of the array.

Summary

In this chapter, I discussed several issues that affect a variable's visibility and its lifetime, including the issue of creating variables dynamically.

PART III

The Microsoft Foundation Class (MFC) Library

8 Object-Oriented Design and Virtual Functions

9 MFC Base Classes

10 Templates and the Standard Template Library

11 Collection Classes

12 Exception Handling and RTTI

Object-Oriented Design and Virtual Functions

To take advantage of the C++ language support for object-oriented programming, you must first understand how object-oriented programs are designed. In this chapter I present some general goals of object-oriented design. I also go over another aspect of polymorphism: the virtual function.

What Is Object-Oriented Design?

What One of the design goals for the C++ language was to provide a language that supported object-oriented programming. Object-oriented programming is not new; Simula, the first language to support object-oriented programming, has been around since the mid-1960s.

Object-oriented design involves classifying real-world objects and actions as classes that can be created, manipulated, and destroyed. The data that makes up an object, and the functions that are performed on that object, are combined to form a class, or a description of that object. Classes can inherit functionality from other objects, and you easily can add new classes that leverage existing classes.

Another key part of object-oriented design is the idea that the class should provide an interface, which is used to manipulate objects that are created from the class. As much as possible, implementation details should be hidden from the user. This enables you to provide complicated classes with a simple interface. It also allows you to change the implementation details of a class if needed.

Why Is Object-Oriented Design Useful?

Why

In traditional, structured design, the data manipulated by a program and the functions that manipulate the data are separate. It often is difficult to reuse parts of a design built with structured design techniques, unless the new design is very similar to the old design.

Object-oriented design is useful because it can be used to create designs that can be reused and extended. A design, or a portion of a design, can be reused in future programs much like a hardware component, such as a computer chip, a disk drive, or a sound card. Because object-oriented designs describe the object's class completely, each class is easily reused, as the data and functions described by the class are integrated.

Because you can hide the implementation of a class behind an interface, it's easy to change the implementation details of a class without affecting users of that class—as long as the interface doesn't change. For example, the Tab control was not available in versions of Windows prior to Windows 95. The MFC CPropertyPage class was rewritten for MFC 4.0 to take advantage of the new Tab control without impacting users of that class, except that the class is now more efficient.

How Is Object-Oriented Design Used?

How

The trickiest part of object-oriented design is finding a good set of objects to work with. An object is just a "thing" that you can use inside your program. The specific objects used in a program really depend on the program's purpose. An object can be a physical item that can be manipulated, like a car or a plane, or it can be more conceptual, like a trip or a visit. Most objects have two important things in common:

- They have some sort of state or properties that make the object unique.
- They have functions or methods that can be applied to the object to change its state, or to take advantage of the object's properties.

Describing Objects in a Class

When using C++, objects are described by a *class*. A class is just a description of the object that can be created, and the actions that can be performed on it. A C++ class has two main parts:

- The *class declaration*. This contains the class interface and information about data members for the class. The class interface usually is located in a header file having a .H suffix. Any file in your program that uses the class must use the #include directive so that the class declaration is added to the source file by the preprocessor.

- The *class implementation*. This includes all of the member functions that have been declared as part of the class. The class implementation usually is located in a file that has a .CPP suffix.

Organizing Classes and Objects

When designing classes, look for similarities in classes, as well as how the different objects relate to each other. If every class that described an object was written "from scratch," there would be a great deal of duplicated code in your programs. Fortunately, by taking a small amount of time to organize your classes, you can avoid much of this extra work.

As you look at different classes that might be contained in a C++ program, you will probably start to intuitively group them. There are two basic ways to organize classes:

- *Hierarchies*. A hierarchy can be used to organize classes like a family tree, with classes "inheriting" member data and functions from their ancestors.

- *Categories*. Often, a set of classes are used together and have some sort of dependency or other form of close relationship with each other. These classes can be organized as a category to simplify their use.

Class Hierarchies

A class in most object-oriented languages, including C++, can inherit functionality from a *base class*. A base class has general properties that are included in classes derived from it. For example, let's say that you have created a class library that you use to display different geometric shapes. All of the shapes in your library have many properties in common that may not seem obvious at first glance. The class declarations for some geometric object classes are shown in Listing 8.1.

Listing 8.1. Class declarations for geometric shapes, without using inheritance.

```
class CSquare
{
public:
            CSquare();
    double  GetSideLength();
    double  GetArea();
    void    GetCenter( int* x, int* y );
```

continues

Listing 8.1. continued

```
    void    SetCenter( int* x, int* y );
    void    Draw();
private:
    double  m_dLength;
    int     m_xCoord;
    int     m_yCoord;
};

class CCircle
{
public:
            CCircle();
    double  GetRadius();
    double  GetArea();
    void    GetCenter( int* x, int* y );
    void    SetCenter( int* x, int* y );
    void    Draw();
private:
    double  m_dRadius;
    int     m_xCoord;
    int     m_yCoord;
};
```

These two classes have several things in common. To name a few similarities: they both refer to shapes, each object can have a unique center, and each object can be drawn. Unfortunately, the declarations in Listing 8.1 do not take advantage of the similarities between the CCircle and CSquare classes. If this pattern was continued, every geometric shape in the collection of classes would be written from scratch.

Organizing classes into a hierarchy before you start writing your class declarations is one way to look for common traits in classes. By organizing your classes, you can quickly see the relationships that exist between all the classes. This should help you in deciding which class you wish to use as your base class. It can also help you in deciding which new classes need to be developed. An example of using base classes can be seen in part of a larger geometric class library design shown in Figure 8.1.

Figure 8.1 is a class diagram drawn using Booch notation, a common way of showing how classes are related. Arrows are drawn from derived classes to their base classes. (Don't worry about being able to draw diagrams in any particular style; the point here is to organize your classes in a way that helps show their relationships with each other.)

The classes for squares, circles, and triangles are used to model those particular types of objects. All of these objects are derived from a base class called CShape. The CShape class defines the common properties for all of the classes derived from it.

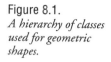

Figure 8.1.
A hierarchy of classes used for geometric shapes.

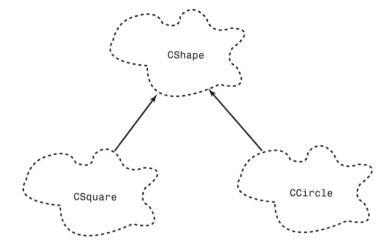

Class Categories

Many times, classes that work together have a strong dependency on each other. Classes that are tightly related are often arranged into categories. Classes arranged into categories are commonly used as a group; it often makes no sense to use a single class that is a part of a larger category.

Using Inheritance

In "Class Hierarchies," I introduced inheritance as a way to organize different types of objects so that common traits could be identified. The classes identified as *ancestor*, or base, classes contain member data and functions that are included in all of the *descendant*, or derived, classes.

In Figure 8.1, all of the classes derived from CShape are called *subclasses* of CShape. Another way of describing the relationships between CShape and the other classes in Figure 8.1 is to use the term IS-A: CSquare IS-A CShape, and CCircle IS-A CShape. Any operation that can be performed on a base class can be performed on a derived class if the two classes have an IS-A relationship.

When using inheritance, a base class establishes a kind of contract that must be followed by all subclasses. If an operation can be performed using a base class, all subclasses must be able to perform that same task. In other words, in a "good" object-oriented design, it must be possible to substitute a subclass for a base class. This is known as the Liskov Substitution Principle, first presented by Barbara Liskov from MIT.

Listing 8.2 declares some classes used to describe geometric shapes, this time using a CShape base class.

Listing 8.2. Declarations for geometric shape classes, using a base class and inheritance.

```
class CShape
{
public:
    CShape();
    double  GetArea();
    void    GetCenter( int* x, int* y );
    void    SetCenter( int* x, int* y );
    void    Draw();
protected:
    int     m_xCoord;
    int     m_yCoord;
};
class CSquare : public CShape
{
public:
            CSquare();
    void    Draw();
    double  GetArea();
    double  GetSideLength();
private:
    double  m_dLength;
};

class CCircle : public CShape
{
public:
            CCircle();
    void    Draw();
    double  GetArea();
    double  GetRadius();
private:
    double  m_dRadius;
};
```

The class declarations in Listing 8.2 use the protected keyword, which often is used in base classes. When a class member is declared as protected, it normally cannot be accessed outside of the class. However, unlike a class member declared as private, it can be used by derived classes.

Using Pointers With Derived Classes

A class object can be allocated and used dynamically, just as if it were one of the fundamental types, like this:

```
CCircle* pCircle = new CCircle;
```

The example above allocates space for a CCircle object, and calls the CCircle constructor to perform any needed initializations. Of course, after the CCircle object is no longer needed, you should make sure that the program calls delete to free the allocated memory and cause the class's destructor to be called.

```
delete pCircle;
```

Using a Pointer to a Base Class

Because a class derived from a base class actually contains the base, it's possible to use a pointer to a base class when working with a derived object. Using the Liskov Substitution Principle that I discussed earlier, you should be able to use a CCircle object in place of a CShape object. This makes a design much easier to implement, because all of the functions that work with shapes can just use pointers to CShape, instead of trying to determine the type of each object. In other words, because CCircle IS-A CShape, we should be able to do this:

```
CShape* pShape = new CCircle;
pShape->Draw();
```

However, this doesn't work. The problem with this code is that it calls the wrong version of Draw. The base-class pointer calls the base-class function, instead of the derived-class's version, as illustrated in the console mode example provided in Listing 8.3.

Listing 8.3. An example of calling the wrong function through a base-class pointer.

```
#include <iostream.h>
//
// Define some shape classes. Most of the member data and
// functions have been removed so that the Draw function
// can be illustrated clearly.
class CShape
{
public:
    void Draw();
};
void CShape::Draw()
{
    cout << "CShape::Draw called" << endl;
}

class CCircle : public CShape
{
public:
    void Draw();
};
void CCircle::Draw()
{
    cout << "Circle::Draw called" << endl;
}

//
// main()
int main()
{
    CShape* pShape = new CCircle;
    pShape->Draw();
    delete pShape;
    return 0;
}
```

In order to solve this problem, you must declare functions used through base-class pointers as virtual functions. When a function is declared with the `virtual` keyword, the compiler generates code that determines the actual type of the object at runtime, and calls the correct function.

Using Virtual Functions

When a virtual function is used, the compiler constructs a special table, called a *virtual function table* or "vtabl." This table is used to keep track of the correct functions to be called for every object of that class. When a virtual function is called, the vtabl is used to access the correct function indirectly, as shown in Figure 8.2.

Figure 8.2.
The virtual function table, used to determine the correct virtual function.

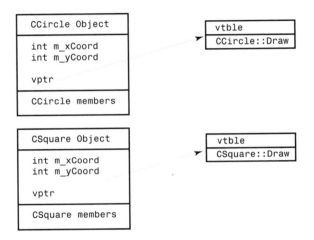

The added overhead of using the vtabl is fairly small, but it could be significant if you have thousands of small objects or if execution speed is critical. For that reason, a function must be specified as virtual; it doesn't happen by default. Listing 8.4 repeats the previous listing, except that Draw is declared as a virtual function.

Listing 8.4. An example of virtual functions and reliable base-class pointer use.

```
#include <iostream.h>
//
// Define some shape classes. Most of the member data and
// functions have been removed so that the Draw function
// can be illustrated clearly.
class CShape
{
public:
    virtual void Draw();
};
void CShape::Draw()
{
    cout << "CShape::Draw called" << endl;
}
```

```
class CCircle : public CShape
{
public:
    virtual void Draw();
};
void CCircle::Draw()
{
    cout << "CCircle::Draw called" << endl;
}

//
// main()
int main()
{
    CShape* pShape = new CCircle;
    pShape->Draw();
    delete pShape;
    return 0;
}
```

Note that the virtual keyword is only used in the class declaration, not in the function definition.

Using Pure Virtual Functions

When a base class declares a virtual function, it sometimes makes no sense for the base class to provide any implementation for the function. A good example of this is shown in the CShape class.

The CShape class should be an abstract class. Abstract classes are allowed to declare functions that are not defined in the base class. An example of a function that should not be implemented in CShape is the Draw member function, shown in the previous examples.

All subclasses of CShape are expected to provide a Draw member function. The CShape base class cannot provide a meaningful Draw function, because it has no way of knowing how a particular shape should be drawn.

To force all subclasses of a class to implement a virtual function, you can declare that function as a "pure" virtual function by adding = 0; to its declaration. Listing 8.5 provides a new version of the shape example, with Draw declared as a pure virtual function.

Listing 8.5. Using a pure virtual function in a base class.

```
#include <iostream.h>
//
// Define some shape classes. Most of the member data and
// functions have been removed so that the Draw function
// can be illustrated clearly.
class CShape
{
public:
    // pure virtual function
```

continues

Listing 8.5. continued

```
    virtual void Draw() = 0;
};

class CCircle : public CShape
{
public:
    virtual void Draw();
};
void CCircle::Draw()
{
    cout << "CCircle::Draw called" << endl;
}

//
// main()
int main()
{
    CShape* pShape = new CCircle;
    pShape->Draw();
    delete pShape;
    return 0;
}
```

If a class has at least one pure virtual function, that class becomes an *abstract* base class, and it can never be instantiated. For example, the code below generates a compiler error:

```
CShape    aShape;
```

Using Virtual Destructors

When you use pointers to base classes to access objects derived from the base class, a serious problem can occur when the object is destroyed. It's possible for the wrong destructor to be called, resulting in a partially destroyed object. Listing 8.6 uses the shape classes to demonstrate this problem.

Listing 8.6. An example of the problems caused by deleting an object without a virtual destructor.

```
#include <iostream.h>
//
// Define some shape classes. Most of the member data and
// functions have been removed so that the Draw function
// can be illustrated clearly.
class CShape
{
public:
    ~CShape();
    // pure virtual function
    virtual void Draw() = 0;
};
CShape::~CShape()
{
```

```
        cout << "Base destructor called." << endl;
}

class CCircle : public CShape
{
public:
    ~CCircle();
    virtual void Draw();
};
CCircle::~CCircle()
{
    cout << "CCircle destructor called." << endl;
}
void CCircle::Draw()
{
    cout << "CCircle::Draw called" << endl;
}

//
// main()
int main()
{
    CShape* pShape = new CCircle;
    pShape->Draw();
    delete pShape;
    return 0;
}
```

The solution in this case is to declare the destructor as `virtual`. Just like all other virtual functions, the correct function is determined at runtime, and the proper object's destructor is called. Unlike other virtual functions, every destructor is called as the object is destroyed. Listing 8.7 corrects the problems found in Listing 8.6, and the `pShape` object is properly destroyed.

Listing 8.7. An example showing the correct destructor chosen at runtime.

```
#include <iostream.h>
//
// Define some shape classes. Most of the member data and
// functions have been removed so that the Draw function
// can be illustrated clearly.
class CShape
{
public:
    virtual ~CShape();
    // pure virtual function
    virtual void Draw() = 0;
};
CShape::~CShape()
{
    cout << "Base destructor called." << endl;
}

class CCircle : public CShape
{
public:
```

continues

Listing 8.7. continued

```
    virtual ~CCircle();
    virtual void Draw();
};
CCircle::~CCircle()
{
    cout << "CCircle destructor called." << endl;
}
void CCircle::Draw()
{
    cout << "CCircle::Draw called" << endl;
}

//
// main()
int main()
{
    CShape* pShape = new CCircle;
    pShape->Draw();
    delete pShape;
    return 0;
}
```

When you use a base class, you should declare its destructor as virtual, even if the destructor consists of just an empty function. If you aren't sure if a class might be used as a base class, declare the destructor as virtual to be safe.

Summary

In this chapter you've looked at object-oriented design, and how you can use it to create programs and components that are more flexible and reusable. You also looked at inheritance and virtual functions, two features of the C++ language that provide support for object-oriented programming.

CHAPTER 9

MFC Base Classes

In this chapter, you look at two base classes that are used for most classes in the MFC class library. The CObject and CWnd classes are commonly used base classes that provide special functionality to classes that are derived from them. In this chapter, you look at both of these classes and build a sample program that demonstrates some of the functions offered by the CObject class.

What Are MFC Base Classes?

What The MFC class library includes a large number of classes well-suited for Windows programming. Most of these classes are derived from CObject, a class that is at the root of the MFC class hierarchy. In addition, any class that represents a window or control is derived from the CWnd class, which handles basic functions that are common to all windows.

The CObject and CWnd classes make use of virtual functions, which enable your program to access general purpose functions through a base pointer. This enables you to easily use any object that is derived from CObject or CWnd when interacting with the MFC framework.

The *CObject* Base Class

Almost every class used in an MFC program is derived from CObject. The CObject class provides four types of services:

- Diagnostic memory management provides diagnostic messages when memory leaks are detected. These leaks are often caused by failing to free objects that have been dynamically created.

- Dynamic creation support uses the CRuntimeClass to enable objects to be created at runtime. This is different from creating objects dynamically using the new operator, which was discussed in Chapter 7, "Scope, Pointers, and Lifetime in C++." This function is discussed in more detail in "How Are the MFC Base Classes Used?"

- Serialization support enables an object to be stored and loaded in an object-oriented fashion. Serialization is discussed in Chapter 41, "Serialization," and Chapter 42, "Serialization and Document/View."

- Runtime class information is similar to runtime type information, or RTTI, which is discussed in Chapter 12, "Exception Handling and RTTI." The MFC class library uses runtime class information to provide diagnostic information when errors are discovered in your program and when you're serializing objects to or from storage.

The *CWnd* Base Class

The CWnd class is derived from CObject and adds a great deal of functionality that is shared by all windows in an MFC program. This also includes dialog boxes and controls, which are just specialized versions of windows. Figure 9.1 shows the major MFC classes derived from CWnd.

Figure 9.1.
The major MFC classes derived from CWnd.

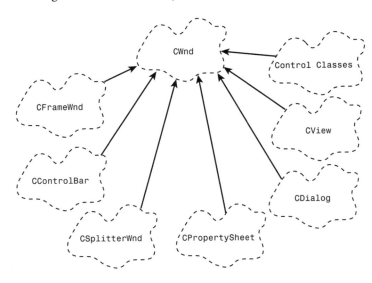

The CWnd class defines functions that can be applied to any CWnd object, including objects that are instances of classes derived from CWnd. For example, to set the caption or title for any window, you can use the CWnd::SetWindowText function.

Why Use MFC Base Classes?

Why

The CObject and CWnd base classes are two examples of base classes that are used to provide basic functionality to a large number of classes through a base class.

Almost every significant object in an MFC program is a CObject instance. This enables you to take advantage of the MFC support for discovering many common memory leaks and other types of programming errors. The CObject class also declares functions that can be used to provide diagnostic dumps during runtime and support for serialization. Serialization is discussed in Chapter 41.

Every window in an MFC program is a CWnd object. CWnd is derived from CObject, so it has all of the CObject functionality built-in. Using the CWnd class to handle all controls and windows in your program enables you to take advantage of polymorphism; the CWnd class provides all of the general window functions for all types of windows. This means you don't need to know exactly what type of control or window is accessed through a CWnd pointer in many cases.

How Are the MFC Base Classes Used?

How

The CObject and CWnd classes are used in different ways. The CObject class is normally used as a base class when you create your own classes. The CWnd class is often passed as a function parameter or return value and is used as a generic pointer to any type of window in an MFC program.

In this section, you create a sample console mode project that demonstrates how the CObject class is used. Following the steps provided in Chapter 3, "Writing Simple C++ Programs," create a new console mode project named Runtime. In addition, configure the project so that it uses the MFC class library by following these steps:

1. Select Settings from the Build menu. This opens the Project Settings dialog box.
2. Click on the General tab.
3. Select Use MFC in a Shared DLL from the Microsoft Foundation Classes combo box.
4. Close the dialog box by clicking the Close button.

Using *CObject* as a Base Class

The CObject class is always used as a base class; there isn't really anything that can be done with a plain CObject. When used as a base class, the CObject class provides a great deal of basic functionality to a class. You can control the amount of functionality provided by CObject by using macros in the derived class's declaration and definition files.

There are four different levels of support offered by CObject to its derived classes.

- Basic support with memory leak detection requires no macros.
- Support for runtime class identification requires the use of the DECLARE_DYNAMIC macro in the class declaration and the IMPLEMENT_DYNAMIC macro in the class definition.
- Support for dynamic object creation requires the use of the DECLARE_DYNCREATE macro in the class declaration and the IMPLEMENT_DYNCREATE macro in the class definition. The use of dynamic object creation is discussed later in this chapter.
- Serialization support requires the use of the DECLARE_SERIAL macro in the class declaration and the IMPLEMENT_SERIAL macro in the class definition. The use of serialization is discussed in Chapters 41 and 42.

Each of the CObject macros is used in a similar way. All DECLARE macros have one parameter—the name of the class. The IMPLEMENT macros generally take two parameters—the name of the class and the name of the immediate base class. IMPLEMENT_SERIAL is an exception because it requires three parameters, as discussed in Chapter 41.

Listing 9.1 is the class declaration for CMyObject, a simple class that is derived from CObject. The CMyObject class supports dynamic creation so it includes the DECLARE_DYNCREATE macro.

Listing 9.1. The CMyObject class declaration, using CObject as a base class.

```
class CMyObject : public CObject
{
    DECLARE_DYNCREATE( CMyObject );
// Constructor
public:
    CMyObject();
//Attributes
public:
    void Set( const CString& szName );
    CString Get() const;
//Implementation
private:
    CString m_szName;
};
```

Save the source code from Listing 9.1 in the Runtime project directory as MyObj.h. It's just an include file, so don't add it to the project.

The source code for the CMyObject member functions is provided in Listing 9.2. Save this source code as MyObj.cpp and add it to the Runtime project. This source file contains the IMPLEMENT_DYNCREATE macro that matches the DECLARE_DYNCREATE macro from the class declaration.

Listing 9.2. Member functions for the `CMyObject` class.

```
#include <afx.h>
#include "MyObj.h"
IMPLEMENT_DYNCREATE( CMyObject, CObject );
CMyObject::CMyObject()
{
}
void CMyObject::Set( const CString& szName )
{
    m_szName = szName;
}
CString CMyObject::Get() const
{
    return m_szName;
}
```

It's important to remember that the DECLARE and IMPLEMENT macros are used in two different places. A DECLARE macro, such as DECLARE_DYNCREATE, is used in the class declaration. An IMPLEMENT macro, such as IMPLEMENT_DYNCREATE, is used only in the class definition.

Creating an Object at Runtime

There are two ways to dynamically create objects. The first method, covered in Chapter 7, uses the C++ operator new to dynamically allocate an object from free storage.

```
CMyObject* pObject = new CMyObject;
```

The second method is used primarily by the MFC framework and uses a special class, CRuntimeClass, and the RUNTIME_CLASS macro. You can use the CRuntimeClass class to determine the type of an object or to create a new object. Listing 9.3 creates a CMyObject instance using the CRuntimeClass::CreateObject function.

Listing 9.3. Creating an object at runtime using `CRuntimeClass`.

```
#include <afx.h>
#include <iostream.h>
#include "MyObj.h"
int main()
{
    CRuntimeClass* pRuntime = RUNTIME_CLASS( CMyObject );
    CObject* pObj = pRuntime->CreateObject();
    ASSERT( pObj->IsKindOf(RUNTIME_CLASS(CMyObject)) );

    CMyObject* pFoo = (CMyObject*)pObj;
    pFoo->Set( "FooBar" );

    cout << pFoo->Get() << endl;

    delete pFoo;
    return 0;
}
```

Save the contents of Listing 9.3 as Runtime.cpp and add the file to the Runtime project. Compile the project and if there are no errors, run the project in a DOS window by following these steps:

1. Open a DOS window from the Start button's Programs menu.
2. Change the current directory to the project directory.
3. Type Debug\Runtime in the DOS window. The program executes and outputs FooBar.

Leave the DOS window open for now because you use it for the next example.

Testing for a Valid Object

The MFC class library offers several diagnostic features. Most of these features are in the form of macros that are used only in a debug version of your program. This gives you the best of both worlds. When you are developing and testing your program, you can use the MFC diagnostic functions to help ensure that your program has as few errors as possible, although it runs with the additional overhead required by the diagnostics. Later, when your program is compiled in a release version, the diagnostic checks are removed, and your program executes at top speed.

There are three macros that are commonly used in an MFC program.

■ ASSERT brings up an error message dialog box when an expression that evaluates to FALSE is passed to it. This macro is compiled only in debug builds.

■ VERIFY works exactly like ASSERT except that the expression that is evaluated is always compiled, even for non-debug builds, although the expression is not tested in release builds.

■ ASSERT_VALID tests a pointer to a CObject instance and verifies that the object is a valid pointer in a valid state. A class derived from CObject can override the AssertValid function to enable testing of the state of an object.

The ASSERT and VERIFY macros are used with all expressions, not just those involving CObject. Although they both test to make sure that the evaluated expression is TRUE, there is an important difference in the way these two macros work. When compiled for a release build, the ASSERT macro and the expression it evaluates are completely ignored during compilation. The VERIFY macro is also ignored, but the expression is compiled and used in the release build.

A common source of errors in MFC programs is placing important code inside an ASSERT macro instead of a VERIFY macro. If the expression is needed for the program to work correctly, it belongs in a VERIFY macro, not an ASSERT macro. These functions are used in examples throughout the rest of the book to test for error conditions.

Providing a *Dump* Function

In addition to the diagnostic functions and macros in the previous section, CObject declares a virtual function for displaying the contents of an object at runtime. This function, Dump, is used to send messages about the current state of the object to a debug window.

If you are debugging an MFC program, the messages are displayed in an output window of the debugger. Add the source code from Listing 9.4 to the CMyObject class declaration. The Dump function is usually placed in the implementation section of the class declaration; in this example, it should be placed after the declaration for m_szName. Because Dump is only called by the MFC framework, it is usually declared as protected or private. Because the Dump function is only called for debug builds, the declaration is surrounded by #ifdef and #endif statements that remove the declaration for Dump for release builds.

Listing 9.4. Adding a Dump function to the CMyObject declaration.

```
#ifdef _DEBUG
    void Dump( CDumpContext& dc ) const;
#endif
```

Add the source code from Listing 9.5 to the MyObj.cpp source code file. The implementation of the function is also bracketed by #ifdef and #endif statements in order to remove the function for release builds.

Listing 9.5. Adding the implementation of Dump to CMyObject.

```
#ifdef _DEBUG
void CMyObject::Dump( CDumpContext& dc ) const
{
    CObject::Dump( dc );
    dc << m_szName;
}
#endif
```

The Dump function in Listing 9.5 calls the base class version of Dump first. This step is recommended to get a consistent output in the debug window. After calling CObject::Dump, member data contained in the class is sent to the dump context using the insertion operator, <<, just as if the data was sent to cout.

Detecting Memory Leaks with *CObject*'s Memory Diagnostics

The Runtime sample program doesn't have any memory leaks. Although this is good in most cases, you need to have a memory leak so that you can see how the Dump function works. To create a typical memory leak, comment out or remove the following delete statement in Runtime.cpp:

```
delete pFoo;
```

Compile and run the program using the Developer Studio debugger. Use one of the following methods to start debugging a program using the integrated debugger:

- Select Debug from the Build menu.
- Click the Go toolbar button.
- Press F5.

After the program runs, the debug window displays messages that look something like the following:

```
Detected memory leaks!
Dumping objects ->
strcore.cpp(76) : {28} normal block at 0x00750D58, 19 bytes long.
 Data: <          FooB> 01 00 00 00 06 00 00 00 06 00 00 00 46 6F 6F 42
{27} client block at 0x00750D28, subtype 0, 8 bytes long.
a CMyObject object at $00750D28, 8 bytes long
Object dump complete.
```

Using *CWnd* as a Base Class

You will rarely create a new class that uses CWnd as a base class, unlike with CObject. The CWnd class is usually used as a generic window pointer. For example, because all windows, including controls, are derived from CWnd, a CWnd pointer is often used in loops and other functions where the exact type of a window is unknown. Listing 9.6 is a function that enables or disables a control using the resource ID passed as a parameter.

Listing 9.6. Disabling and enabling a control using a CWnd pointer.

```
void CMyDialog::EnableControl( UINT nID, BOOL bEnable )
{
    CWnd* pWnd = GetDlgItem( nID );
    ASSERT( pWnd != NULL );
    pWnd->EnableWindow( bEnable );
}
```

The CWnd class contains additional functions that can be applied to most windows. Although there are dozens of CWnd functions, here is a list of the more commonly used ones:

- ShowWindow is used to either hide or display the window. You must pass a parameter that determines how the command should affect the window. There are ten possible parameters; the most commonly used ones are SW_HIDE to hide the window and SW_SHOW, which displays the window using its current size and position.
- SetWindowText is used to set the caption or title bar for a window. If the window is an edit control, calling SetWindowText sets the text contained in the edit control.
- GetWindowText returns the current caption or title bar for a window. If the window is an edit control, the contents of the control are returned.
- MoveWindow is used to specify a new position for a window or control.

- `SetFont` enables you to define the font used for a window. This function works for all windows, including edit controls. Using fonts is discussed in Chapter 32, "Fonts."
- `GetFont` returns the current font used by a particular window.

In addition, there are more member `CWnd` functions that are discussed in upcoming chapters.

Summary

In this chapter, I discussed the two main base classes used in the MFC class library, `CObject` and `CWnd`. I discussed features provided by these two base classes and created an example of how to use `CObject` as a base.

Templates and the Standard Template Library

In this chapter, I discuss C++ templates and the Standard Template Library, or STL. You use templates to build a CStack collection class that can be used to store any type of object, and you create a sample program that uses the STL.

Collections and containers are two names for objects that are used to store other objects. MFC collections are discussed in more detail in Chapter 11, "Collection Classes."

What Are Templates?

What Templates are used with classes and functions that accept parameters when the class is used. You can think of a class or function template as an order form with some blank spaces provided that can be filled in when the order is placed. Instead of creating a list class for pointer arrays and another list class for CStrings, a single template class can be used as a list class for both types.

Why Use Templates?

Why

Templates are very useful in collections because a single, well written collection class that uses templates can be immediately reused for all of the built-in types and any MFC- or user- created class as well. In addition, using templates for your collection classes helps eliminate one of the major reasons that casting is often required.

How Are Templates Used?

How

The syntax used for declaring and using templates might be difficult to understand at first. As with most things, practice makes perfect. The syntax for using a template is fairly simple. A CStack collection of integers is declared as

```
CStack<int>    stackOfInt;
```

The <int> part of the declaration is the parameter list for the template. The parameter list is used to tell the compiler how to create this particular instance of the template. This is also known as an instantiation because a new instance of the template with these arguments will be created. Don't worry about the actual meaning of the template parameters used for CStack right now; I discuss those in the next section.

You can also use the typedef keyword to make your declarations easier to read. If you use typedef to create a new type, you can use the new name in place of the longer template syntax, as shown in Listing 10.1.

Listing 10.1. Using typedef to simplify template declarations.

```
typedef      CStack<int>    INTSTACK;
INTSTACK    stackOfInt;
INTSTACK    stackOfIntToo;
```

A *CStack* Template Class

Creating a template-based class is only a little bit more work than creating a non-template class. In this section, you create your own template-based stack class.

A stack is a collection of objects that enables items to be added or removed from only one logical point in the collection, the "top." Items are pushed on and popped off the stack. If two or more items are stored in a stack, you can access only the last item added to the stack, as shown in Figure 10.1.

Figure 10.1.
A stack enables you to
access only the top item.

When you create a definition for your templates, it's common practice to use the placeholder T to represent the type that will be provided later when the template is instantiated. An example of a simple stack template is provided in Listing 10.2.

Listing 10.2. The CStack template class.

```cpp
template <class T> class CStack
{
    public:
        CStack();
        virtual ~CStack();
        BOOL    IsEmpty() const;
        T       Pop();
        void    Push( const T& item );
    private:
        CStack<T>( const CStack& T){};
        T*      m_p;
        int     m_nStored;
        int     m_nDepth;
        enum    { GROW_BY = 5 };
};
//Constructors
template <class T> CStack<T>::CStack()
{
    m_p = 0;
    m_nStored = 0;
    m_nDepth  = 0;
}
template <class T> CStack<T>::~CStack()
{
    delete [] m_p;
}
// Operations
template <class T> BOOL CStack<T>::IsEmpty() const
{
    return m_nStored == 0;
}
template <class T> void CStack<T>::Push( const T& item )
{
    if( m_nStored == m_nDepth )
    {
        T* p = new T[m_nDepth + GROW_BY];
        for( int i=0; i < m_nDepth; i++ )
        {
            p[i] = m_p[i];
        }
        m_nDepth += GROW_BY;
        delete [] m_p;
        m_p = p;
    }
```

Listing 10.2. continued

```
    m_p[m_nStored] = item;
    m_nStored++;
}
template <class T> int CStack<T>::Pop()
{
    ASSERT( m_nStored );
    m_nStored--;
    return m_p[m_nStored];
}
```

The template declaration tells the compiler to use a type that will be provided later when the template is actually instantiated. The following syntax is used at the beginning of the declaration:

```
template <class T> class CStack
```

This tells the compiler that a user of CStack will provide a type when the template is instantiated and that type should be used wherever T is found in the rest of the template declaration.

The CStack member functions also use a similar declaration. If CStack was a non-template class, the IsEmpty member function might look like the following:

```
BOOL CStack::IsEmpty() const
{
    return m_nStored == 0;
}
```

Because CStack is a template class, the template information must be provided. Another way to define the IsEmpty function is to place the template information on a separate line before the rest of the function.

```
template <class T>
BOOL CStack<T>::IsEmpty() const
{
    return m_nStored == 0;
}
```

Listing 10.3 is a simple example that uses CStack.

Listing 10.3. Using the CStack template.

```
#include <afx.h>
#include <iostream.h>
#include "stack.h"

int main( int argc, char* argv[] )
{
    CStack<int> theStack;
    int i = 0;
    while( i < 5 )
    {
        cout << "Pushing a " << i << endl;
        theStack.Push( i++ );
```

```
    }
    cout << "All items pushed" << endl;
    while( theStack.IsEmpty() == FALSE )
    {
        cout << "Popping a " << theStack.Pop() << endl;
    }
    return 0;
}
```

Using Template Functions

Another important use of templates is function templates. If you are familiar with C, you have probably used preprocessor macros to create low-overhead functions. Unfortunately, preprocessor macros aren't really functions, and they have absolutely no parameter checking whatsoever.

Function templates enable a function to be used for a wide range of different types. Listing 10.4 is a function template that exchanges the values of the two parameters passed to it.

Listing 10.4. An example of a function template that exchanges its parameters.

```
template< class T >
void ArgSwap( T& foo, T& bar )
{
    T       temp;
    temp = foo;
    foo  = bar;
    bar  = temp;
}
```

Using a function template is very easy. The compiler handles everything for you. The example in Listing 10.5 displays a message before and after calling the ArgSwap function template.

Listing 10.5. Using ArgSwap to exchange the contents of two CString objects.

```
#include <afx.h>
#include <iostream.h>
#include "argswap.h"

int main()
{
    CString     szFirstMsg( "Hello" );
    CString     szSecondMsg( "GoodBye" );

    cout << szFirstMsg << "\t" << szSecondMsg << endl;
    ArgSwap( szFirstMsg, szSecondMsg );
    cout << szFirstMsg << "\t" << szSecondMsg << endl;

    return EXIT_SUCCESS;
}
```

What Is the Standard Template Library?

What
The Standard Template Library is a set of collections, algorithms, and functions that have recently been added to the C++ Draft Standard. As part of the C++ standardization process, some of the members of the C++ community thought that there was a need for a basic C++ library that would take advantage of the C++ language and would be available on all compilers. The STL was selected by the C++ standardization committees to be this standard library.

As its name suggests, the STL makes heavy use of templates in its library classes and functions. The STL classes grew out of research work that was performed at Hewlett-Packard on generic programming; the STL uses templates extensively to provide a set of collections and algorithms that are truly generic. Functions and objects in the STL are classified by what they do, not by the way they are implemented.

The Standard Template Library includes five different types of components:

- Containers, also known as collections, are used to store other objects. Containers are classified according to the methods used to access items stored in the container. Collections and containers are also discussed in Chapter 11.

- Iterators are used to move through items stored in a container. An iterator is similar to a cursor in a word processor. In the STL, there are several different types of iterators.

- Function objects are used to wrap a commonly performed function in a generic object. Function object classes use templates that makes them flexible, as well as type-safe.

- Adapters are used to map a new interface for an existing class. For example, in the STL, stack is an adapter class applied on top of another class, such as list or vector.

- Algorithms are used to perform specified operations on objects. For example, the sort algorithm is used to sort a container.

Why Use the Standard Template Library?

Why
The STL offers generic containers and algorithms that can be applied to any type of object. This is the major strength of the Standard Template Library because it enables the containers and algorithms in an application to be completely separated from the application's data.

All STL containers and algorithms use templates that can be easily used for almost any data type. The containers, functions, and algorithms used by the STL can be adapted to any data type and in many cases can be used interchangeably with C++ arrays. For example, the functions and helper objects that are used with STL vectors can also be used with built-in arrays.

How Is the Standard Template Library Used?

In order to use the Standard Template Library, you must add the STL files to the `#include` file search path. You might also consider copying the \MSDEV\STL directory to your hard drive to speed up access time, especially if your other `#include` files are located on the hard disk.

How

To add the STL directory to the `#include` file search path, follow these steps:

1. Select Options from the Tools menu.
2. Select the Directories tab in the Options dialog box.
3. Add the STL directory to the Directories list box. The STL directory on the CD is \MSDEV\STL. If you copied the STL files to your hard disk, enter that location.
4. Click the OK button.

The STL was not created by Microsoft; the version on the distribution CD is the public domain version available to everyone. A reference manual for the STL is included in the STL directory. Although the Visual C++ compiler offers excellent support for the STL, be aware that some of the template constructions used by the library push the envelope as far as template support is concerned, and it's not uncommon to receive warning messages when using the STL.

Using Containers

One of the strengths of the STL is the support for generic containers. Using containers and collections is detailed in Chapter 11, so I introduce here a very simple container, the `vector`. An STL `vector` is similar to an array except that it automatically expands as needed when additional items are added. To declare a `vector` of integers named `v`, the syntax is

```
vector<int> v;
```

To add an item to a `vector`, you use the `push_back` function.

```
v.push_back(42);
```

The `vector` class is only one of several containers provided by the STL. The STL containers are separated into two types: sequences and associative containers, as shown in Figure 10.2.

Figure 10.2.
The containers provided by the Standard Template Library.

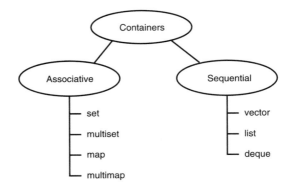

Sequences are collections that imply that items are stored based on the order in which they were inserted into the collection. Associative containers are sorted or retrieved on the basis of a key or other mapping.

Using Iterators

An STL iterator works very much like a pointer. An iterator is used to move forward or backward through a container or other structure, and it is declared in the following way:

```
vector<int>::interator    nIterator;
```

This line declares nIterator to be an iterator for a vector of integers. Before an iterator is used, it must be given a position, much like a pointer must be initialized.

```
nIterator = v.begin();
```

The begin function returns an iterator position that points to the first element in a container. There is also a function named end that returns a position *past* the end of the container.

```
for( nIter = v.begin(); nIter != n.end(); nIter++ )
    cout << *nIter << endl;
```

This code looks almost exactly like a for loop that would be used to display the contents of a built-in array. In fact, you can use STL iterators with built-in arrays.

```
int     arAges[] = { 5, 27, 38, 45 };
vector<int>::iterator nIter = arAges;
for(nIter = arAges; nIter != arAges + 4; nIter++)
    cout << *nIter << endl;
```

Iterators can be declared and used for all types of STL containers. This helps make the STL very flexible; not only are the containers generic, but also your algorithms can be generic.

There is also a set of iterators that can be used to iterate a container in reverse. A reverse iterator works very much like the forward iterators discussed previously except that when incremented, it moves to the previous item in a container. A reverse iterator must be explicitly declared.

```
vector<int>::reverse_iterator   revIter;
```

A different set of positioning functions are used with reverse iterators. The rbegin function returns the iterator position to the last collection item, and the rend function returns an iterator position *before* the first container item.

```
for( revIter = v.rbegin(); revIter != v.rend(); revIter++ )
```

Using Function Objects

An STL function object provides a generic function that can be applied to any object type. Containers and algorithms in the STL often use function objects to perform a task, such as comparing two objects, or to test if a certain condition has been met. For example, a greater function object is often used when sorting a container. An instance of greater used to compare integers looks like the following:

```
greater<int>    IsGreater;
```

Using the STL Algorithms

The STL also offers generic algorithms that can be applied to any type of object or container. This is the major strength of the Standard Template Library. All STL algorithms are template functions that can be used for almost any data type. This enables the STL to be truly generic; the STL source code is a good role model for designing extendible libraries.

As an example of the algorithms provided in the STL, let's look at the sorting algorithms. Each of the sorting algorithms comes in two flavors: one version that automatically uses the < operator to compare items and another version that uses a function object to compare items. The sorting algorithms in the STL are the following:

- sort is used to order a container with fairly good performance on average, although its worst-case time can be very poor. On average, the sort is logarithmic, meaning that the time required to sort the collection will approach *NlogN*, where *N* is the number of items in the collection. This is good performance for a general-purpose sort algorithm.
- stable_sort guarantees that the relative order of objects that compare equally will be preserved. If enough resources are available, the sort time is *NlogN*.
- partial_sort is used to order only part of a container.
- partial_sort_copy is used to copy the results of a partial sort into a new container.

Using an STL algorithm is just like calling any other function. For example, to sort a vector of integers named v using the greater function object, the function call looks like the following:

```
sort( v.begin(), v.end(), greater<int> );
```

Essential Example

An STL Example

The source code in Listing 10.6 is a complete console mode program that demonstrates the STL discussed in this chapter. This example uses the vector class, forward and reverse iterators, and the sort algorithm.

Listing 10.6. A sample program that uses the STL.

```
#include <iostream.h>
#include <vector.h>
#include <algo.h>

int arAges[] = { 105, 27, 89, 45 };
int main()
{
    vector<int> v;
    v.push_back( 434 );
    v.push_back( 356 );
    v.push_back( 267 );
    v.push_back( 987 );
    sort( v.begin(), v.end(), greater<int>() );
    vector<int>::iterator fwdIter = v.begin();
    vector<int>::reverse_iterator revIter = v.rbegin();

    while( fwdIter != v.end() )
    {
        cout << *fwdIter << endl;
        ++fwdIter;
    }
    while( revIter != v.rend() )
    {
        cout << *revIter << endl;
        ++revIter;
    }
    sort( arAges, arAges + 4, less<int>() );
    fwdIter = arAges;
    while( fwdIter != arAges + 4 )
    {
        cout << *fwdIter << endl;
        ++fwdIter;
    }
    return 0;
}
```

Summary

In this chapter, I introduced C++ templates and created a sample stack class, CStack. I also discussed the Standard Template Library and used it to create a small console mode application.

Collection Classes

In Chapter 5, "Control Structures and Classes," I discussed using classes to model real-world objects. Most of the examples of classes that you have seen so far are used to represent things that you can see or interact with, such as CString.

This chapter covers another useful type of class, the collection. The MFC class library includes three basic types of collection classes, and this chapter includes examples showing how to use all of them.

Also covered in this chapter are class and function templates. The MFC collection classes are implemented as templates, and you will see how to use them in your own programs. You also create and use a new CStack collection class from scratch.

What Are Collections?

What A collection class is used to create objects that are capable of storing other objects, as with the STL container classes discussed in Chapter 10, "Templates and the Standard Template Library." The objects that are stored may be built-in types, such as int, char, or long, or they may be objects like CStrings. There are three basic types of collection classes offered as part of the MFC class library.

■ **Arrays**. An array collection class enables you to store and access data using the subscript, or [ ], operator. The array class is optimized to enable easy access to a particular item in the array if its position is known. However, it can be very costly, in terms of processing time, to add an item into the middle of the array.

■ **Lists**. A list-based collection stores its items in a chain-like list. This makes it very easy to add or remove items located anywhere in the collection. List collections have a "head" and a "tail." Items are easily inserted at the head or tail of a list. However, it can be very difficult to search for an item in a large list because the items stored in a list must be tested in order to find a particular item; on average this means that half the items in a list are tested for every search.

■ **Maps**. A map is a slightly more complex collection. Each item stored in a map has a unique key associated with it. For example, a map of customers might use customer number values as keys to the customer names stored in the map. The key for each item must be unique, and the key is used to access the item stored in the map. Adding, removing, or accessing any individual item stored in a map is very easy; however, you must have the key for the item to be retrieved. This key is converted into an index that is used to access each individual item. Each key is first converted into a *hash value*, which is used as an index to an array of collection items known as a *hash table*. You can specify the size of the hash table when the map is created; a large hash table requires more storage, whereas a small hash table increases the chance that two keys result in equal hash values, known as a collision. The MFC map classes handle collisions by creating a list of items that have equal keys.

The three collection types are available in template and non-template versions. The non-template versions specify a certain type of item to be stored in the collection. For example, the CObArray class manages a collection of pointers to objects derived from CObject and treats the collection just like an array. Using the non-template versions of the MFC collection classes is generally more complicated than using the template versions. The non-template versions of these collection classes were part of the MFC library before templates were widely used, and they are still included for historical reasons.

Why Use Collections?

Why The MFC collection classes offer a wide variety of collection types that you can use in your MFC-based programs. The collection classes are provided as part of the class library, so using them requires very little code writing on your part. Reusing these classes enables you to leverage thousands of lines of trusted code in your application.

Unlike the STL container classes discussed in Chapter 10, the MFC collection classes have been designed to work in MFC-based programs. For example, all collection classes can be stored to an archive by calling the collection's Serialize member function. Serialization is discussed in Chapter 41, "Serialization," and Chapter 42, "Serialization and Document/View."

How Is the *CList* Collection Class Used?

The CList collection is often used when a collection of items is used as a chain of related items, as shown in Figure 11.1. If you need to access items at the beginning and end of a list, the CList collection is perfect for you.

How

Figure 11.1.
A list-based collection resembles a chain of related items.

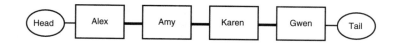

For an example of using the CList class, let's create a quick console mode application that simulates a restaurant waiting list. In the example shown in Listing 11.1, several names will be added and removed from a waiting list, implemented using CList.

Listing 11.1. Using the CList collection class to create a waiting list.

```
#include <afx.h>
#include <iostream.h>
#include <afxtempl.h>

int main()
{
    CList< CString, CString& >  waitingList;

    CString     szAlex( "Alex" );
    CString     szJames( "James" );
    CString     szRoger( "Roger" );

    //
    // Add the three names to the end of the list.
    //
    waitingList.AddTail( szAlex );
    waitingList.AddTail( szJames );
    waitingList.AddTail( szRoger );

    //
    // Display the number of items stored in the list.
    //
    int cWaiting = waitingList.GetCount();
    cout << "There are " << cWaiting << " people waiting:" << endl;

    //
    // Traverse the waiting list, and display the list contents.
    //
    POSITION     pos = waitingList.GetHeadPosition();
    while( pos != NULL )
    {
        CString szWaiting = waitingList.GetNext( pos );
        cout << "\t" << szWaiting << endl;
```

continues

Listing 11.1. continued

```
    }

    //
    // Remove the items stored in the waiting list.
    //
    waitingList.RemoveAll();

    return EXIT_SUCCESS;
}
```

The example starts out by instantiating a CList template that will store CString objects. The first parameter for the CList template is the type of object stored inside the list. The second parameter is the type of object that is passed as an argument for CList functions. As discussed in Chapter 7, "Scope, Pointers, and Lifetime in C++," a reference to CString is used to help reduce temporary copies during function calls.

The CList collection enables items to be added at the head and tail of the list. In this example, you add three names to the end of the list by using the AddTail member function. To add an item to the head of a CList, use the AddHead member function.

To traverse or examine every item stored in the collection, a POSITION variable is used. A POSITION variable works a lot like a cursor in a word processing program. Calling the GetHeadPosition member function places the POSITION variable just before the first item stored in the list. The GetNext member function does two things: it returns the next item stored in the list and advances the POSITION variable to next item in the CList. If the POSITION variable is NULL, there are no more items in the CList.

All of the collection classes have a RemoveAll member function, which is used to remove and delete all of the items stored in the collection.

How Is the *CArray* Collection Class Used?

How The CArray class is used to create collections that are more useful than the simple built-in arrays available in C++. As discussed in Chapter 6, "Arrays, Strings, and Polymorphism," an array of integers can be declared as the following:

```
int     rgScore[5];
```

However, the C++ language does not provide any sort of range checking, so if you attempt to access the ninth element by using rgScore[8], you'll create a difficult-to-find bug in your program.

In contrast, the CArray class provides range checking in the form of ASSERT calls when your program is compiled with debugging options enabled. It also automatically enables the array to grow dynamically as new elements are added—something that can't be done with built-in arrays. An example using the CArray class is shown in Listing 11.2.

Listing 11.2. Using the CArray collection to store a hand of cards.

```cpp
#include <afx.h>
#include <iostream.h>
#include <afxtempl.h>

int main()
{
    CArray< CString, CString& >  rgCards;

    CString szAce( "Ace of Spades" );
    CString szKing( "King of Spades" );
    CString szQueen( "Queen of Spades" );
    CString szJack( "Jack of Spades" );
    CString szTen( "Ten of Spades" );
    //
    // Add five cards to the card array.
    //
    rgCards.SetAtGrow( 0, szAce );
    rgCards.SetAtGrow( 1, szKing );
    rgCards.SetAtGrow( 2, szQueen );
    rgCards.SetAtGrow( 3, szJack );
    rgCards.SetAtGrow( 4, szTen );
    //
    // Display the contents of the card array.
    //
    cout << "It looks like I have the winning hand!" << endl;
    int cCards = rgCards.GetSize();
    for( int nCardIndex = 0; nCardIndex < cCards; nCardIndex++ )
    {
        cout << "\t" << rgCards[nCardIndex] << endl;
    }
    //
    // Remove the items stored in the card array.
    //
    rgCards.RemoveAll();

    return EXIT_SUCCESS;
}
```

This example is similar to the waiting list given in Listing 11.1. The template parameter list for CArray is identical to the parameter list for CList. The first parameter is the type of item stored in the array, and the second parameter is the argument type for CArray member functions.

The SetAtGrow member function stores an item in the CArray at the provided index. If the CArray is not large enough, it grows to accommodate the new item. There is also a SetAt member function that does not automatically increase the size of the CArray if needed.

The number of items stored in the CArray is available by calling the GetSize member function. Access to individual items in the CArray is available by using the subscript operator, as it is with built-in arrays. However, note that GetSize is used in this example to ensure that the item exists. If you aren't sure that an item is stored, use the GetAt member function instead.

How Is the *CMap* Collection Class Used?

How

The CMap class is used to create collections that are indexed using a unique key for every item stored in the collection. Every item stored in the collection must have a unique key; if you attempt to store two items with the same key, the first item will be replaced by the second item.

The CMap collection class is ideal for storing items that have unique serial or identification numbers. For example, employee numbers, Social Security numbers, and ISBN numbers are all examples of good keys because they are guaranteed to be unique. The example in Listing 11.3 uses the CMap class to store a collection of customer names, using a customer ID as a key for each item.

Listing 11.3. A customer list that uses the CMap class.

```
#include <afx.h>
#include <iostream.h>
#include <afxtempl.h>
int main()
{
    CMap< int, int, CString, CString& >  customerNumbers;
    CString     szAlex( "Alex" );
    CString     szRene( "Rene'" );
    CString     szMaynard( "Maynard" );

    customerNumbers.SetAt( 12564, szAlex );
    customerNumbers.SetAt( 12453, szRene );
    customerNumbers.SetAt( 16342, szMaynard );
    //
    // Display the number of items stored in the list.
    //
    int cCustomers = customerNumbers.GetCount();
    cout << "We have " << cCustomers << " customers:" << endl;
    cout << "\nName\tCustomer Number" << endl;
    //
    // Iterate over the map, displaying the items one at a time.
    //
    POSITION    pos = customerNumbers.GetStartPosition();
    while( pos != NULL )
    {
        CString szCustomer;    // Customer Name
        int     idCustomer;    // Customer ID
        customerNumbers.GetNextAssoc( pos, idCustomer, szCustomer );
        cout << szCustomer << "\t" << idCustomer << endl;
    }
```

```
//
// Retrieve a customer from the collection using the key.
//
CString szCustomer;
BOOL fFound = customerNumbers.Lookup( 12453, szCustomer );
if( TRUE == fFound )
{
    cout << "\nCustomer ID 12453 belongs to " << szCustomer << endl;
}
//
// Remove the items stored in the waiting list.
//
customerNumbers.RemoveAll();
return EXIT_SUCCESS;
}
```

The CMap template parameter list is much more complicated than the parameter lists used for CList or CArray. The first two parameters are used for the key type. The first parameter is the type of key that is used inside the collection, and the second parameter is the type of key used as an argument in member functions. In our example, the key is an int, but it's possible to create an advanced collection derived from CMap that uses almost any type as a key.

The next two parameters refer to the item stored in the collection. The third parameter is the type of item stored inside the collection, and the fourth parameter is the type of item used as an argument in member functions.

The SetAt member function is used to store an item and a key in the CMap collection. The Lookup member function is usually used to retrieve an item from the collection based on a key. In large collections, CMap is much faster than CList or CArray at searching, inserting, or deleting an arbitrary single item based on a key.

You can search a CMap very much like a CList. The GetStartPosition member function returns a POSITION variable that is advanced to the next item using the GetNextAssoc member function. However, there is no order for the items stored in a CMap, other than their key values. If the CMap is traversed using GetNextAssoc, the items in the collection are returned based on the internal structure of the CMap, not the order in which they were inserted.

Summary

In this chapter, I discussed the way that the MFC class library uses templates in its collection classes.

Exception Handling and RTTI

Developer Studio includes Run Time Type Information, or RTTI, for the first time with Visual C++ 4.0. Previous versions of Visual C++ and the MFC class library included a crude version of RTTI, but true support of this language feature is new to Developer Studio.

What Is Run Time Type Information?

What Run Time Type information is used to determine the type of an object. Under the general name of RTTI, there are two main features:

- Type identification, where the type_id expression can be used to determine if an object is of a certain type.
- Improved casting, where a pointer to a type can be converted to another type.

The ability to determine the type of an object is used to offer improved casts. There are several different operators used for casting:

- `dynamic_cast`
- `reinterpret_cast`
- `static_cast`
- `const_cast`

Each of these cast operators is used for a specific purpose, and together they replace the traditional, error-prone cast often used in C programs.

Why Use RTTI?

Why

RTTI is useful when dealing with pointers to base classes when you must determine the exact type of an object. This information is sometimes needed when using class libraries, especially when two or more libraries from different sources are used together.

Determining the type of an object is not usually needed in a well-designed program, although the actual type of an object is sometimes used when debugging.

How Is RTTI Used?

How

Information about an object's type is stored in a `type_info` structure, which can be accessed using the `typeid` operator. For example, you can easily display the name of an object by using `cout`:

```
cout << typeid( *pDoc ).name();
```

When programming a Windows program, RTTI is most often used to help make casts safer. The traditional method of casting forces the compiler to accept the suggested conversion, even if the cast is unsafe or unwise. The traditional cast, shown here, attempts to cast the return value of `GetDocument` into a pointer to `CMyDocument`:

```
CMyDocument pDoc = (CMyDocument*)GetDocument();
```

Because `GetDocument` is guaranteed only to return a pointer to a class derived from `CDocument`, this cast may fail. If the object cannot be cast, disaster probably will result when the pointer is used. In contrast, a dynamic cast like the following converts the return value from a pointer to `CDocument` to a `CMyDocument` pointer:

```
CMyDocument pDoc = dynamic_cast<CMyDocument*>(GetDocument());
```

If the conversion is not possible, `pDoc` will have a value of zero.

Each of the four types of RTTI casts is used for a specific, narrow purpose. This allows the compiler to reject a case in some cases, if appropriate.

When casting from a base class to a derived class, there usually is no way to be completely sure that the cast will succeed. This type of casting, called *down-casting*, is exactly what the dynamic_cast operator is used for.

Figure 12.1 is a class diagram of three classes used in the examples for this section. Class CBase is a base class, and there are two derived classes: CDerived and COther.

Figure 12.1.
Three classes used as RTTI examples in this section.

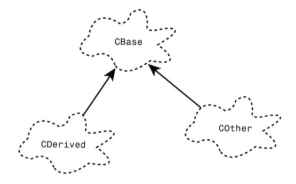

The dynamic_cast expression is used to convert a pointer or reference of one type to another. If the conversion fails, the value of the expression is zero. If the conversion is successful, the value is a pointer to the new type. This type of conversion is most useful for converting pointers from base to derived class types. Listing 12.1 is an example of using dynamic_cast.

Listing 12.1. Using the dynamic_cast operator.

```
#include <iostream.h>
// CBase class
class CBase
{
public:
    virtual void Print() { cout << "Base class print" << endl; }
};
// CDerived class, derived from CBase
class CDerived : public CBase
{
public:
    virtual void Print() { cout << "Derived class print" << endl; }
};
// COther class, derived from CBase
class COther : public CBase
{
public:
    virtual void Print() { cout << "Other class print" << endl; }
};

void p( CBase* p )
{
    // Call Print only for COther objects.
```

continues

Listing 12.1. continued

```
    COther* od = dynamic_cast<COther*>(p);
    if( od )
    {
        od->Print();
    }
    else
    {
        cout << "Skipping Print for non-COther type" << endl;
    }
}

int main()
{
    CDerived    d;
    COther      o;

    p( &d );
    p( &o );

    return 0;
}
```

Due to the overhead imposed by RTTI, it is usually disabled by the Visual C++ compiler. Before compiling the example in Listing 12.1, you must enable the compiler options for RTTI by following these steps:

1. Select Settings from the Build menu; this pops up the Compiler settings dialog box.

2. Click the tab labeled C/C++.

3. Select C++ Language from the Category drop-down combo box.

4. Select the checkbox labeled Enable Run Time Type Information (RTTI).

5. Click the OK button to dismiss the dialog box.

What Is Exception Handling?

What At times we must face the fact that not all things are perfect and that occasionally even our best plans fail. Exception handling is designed for those occasions. Rather than just failing an operation, the C++ environment gives us the opportunity to try an operation and have a safety net if it fails.

Why Use Exception Handling?

Why Without exception handling, a program that encounters an unrecoverable error, such as divide by zero, would just raise an error flag and the system would abort the program.

How Is Exception Handling Used?

In most real-world programs, much of the C++ code is used to handle error conditions. In many of these applications, more than half of the code is used for error cases or special conditions that rarely occur. This "special case" code often is sprinkled throughout the program, as shown in Listing 12.2.

How

Listing 12.2. The traditional way to detect errors: test function return values.

```
BOOL LoadImageListFromID( CImageList* pImage, UINT nResourceID )
{
    CBitmap  bmp;
    CBitmap* pBmpNull = 0;
    BOOL     bReturn = TRUE;

    if( bmp.LoadBitmap( nResourceID ) == FALSE )
    {
        bReturn = FALSE;
    }
    else if( m_imageList.Add( &bmp, pBmpNull ) == -1 )
    {
        bReturn = FALSE;
    }
    else if( bmpCross.DeleteObject() == FALSE )
    {
        bReturn = FALSE;
    }
    return bReturn;
}
```

Detecting Error Conditions

As shown in Listing 12.2, the traditional way to detect error conditions is to use a function return value to indicate that an error has occurred. There are several problems with relying on function return values; the biggest is that it is easy to forget to use them. Testing for function return values also tends to make code difficult to read, because the error-detection code is embedded in the functional code. Also, when using C++, there is no return value for a constructor, so there is no way to test whether an object has been constructed properly. Exception handling was created to address all of these problems.

Using Exceptions to Detect Errors

The general idea behind C++ exception handling is that a section of code that fails can *throw*, or *raise*, an exception that can be caught by an exception handler. The simplest example is when an exception is handled within a single function, as shown in Listing 12.3.

Listing 12.3. Simple exception handling.

```
#include <iostream.h>
#include <stdexcpt.h>

int Divide( int n1, int n2 )
{
    int nReturn;

    try{
        if( n2 == 0 )
            throw exception();
        else
            nReturn = n1/n2;
    }
    catch(...)
    {
        cout << "caught runtime error" << endl;
    }
    return nReturn;
}

int main()
{
    int n = Divide( 15, 0 );
    return 0;
}
```

The try keyword marks the beginning of a try block. Inside a try block, any exceptions that are thrown are handled by exception handlers that follow the try block. Exceptions that are thrown by functions called from inside a try block also are handled by a suitable catch statement. An exception handler specifies the exceptions that it handles by using the catch keyword. A single try block can throw several different types of exceptions, as shown in Listing 12.4.

Listing 12.4. A single try block that throws two different types of expressions.

```
    try
    {
        if( nIndex < 0 )
            throw exception();
        else if( nIndex >= m_nLength )
            throw exception();
        else if( check_lock( nIndex ) == LOCKED )
            throw "Array element is locked";
        else
        {
            // normal processing
        }
    }
    catch( const char* pszErr )
    {
        cout << *pszErr << endl;
    }
```

```
catch( exception e )
{
    cout << e.what() << endl;
}
```

In Listing 12.4, a pointer to char is thrown to the exception handler. A throw statement looks very much like a return statement, as far as its syntax is concerned. The result of the throw expression is used to evaluate which catch expression should be used to resume processing.

Normally, a function will throw exceptions that are intended to be caught by the calling function. If no suitable catch expression can be found in the calling function, the next higher-level function is checked for a try block and suitable exception handler. If no exception handler can be found, a special, high-level function named terminate is called. This function normally terminates the program.

A catch expression matches the thrown exception if it is an exact match for the thrown object. The standard conversions are also allowed; for example, a pointer to a base class will catch a pointer to a derived class. A catch expression that contains an ellipsis (. . .) will catch all exceptions. The block of code following a catch expression is called a catch block and must be enclosed in curly braces.

Using Exceptions to Clean Up When Errors Are Detected

When an exception is thrown, any objects that have been constructed are guaranteed to be properly destroyed. This is one of the big benefits of using exception handling, because it ensures that your program cleans up properly, even in error conditions.

Detecting Errors During Construction

As discussed earlier, one of the reasons exceptions were added to the C++ language was to handle errors that occur inside constructors. Because a constructor does not have a return value, there are only two ways to handle errors during construction if exceptions are not used:

- Two-stage construction, where only "safe" operations that cannot fail are performed during construction. A separate Create or Init function is then used to complete construction of the object.
- Using a test function that returns an error code if construction failed.

Each of the above methods has drawbacks. Two-stage construction results in code that is difficult both to read and write. One of the advantages to using constructors is that initialization is done automatically, inside the constructor. When two-stage construction is used, this benefit is reduced. Also, two-stage construction cannot be used for copy constructors and doesn't work well with assignment operators, so those operations must be handled in other ways.

The primary difficulty with using a function to determine whether construction was successful is that a great deal of extra source code must be added. There is also a problem using copy constructors and assignment operators, because it may not always be obvious when a test function should be called.

Exception handling is easier to use than either of the above methods. As shown in the console mode program provided in Listing 12.5, the try block should enclose all objects that might throw exceptions when they are constructed.

Listing 12.5. Throwing and catching errors during construction.

```
CSafeArray::CSafeArray( int nArraySize )
{
    try
    {
        m_nData = new int[nArraySize];
        m_pLogger = new CLog;
    }
    catch(...)
    {
        cout << "Error constructing CSafeArray" << endl;
        throw;
    }
}
```

Using throw with no argument inside a catch block re-throws the currently executing exception, just as if it had not been handled. This allows the expression to be caught and handled by an enclosing set of try and catch blocks.

Summary

In this chapter I have discussed exception handling and RTTI, two features of the C++ language that you can use to make your programs safer and more robust. I covered using the standard exception library, as well as using dynamic_cast for safe down-casting operations.

PART IV

The Windows Environment

13 Using Visual C++ for Windows Programming

14 Messages and Event-Driven Programming

15 Menus

16 Dialog Boxes

Using Visual C++ for Windows Programming

Windows programs differ from most of the programs that you have seen so far in this book. The programs you saw in earlier chapters consisted of short listings that created small sequential programs that assumed complete control over a console mode window. In this chapter, I present some of the properties shared by programs written using Developer Studio, and a simple AppWizard application is created.

What Is a Visual C++ Windows Program?

What Although sequential programs work well for explaining simple concepts like the basics of the C++ language, they don't work well in a multitasking environment like Microsoft Windows. In the Windows environment everything is shared: the screen, keyboard, the mouse—even the user.

Programs written for Windows must cooperate with Windows and with other programs that may be running at the same time.

In a cooperative environment like Windows, messages are sent to a program when an event occurs that affects the program. Every message sent to a program has a specific purpose. For example, messages are sent when a program should be initialized, when menu selections are made, and when a window should be redrawn. I examine messages in detail in Chapter 14, "Messages and Event-Driven Programming," but for now let's just say that responding to event messages are a key part of most Windows programs.

Another characteristic of Windows programs is that they must share resources. Many resources must be requested from the operating system before they are used and, once used, must be returned to the operating system so that they can be used by other programs. This is one way Windows controls access to resources like the screen and other physical devices.

In short, a program that runs in a window has to be a good citizen. It cannot assume that it has complete control over the computer on which it's running; it must ask permission before taking control of any central resource; and it must be ready to react to events that are sent to it.

Why Write a Windows Program Using Visual C++?

Why　When using Visual C++, much of the complexity of writing a Windows program is easily handled. The integrated tools you use to create your program can make your job much easier by writing much of the required source code for you, and also by taking advantage of the MFC class library.

Three different parts of the Visual C++ package simplify writing programs for Windows:

- The actual C and C++ compilers. Even if you choose not to use the MFC class library or any of the Wizards included in the Developer Studio, you still can write programs using the C and C++ compiler. Developer Studio includes an advanced text editor with syntax highlighting, an integrated help system, and an integrated debugger.
- The MFC class library. Version 4.0 of the MFC class library includes new classes that enable you to add advanced features to your programs with just a few lines of code.
- Tools such as AppWizard and ClassWizard. The Wizards that are included as part of the Developer Studio enable you to quickly get started writing Windows programs by generating skeleton applications for you, and by managing the process of writing a Windows program.

What Is the MFC Class Library?

As discussed earlier, the MFC Class Library is a collection of C++ classes that simplify writing C++ programs. Although a few of the MFC classes can be used in console mode programs, most of the MFC classes have been created specifically for use in Windows programs.

What

The classes contained in the MFC class library are arranged into the following categories:

- General purpose classes. This category includes classes that are used to handle files and strings. A hierarchy of exception classes is also included in this category. Other commonly used classes include CRect and CPoint, which are used to represent areas of the screen.

- Visual object classes. These classes handle almost everything that is visible in a Windows program. Included in this category are classes to handle menus, graphics, windows, controls, and drawing objects such as pens and brushes.

- Application classes. This category includes classes that manage application-level objects, like threads of execution, or the MFC Document/View architecture. Document/View is the basis for most programs built with MFC, and I discuss it later in this chapter.

- Collection classes. As I discussed in Chapter 11, "Collection Classes," these classes are used to create containers that store other objects.

- OLE2 classes. These classes simplify writing programs that take advantage of OLE2 features.

- Database classes. These classes provide database access.

- Common control classes. Windows 95 introduced a number of new controls, such as list views, tree controls, and progress controls. These classes provide easy access to the controls.

- Windows Socket classes. These classes are used for socket-based communication. Sockets typically are used for communication in client/server and network programming.

Why Use the MFC Class Library?

The MFC classes cover most aspects of Windows programming. No matter what you do with Windows, there's probably an MFC class that can help make your life easier. The MFC class library gives you easy access to advanced features such as floating toolbars and palettes, printing and print preview, and OLE2.

Why

The code contained in the MFC class library is used by Windows developers worldwide, including developers at Microsoft and other large companies. You can treat this source code as "trusted code," as it has been tested and debugged by programmers working on a wide variety of applications.

One of the best reasons to use the MFC class library is that doing so can dramatically shorten the learning curve required for Windows programming. Using MFC reduces the amount of source code that you have to write. The source code that you supply can be much simpler.

How Is the MFC Class Library Used?

How

When you write a program using MFC, you usually use AppWizard or other tools provided with Visual C++. However, you can get all of the benefits of using MFC even without using any of the Wizards.

A simple Windows program that uses C takes about 80 lines of source code, not counting comments or white space. A program written using the MFC class library is about half that size, as is shown in Listing 13.1.

Listing 13.1. A simple MFC Windows program, written without AppWizard.

```
#include <afxwin.h>
// The CHelloApp class
class CHelloApp : public CWinApp
{
    public:
        BOOL InitInstance();
};
// The CHelloWnd class
class CHelloWnd : public CFrameWnd
{
    public:
        CHelloWnd();
    protected:
        afx_msg void OnPaint();
        DECLARE_MESSAGE_MAP()
};
BOOL CHelloApp::InitInstance()
{
    m_pMainWnd = new CHelloWnd;
    m_pMainWnd->ShowWindow( m_nCmdShow );
    m_pMainWnd->UpdateWindow();
    return TRUE;
}
// Create a message map that handles one message - WM_PAINT
BEGIN_MESSAGE_MAP( CHelloWnd, CFrameWnd )
    ON_WM_PAINT()
END_MESSAGE_MAP()

CHelloWnd::CHelloWnd()
{
    Create( NULL, "Hello" );
}
```

```
// OnPaint - Handles the WM_PAINT message from Windows.
void CHelloWnd::OnPaint()
{
    CRect       rcClient;
    GetClientRect( rcClient );

    CPaintDC    dc( this );
    dc.DrawText( "Hello World!", -1, rcClient,
                 DT_SINGLELINE | DT_CENTER | DT_VCENTER );
}
// Create a single instance of the application.
CHelloApp   theApplication;
```

To compile and run the program in Listing 13.1, you must first create a Windows application project. To create a project that builds a Windows program that uses MFC, follow these steps:

1. Create a new project, as described in Chapter 4, "C++ Basics," except that the project type is "Application." Create a new directory and name the new project "Hello."

2. Check the project settings to make sure the compiler will build a project using the MFC class library. Select Settings from the Build menu. When the dialog box appears, select "Use MFC in a shared DLL" from the Microsoft Foundation Classes drop-down list. This tells the compiler to generate a program that uses MFC code contained in a Dynamic Link Library, or DLL, and makes your program much smaller.

3. Open a new source file document and type the contents of the program exactly as shown in Listing 13.1. Save the source file in the project directory you created in Step 1, and add the source file to the project.

4. Build the project by selecting Build | Build, or by pressing the Build button on the toolbar. If the program compiles successfully, it's ready to run. If there is a syntax error, check to make sure you have entered the program exactly as shown in Listing 13.1. If there is an error while linking, check to make sure the project settings were changed as I described in Step 2.

5. Because this is a Windows program, you can run it directly from Developer Studio. Select Build | Execute from the main menu, or press the Go button on the toolbar.

Examining the MFC Hello Program

The simple Windows program I provided in Listing 13.1 might seem large, but it's actually about half the size of an equivalent program written in C. Using the MFC class library allows us to leverage a large amount of source code that has already been written for you.

There are two classes included in Listing 13.1:

■ CHelloWnd, which handles the main window "frame" for the program. CHelloWnd is a very small class because this program doesn't have any menu or toolbars. It handles a single window message, WM_PAINT.

■ CHelloApp, a class derived from CWinApp. The constructor for the CHelloApp class contains the code that actually starts the program. The InitInstance member function creates and displays a CHelloWnd object.

As I discussed earlier in this chapter, Windows programs receive event messages from Windows in the form of messages. The only message handled by the program in Listing 13.1 is WM_PAINT, which is processed by the CHelloWnd::OnPaint member function. The WM_PAINT message is sent to an application from Windows when the window must be repainted. This can happen for several reasons, including:

■ The application has just started, and the window must be painted for the first time.

■ The window has been uncovered, and must be repainted.

■ The window was marked as invalid, and must be repainted.

Event-driven programming and messages are covered in detail in Chapter 14. For now, just accept the fact that Windows will send you a WM_PAINT message when your program needs it.

Using Rectangles and the *CRect* Class

A Windows program is almost entirely made up of rectangles: The menu bar, status bar, dialog boxes, and main windows are all rectangular. For that reason, the RECT structure often is used to provide the dimensions of displayed objects.

One commonly used MFC class is CRect, which is used to represent a rectangular area of the screen. CRect is a class derived from a RECT structure, which is often used when programming using C and the SDK. Both the CRect class and RECT structure have four data members, which can be used to give the coordinates for each corner of a rectangle.

The CHelloWnd::OnPaint function uses a CRect object, rcClient, to determine the size of the window client area, like this:

```
CRect        rcClient;
GetClientRect( rcClient );
```

The client area is the entire window, not including any caption bars, menu bars, or anything else added to the window by the operating system. The rcClient object is used to store the dimensions of the client area. The prefix rc commonly is used for CRect objects. The CRect class is used whenever a rectangle needs to be stored or manipulated.

Using Device Contexts

A device context is used whenever output is carried out in a Windows program. A device context contains information about the drawing or display characteristics for a screen display or printer. Windows uses device contexts to control screen access and to provide a logical drawing interface.

A common source of errors in Windows programs written using C or other languages is misuses of a device context. Device contexts are scarce resources, and serious problems often result when they are mishandled. The MFC class library has four different classes that make it easy to safely use device contexts. I cover device contexts in detail in Chapter 29, "Device Contexts."

In Listing 13.1, the most commonly used device context, known as a paint device context, or PaintDC, is defined and associated with the CHelloWnd object with:

```
CPaintDC    dc( this );
```

The keyword this is used to represent a pointer to the current object. The this pointer always contains the address of the current object. During construction, the CPaintDC object allocates a device context from the operating system, and performs some initialization work. After the CPaintDC object is constructed, the output string is displayed using the DrawText function, which is a member of the CPaintDC class:

```
dc.DrawText( "Hello World!", -1, rcClient,
             DT_SINGLELINE | DT_CENTER | DT_VCENTER );
```

The DrawText function is the simplest string output function available in Windows. DrawText has these parameters:

- Output string.
- Output string length, or –1 to indicate that the string is zero-terminated.
- Bounding rectangle for the string.
- Attributes for output. In this case we specify the string as a single line, centered vertically and horizontally. The C++ bitwise OR operator (|) is used to combine the output attributes.

After the string is displayed, the CPaintDC object dc is destroyed at the end of the function body. The CPaintDC destructor releases all resources that were allocated during construction, and returns the device context to the operating system. A common practice in the MFC class library is to use the class constructor to allocate system resources, and the destructor to return resources. This cuts down significantly on the amount of code you must write, and helps to reduce errors.

What Is AppWizard?

As was discussed in Chapter 1, "Introducing Visual C++ 4 Developer Studio," Developer Studio includes a tool, AppWizard, which is used for creating a skeleton application. AppWizard asks you a series of questions about your program, then generates a project and much of the source code for you, allowing you to concentrate on the code that makes your program unique.

What

Why Use AppWizard?

Why

Even if you use the MFC class library, there still is a learning curve before you can write a moderately sized Windows program with it. In addition, much of the code that is used as a starting point for many Windows programs is generic "skeleton" code similar for all Windows applications.

The MFC class library is built around the Document/View programming model. Using AppWizard to create the skeleton code for your program is the quickest way to get started writing Document/View programs.

A Quick Overview of the Document/View Architecture

The AppWizard uses MFC classes to create applications that are based on the MFC Document/View architecture. The basic idea behind Document/View is to separate the data handling classes from the classes that handle the user interface.

Separating the data from the user interface allows each of the classes to concentrate on performing one job, with a set of interfaces defined for interaction with the other classes involved in the program. A view class is responsible for providing a "viewport" through which you can see and manage the document. A document class is responsible for controlling all of the data, including storing it when necessary. Figure 13.1 shows how the document and view classes interact with each other.

Figure 13.1.
The Document/View architecture.

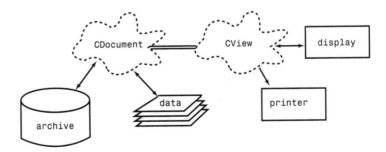

I discuss the Document/View architecture in detail in Chapter 25, "Document/View Architecture." For now, just be aware that there are four main "super classes" used in a Document/View application:

- The document class, which controls the data used by an application. The data does not have to be an actual page of text; for example, a spreadsheet or project plan can easily be represented as a document.
- The view class, used to display information about the document to the user, and to handle any interaction that is required between the user and the document.

- The frame class, used to physically contain the view, menu, toolbar, and other physical elements of the program.
- The application class, which controls the application-level interaction with Windows.

In addition to the four classes above, there are some specialized classes that are used in Document/View programs I discuss in Chapter 25.

How Is AppWizard Used?

AppWizard sets up the following types of generic programs for you:

How

- Single Document, or SDI; a program that controls a single document at a time
- Multiple Document, or MDI; a program that can control several different documents at once
- Dialog Based; a program that has a dialog box as its main display window

After you select one of these application types, you are asked for more information about the new program. The opening screen for AppWizard is shown in Figure 13.2.

Figure 13.2.
The opening screen for AppWizard.

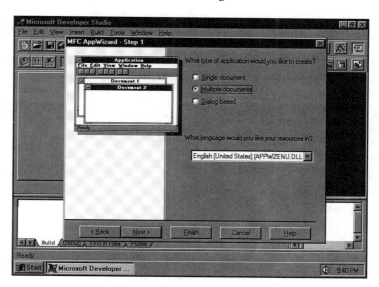

Using AppWizard to Create an SDI Application

To create a simple SDI program, select Single Document on the opening AppWizard screen. AppWizard displays six Wizard pages filled with default information for a typical SDI program. You can move to the next page by pressing the button labeled Next and to the previous page by pressing the button labeled Previous. At any time you can tell AppWizard to create the project for you by pressing the button labeled Finish.

AppWizard will create several classes and files for you, and create a project that you can use to manage the process of compiling the program. AppWizard creates these classes for a program named Hello:

- CHelloApp, derived from CWinApp, the application class for the program
- CHelloDoc, the program's document class, derived from CDocument
- CHelloView, the program's view class derived from CView
- CMainFrame, the main frame class for the program

In addition, there are a number of files that are created by AppWizard that are not used for C++ classes. AppWizard creates these files:

- readme.txt, a file that has information about all of the files created by AppWizard
- hello.rc, a resource file that contains information about dialog boxes, menus, and other resources used by the program
- hello.mak, the project file used by Developer Studio to build the program
- stdafx.cpp, a file included in all AppWizard programs, which includes all the standard include files
- stdafx.h, a standard header file included in all AppWizard programs, which is used to include other files that are included in the precompiled headers

Creating a Windows program using AppWizard is easy. In fact, you can compile and run the program as it is now, although it doesn't really do anything.

How to Customize a Skeleton Program Built Using AppWizard

How

To add a "Hello World!" message to this simple SDI program, as was done in Listing 13.1, open the file hellovw.cpp by clicking on the project tree and then selecting the FileView tab at the bottom of the project tree or by using the Open File icon on the toolbar. Locate the CHelloView::OnDraw function and edit the function so that it looks like the code provided in Listing 13.2.

Listing 13.2. The CHelloView::OnDraw function for the SDI version of Hello World!

```
void CHelloView::OnDraw(CDC* pDC)
{
    CHelloDoc* pDoc = GetDocument();
    ASSERT_VALID(pDoc);

    // TODO: add draw code for native data here
    CRect   rcClient;
    GetClientRect( rcClient );
    pDC->DrawText( "Hello World!", -1, rcClient,
                DT_SINGLELINE ¦ DT_CENTER ¦ DT_VCENTER );

}
```

The `CHelloView::OnDraw` function is called whenever the view must be drawn. In a Document/View application, it also is called when the view is printed, or during a print preview. I discuss these topics later, in Chapter 35, "Printing."

Summary

In this chapter, I discussed some of the common features of Windows programs and how the Visual C++ Developer Studio can be used to write programs for Windows. I also presented short overviews of the Document/View architecture and MFC class library, and I showed you an SDI program built using AppWizard.

Messages and Event-Driven Programming

Messages are at the heart of every Windows program. Even the 50-line MFC program I provided in Chapter 13, "Using Visual C++ for Windows Programming," had to handle the WM_PAINT message. A good understanding of how the Windows operating system sends messages will be a great help to you as you write your own programs.

What Are Messages?

What Programs written for Microsoft Windows react to events that are sent to a program's main window. These events are sent to the window in the form of messages. Each message has a specific purpose: redraw the window, resize the window, close the window, and so on. For many messages, the application can just pass the message to a special function called the *default window procedure*, which handles the message if no special processing is required.

A Windows program can also send messages to other windows. Because every control used in a Windows program is also a window, messages are also often used for communication with controls.

There are two different types of messages handled by a Windows program:

- Messages sent from the operating system
- Messages sent to and from controls that deal with user input

Examples of messages sent from the operating system include messages used to tell the program that it should start or close, or to tell a window that it is being resized or moved. Messages sent to controls can be used to change the font used by a window or its title. Messages received from a control include notifications that a button has been pressed or that a character has been entered in an edit control.

Why Are Messages Used?

Why There are two reasons why messages are used so heavily in Windows programs:

- Unlike a function call, a message is a physical chunk of data, so it can easily be queued and prioritized.
- A message is not dependent on a particular language or processor type, so a message-based program can easily be ported to other CPUs as is often done with Windows NT.

Queues work well for event-driven programming. When an event occurs, a message can be created and quickly queued to the appropriate window or program. Each message that is queued can then be handled in an orderly manner.

The fact that messages are language-independent has allowed Windows to grow over the years. Today, you can write a Windows program using diverse languages, such as Visual Basic, Delphi, Visual C++, or PowerBuilder. Because messages are language-independent, messages can easily be sent between these programs. The message interface enables you to add new features to the programs you write and also allows Windows to grow in the future.

Since it was first introduced, every release of Microsoft Windows has added new messages and new functionality. However, most of the core messages used in the initial version of Windows still are available, even on multiprocessor machines that are running Windows NT.

> **Caution** When using an event-driven programming model such as Microsoft Windows, you cannot always be certain about message order. A subtle difference in the way different users make use of a program may cause messages to be received in a different sequence. This means that every time you handle an event, you should handle only *that particular event*, and not assume that any other activity has taken place.

What Are Message Queues?

Messages are delivered to all windows that must receive events. For example, the simple act of moving the mouse cursor across the main window of a Windows program generates a large number of messages. Messages sent to a window are placed in a queue, and a program must examine each message in turn. Typically, a program examines messages that are sent to it and responds only to messages that are of interest, as shown in Figure 14.1.

What

Figure 14.1.
Messages queued and handled in order by an application.

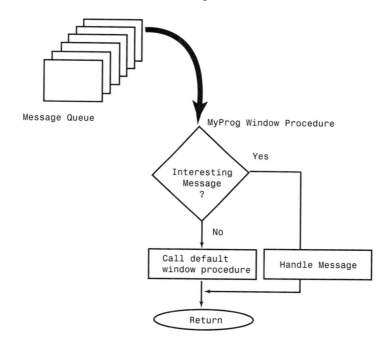

As shown in Figure 14.1, messages sent to a program are handled by a window procedure that is defined for the program. I show you an example of a window procedure written in C later, in Listing 14.1.

How Are Messages Handled?

When a user moves the mouse over a program's main window, WM_NCMOUSEMOVE and WM_MOUSEMOVE messages are sent to the program's window procedure. WM_NCMOUSEMOVE is sent when the mouse is moved over the menu or caption bar. The WM_MOUSEMOVE message is sent when the mouse is over the window's client area. (The *client area* is the part of a window that is not covered by the caption and menu bar. In other words, it's the "real" part of a window.)

How

Another type of mouse message is the WM_LBUTTONDOWN message, sent when the primary mouse button is pressed. Because this is the left button for most mouse users, the message is named WM_LBUTTONDOWN. A similar message is WM_RBUTTONDOWN, sent when the secondary, usually right, mouse button is pressed.

These and other messages are sent to a window's *window procedure*. A window procedure is a function that handles messages sent to it. When a window procedure receives the message, the parameters passed along with the message are used to help decide how the message should be handled.

Using a Traditional Windows Procedure

An example using a traditional Windows procedure will help illustrate how messages are handled. When you program with MFC, the Window procedure is hidden from you. In C, however, the messages would be handled as shown in Listing 14.1.

Listing 14.1. Handling mouse and WM_PAINT messages using a window procedure written in C.

```c
LRESULT WndProc( HWND hWnd, UINT msg, WPARAM wParam, LPARAM lParam )
{
    // Variables set during mouse messages
    static int cx = 0;
    static int cy = 0;
    static UINT fwKeys = 0;

    switch( msg )
    {
        // Handle left or right mouse clicks, store mouse coords
        // for use later during WM_PAINT.
        case WM_LBUTTONDOWN:
        case WM_RBUTTONDOWN:
        {
            cx = LOWORD( lParam );
            cy = HIWORD( lParam );
            fwKeys = wParam;
        }
        break;

        case WM_PAINT:
        {
            PAINTSTRUCT ps;
            HDC         hdcPaint = BeginPaint( hWnd, &ps );
            RECT        rcClient;
            char        szPosition[35];

            wsprintf( szPosition, "The mouse is at %d x, %d y, (int)cx, (int)cy );

            GetClientRect( hWnd, &rcClient );
            DrawText( hdcPaint,
                    szPosition,
                    -1,
                    &rcClient,
                    DT_CENTERLINE | DT_VCENTER | DT_CENTER );

            EndPaint( hWnd, &ps );
        }
```

```
        default:
            lResult = DefWindowProc( hWnd, msg, wParam, lParam );
    }
    return lResult;
}
```

In Listing 14.1, `WndProc` is an example of a window procedure. Each message handled by the window procedure must use the parameters passed to it differently. Many times these parameters are cast into new types, potentially leading to hard-to-find errors. Each message also must be handled correctly for your program to work properly. Fortunately, as you see later in this chapter, Visual C++ offers a better way to handle messages for your programs.

What Are the Different Types of Messages?

There are several categories of messages. The messages you've seen so far are general-purpose windows messages, which all begin with `WM_`. These messages apply to most windows. Specialized control windows also have their own series of messages. Table 14.1 lists some of the more common prefixes for messages that can be sent to your program along with each type of control. For example, messages that begin with `LV` refer to List view controls.

Table 14.1. Prefixes used for common messages in windows.

Prefix	Type of Window
AC	Animated control
BM	Button control
CB	Combo-box control
DM	Default pushbutton control
EM	Edit control
LB	List-box control
LV	List-view control
PB	Progress-bar control
SB	Status-bar control
SBM	Scroll-bar control
TB	Toolbar control
TC	Tab control
TT	Tool-tip control
TV	Tree-view control
WM	General window

What Is ClassWizard?

What

Visual C++ Developer Studio includes ClassWizard, a tool that you can use to configure classes used in MFC programs you write for Windows. Using ClassWizard, you can add new classes and member variables, bind resources and controls to classes, and add message-handling functions. Using ClassWizard helps you eliminate common coding errors, because much of the code can be written automatically.

You can think of ClassWizard as an extension of AppWizard. When you initially create a program, you use AppWizard to create the classes and skeleton code needed for that program. After you create the program, use ClassWizard to add classes, functions, and member data to your program.

Why Use ClassWizard to Handle Messages?

Why

As shown in Listing 14.1, handling the messages sent to your program can be a significant chore if you use the traditional, straight C approach. Fortunately, ClassWizard helps you track and handle windows messages at the click of a button.

You can use ClassWizard to greatly simplify handling messages sent to your application. ClassWizard and the MFC class library work together to eliminate a common source of errors by cracking the parameters of the message for you, so that casts and other contortions aren't needed.

How Is ClassWizard Used to Handle Messages?

How

Using ClassWizard adds code that typically is used for a particular message-handling function. This commonly reused, or "boilerplate," code can help reduce the number of errors still further, because it's guaranteed to be correct. Listing 14.2 is an example of a function created by ClassWizard to handle the WM_LBUTTONDOWN message.

Listing 14.2. The OnLButtonDown function created by ClassWizard.

```
void CMyView::OnLButtonDown(UINT nFlags, CPoint point)
{
    //TODO: Add your message handler code here and/or call default

    CView::OnLButtonDown(nFlags, point);
}
```

What Is a Message Map?

A *message map* is used to connect messages sent to a program with the functions that are meant to handle those messages. When AppWizard or ClassWizard add a message-handling function, an entry is added to the class message map. Listing 14.3 shows an example of a message map.

What

Listing 14.3. A message map for the CMyView class.

```
BEGIN_MESSAGE_MAP(CMyView, CView)
    //{{AFX_MSG_MAP(CMyView)
    ON_WM_LBUTTONDOWN()
    //}}AFX_MSG_MAP
    // Standard printing commands
    ON_COMMAND(ID_FILE_PRINT, CView::OnFilePrint)
    ON_COMMAND(ID_FILE_PRINT_DIRECT, CView::OnFilePrint)
    ON_COMMAND(ID_FILE_PRINT_PREVIEW, CView::OnFilePrintPreview)
END_MESSAGE_MAP()
```

The message map begins with the BEGIN_MESSAGE_MAP macro and ends with the END_MESSAGE_MAP macro. The lines reserved for use by ClassWizard start with //{{AFX_MSG_MAP and end with //}}AFX_MSG_MAP. If you make manual changes to the message map, do not change the entries reserved for ClassWizard; they are maintained automatically.

Essential Example

A Program to Test for Mouse Clicks

As an example, you're about to create a program that actually shows how messages are used to notify your application about events. This program, MouseTst, will be an SDI application that displays a message whenever the mouse is clicked inside the client area.

The first step in creating MouseTst is to use AppWizard to create an SDI application. I listed the steps needed to create an SDI application in Chapter 13. Feel free to select or remove any options offered by AppWizard, because none of the options have any bearing on the demonstration. Name the application MouseTst.

Messages Handled by MouseTst

The MouseTst program must handle four messages used to collect mouse events. The messages used by MouseTst are listed in Table 14.2.

Table 14.2. Messages handled by MouseTst.

Message	Function	Description
WM_LBUTTONDOWN	OnLButtonDown	Left mouse button pressed
WM_LBUTTONDBLCLK	OnLButtonDblClk	Left mouse button clicked twice
WM_RBUTTONDOWN	OnRButtonDown	Right mouse button pressed
WM_RBUTTONDBLCLK	OnRButtonDblClk	Right mouse button double-clicked

In addition, when the WM_PAINT message is received, the MFC framework calls the OnDraw member function. MouseTst will use OnDraw to update the display with the current mouse position and last message.

Updating the *CMouseTstView* Class

All of the work that keeps track of the mouse events will be done in the CMouseTstView class. There are two steps to displaying the mouse event information in the MouseTst program, as shown in Figure 14.1:

1. When one of the four mouse events occur, the event type and the mouse position are recorded, and the view's rectangle is invalidated, causing a WM_PAINT message to be generated.

2. When a WM_PAINT message is received, the OnDraw member function is called, and the mouse event and position are displayed.

All output is done in response to a WM_PAINT message. WM_PAINT is sent when a window's client area is invalidated. This often is due to the window being uncovered, or *reopened.* Because the window must be redrawn in response to a WM_PAINT message, most programs written for Windows do all of their drawing in response to WM_PAINT, and just invalidate their display window or view when the window should be updated.

In order to keep track of the mouse event and position, you must add two member variables to the CMouseTstView class. Add the three lines from Listing 14.4 as the last three lines before the closing curly brace in CMouseTstView.h.

Listing 14.4. New member variables for the CMouseTstView class.

```
private:
    CPoint    m_ptMouse;
    CString   m_szDescription;
```

The constructor for CMouseTstView must initialize the new member variables. Edit the constructor for CMouseTstView, found in CMouseTstView.cpp, so it looks like the source code in Listing 14.5.

Listing 14.5. The constructor for CMouseTstView.

```
CMouseTstView::CMouseTstView()
{
    m_ptMouse = CPoint(0,0);
    m_szDescription.Empty();
}
```

Using ClassWizard, add message-handling functions for the four mouse events that you're handling in the MouseTst program. Open ClassWizard by pressing Ctrl+W, or by right-clicking in a source-code window and selecting ClassWizard from the menu. After ClassWizard appears, follow these steps:

1. Select the CMouseTstView class in the Object ID list box; a list of messages sent to the CMouseTstView class will be displayed in the Message list box.

2. Select the WM_LBUTTONDOWN message from the message list box, and press the button labeled Add Function.

3. Repeat Step 2 for the WM_RBUTTONDOWN, WM_LBUTTONDBLCLK, and WM_RBUTTONDBLCLK messages.

4. Click the OK button to close ClassWizard.

Edit the message-handling functions so they look like the function provided in Listing 14.6. You must remove some source code provided by ClassWizard in each function.

Listing 14.6. The four mouse-handling functions for CMouseTstView.

```
void CMouseTstView::OnLButtonDblClk(UINT nFlags, CPoint point)
{
    m_ptMouse = point;
    m_szDescription = "Left Button Double Click";
    InvalidateRect( NULL );
}

void CMouseTstView::OnLButtonDown(UINT nFlags, CPoint point)
{
    m_ptMouse = point;
    m_szDescription = "Left Button Down";
    InvalidateRect( NULL );
}

void CMouseTstView::OnRButtonDblClk(UINT nFlags, CPoint point)
{
    m_ptMouse = point;
    m_szDescription = "Right Button Double Click";
    InvalidateRect( NULL );
}

void CMouseTstView::OnRButtonDown(UINT nFlags, CPoint point)
{
    m_ptMouse = point;
    m_szDescription = "Right Button Down";
    InvalidateRect( NULL );
}
```

Each of the message-handling functions in Listing 14.6 stores the position of both the mouse event and a text string that describes the event. Each function then invalidates the view rectangle. The next step is to use the CMouseTstView::OnDraw function to display the event. Edit CMouseTstView::OnDraw so it contains the source code in Listing 14.7. Remove any existing source code provided by AppWizard.

Listing 14.7 The OnDraw member function for CMouseTstView.

```
void CMouseTstView::OnDraw(CDC* pDC)
{
    pDC->TextOut( m_ptMouse.x, m_ptMouse.y, m_szDescription );
}
```

The OnDraw member function uses TextOut to display the previously saved event message. The CPoint object, m_ptMouse, was used to store the mouse event's position. A CPoint object has two member variables, x and y, which are used to plot a point in a window.

Running MouseTst

Build and run MouseTst, then click in the main window's client area. A message is displayed whenever you click the left or right mouse buttons.

Summary

In this chapter you looked at how messages are handled by a program written for Windows. You also wrote a sample program that handles and displays some commonly used mouse event messages.

CHAPTER

15

Menus

Menus are an essential part of most Windows programs. Except for some simple dialog box–based applications, all Windows programs offer some type of menu. In this chapter, I discuss how menu resources and the MFC CMenu class are used in Windows programs. You modify a menu created by AppWizard and also create a floating pop-up menu as examples.

What Is a Menu?

What A menu is a list of command messages that can be selected and sent to a window. To the user, a menu item is a string that indicates a task that can be performed by the application. Each menu item also has an ID that is used to identify the item when routing window messages. This ID is also used when modifying attributes for the menu item.

Menus are usually attached to a window, although many applications support floating pop-up menus that can appear anywhere on the desktop. Later in this chapter, you create a floating pop-up menu that is displayed when the right mouse button is clicked. These menus are often used to provide context-sensitive help and offer different menu choices depending on the window that creates the menu.

Common User Interface Elements

In order to make Windows programs easier to use, most programs follow a common set of guidelines regarding the appearance of their menus. For example, menu items leading to dialog boxes that require additional user input are usually marked with an ellipsis . . . .

Another user interface requirement is a mnemonic, or underlined letter, for each menu item. When this letter is pressed, the appropriate menu item is selected. This letter is usually the first letter of the menu item; however, in some cases another letter is used. For example, the Exit menu item found in the File menu uses x as its mnemonic.

Menus are sometimes nested, meaning that one menu item is actually a submenu with a series of additional menu items. A menu item that leads to a nested submenu has a right arrow to indicate that more selections are available. You can see an example of a nested menu structure in the menus used by the Windows 95 Start button, as shown in Figure 15.1.

Figure 15.1.
The nested menu structure used by the Start button.

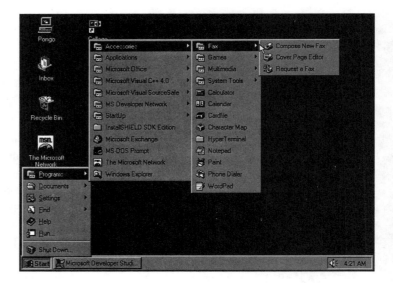

Why Use a Menu?

You use menus to indicate a list of actions that can be applied to a Windows program. Although AppWizard creates a default set of menus for your program, you must modify these menus when adding functionality to your programs.

Floating pop-up menus are another way to make your program easier to use. By supplying a context-sensitive menu that is displayed when the right mouse button is clicked, you make your program more user-friendly.

How Are Menus Used?

You can create menus dynamically or as static resources that are added to your program. The MFC class library provides a CMenu class that simplifies handling menus and is used for the examples in this chapter.

How

AppWizard generates a menu resource for programs that it creates. This menu resource can be edited to add extra menu items for your application, or you can create new menu resources for your application.

For the examples used in this chapter, create a sample SDI application called Menu. This program is used to demonstrate how menu resources are created and modified.

Message Routing

Before I look at creating and modifying menus, let's look at the way that menu messages are handled by Windows programs in general and MFC programs in particular.

A menu is always associated with a particular window. In most MFC programs, it is associated with the main frame window, which also contains the application's toolbar and status bar. When a menu item is selected, a WM_COMMAND message is sent to the main frame window; this message includes the ID of the menu item. The MFC framework and your application convert this message into a function call, as described in Chapter 14, "Messages and Event-Driven Programming."

In an MFC application, there are many windows that can receive a menu selection message. In general, any window that is derived from CCmdTarget is plugged into the MFC framework's message loop. When a menu item is selected, the message is offered to all of the command target objects in your application, in the following order:

- The CMainFrame object
- The main MDI frame window
- The active child frame of an MDI frame window
- The view that is associated with the MDI child frame
- The document object associated with the active view
- The document template associated with the document object
- The CWinApp object

This list might seem like a large number of steps to take, but it's actually not very complicated in practice. Usually, a menu item is handled by one type of object—a view or main frame. Menu messages are rarely handled directly by the document template or child frame objects. Figure 15.2 shows a simplified map of how commands are routed in an MFC application.

Figure 15.2.
Menu command routing in an MFC application.

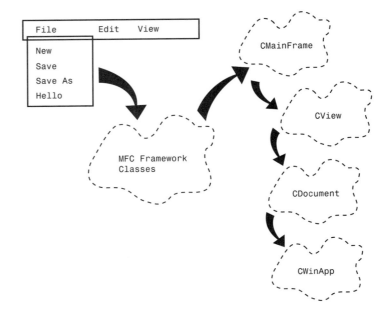

In most cases, you can use ClassWizard to configure the message maps required to route menu selection messages to their proper destinations.

Adding New Menu Items

One of the easiest tasks to perform with a menu is adding a new menu item. In order to use a new menu item, you must do two things:

- Modify the menu resource to include the new menu item.
- Add a message-handling function using ClassWizard.

These steps are explained in the next two sections.

Opening the Menu Resource

To display the current menu resources, select the ResourceView tab in the project workspace window. Expand the resource tree to show the different resource types defined for the current project; one of the folders is labeled Menu.

Open the menu folder to display the resources defined for the menus of the project. Every multiple-document application created by AppWizard has two menu resources. MDI applications use an IDR_MAINFRAME menu when no views are active. They also have an additional menu item used when a view is active. The name of this menu resource is based on the application name, as IDR_xxxTYPE, where xxx is replaced by the program's name. For example, IDR_FOOTYPE is the second menu resource created for a program named Foo.

SDI applications have a single menu created by AppWizard named IDR_MAINFRAME. This is the menu displayed by default for single-document applications. Every AppWizard program begins with the exact same menu; it's up to you to supply any modifications that are required for your application.

Editing the Menu Resource

Open the menu resource by double-clicking the menu resource icon. The menu is displayed in the resource editor ready for editing. When the menu is initially loaded into the editor, only the top-level menu bar is displayed. Clicking any top-level menu item displays the pop-up menu associated with that item, as shown in Figure 15.3.

Figure 15.3.
Using the Developer Studio resource editor to edit a menu resource.

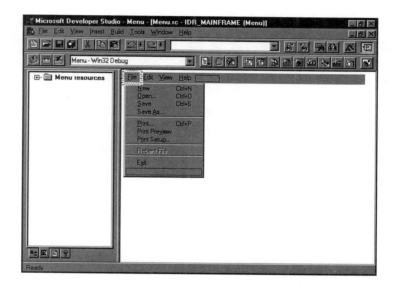

The last item of every menu is an empty box. This box is used to add new menu items to the menu resource. All menu items are initially added to the end of a menu resource and then moved to their proper position. To add a new menu item, follow these steps:

1. Double-click the empty box on the File menu to display the menu properties dialog box.

2. To add a menu item, provide a menu ID and caption for the new menu item. By convention, menu IDs begin with ID_ and then you include the name of the top-level menu. For this example, enter ID_FILE_HELLO as the menu ID and &Hello as the menu caption.

3. Optionally, you can provide a prompt that is displayed in the status bar when the new menu item is highlighted.

4. Click anywhere outside the properties dialog box to return to the editor.

After you've added the new menu item, it can be moved to a new position by dragging it with the mouse. Changing the menu position does not change any of its attributes.

Menu Item Properties

There are several optional properties that can be applied to a menu item via the properties dialog box. These properties are the following:

- **ID** is used for the menu's resource ID. This ID is sent as part of the WM_COMMAND message to your application and is used by ClassWizard to identify the menu item.
- **Caption** is the name used to identify the menu item. The mnemonic letter is preceded by an ampersand (&) and is used to select the item without using the mouse.
- **Separator** is used to indicate that this menu item is a separator, or horizontal line that divides logical sections of a menu. This checkbox is usually cleared.
- **Checked** is used to indicate that the menu item should display a checkmark to indicate the menu item is selected. This checkbox is usually cleared.
- **Pop-up** is used to indicate that this menu item is the top level of a pop-up or submenu. This option is usually cleared except on the top-level menu bar.
- **Grayed** indicates that this menu item is grayed. This checkbox is usually cleared.
- **Inactive** indicates that this menu item is inactive. This checkbox is usually cleared.
- **Help** places the menu item to the far right side of the menu bar. This option is rarely used, even for the Help menu.
- **Break** is used to split the menu at this menu item. The default choice is none and is used in almost all cases.
- **Prompt** is used to specify the text that will be displayed in the status bar when the menu item is highlighted.

Adding a Message-Handling Function

After adding a menu item to the application's menu, the next step is to add a message-handling function to handle the new menu item. As discussed in Chapter 14, ClassWizard is used to create message-handling functions for MFC-based Windows programs. To add a message-handling function for the ID_FILE_HELLO menu item, follow these steps:

1. Open ClassWizard by pressing Ctrl+W or by right-clicking in a source code window and selecting ClassWizard from the menu.
2. Select the tab labeled Message Maps and select the class that will handle the message from the Class Name combo box—in this case, CMainFrame.
3. Select the object that is generating the message from the Object ID list box—in this case, ID_FILE_HELLO. Two message-handling functions are displayed in the Messages list box.

4. Select the COMMAND message from the Messages list box and click the Add Function button. Accept the default name suggested by ClassWizard for the function name—OnFileHello.

5. Click the OK button to close ClassWizard.

Edit the CMainFrame::OnFileHello function so that it looks like the function provided in Listing 15.1. The AfxMessageBox function displays a simple message dialog box and is discussed in detail in the next chapter.

Listing 15.1. The CMainFrame::OnFileHello message-handling function.

```
void CMainFrame::OnFileHello()
{
    AfxMessageBox( "Hello from the File menu" );
}
```

These basic steps are used to add all of the menu items used in examples for the remaining chapters in this book. The Developer Studio tools are so easy to use that adding a new menu item will be second nature in no time.

Creating a Pop-Up Menu

Creating a floating pop-up menu is similar to modifying an existing menu except that a new menu resource must be created as the first step. Most floating pop-up menus are displayed in response to the WM_RBUTTONDOWN message, which is sent when the right mouse button is clicked.

Creating the Resource

Use the Developer Studio resource editor to create the floating pop-up menu. To create the new menu resource, use one of the following techniques:

- Select Resource from the Insert menu and then select Menu from the Insert Resource dialog box; or

- Right-click on the Menu folder in the ResourceView and then select Insert Menu from the pop-up menu.

Both of these methods opens a new menu resource for editing. Add a dummy caption for the first top-level item on the menu bar. This caption is not displayed by the pop-up menu; it is only used as a placeholder.

Open the properties dialog box for the menu resource by double-clicking the edge of the menu resource and change the resource ID to ID_POPUP. Using the values from Table 15.1, add three menu items under the dummy label.

Table 15.1. Menu items added to the ID_POPUP menu resource.

Menu ID	Caption
ID_LIONS	&Lions
ID_TIGERS	&Tigers
ID_BEARS	&Bears

Adding Message-Handling Functions

The new pop-up menu is displayed when a right mouse click is detected on the application's view. After a menu item has been selected, a message is displayed at the menu's location, similar to the message displayed in the MouseTst example from Chapter 14.

You must add two new variables to the CMenuView class: a CString variable that stores the message and a CPoint variable that stores the location of the pop-up menu. Add the source code provided in Listing 15.2 to the CMenuView class after the //Implementation comment.

Listing 15.2. New member variables for the CMenuView class.

```
// Implementation
protected:
    CPoint  m_ptMsg;
    CString m_szMsg;
```

The CMenuView::OnDraw member function resembles the OnDraw member function from CMouseTestView in Chapter 14. Both functions use the TextOut function to display a message at a certain point in the view. Edit the CMenuView::OnDraw function so that it looks like the function provided in Listing 15.3. You need to remove a few lines of AppWizard-supplied code.

Listing 15.3. The CMenuView::OnDraw member function.

```
void CMenuView::OnDraw(CDC* pDC)
{
    pDC->TextOut( m_ptMsg.x, m_ptMsg.y, m_szMsg );
}
```

Trapping Messages

Use ClassWizard to add four new message-handling functions to the CMenuView class: three message-handling functions for the new menu items and one message-handling function to detect the right-click from the mouse button. The steps used to add the message-handling functions are similar to the ones used earlier when modifying an existing menu except these messages are handled by the CMenuView class.

1. Open ClassWizard by pressing Ctrl+W or right-clicking in a source code window and selecting ClassWizard from the menu.
2. Select the tab labeled Message Maps and select the class that will handle the message from the Class Name combo box—in this case, CMenuView.
3. Select the object that is generating the message from the Object ID list box—in this case, use one of the values from Table 15.2.
4. Select a message from the Messages list box and click the Add Function button. Accept the default name suggested by ClassWizard for the function name.
5. Repeat this process for all entries in Table 15.2.
6. Click the OK button to close ClassWizard.

Table 15.2. Values used to create message-handling functions.

Object ID	Message	Function
CMenuView	WM_RBUTTONDOWN	OnRButtonDown
ID_LIONS	COMMAND	OnLions
ID_TIGERS	COMMAND	OnTigers
ID_BEARS	COMMAND	OnBears

The source code for the CMenuView::OnRButtonDown message-handling function is provided in Listing 15.4.

Listing 15.4. Popping up a menu when a right mouse click is detected.

```
void CMenuView::OnRButtonDown(UINT nFlags, CPoint point)
{
    CMenu    zooMenu;
    // Store popup point, and convert to screen coordinates
    // for the menu functions.
    m_ptMsg = point;
    ClientToScreen( &point );
    zooMenu.LoadMenu( ID_POPUP );
    CMenu* pPopup = zooMenu.GetSubMenu( 0 );
    pPopup->TrackPopupMenu( TPM_LEFTALIGN|TPM_RIGHTBUTTON,
                            point.x,
                            point.y,
                            this );
}
```

When a right mouse click is detected, the WM_RBUTTONDOWN message is sent to the application, and the MFC framework calls the OnRButtonDown message. The OnRButtonDown function creates a CMenu object and loads the ID_POPUP menu resource. The floating menu is displayed by calling GetSubMenu and TrackPopupMenu.

The GetSubMenu function is used to skip past the dummy menu item at the top of the ID_POPUP menu resource. The GetSubMenu function returns a temporary pointer to the pop-up menu. Calling TrackPopupMenu causes the pop-up menu to be displayed and the menu item selection to automatically follow the mouse cursor.

The source code for handling menu selection messages sent to the CMenuView class is provided in Listing 15.5.

Listing 15.5. Message-handling functions for floating menu items.

```
void CMenuView::OnLions()
{
    m_szMsg = "Lions are out";
    InvalidateRect( NULL );
}
void CMenuView::OnTigers()
{
    m_szMsg = "Tigers are afoot";
    InvalidateRect( NULL );
}
void CMenuView::OnBears()
{
    m_szMsg = "Bears are hungry";
    InvalidateRect( NULL );
}
```

Each of the message-handling functions in Listing 15.5 work in a similar way: a message is stored in the m_szMsg member variable, and the view rectangle is invalidated. This causes a WM_PAINT message to be sent to the MFC framework, which in turn calls the OnDraw function to display the message.

Summary

In this chapter, I discussed the use of menus in Windows applications. I discussed the routing of menu command messages, as well as methods for modifying and creating menu resources. As an example, you created an application that displays a floating pop-up menu when the right mouse button is clicked.

Dialog Boxes

Dialog boxes are used for much of the interaction between the user and a Windows program. In this chapter, I discuss the different types of dialog boxes and the steps required to add them to a project using Developer Studio.

What Is a Dialog Box?

What Dialog boxes, often just called *dialogs*, are used to present information and collect input from the user. Dialog boxes come in all shapes and sizes, ranging from simple message boxes that display a single line of text to large dialog boxes that contain sophisticated controls.

Dialog boxes normally are used to collect information and to provide feedback to a program's user. The most commonly used type of dialog box is a *modal dialog box*, which usually contains several controls used to interact with a program.

Dialog boxes are also used for one-way communication with a user, such as "splash screens" used to display copyright and startup information as a program is launched. The opening screen displayed by the Visual C++

Developer Studio and Microsoft Word are two examples of dialog boxes used for one-way communication. Dialog boxes are sometimes used to notify the user about the progress of a lengthy operation.

Another commonly used type of dialog box is the message box, which I used in Chapter 14, "Messages and Event-Driven Programming." Most message boxes are used to give short messages to a user, and are sometimes used to collect simple feedback.

Why Use Dialog Boxes?

Why

Dialog boxes provide a convenient way for users to interact with Windows programs. Users expect most interaction with a Windows program to take place through dialog boxes. As I discuss later in the section "Using Dialog Boxes for Input," all dialog boxes have certain things incommon; these common characteristics make the user's life easier, because users don't need to learn and relearn how dialog boxes work from program to program.

There are several different types of dialog boxes, and each of them has a specific purpose. In this chapter, I discuss these three main types of dialog boxes:

- Message Boxes
- Modal Dialog Boxes
- Modeless Dialog Boxes

Understanding Message Boxes

The simplest type of dialog box is the message box, which is used to display information to the user. This type of dialog box is so simple you can call it with just one line of code, using the MFC class library. For example, to display a message box using default parameters supplied by MFC, just use this line:

```
AfxMessageBox( "Hello World" );
```

This line of code creates a message box with a exclamation mark inside a yellow triangle. There are several additional options for the icon displayed in a message box, as I discuss later.

Using Dialog Boxes for Input

When most people think of dialog boxes, they think of the dialog boxes that collect input from a user. Dialog boxes are often used to contain controls that are used to handle user input. There are a wide range of controls that you can include in a dialog box. In fact, a major portion of this book covers the various types of controls available in Windows.

Some dialog boxes are needed so often in Windows programs that they have been included as part of the operating system. These dialog boxes, known as *common dialog boxes*, are available by calling a function and don't require that you create a dialog box resource. There are common dialog boxes for opening and selecting files, choosing fonts and colors, and performing find and replace operations. I cover each of these dialog boxes later in the book. For example, in Chapter 32, "Fonts," I discuss using a common dialog box to select a font.

Most dialog boxes are *modal*, which means that they must be closed before a user can perform another task. A dialog box that is *modeless* allows other activities to be carried out while the dialog box is still open.

An example of a modeless dialog box is the Find and Replace dialog box used by Developer Studio. When the dialog box is open, you can still make selections from the main menu, and even open other dialog boxes. In contrast, all other Developer Studio dialog boxes are modal. As long as they are open, the user cannot interact with the other parts of Developer Studio.

How Are Dialog Boxes Used?

Developer Studio makes it easy to use dialog boxes in a Windows program. All of the necessary steps are automated, and the tools used to create the dialog box and include it in a project are all integrated.

How

Adding Message Boxes

As I discussed earlier, you can add message boxes to your program by using one line of code. You must supply at least a single parameter: the text that is displayed inside the dialog box. Optionally, you can also specify an icon style and a button arrangement pattern. The types of icons that are available for message boxes are shown in Figure 16.1.

Figure 16.1.
Icons you can include in
a message box.

Each of the icons in Figure 16.1 has a specific meaning. When most Windows programs display a message box, they use a standard icon for each message. When programs use the same icons consistently, users find it much easier to understand the meanings of information provided with message boxes. The meaning and style name for each icon is shown in Table 16.1.

Table 16.1. Icons used in Windows message box dialog boxes.

Icon Displayed	Meaning	Message Box Style
Exclamation mark	Warning	`MB_ICONEXCLAMATION`
An "i" in a circle	Information	`MB_ICONINFORMATION`
Question mark	Question	`MB_ICONQUESTION`
Stop sign	Error	`MB_ICONSTOP`

In addition, you can specify a button arrangement to be used in the message box. By default, a single button labeled OK is included in the message box. However, sometimes it's convenient to ask a user a simple question and collect an answer. One use for these button arrangements is to ask the user what action to take during an error. For example, this code displays a message box that contains a question mark icon, and asks the user if the current file should be deleted:

```
int nChoice = AfxMessageBox( "Overwrite existing file?",
                        MB_YESNOCANCEL | MB_ICONQUESTION );
if( nChoice == IDYES )
{
    // Overwrite file
}
```

The user can choose between buttons marked Yes, No, and Cancel. Table 16.2 gives the different button arrangements possible for a message box.

Table 16.2. Button arrangements.

Message Box style	Buttons Included in Dialog Box
MB_ABORTRETRYIGNORE	Abort, Retry, and Ignore
MB_OK	OK
MB_OKCANCEL	OK and Cancel
MB_RETRYCANCEL	Retry and Cancel
MB_YESNO	Yes and No
MB_YESNOCANCEL	Yes, No, and Cancel

The message box return value indicates the button selected by the user. Table 16.3 is a list of possible return values, and the choice made by the user.

Table 16.3. Message box return values.

Return Value	Button Pressed
IDABORT	Abort
IDCANCEL	Cancel
IDIGNORE	Ignore
IDNO	No
IDOK	OK
IDRETRY	Retry
IDYES	Yes

Using the Bitwise *OR* Operator

In the code above Table 16.2, I used a vertical bar to separate two different options for the AfxMessageBox function. The vertical bar is the *bitwise OR operator*, which is used to combine the bit patterns of two or more values.

Unlike adding two operands, the values are combined "bitwise," meaning that the two values are compared bit by bit. If a particular bit is high in either operand, the result will have that bit enabled. If a particular bit is low in both operands, the result will be zero. For example, this expression also is equal to seven:

```
4 | 3
```

is equal to seven. However, the result of:

```
4 | 7
```

is also equal to seven. Each possible parameter has a unique bit pattern, enabling you to use the bitwise OR operator when you combine parameter values in AfxMessageBox or other MFC function calls.

When using the bitwise OR operator with AfxMessageBox, you can combine one icon style and one button style. You can't combine two icon styles, or two button styles. If no styles are provided, the message box will contain the exclamation mark icon and an OK button.

Adding a Dialog Box

Adding a dialog box to a program usually takes four steps:

1. Design and create a dialog box resource using the Developer Studio resource tools.
2. Use ClassWizard to create a C++ class derived from CDialog that will manage the dialog box.
3. Add functions to handle messages sent to the dialog box, if needed.
4. If the dialog box is selected from the main menu, the menu resource must be modified, and message-handling functions created using ClassWizard.

I cover each of these steps in the following sections.

Understanding Resources

Dialog boxes are just a specialized type of window. However, because they commonly are used for short periods of time, they usually are stored as program resources and only loaded when needed. Program resources are stored in a program's EXE file, but are loaded only when they are actually needed. You can see this behavior when running a Windows program on a machine that has little free memory. Every time a dialog box is opened, the hard disk is accessed to load the dialog box resources from the EXE.

Menus and accelerators, which I cover in Chapter 15, "Menus," are two types of resources. Here are some of the other resource types used by Windows programs:

- *Bitmaps,* used to store images such as the logo from the Visual C++ opening, or "splash" screen. I cover bitmaps in more detail in Chapter 20, "Using Image Lists and Bitmaps," and in Chapter 33, "Icons."

- *Cursors,* used to indicate the current mouse position. A program can modify the cursor to indicate that a specific action can be taken with the mouse at its current position, or for other user-feedback purposes. I cover cursors in detail in Chapter 34, "Cursors."

- *Dialog Boxes,* which are just windows that are used for interaction with a program's user. The message box I covered earlier in this chapter is one example of dialog boxes.

- *Icons,* which are small bitmaps in a special format that can be used to represent another object in a Windows program. For example, icons are often used to represent programs and documents that aren't currently visible.

In this chapter I discuss creating and using dialog box resources. Later chapters deal with the other resource types.

Creating the Dialog Box Resource by Hand

There are two ways to create a dialog box resource. The first way, which is tedious and error-prone, is to code the resource statements by hand, and add them to your resource file. A dialog box resource definition is provided in Listing 16.1.

Listing 16.1. A typical resource definition for a dialog box.

```
IDD_ABOUTBOX DIALOG DISCARDABLE  34, 22, 217, 55
STYLE DS_MODALFRAME ¦ WS_POPUP ¦ WS_CAPTION ¦ WS_SYSMENU
CAPTION "About Hello World"
FONT 8, "MS Sans Serif"
BEGIN
    ICON            IDR_MAINFRAME,IDC_STATIC,11,17,20,20
    LTEXT           "Hello World 1.0",IDC_STATIC,40,10,119,8
    LTEXT           "Copyright \251 1994",IDC_STATIC,40,25,119,8
    DEFPUSHBUTTON   "OK",IDOK,176,6,32,14,WS_GROUP
END
```

The first five lines of Listing 16.1 describe the dialog box, and the remaining lines define the controls that are contained by the dialog box. Each element of the definition, including the dialog box and all of the controls, is given a name and position. Creating a dialog box resource this way is almost impossible without a lot of time and effort. You will almost always want to use the easier method described in the next section, which takes advantage of the tools included in Developer Studio.

Creating a Dialog Box Resource Using Developer Studio

Developer Studio enables you to create a dialog box and configure it visually. You can add and size controls by using a mouse. You can set attributes for the dialog box and its controls with the click of a mouse button.

Before using the following steps, either create a new Windows project, as discussed in Chapter 13, "Using Visual C++ for Windows Programming," or open an existing project. To create a new dialog box resource for an existing project, use either of the following methods:

- Select Resource from the Insert menu, then select Dialog as the resource type.
- Right-click the Dialog folder in the Resource tree, and select Insert Dialog from the pop-up menu.

With either of the methods described above, the dialog box editor is displayed, as shown in Figure 16.2.

Figure 16.2.
The Developer Studio dialog box editor.

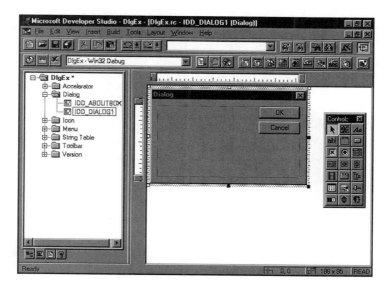

The dialog box that is displayed for editing initially contains two button controls, one marked OK and another labeled Cancel. As I discuss in Chapter 17, "Button Controls," these are two standard dialog box controls. The MFC class library handles the operation of these controls in most cases.

Customizing the Dialog Box's Properties

Every dialog box has properties that you can display by double-clicking the dialog box or by right-clicking and then selecting Properties from the pop-up menu. Here are the dialog box properties under the tab labeled General:

- `Dialog ID`, normally set to something like `IDD_DIALOG1`. Naming dialog boxes with an identifier that begins with `IDD_` is an MFC convention, although you should try to name your dialog boxes with a more meaningful name, like `IDD_HELLO`.
- `Dialog Caption`, normally set to a default of Dialog. You should change this to something more meaningful as well, such as Hello for the sample dialog box.
- `Menu`, normally cleared as few dialog boxes use a menu.
- `Font`, normally cleared to use the system-provided font.
- `Position`, normally cleared.

Like all windows, a dialog box has a number of style attributes. You can display these attributes by selecting the tab labeled Styles. Here are the default values for the following attributes:

- `Style`, usually set to Popup for most dialog boxes. In the case of special dialog box templates used in Form Views or Dialog Bars, the style is set to Child.
- `Border`, set to Dialog Frame for most dialog boxes.
- `Minimize box`, which creates a minimize box for the dialog box. This checkbox is cleared for most dialog boxes, indicating that no minimize box is provided.
- `Maximize box`, used to create a maximize box for the dialog box. This checkbox is cleared for most dialog boxes, indicating that no maximize box is provided.
- `Titlebar`, which creates a title bar for the dialog box. This checkbox is almost always checked, because most dialog boxes have a title bar.
- `System menu`, used to indicate that a system menu should be provided for the dialog box. This checkbox is normally checked.
- `Horizontal scroll`, used to create a scroll bar for the dialog box. This checkbox is almost always cleared, because dialog boxes rarely use a scroll bar.
- `Vertical scroll`, used to create a vertical scroll bar for the dialog box. Like the horizontal scroll bar, this attribute is rarely used.
- `Clip siblings`, which is only used with child windows. This checkbox is normally cleared.
- `Clip children`, used for parent windows. This checkbox is rarely checked for most dialog boxes.

The tab labeled More Styles contains additional properties for the dialog box, including:

- `System Modal`, which creates a system-modal dialog box. If this option is enabled, the user cannot switch to any other program.

- Absolute align, used to indicate how the dialog box is positioned when initially displayed. If this checkbox is checked, the dialog box is aligned with the screen instead of the parent window.

- No idle msg, which prevents a particular window message, WM_ENTERIDLE, from being sent when the dialog box's message queue is empty. This checkbox is normally cleared.

- Local edit, used to specify how an edit control's memory is allocated. This checkbox is normally cleared, which means edit controls use memory outside the program's data segment.

- Visible, used to specify that the dialog box should be visible when first displayed. This checkbox is usually checked. In the case of Form Views, this checkbox is cleared. I cover form views in Chapter 26, "Using Form Views."

- Disabled, which indicates that the dialog box should be disabled when initially displayed. This checkbox is usually cleared.

- 3D-look, which gives the dialog box a three dimensional appearance. This checkbox is usually cleared.

- Set foreground, which forces the dialog box to be placed into the foreground. This checkbox is usually cleared.

- No fail create, which tells Windows to create the dialog box, even if an error occurs. This checkbox is usually cleared.

- Control, which creates a dialog box resource that can be used as a child control. This checkbox is usually cleared.

- Center, which causes the dialog box to be centered when it is initially displayed. This checkbox is usually cleared.

- Center mouse, which places the mouse cursor in the center of the dialog box. This checkbox is usually cleared.

There are also advanced styles located under the tab labeled Extended Styles. These styles are rarely used and aren't discussed in this book.

Adding a Control

A simple control that you can add to the dialog box is a static text control. The static text control requires no interaction with the dialog box; it is often used as a plain text label for other controls contained by the dialog box. To add a static text control, follow these steps:

1. Select the static text control icon on the control toolbar. The cursor changes shape to a plus sign when moved over the dialog box.

2. Center the cursor over the dialog box, and click the left mouse button. A static text control is created, and contains the label Static.

3. Change the label of the static text control by double-clicking the control, then changing the caption to "Hello World."

The static text control is visible whenever the dialog box is displayed. Text controls are an excellent choice for labeling controls, or messages that are not likely to change. Experiment with changing the size and position of the static text control by dragging its edges with the mouse.

Creating a Class for the Dialog Box

You can use the CDialog class to manage most of the interaction with a dialog box in your program. The CDialog class provides member functions that make a dialog box easy to use. You should derive a class from CDialog that is specifically tailored for your dialog box, using ClassWizard.

To start ClassWizard, use any of these methods:

- Press Ctrl+W almost anytime in Developer Studio.
- Select ClassWizard from the View menu.
- Right-click anywhere in the dialog box editor, and select ClassWizard from the pop-up menu.

If ClassWizard knows that a new resource has been added, such as IDD_HELLO, a dialog box asks you to choose between three options for the new dialog box resource:

- Create a new class.
- Import an existing class.
- Select an existing class.

You should almost always choose to create a new dialog box class, unless you are reusing some existing code. A Create New Class dialog box is displayed, as shown in Figure 16.3.

Figure 16.3.
The ClassWizard and Create New Class dialog box.

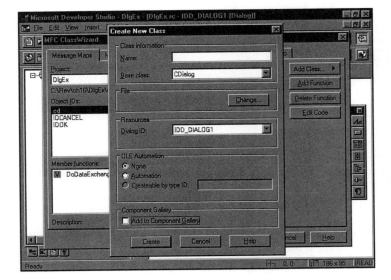

Values provided to the Create New Class dialog box are used by ClassWizard to create a class that will manage the new dialog box resource. Use the values from Table 16.4 to fill in the values for the IDD_HELLO dialog box.

Table 16.4. Sample values for the Create New Class dialog box.

Control	Value
Name	CHelloDlg
Base Class	CDialog
File	HelloDlg.cpp
Dialog ID	IDD_HELLO
OLE Automation	None
Add to Component Gallery	Cleared

Click the button labeled Create. The CHelloDlg class is generated, and two files will be added to your project:

- The HelloDlg.h file contains the class declaration.
- The HelloDlg.cpp file contains the class definitions.

Adding a Message Handler for *WM_INITDIALOG*

After you have added the CHelloDlg class to your project, ClassWizard can be used to add a message-handling function. The WM_INITDIALOG message is sent to the dialog box just before it is displayed. Most dialog box classes use the WM_INITDIALOG message to initialize member variables.

To add a message handler for WM_INITDIALOG, follow the same steps I outlined in Chapter 14, "Messages and Event-Driven Programming":

1. Using ClassWizard, select the CHelloDlg class.
2. Select CHelloDlg from the Object ID list box.
3. Scroll through the list of messages, and select WM_INITDIALOG.
4. Press the button labeled Add Function.
5. Press the button labeled Edit Code.

The CHelloDlg::OnInitDialog function doesn't really have to initialize any variables, so you can just display a message box instead. Edit OnInitDialog so it looks like the function in Listing 16.2.

Listing 16.2. The `CHelloDlg::OnInitDialog` function.

```
BOOL CHelloDlg::OnInitDialog()
{
    CDialog::OnInitDialog();
    AfxMessageBox( "WM_INITDIALOG received" );
    return TRUE;
}
```

Adding a Menu Choice for the New Dialog Box

Add a menu choice to the View menu named "Hello...," using the procedure I discussed in Chapter 15, "Menus." Use the values from Table 16.5 for the menu item.

Table 16.5. Values for the Hello menu item.

Control	Value
Menu ID	ID_VIEW_HELLO
Caption	&Hello...

The `CMainFrame` class will create the dialog box when the new menu item is selected. Use the following steps to add a message-handling function for the new menu item and display the `IDD_HELLO` dialog box.

1. Using ClassWizard, add a message-handling function to `CMainFrame` for the menu ID, named `OnViewHello`. This function creates a `CHelloDlg` object and executes the dialog box.

2. Add an #include statement in MainFrm.cpp that includes the class definition for `CHelloDlg`, found in HelloDlg.h.

3. Add the following line just above the include statement for MainFrm.h:

   ```
   #include "HelloDlg.h"
   ```

Listing 16.3 provides the source for `MainFrame::OnViewHello`.

Listing 16.3. The message-handling function for the Hello menu item.

```
void CMainFrame::OnViewHello()
{
    CHelloDlg    dlgHello;

    if( dlgHello.DoModal() == IDOK )
        AfxMessageBox( "OK button pressed" );
    else // IDCANCEL
        AfxMessageBox( "Cancel button pressed" );
}
```

Compile and run the project containing the new dialog box. When the DoModal member function is called, the IDD_HELLO dialog box is displayed. The function call does not return until the dialog box is closed by pressing one of the dialog box's buttons. If OK is pressed, the return value is IDOK. If Cancel is pressed, the return value is IDCANCEL.

Summary

In this chapter, I discussed dialog boxes and how they are used in programs written for Windows. I also covered the support provided by Developer Studio, including ClassWizard, the MFC class library, and the dialog box editor.

PART V

Control Classes

17   Button Controls

18   Using Edit Controls

19   Using List-Box and Combo-Box Controls

20   Using Image Lists and Bitmaps

Button Controls

Button controls are probably the most flexible control available in Windows. In this chapter I discuss the different types of button controls provided by Windows. You add each type of button to a dialog box-based project and use ClassWizard to add button events and member variables for the dialog box's button controls.

What Is a Button?

What A button is a special type of window that contains a text or bitmap label, usually found in a dialog box, toolbar, or other window containing controls. Five different types of buttons are provided by Windows:

- *Pushbuttons*, which have a raised, three-dimensional appearance and seem to be depressed as they are clicked with the mouse. Pushbuttons normally have a text label on the face of the control.

- *Radio buttons*, which consist of a round button with a label adjacent to it.

- *Checkboxes*, made up of a square box that contains a checkmark when selected, and a label next to the control.

- *Owner-drawn* buttons, which are painted by the button's owner instead of by Windows. I present owner-drawn buttons in Chapter 39, "Owner-Drawn Controls."
- *Group boxes*, which are simply rectangles that are used to surround other controls that have a common purpose.

Why Are Buttons Used?

Why In general, buttons are used to indicate a selection by the user. Buttons are used in Windows programs because they are convenient and easy for users to operate. Users have come to expect buttons to be presented in a large number of cases, especially when dialog boxes are present in a program.

What Are Pushbuttons?

Almost every dialog box has at least one pushbutton control to indicate actions that can be invoked by a user. Some common uses for pushbuttons include closing a dialog box, beginning a search, or asking for help.

What Are Radio Buttons?

Radio buttons are used when a selection must be made from several mutually exclusive options, such as a user's sex. Only one of the radio buttons, which usually are grouped together, is checked at any particular time.

What Are Checkboxes?

Checkboxes are used as Boolean flags that indicate whether or not a particular condition is true or false. Unlike radio buttons, several checkboxes in a group can be checked. Optionally, a checkbox can support a third state—disabled—meaning that the control is neither true or false.

What Are Group Boxes?

A group box is used to logically group controls that are used for similar purposes. This helps the user understand the relationships between controls and makes a dialog box easier to use. Radio buttons are almost always enclosed in a group box so that it's obvious which controls are associated with each other.

How Are Buttons Used?

How Button controls normally are created as part of a dialog box. After you add a button to a dialog box, you can use ClassWizard to add functions that can be used to handle events created when the button is pressed, checked, or selected. ClassWizard is also used to create CButton objects that are associated with individual button controls.

You can use the MFC class CButton to interact with button controls: both buttons that have been added to a dialog box resource and buttons that have been created dynamically. Use ClassWizard to associate a button control with a specific CButton object.

In order to see how button controls can be used with dialog boxes, you can create a project using AppWizard that consists of a single dialog box as the program's main window. I use this project, named Button, for the rest of this chapter as an example of how to use buttons in a dialog box.

What Is a Dialog Box-Based Project?

A dialog box-based project uses a dialog box as the main window of a simple program. For example, many of the utilities found in the Windows 95 Control Panel are dialog box-based.

What

A dialog box-based program has a menu that is accessed through the System Menu at the upper-left corner of the dialog box's caption bar. If your program needs to have sophisticated menus, it should not be dialog box-based. However, this type of program is perfect for demonstrating button controls or other simple programs.

Why Use a Dialog Box-Based Project?

A dialog box-based project is often used to build very small programs that interact with the user through a single dialog box. The program can be much smaller and easier to program, because the number of classes created by AppWizard is reduced by about half.

Why

A dialog box-based program is easily operated by a user. There is only one dialog box window, no menu, and all of the available controls usually are initially visible. There are no hidden dialog boxes or menu items, and the user can usually see exactly which operations should be carried out.

How Is a Dialog Box-Based Project Created?

You can create a dialog box-based program using AppWizard, just like the SDI program you built in Chapter 13, "Using Visual C++ for Windows Programming." Building a dialog box-based project is one of the initial options offered by AppWizard. I cover the third choice, building an MDI project, in Chapter 25, "Document/View Architecture."

How

Because a dialog box-based project is much simpler than an SDI or MDI project, there are fewer steps required when using AppWizard. Only four wizard pages are presented by AppWizard when building a dialog box-based project, versus the six pages required for an SDI or MDI project.

To create a dialog box-based project using AppWizard, follow these steps:

1. Open AppWizard by creating a new project workspace, as you have in previous chapters. For the purpose of building an example for this chapter, use the name "Button."

2. When the opening screen for AppWizard appears, select a dialog box-based project as the project type.

3. Accept the default project settings suggested by AppWizard and press the Finish button. You can also browse through the Wizard pages and change the default settings, if you wish. AppWizard creates the dialog box-based project for you, just as it created the SDI project in Chapter 13.

Adding Buttons to a Dialog Box

After AppWizard has created the files used by the Button project, open the Button.rc resource file, located under the Win32 Debug tree. Open the resource file by double-clicking the icon labeled Button.rc, or by right-clicking the icon and selecting Open from the pop-up menu.

A tree representing the resource types used in the Button project appears. Click the Dialog folder. Two dialog box resources appear: IDD_ABOUTBOX and IDD_BUTTON_DIALOG. The program's main dialog box uses the IDD_BUTTON_DIALOG resource.

Using the Dialog Box Editor

Open the dialog box editor by double-clicking the IDD_BUTTON_DIALOG icon or by right-clicking the icon and selecting Open from the pop-up menu. The IDD_BUTTON_DIALOG dialog box is displayed in the dialog box editor, along with a dockable control toolbar or palette. The floating control palette contains all of the controls available for a dialog box, as shown in Figure 17.1.

There are four different icons on the control palette for buttons, each used for a particular button type. Use one of the following steps to add a button control to a dialog box:

- Drag a button control from the palette to the dialog box by pressing the left mouse button while over the control button, then "dragging" the mouse cursor to the dialog box with the left mouse button still pressed. Release the mouse button when the cursor is over the desired spot in the dialog box.

- Select a button control by clicking a control in the control palette. Click the desired location for the control in the dialog box, and the dialog box editor creates a control for you in that location.

These steps apply for all controls in the control palette. After you've added a control to the dialog box, you can reposition and resize it using the mouse.

Figure 17.1.
The floating control palette.

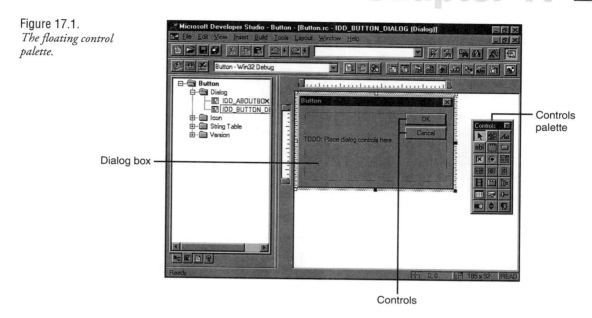

Controls palette

Dialog box

Controls

As a demonstration, add several buttons to the main dialog box used in the Button project. I use these controls later in the chapter to demonstrate button events. Refer to Figure 17.2 for the location of the added buttons.

Figure 17.2.
The main dialog box used by the Button project.

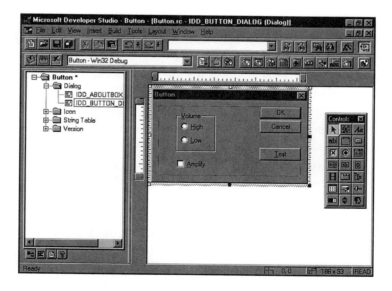

There are a total of five buttons added to IDD_BUTTON_DIALOG. Use the values from Table 17.1 to set the properties for each control. Except for the ID and caption, all controls use the default set of properties.

Table 17.1. Values used for controls in IDD_BUTTON_DIALOG.

Control ID	Button Type	Caption
IDC_BTN_TEST	Pushbutton	&Test
IDC_RADIO_HIGH	Radio Button	&High
IDC_RADIO_LOW	Radio Button	&Low
IDC_GROUP_VOLUME	Group Control	&Volume
IDC_CHECK_AMP	Checkbox	&Amplified

Button Control Properties

Like all controls, buttons have a set of properties that define the behavior of each control. Although there are four different types of button controls, they share a common set of properties. You can display the properties for a particular control by double-clicking the control, or by selecting Properties from the menu displayed when you right-click the control. These properties are shared by all button controls:

- ID, used for the button's resource ID. A default resource ID, such as IDC_BUTTON, is supplied by Developer Studio. Using IDC_ as a prefix for control resource IDs is a Microsoft naming convention.

- Caption, which indicates the text that appears as the button's label. Developer Studio supplies a default name, such as Button. To make one of the letters in the caption of a control the mnemonic key, precede it with an ampersand (&).

- Visible, which indicates that the button is initially visible. This checkbox is normally checked.

- Disabled, which indicates that the button should be initially disabled. This checkbox is normally cleared.

- Group, which marks the first control in a group. All controls following a control with this attribute are considered part of the same group if this checkbox is cleared. A user can move between controls in the same group using the arrow keys.

- Tabstop, which indicates that this control can be reached by pressing Tab on the keyboard. This checkbox is normally checked.

- Default Button, which marks this control as the dialog box's default button. There can only be one default button in a dialog box, and it is executed if the user presses Enter without using any other controls in the dialog box. This checkbox is normally cleared.

- Owner Draw, which indicates that the button will be drawn by the button's owner; in this case, the dialog box. I cover using owner-drawn controls in Chapter 39. In most cases, this checkbox is cleared.

Group boxes support the fewest properties of any button control. All button properties are supported except default button and owner draw.

Radio buttons do not use the default button property, because they aren't used as default buttons. However, radio buttons do support two properties not used by pushbutton controls:

- `Auto`, which automatically changes the state of the control when it is selected. This checkbox is normally selected.
- `Left Text`, which places the control's label on the left side of the checkbox, instead of the right. This checkbox is normally cleared.

Checkboxes support the same properties as radio controls, except that they are used with one additional attribute:

- `Tri State`, meaning that the checkbox can have three states instead of two. In addition to true and false, the control can be disabled, meaning that the value is neither true or false.

Using Standard Pushbutton Layouts in Your Dialog Boxes

Several pushbuttons are commonly used in dialog boxes that contain controls. As each of these pushbuttons carries a specific meaning, you should try to use the standard terminology whenever possible, because it minimizes the amount of work required for users of your programs. Here are the standard meanings for these buttons:

- OK, used to close and accept any information that is present in the dialog box. Any user-supplied information in the dialog box is used by the program. Note that the OK pushbutton is the only button spelled with all capital letters.
- Cancel, used to close the dialog box and remove any changes that may have been performed while the dialog box was open. If there are changes that cannot be reversed, the label for this button should be changed to read "Close." I discuss changing the label for a button later in this chapter.
- Close, used to close the dialog box. It does not necessarily imply that any action is taken by the program. Close is most often used when a Cancel button cannot be used to remove changes made while the dialog box is open. Many programs change a Cancel button into a Close button.
- Help, used to request context-sensitive help for the open dialog box.
- Apply, used to perform changes based on data that has been entered in the dialog box. Unlike the OK button, the dialog box should remain open after the Apply button is pressed.

Binding a Button Control to a *CButton* Object

The easiest way to set or retrieve the value of a control is to associate it with a class-member variable using ClassWizard. When associating a member variable with a control, you can associate the member variable either with the control or with the control's value. Member variables representing buttons are rarely associated by value; rather, the CButton class is used to represent most button controls. I discuss associating member variables by value with dialog box controls in Chapter 18, "Using Edit Controls."

To add a member variable to a CDialog-derived class, follow these steps:

1. Open ClassWizard.
2. Select the CDialog-derived class that manages the dialog box; in this case, CButtonDlg.
3. Select the tab labeled Member Variables.
4. Select the control ID representing the control associated with the new member variable.
5. Press the button labeled Add Variable. An "Add Member Variable" dialog box appears. Enter the control's name, category, and variable type, then press OK.
6. Close ClassWizard.

Follow these steps for all controls added to the IDD_BUTTON_DIALOG earlier. Use the values from Table 17.2 for each new member variable added to CButtonDlg.

Table 17.2. Values used to add member variables for CButtonDlg.

Control ID	Variable Name	Category	Type
IDC_BTN_TEST	m_btnTest	Control	CButton
IDC_RADIO_HIGH	m_btnHigh	Control	CButton
IDC_RADIO_LOW	m_btnLow	Control	CButton
IDC_GROUP_VOLUME	m_btnVolume	Control	CButton
IDC_CHECK_AMP	m_btnAmp	Control	CButton

ClassWizard automatically adds the member variables to the CButtonDlg class declaration for you.

Adding Button Events to a Dialog Box Class

Although the buttons are part of the dialog box resource, and appear whenever the dialog box is displayed, nothing happens when the buttons are used because no button events are handled by the dialog box class.

In order to do some work when the button is pushed, a message-handling function must be added to the dialog box class. As I discussed in Chapter 14, "Messages and Event-Driven Programming," ClassWizard is used to add message-handling functions to classes.

Pushbuttons are normally associated with button events in a dialog box class. To add a button event for IDC_BTN_TEST, follow these steps:

1. Open ClassWizard.
2. Select the tab labeled Message Maps.

3. Select CButtonDlg as the Class name.
4. Select IDC_BTN_TEST as the Object ID.
5. Select BN_CLICKED from the Messages list box.
6. Press the button labeled Add Function and accept the default name for the member function.
7. Close ClassWizard.

Checkboxes and radio buttons sometimes use BN_CLICKED messages, but not as often as pushbuttons. Add the source code from Listing 17.1 to the CButtonDlg::OnBtnTest function, then compile and run the project.

Listing 17.1. The CButtonDlg::OnBtnTest member function.

```
void CButtonDlg::OnBtnTest()
{
    AfxMessageBox( "Test button pressed" );
}
```

Changing a Button's Label

Like all controls, a button is a just a special type of window. For that reason, the MFC class library uses the CWnd class as a base class for all control classes. To change the label for a button, you can use the SetWindowText function.

This function commonly is used to change the label for buttons after the dialog box has been created. You can use the SetWindowText function to change the Amplify button from the earlier example into a Record button. To do so, replace the CButtonDlg::OnBtnTest function with the function provided in Listing 17.2.

Listing 17.2. Changing the label for several buttons.

```
void CButtonDlg::OnBtnTest()
{
    static BOOL bSetWaterLevel = TRUE;
    if( bSetWaterLevel == TRUE )
    {
        m_btnVolume.SetWindowText( "&Water Level" );
        m_btnAmp.SetWindowText( "&Record" );
        bSetWaterLevel = FALSE;
    }
    else
    {
        m_btnVolume.SetWindowText( "&Volume" );
        m_btnAmp.SetWindowText( "&Amplify" );
        bSetWaterLevel = TRUE;
    }
}
```

After you build the Button example using the code from Listing 17.2, the radio button group will alternate between Volume and Unplugged.

Enabling and Disabling Buttons

Most controls are enabled by default, although a control can be initially disabled by setting that attribute in its property list. A control can be selected only if it is enabled. The CWnd class includes the EnableWindow member function that allows a CWnd object to be enabled or disabled. Because CButton and all other control classes are derived from CWnd, you can disable a button like this:

```
pButton->EnableWindow( FALSE );   // Disables control
```

The parameter for EnableWindow is TRUE if the window or control should be enabled, and FALSE if it should be disabled. The default parameter for EnableWindow sets the parameter to TRUE, as no parameter is needed to enable the control:

```
pButton->EnableWindow();   // Enables control
```

It is common practice for buttons and other controls to be enabled or disabled based on events that are received by the dialog box. As an example, pressing one button can cause another button to be disabled or enabled. To disable a dialog box control, replace the CButtonDlg::OnBtnTest function with the source code provided in Listing 17.3.

Listing 17.3. Using CWnd::EnableWindow to disable a dialog box control.

```
void CButtonDlg::OnBtnTest()
{
    static BOOL bEnableControl = FALSE;

    m_btnAmp.EnableWindow( bEnableControl );

    if( bEnableControl == TRUE )
        bEnableControl = FALSE;
    else
        bEnableControl = TRUE;
}
```

Now when you click the Test button, the Amplify checkbox is disabled. When you click the Test button again, the checkbox is enabled.

Hiding a Button

It's not unusual to need to hide a button that is located in a dialog box. Often, a button has its properties set to be hidden by default. Once again, the CWnd class has a member function that can be used to hide or display a window as needed. Use the CWnd::ShowWindow member function like this:

```
pButton->ShowWindow( SW_HIDE );   // Hide control
```

This code hides the pButton window, which is a button control in this case. To display a hidden window, the ShowWindow function is used with the SW_SHOW parameter:

```
pButton->ShowWindow( SW_SHOW );   // Display control
```

Listing 17.4 provides a function that uses CWnd::ShowWindow to alternately hide and display some of the other buttons in the main dialog box.

Listing 17.4. Using CWnd::ShowWindow to hide a dialog box control.

```
void CButtonDlg::OnBtnTest()
{
    static int nShowControl = SW_HIDE;

    m_btnAmp.ShowWindow( nShowControl );

    if( nShowControl == SW_SHOW )
        nShowControl = SW_HIDE;
    else
        nShowControl = SW_SHOW;
}
```

What Is Tab Order?

When a dialog box is presented to the user, one control will have the *keyboard focus*, sometimes just called the *focus*. The control that has the focus receives all input from the keyboard. When a control has the focus, it has a dotted focus rectangle drawn around it.

What

A user can change the focus to a new control by pressing the Tab key on the keyboard. Each time the Tab key is pressed, a new control receives the focus. If you aren't familiar with how this works, you may want to experiment with a few dialog boxes from Developer Studio.

The controls are always selected in a fixed order. The same control always has the focus when a dialog box is displayed, and the focus is always distributed in the same order when the users press the Tab key.

Why Is Tab Order Used?

Tab order lets users select controls without using the mouse. Although almost all Windows users have access to a mouse, it's sometimes more convenient to use the keyboard. Also, because tabbing between controls is a standard feature in Windows dialog boxes, you should use it correctly.

Why

The tab order should follow a logical pattern through the dialog box. If the tab order follows a predictable pattern, users of the dialog box will find it much easier to navigate using the Tab key. Usually, the first editable control receives the focus when the dialog box is opened. After that, the focus should be passed to the next logical control in the dialog box, with the buttons that control the dialog box—OK, Cancel, and Apply—receiving the focus last.

How Is the Tab Order Set?

How In a dialog box, the tab order follows the sequence in which controls were defined in the resource script. As new controls are added, they are placed at the end of the tab order. You can use the resource tools included in the Developer Studio to change this sequence, thereby altering the tab order.

With the dialog box displayed in the Developer Studio, select Tab Order from the Layout menu, or press Ctrl+D. Each control in the dialog box that has the tabstop attribute is tagged with a number, as shown in Figure 17.3.

Figure 17.3.
Displaying the tab order
for dialog box controls.

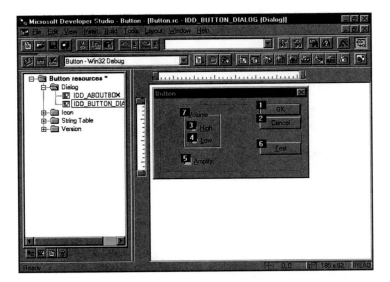

To change the tab order, just click the control that should be in tab position one; the tag associated with that control changes to reflect its new tab order. Repeat the process of clicking controls until the displayed tab order is correct.

Summary

In this chapter, I discussed the different types of button controls provided by Windows and used the controls in a variety of ways, and you built a dialog box-based project. I also discussed control tab order.

Using Edit Controls

In Windows programs, user input is often collected using edit controls. This chapter covers using edit controls to collect and display free-form text supplied by the user. I also discuss associating an edit control with `CEdit` or `CString` objects using ClassWizard, and using DDV and DDX routines for data validation and verification.

What Is an Edit Control?

What An edit control is a window used to store free-form text input by a user. Edit controls can be *single-line edit controls*, meaning that a single line of text can be entered, or they can be *multiple-line edit controls*, sometimes known as MLE controls.

Edit controls are usually found in dialog boxes. Although the edit control can be highly customized, almost anywhere user input is required, you can usually find an edit control. You can find some examples of customized edit controls in Chapter 38, "Subclassing and Superclassing Controls."

Why Use an Edit Control?

Why

Single-line edit controls are used when text must be collected. For example, when a name or address must be entered in a dialog box, an edit control is used to collect that information. Multiline edit controls often use scroll bars that allow more text to be entered than can be displayed.

A prompt in the form of default text can be provided for an edit control. In some situations, this can reduce the amount of typing required by a user. All edit controls also support a limited amount of editing, without any need for extra programming on your part. For example, the standard cut-and-paste commands work as expected in an edit control. Table 18.1 lists the editing commands available in an edit control.

Table 18.1. Editing commands available in an edit control.

Command	Keystroke
Cut	Control + X
Paste	Control + V
Copy	Control + C
Undo	Control + Z

Because of the built-in editing capabilities of the edit control, it's possible to create a simple text editor using a multiple-line edit control. Although an MLE cannot replace a real text editor, it does provide a simple way to collect multiple lines of text from a user.

One difference between edit controls and the pushbutton controls I've discussed in the previous chapter is that a button control is normally used to generate events. An edit control can generate events also but is most often used to actually store data.

How Is an Edit Control Used?

How

You normally add edit controls to a dialog box just as you added buttons in Chapter 17, "Button Controls." After you add the control to a dialog box, use ClassWizard to configure the control for use in the program.

The MFC class CEdit is often used to interact with edit controls. As I discuss in the next section, ClassWizard can be used to associate an edit control with a specific CEdit object. An edit control can also be associated with a CString object, which can simplify the use of edit controls in dialog boxes. I cover using edit controls associated with CString objects in detail beginning with the section "What Are DDV and DDX Routines?" later in this chapter.

Of course, edit controls can be used in dialog box-based programs, which were discussed in Chapter 17. However, I use an SDI program to show off some of the data exchange and validation features often used with edit controls.

Building an SDI Test Project

Some of the sample programs in this book require you to build an SDI project and add a test dialog box. You can use the following five steps to build a test project that includes a test dialog box:

1. Create an SDI project named EditTest using AppWizard, as discussed in Chapter 13, "Using Visual C++ for Windows Programming." Feel free to add or remove any of the optional features suggested by AppWizard, as they aren't used in this chapter.

2. As discussed in Chapter 16, "Dialog Boxes," add a dialog box resource to the program. Name the dialog box IDD_TEST, and set the caption to Test Dialog. Using ClassWizard, create a dialog box class for the new dialog box called CTestDlg.

3. Add a menu choice named ID_VIEW_TEST, with a caption of Test... that brings up the edit dialog box by adding a new menu choice on the View menu. Add a message-handling function for the new menu item using ClassWizard. The steps required to add a message-handling function that uses a CDialog-based object were discussed in Chapter 16. Use the source code provided in Listing 18.1 for the CMainFrame message handling function.

4. Include the class declaration for CTestDlg in the MainFrame.cpp file by adding the following line after all of the #include directives in MainFrame.cpp:

   ```
   #include "testdlg.h"
   ```

5. Add a pushbutton control, IDC_TEST, labeled Test, to the dialog box, as was done in Chapter 17. Using ClassWizard, add a function that handles the BN_CLICKED message, which I use in later examples.

6. After following these steps, make sure that the project compiles properly by pressing the Build icon on the toolbar, or by selecting Build|Build EditTest.exe from the main menu. Try the menu item to make sure the IDC_TEST dialog box is displayed when View|Test... is selected.

Listing 18.1. Handling a menu-item selection for EditTest.

```
void CMainFrame::OnViewTest()
{
    CTestDlg    dlg;

    dlg.DoModal();
}
```

Adding an Edit Control to a Dialog Box

You add an edit control to a dialog box just as you added a button control in Chapter 17, using either of these two basic methods:

- Using drag-and-drop, drag an edit control from the control palette and drop at a desirable location in the dialog box.

- Select an edit control by clicking the edit-control icon in the tool palette, and click over the location in the dialog box where the edit control should be located.

Arrange the edit control so that the dialog box resembles the one in Figure 18.1.

Figure 18.1.
*The dialog box used
in the edit-control
examples.*

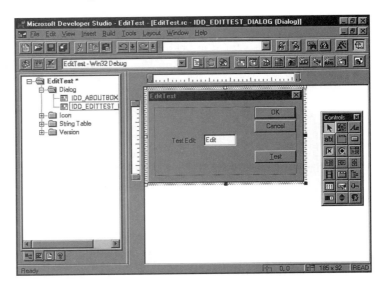

In Figure 18.1, there is a static-text control immediately to the left of the edit control. Edit controls are usually labeled with a static text so a user can determine the type of input needed. I discussed static-text controls in Chapter 17.

The ID for the new edit control is set by default to IDC_EDIT1, or a similar name. Change the ID to IDC_EDIT_TEST, leaving the other properties set to their default values.

Edit Control Properties

You can examine the properties for an edit control, just as with other resources, by double-clicking the control, or by right-clicking over the control and selecting Properties... from the pop-up menu. These general properties are available for an edit control:

- ID, used for the edit control's resource ID. Like other controls, a default resource ID is supplied by Developer Studio.

- Visible, which indicates that the edit control is initially visible. This option is normally selected.

- Disabled, which indicates the edit control should be initially disabled. This option is not normally selected.

- Group, used to mark the first control in a group. All controls following a control with this attribute are considered part of the same group, if the attribute is cleared. A user can move between controls in the same group using the arrow keys.

- `Help ID`, which creates a context-sensitive help ID for this control.
- `Tabstop`, which indicates that this control can be reached by pressing the Tab key. This option is normally selected.

There also is a group of properties that apply specifically to edit controls. The properties below are displayed by pressing the Styles tab in the Properties dialog box:

- `Align Text`, a drop-down list box that is enabled if the edit control is an MLE. The text can be aligned to the left, center, or right, with left as the default.
- `Multi-line`, which defines the control as an MLE. This option is not selected by default.
- `Number`, which restricts the edit control to digits only. This feature is available only in Windows 95 or Windows NT version 3.51 or later.
- `Horizontal Scroll`, which is enabled only for an MLE and provides a horizontal scroll bar. The option is not selected by default.
- `Auto HScroll`, which scrolls text to the right if needed. This option is normally selected.
- `Vertical Scroll`, which is enabled only for an MLE, and provides a vertical scroll bar. The option is not selected by default.
- `Auto VScroll`, which is enabled only for an MLE, and provides automatic scrolling when the user presses return on the last line. The option is not selected by default.
- `Password`, which hides the user's input by displaying an asterisk instead of each character. This option is available only in single-line controls and is not selected by default.
- `No Hide Selection`, which changes the way an edit control handles the focus. When this option is enabled, text appears to be selected at all times. This option is not selected by default.
- `OEM Convert`, which performs conversions on the user's input so that the `AnsiToOem` function works correctly if called by your program. This option is not selected by default.
- `Want Return`, which applies to MLE controls. This option allows an edit control to accept an Enter keypress instead of an Enter keypress affecting the dialog box's default pushbutton.
- `Border`, which creates a border around the control. This option is selected by default.
- `Uppercase`, which converts all input to uppercase characters. This option is not selected by default.
- `Lowercase`, which converts all input to lowercase characters. This option is not selected by default.
- `Read-only`, which prevents the user from typing or editing text in the edit control. This option is not selected by default.

Attaching a *CEdit* Object to an Edit Control

As I discussed earlier, one way to interact with an edit control is through a CEdit object that is attached to the control. To attach a CEdit object to an edit control, you use ClassWizard much as you did for button controls in the previous chapter:

1. Open ClassWizard.
2. Select the CDialog-derived class that manages the dialog box; in this case, CTestDlg.
3. Select the tab labeled Member Variables.
4. Select the control ID representing the control associated with the new member variable; in this case, IDC_EDIT_TEST.
5. Click the button labeled Add Variable. An Add Member Variable dialog box appears. Enter the control's name, category, and variable type, then click OK. For this example, use the values from Table 18.2.

Table 18.2. Values used to add a CEdit member variable for CTestDlg.

Control ID	Variable Name	Category	Type
IDC_EDIT_TEST	m_editTest	Control	CEdit

The default value displayed in the Category control is Value. I use Value for some member variables later in the chapter, when I discuss DDV and DDX routines.

Collecting Entered Text from an Edit Control

The primary reason for using an edit control, of course, is to collect information from a user. In order to do that, you need to get the information from the edit control. Using the CEdit class simplifies this process.

There are several CEdit member functions that are useful when collecting information from an edit control, such as the GetWindowText and LineLength member functions. As an example, add the source code in Listing 18.2 to the CTestDlg::OnTest member function, created earlier.

Listing 18.2. Collecting input from an edit control using CEdit.

```
void CTestDlg::OnTest()
{
    CString szEdit;
    CString szResult;

    int nLength = m_editTest.LineLength();
    m_editTest.GetWindowText( szEdit );
    szResult.Format( "%s has %d chars", szEdit, nLength );

    AfxMessageBox( szResult );
}
```

When the Test button is clicked, the text entered in the edit control is retrieved by using the `m_editTest` object. Normally, you are interested only in data contained in an edit control if the OK button is clicked. If the Cancel button is clicked, the dialog box should be closed and, usually, any entered information is simply discarded.

Setting Default Text for an Edit Control

By default, an edit control is empty when it is initially displayed to a user. However, edit controls often are used to display current information to a user that can either be changed or accepted. In other words, you can use an edit control to prompt a user by displaying a default entry.

An edit control is a special type of window in the same way that a button is a special type of window. The `CEdit` control also has complete access to all of the `CWnd` member functions. The `CWnd::SetWindowText` member function can be used to insert text into an edit control, just as though it had been entered by a user. Using ClassWizard, create a message-handling function for the `WM_INITDIALOG` message, which is sent to the main dialog box just before it is displayed. Add the source code from Listing 18.3 to the `CTestDlg::OnInitDialog` member function.

Listing 18.3. Adding default text to an edit control.

```
BOOL CTestDlg::OnInitDialog()
{
    CDialog::OnInitDialog();

    m_editTest.SetWindowText( "Default" );

    return TRUE;
}
```

After the default text has been added, the user can either accept the text in the edit control, or edit the text as needed.

What Are DDV and DDX Routines?

The DDV and DDX routines are helper functions that help manage data for dialog boxes. DDV, or Dialog Data Validation, routines are used for data validation. DDX, or Dialog Data Exchange, routines are used for exchanging data to and from the controls in a dialog box.

What

Although you can use the DDV and DDX routines in your dialog boxes directly, ClassWizard adds the code for you at the click of a button. Normally, you add the DDV and DDX routines with ClassWizard, instead of trying to hand-code the necessary function calls.

Why Are DDV and DDX Routines Used?

Why

The DDV routines are useful when collecting data from an edit control. In general, you have little control over how a user enters data in an edit control. There are some steps you can take, some of which I cover in Chapter 38. However, using a DDV is much simpler and less error prone. A DDV enables you to perform some simple validation based on range or string length.

For example, if an edit control is used to collect an abbreviated state name, you want to limit the entered text to two characters. Using a DDV routine, it's easy to make sure that two characters have been entered.

DDX functions link member variables from the dialog box class to controls that are contained in the dialog box. DDX routines allow data to be transferred to and from the controls much easier than is otherwise possible. As discussed in Chapter 16, a dialog box is normally used something like this:

```
CMyDialog    dlgMine;
dlgMine.DoModal();
```

In this example, the dialog box is created when DoModal is called, and the function does not return until the dialog box is closed by the user. This presents a problem if data must be passed to or from the dialog box. Because none of the controls exist until the dialog box is created, it's not possible to use SetWindowText, GetWindowText, or other functions to interact directly with controls contained in the dialog box. Once the dialog box has been dismissed, it is too late to use those functions to collect user input.

When DDX routines are used to exchange information with a dialog box, the dialog box can be used like this:

```
CMyDialog    dlgMine;
dlgMine.m_szTest = "Hello World";
dlgMine.DoModal();
```

The DDX routines enable you to have access to the dialog box's controls before and after the dialog box has been created. This simplifies dialog box programming because it is a much more flexible method than adding code in the InitDialog member function, as I discussed earlier.

How Are DDV and DDX Routines Used?

How

The easiest and most useful way to add DDV and DDX routines to your dialog box class is by using ClassWizard. Member variables associated with dialog box controls by value automatically use the DDV and DDX routines provided by MFC.

For example, CString member variables are often associated with edit controls. ClassWizard adds source code to handle the exchange and validation of data in two places:

- In the dialog box's constructor, source code is added to initialize the member variable.
- In the dialog box's DoDataExchange member function, ClassWizard adds DDV and DDX routines for each member variable associated with a control's value.

`DoDataExchange` is a virtual function that is called to move data between the control and the dialog box's member data. As shown in Figure 18.2, `DoDataExchange` has a single parameter that controls the direction that data is copied.

Figure 18.2.
DDV and DDX
routines used to handle
dialog box data.

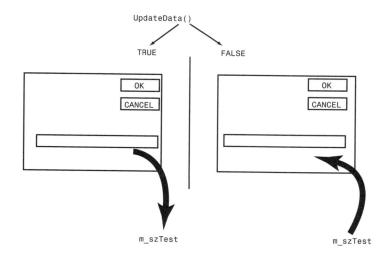

`DoDataExchange` takes a single parameter, either `TRUE` or `FALSE`, with `TRUE` as the default parameter. When `DoDataExchange( FALSE )` is called, data is moved from the member variable to the control. When `DoDataExchange( TRUE )` is called, data is copied from the control to the member variable.

When the dialog box is initially displayed, during `CDialog::OnInitDialog`, `UpdateData(FALSE)` is called to transfer data from the member variables to the dialog box's controls. Later, during `CDialog::OnOk`, `UpdateData()` is called to transfer data from the dialog box's controls to member variables. Normally, these two calls to `UpdateData` are sufficient. However, you can add a call to `UpdateData` if you want to update or reset control values inside dialog box's member function.

Associating a Control's Value with a Member Variable

You add member variables that are associated with a control's value almost exactly the way you added control-type variables earlier in this chapter. For example, to create a member variable associated with the `IDD_EDIT_TEST` edit control, follow these steps:

1. Open ClassWizard.
2. Select the `CDialog`-derived class that manages the dialog box; in this case, `CTestDlg`.
3. Select the tab labeled Member Variables.
4. Select the control ID representing the control associated with the new member variable; in this case, `IDC_EDIT_TEST`.

5. Click the button labeled Add Variable. An Add Member Variable dialog box appears. Enter the control's name, category, and variable type, then click OK. For this example, use the values from Table 18.3.

Table 18.3. Values used to associate a CString member variable with an edit control.

Control ID	Variable Name	Category	Type
IDC_EDIT_TEST	m_szTest	Value	CString

The steps above are exactly like the steps used to add a control-type variable earlier in this chapter, except that the control type is set to Value. A member variable associated by value with an edit control can also be an int, UINT, long, DWORD, float, double, or BYTE, although it is most commonly a CString.

After closing the Add Member Variable dialog box, ClassWizard displays an edit control that you can use to specify the type of validation to be performed on the member variable. If a CString object is associated with an edit control, the maximum string length can be specified. If a numeric variable is used, the allowed range can be defined.

Exchanging Edit-Control Information Using DDX Functions

The member variables associated with dialog box controls by ClassWizard are added to the dialog box class as public variables. This allows the member variables to be easily accessed and used. For example, to use the m_szTest variable that was added in previous section, edit the CMainFrame::OnViewTest member function so it looks like the function in Listing 18.4. Before compiling the project, remove the line:

```
m_editTest.SetWindowText( "Default" );
```

that was added to CTestDlg::OnInitDialog earlier.

Listing 18.4. Using member variables to exchange information with an edit control.

```
void CMainFrame::OnViewTest()
{
    CTestDlg    dlg;

    dlg.m_szTest = "DDX Test";

    if( dlg.DoModal() == IDOK )
    {
        AfxMessageBox( dlg.m_szTest );
    }
    else
    {
```

```
        AfxMessageBox( "Dialog cancelled" );
    }
}
```

Listing 18.4 sets the value of m_szTest before the dialog box is displayed to the user. CDialog::OnInitDialog calls the CWnd::UpdateData function, which calls UpdateData. Because UpdateData is a virtual function, the proper version of the function is called: the version that is part of the CDialog-derived class that handles the dialog box.

After the dialog box is closed, the CMainFrame::OnViewTest function checks the return value of DoModal. If IDOK was returned, the dialog box was closed using the OK button, and the value of m_szTest is displayed.

Summary

In this chapter, I discussed the Windows edit control and how it is usually used in a dialog box. I also presented associating an edit control with a CEdit object using ClassWizard, as well as data exchange and validation.

Using List-Box and Combo-Box Controls

List boxes and combo boxes are two types of controls that are used often in Windows programming. The list box often is used to allow a user to select from a large number of possible choices, while the combo box is a combination of the list box and edit controls. In this chapter, I discuss these controls and use them in simple examples.

What Are List Boxes?

What A list box normally is found in a dialog box, control bar, or other window that contains controls. List-box controls are used to contain a list of items available for selection. The user can select items by using the keyboard or by clicking an individual item using a mouse. List boxes can be *single selection*, meaning that only one item is selected at a time, or *multiple selection*, meaning that multiple items can be selected. By default, list boxes are single selection.

List boxes often are used to contain a large number of items. If some items cannot be displayed, a scroll bar is displayed to help the user navigate through the list. When a list box contains several items, the list box usually is sorted; this is a list-box property and can usually be done by the control as each item is inserted, with no programmer intervention.

Why Use a List Box?

Why

List boxes are the simplest control that allows an arbitrary number of items to be displayed to a user. List boxes are often used to display lists of information that are extracted from databases or reports. Because the list box doesn't have to be sized, it is well suited for this type of data. When a sorted list box is used, it's easy for a user to search through a large number of text items and make a selection.

List boxes are also extremely easy to program. If you have created a list-box object, you can add an item to the list box with just one line of code, like this:

```
listBox.AddString( "Mickey" );
```

No other control is as flexible and easy to use for both the programmer and the user.

The list box is also the first control I've discussed that uses indexes. Whenever an item is selected, inserted, or deleted, a zero-based index is used to identify the item. This index can be synchronized with a database index, or used to identify the item in other ways. I discuss more controls that use indexes in upcoming chapters.

How Is a List Box Used?

How

You normally add list boxes to a dialog box resource just as you added buttons and edit controls in the previous two chapters. Once you have added the control, use ClassWizard to add message-handling functions and associate the control with a CListBox object.

The MFC CListBox class can be used to manage and interact with the list-box control. Like other control classes, CListBox is derived from CWnd, and most CWnd functions can be used with CListBox objects. I cover the details about CListBox later, in the section, "Using the *CListBox* Class."

Adding a List Box to a Dialog Box

For demonstration purposes, create a dialog box-based project named ListBox using AppWizard. After AppWizard has created the project, the ListBox.rc resource file is found in the project workspace, under the "Win32 Debug" tree. Open the resource file by double-clicking the icon labeled ListBox.rc, or by right-clicking on the icon and selecting Open from the pop-up menu.

Adding a list box to IDD_LISTBOX_DIALOG, the main dialog box, is just like adding a button or edit control. Either drag and drop a list-box control from the control palette to the main dialog box, or select the list-box control on the tool palette using the mouse, and click the desired position in the main dialog box. Figure 19.1 shows the IDD_LISTBOX_DIALOG with a list-box control.

Figure 19.1.
The main dialog box used in the ListBox sample program.

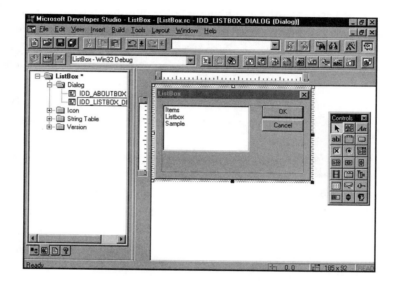

Open the properties dialog box for the list box by double-clicking the list-box control, and change the resource ID to IDC_LIST. Set all other properties to their default values.

List-Box Properties

Just like other controls, list boxes have properties that you can configure using the Developer Studio resource editor. Some of these properties are available in other controls, and some are unique to list boxes. These properties are available for a list-box control:

- ID, used for the list-box resource ID. A default resource ID, such as IDC_LIST, is supplied by Developer Studio.
- Visible, which indicates that the list is initially visible. This checkbox is normally checked.
- Disabled, which indicates the list should be initially disabled. This checkbox is normally cleared.
- Group, which marks the first control in a group. This checkbox is normally cleared.
- Tabstop, which indicates that this control can be reached by pressing the Tab key. This checkbox is normally checked.

- `Help ID`, which creates a context-sensitive help ID for this control.

- `Selection`, which determines how items in a list box can be selected. A single-selection list box allows one item to be selected at any given time. Multiple-selection list boxes allow several selections at once, but ignore the Shift and Control keys. Extended selection list boxes use the Shift and Control keys during selection.

- `Owner Draw`, which indicates that the button will be drawn by the button's owner, in this case the dialog box. I cover using owner-drawn controls in Chapter 39, "Owner-Drawn Controls." In most cases, this option is set to no.

- `Has strings`, which specifies that an owner-drawn list box contains strings. All other list boxes contain strings by default.

- `Border`, which specifies a border for the list box. This option is enabled by default.

- `Sort`, which indicates that the list-box contents should be sorted. This option is normally selected.

- `Notify`, which indicates that notification messages should be sent to the dialog box. This option is normally selected.

- `Multi-column`, which creates a multicolumn list box. This option is normally cleared.

- `Horizontal Scroll`, which creates a list box with a horizontal scroll bar. This option is normally cleared.

- `Vertical Scroll`, which creates a list box with a vertical scroll bar. This option is normally selected.

- `No redraw`, which indicates that the list box should not update its appearance when its contents are changed. This option is rarely selected, and is cleared by default.

- `Use tabstops`, which specifies that text items displayed in the list box may contain tabs. This option is normally cleared.

- `Want key input`, which indicates that the list-box owner should receive WM_VKEYTOITEM or WM_CHARTOITEM messages when keys are pressed while the list box has the input focus. This option is normally cleared.

- `Disable no scroll`, which displays a vertical scroll bar, even if it's not needed. This option is normally cleared.

- `No integral height`, which indicates that Windows should display the list box exactly as specified in the resource description, displaying partial items if needed. This option is normally selected.

Using the *CListBox* Class

Like control classes used in previous chapters, the MFC CListBox class makes your life much easier by providing a C++ class that hides control messages and provides an easy to use interface.

To attach a `CListBox` object to a list-box control, use ClassWizard as you have for controls in previous chapters:

1. Open ClassWizard.
2. Select the `CDialog`-derived class that manages the dialog box; in this case, `CListBoxDlg`.
3. Select the tab labeled "Member Variables."
4. Select the control ID representing the control associated with the new member variable; in this case, `IDC_LIST`.
5. Click the button labeled Add Variable. An Add Member Variable dialog box appears. Enter the control's name, category, and variable type, then click OK. For this example, use the values from Table 19.1.

Table 19.1. Values used to add a `CListBox` member variable for `CListBoxDlg`.

Control ID	Variable Name	Category	Type
IDC_LIST	m_listBox	Control	CListBox

Adding an Item to a List Box

There are two ways to add a text string to a list box:

- To add a string to a list box, the `AddString` member function can be called:

```
m_listBox.AddString( "Mickey" );
```

Any strings added to a sorted list box are sorted as they are added. If the list box is not sorted, the item is added after the last item in the list.

- To add an item at a specified position in a list box, use the `InsertString` member function:

```
m_listBox.InsertString( 0, "Mickey" );
```

All positions in a list box are numbered beginning with zero. Any existing list box items are shifted down, if needed, to make room for the new item.

Both the `InsertString` and `AddString` functions return the position of the new item. If an error occurs when adding an item, `LB_ERR` is returned from the `AddString` or `InsertString` functions. If the list box is full, `LB_ERRSPACE` is returned. Using the source code from Listing 19.1, add three strings to the `IDC_LIST` list box during the `CListBoxDlg::OnInitDialog` member function. There already are several lines of code in `CListBoxDlg::OnInitDialog`; add the three `AddString` statements after the `//TODO` comment supplied by AppWizard.

Part V

Listing 19.1. Using `AddString` to add strings to a list box.

```
// TODO: Add extra initialization here
m_listBox.AddString( "Foo" );
m_listBox.AddString( "Bar" );
m_listBox.AddString( "Baz" );
```

To determine the number of items currently in a list box, use the `GetCount` member function:

```
nItems = listBox.GetCount();
```

The `GetCount` function returns the total number of items in a list box, not the value of the last valid index. If a list box contains five items, `GetCount` returns five, but the last valid index is four.

Removing Items from a List Box

Remove items in a list box by specifying the item position to be removed in a call to the `DeleteString` member function:

```
listBox.DeleteString( 8, "Mickey" );
```

This line removes the item in the ninth position of the list box. Remember, all list-box position indexes start from zero. The return value from the `DeleteString` member function is the number of items remaining in the list box, or `LB_ERR` if any errors occur. The return value can be used like this:

```
int nLastPos = listBox.GetCount() - 1;
while( nLastPos > 2 && nItems != LB_ERR )
    nItems = listBox.DeleteString( nLastPos );
```

This code removes the contents of a list box, except for the first three items. To clear a list box completely, use the `ResetContent` function:

```
listBox.ResetContent();
```

The `ResetContent` function returns void.

Receiving List-Box Messages

There are several messages that are sent to the parent of a list box for notification purposes when certain events occur. All of these messages are prefixed with `LBN_`, for List Box Notification. For these messages to be sent, the list box must have the `Notify` property enabled. The messages sent from the list box to its parent are:

- `LBN_DBLCLK` is sent when a user double-clicks a list-box item.
- `LBN_ERRSPACE` indicates that an item could not be removed due to a lack of memory.
- `LBN_KILLFOCUS` is sent just before the list box loses the input focus.
- `LBN_SELCANCEL` is sent when a user cancels a list-box selection.
- `LBN_SELCHANGE` is sent when the selection state in a list box is about to change.
- `LBN_SETFOCUS` is sent when a list box receives the input focus.

The LBN_DBLCLK message is the most frequently used notification message. Most users expect some sort of default action to take place when a list-box item is double-clicked. For example, when a list of filenames is displayed, double-clicking a particular filename might be expected to open that file for editing.

The steps to add message-handling functions for any of the controls used in Windows are very similar. To create a message-handling function for the LBN_DBLCLK notification message, follow these steps:

1. Open ClassWizard and click the tab labeled "Message Maps."
2. Select the CListBoxDlg class, and the IDC_LIST Object ID.
3. Select LBN_DBLCLK, and click the "Add Function" button.
4. Accept the suggested function name CListBoxDlg::OnDblclkList.
5. Click the button labeled Edit Code.
6. Add the source code from Listing 19.2 to the CListBoxDlg::OnDblclkList function.
7. Compile and run the ListBox project and then double-click any of the list-box items. The LBN_DBLCLK message is sent to the CListBoxDlg::OnDblclkList function, and a message box is displayed with information about the selected item.

Listing 19.2. Handling a list-box notification message.

```
void CListBoxDlg::OnDblclkList()
{
    int nSelection = m_listBox.GetCurSel();
    if( nSelection != LB_ERR )
    {
        CString szSelection;
        m_listBox.GetText( nSelection, szSelection );

        AfxMessageBox( szSelection );
    }
}
```

When a dialog box that contains a list box is closed by using the OK button, the currently selected item in the list box can be determined by using the CListBox::GetCurSel member function, as shown in Listing 19.2.

The GetCurSel member function returns the position of the currently selected item, with the first item position starting at zero. If no item is selected, or if the list box has the multiple-selection property, LB_ERR is returned.

What Are Combo Boxes?

A combo-box control is a single control that combines an edit control and list box. A combo box allows a user to enter data either by entering text like an edit control, or by selecting an item from several choices like a list box, as shown in Figure 19.2.

What

Figure 19.2.
A combo box combines
an edit control and a list
box in one control.

There are three types of combo boxes:

- Simple combo boxes, which display an edit control and list box. Unlike the other combo-box types, the list box is always visible. When the list box contains more items than can be displayed, a scroll bar is used to scroll through the list box.

- Drop-down combo boxes, which hide the list box until the user opens it. This lets the list use much less room in a dialog box than that used by the simple combo box.

- Drop-down list boxes, which are similar to drop-down combo boxes, only displaying the list box when opened by the user. However, a static-text control is used to display the selection instead of an edit control. Therefore, the user is limited to selecting items from the list box.

Why Use a Combo Box?

Why   Combo boxes are quite useful when a user is not limited to selecting only the items presented in a list box. The list box portion of the combo box can be used to display recent selections, allowing the user the freedom to enter a new selection in the edit control.

Combo boxes combine the features of a list box and an edit control. Any time an edit control is used, a combo box can be used to store previous user entries.

Combo boxes also are used when space in a dialog box is at a premium. A large number of choices in a combo box can be hidden until the combo box is opened, allowing more controls to be placed in a smaller area than that required for a list box.

How Is a Combo Box Used?

How   Just like list boxes and other controls, you normally add combo boxes to dialog box resources using the Developer Studio dialog box editor. After you add the control, use ClassWizard to add message-handling functions and associate the control with a CComboBox object.

The MFC CComboBox class is used to manage and interact with the combo box control, and contains many of the member functions that are available in the CListBox and CEdit classes. For example, you can use GetCurSel to get the currently selected item from the list-box part of a combo box.

Combo-Box Properties

A combo box has a large number of properties because it combines an edit control and a list box. Most edit-control and list-box styles have similar properties that can be applied to combo boxes. These combo-box properties are identical to the list-box properties discussed earlier:

- `ID`
- `Visible`
- `Disabled`
- `Group`
- `Tabstop`
- `Owner Draw`
- `Has strings`
- `Sort`
- `Vertical scroll`
- `No integral height`
- `Help ID`
- `Disable no scroll`

The following combo-box properties are identical to properties offered for edit controls (discussed in Chapter 18, "Using Edit Controls"):

- `Auto HScroll`
- `OEM convert`

These two properties are unique to combo-box controls:

- `List choices`, used to list items that appear by default when the dialog box is created. Press Ctrl+Enter after each entry.
- `Type`, used to specify the type of the combo box. You can choose between Simple, Dropdown, and Drop List. Dropdown is the default choice.

Adding Items to a Combo Box

You add strings to combo boxes just as you add them to list boxes. Just like `CListBox`, the `CComboBox` class contains `AddString` and `InsertString` member functions:

```
comboBox.AddString( "Mickey" );
```

or

```
comboBox.InsertString( 0, "Mickey" );
```

All positions in a combo box are numbered beginning with zero, just like list boxes. However, if an error occurs, `CB_ERR` is returned instead of `LB_ERR`. If an item cannot be added due to insufficient space, `CB_ERRSPACE` is returned.

To determine the number of items currently in a combo box, CComboBox includes the GetCount member function:

```
nItems = comboBox.GetCount();
```

Remember, CB_ERR is returned instead of LB_ERR when using a CComboBox object.

Collecting Input from a Combo Box

You can collect input from a combo box by using the GetWindowText member function, just like an edit control. For simple combo boxes and drop-down combo boxes, this is the easiest way to get the current selection. You can also use the GetCurSel member function to determine the current selection position from the list box.

A Combo-Box Example

To create a sample project using a combo box and the CComboBox class, follow these steps:

1. Create a dialog box-based project named ComboList using AppWizard, as described in previous examples.

2. Add a drop-down combo list to the IDD_COMBOLIST_DIALOG resource, as you did for the list box earlier in this chapter.

3. Give the combo box the resource ID IDC_COMBO. Use the default values for all other properties.

4. Add a static-text control to the dialog box, and give it the resource ID IDC_RESULT. This text control will be used to display information about messages received from the combo box.

5. Using ClassWizard, add a member variable to the CComboListDlg class named m_comboList. Set the control type to Control.

6. Using ClassWizard, add a message-handling function for the IDOK control BN_CLICKED message to the CComboListDlg class.

7. Using ClassWizard, add message-handling functions for IDC_COMBO control messages to the CComboListDlg class. Add functions to handle CBN_CLOSEUP and CBN_EDITUPDATE messages.

Adding Strings to a Combo Box

After completing these steps, add the source code in Listing 19.3 to the CComboListDlg::OnInitDialog member function. This code adds three entries to the combo box. There are already several lines of code in the function; don't remove them. Just add the code from Listing 19.3 after the //TODO comment provided by AppWizard.

Listing 19.3. Source code added to the `CComboListDlg::OnInitDialog` function.

```
// In OnInitDialog...
// TODO: Add extra initialization here
    m_comboList.AddString( "Foo" );
    m_comboList.AddString( "Bar" );
    m_comboList.AddString( "Baz" );
```

Getting the Current Combo-Box Selection

Edit the `CComboListDlg::OnOk` member function so it looks like the source code provided in Listing 19.4. This code uses member functions from the `CComboBox` class to display information about the current combo box selection.

Listing 19.4. Source code added to the `CComboListDlg::OnOk` function.

```
void CComboListDlg::OnOK()
{
    CString szCombo;

    m_comboList.GetWindowText( szCombo );
    AfxMessageBox( szCombo );

    int nChoice = m_comboList.GetCurSel();
    szCombo.Format( "The current selection is %d", nChoice );
    AfxMessageBox( szCombo );

    CDialog::OnOK();
}
```

Detecting Combo-Box Events

Add the source code provided in Listing 19.5 to the `CComboListDlg::OnCloseupCombo` function. When the `CBN_CLOSEUP` message is received, a message is displayed on the static-text control `IDC_RESULT`.

Listing 19.5. Source code added to the `CComboListDlg::OnCloseupCombo` function.

```
void CComboListDlg::OnCloseupCombo()
{
    CString     szChoice;
    CString     szResult;
    int         nChoice;

    // Get current selections from edit and list-box controls
    m_comboList.GetWindowText( szChoice );
    nChoice = m_comboList.GetCurSel();

    if( nChoice != CB_ERR )
    {
```

continues

Listing 19.5. continued

```
        // If a valid choice was made from the list box, fetch
        // the item's text string.
        m_comboList.GetLBText( nChoice, szChoice );
        szResult = "Closing after selecting " + szChoice;
    }
    else if( szChoice.IsEmpty() == TRUE )
    {
        // No choice was made from the list box, and the edit
        // control was empty.
        szResult = "No choice selected";
    }
    else if( m_comboList.FindStringExact(-1, szChoice) != CB_ERR )
    {
        // The string from the edit control was found in the
        // list box.
        szResult = "Closing after selecting " + szChoice;
    }
    else
    {
        // The edit control contains a new string, not currently
        // in the list box. Add the string.
        m_comboList.AddString( szChoice );
        szResult = "Adding " + szChoice + " to list";
    }

    // Get a pointer to the static-text control, and display an
    // appropriate result message.
    CWnd* pWnd = GetDlgItem( IDC_RESULT );
    ASSERT( pWnd );
    if( pWnd )
        pWnd->SetWindowText( szResult );
}
```

The `CComboListDlg::OnCloseupCombo` function collects the contents from the edit-control section of the combo box, and the selected item from the list-box section of the combo box. If a selection has been made in the list box, the item's string is retrieved and displayed. Otherwise, if a string was entered in the edit control, it is displayed. The string is not currently in the list box; it is added to it.

Add the source code provided in Listing 19.6 to the `CComboListDlg::OnEditupdateCombo` member function. `CBN_EDITUPDATE` is received when the user types inside the edit control. When the `CBN_EDITUPDATE` message is received, the contents of the edit control are displayed on the `IDC_RESULT` text control.

Listing 19.6. Source code added to the `CComboListDlg::OnEditupdateCombo` function.

```
void CComboListDlg::OnEditupdateCombo()
{
    CString     szChoice;
    CString     szResult;

    m_comboList.GetWindowText( szChoice );
    szResult = "Choice changed to " + szChoice;
```

```
    CWnd* pWnd = GetDlgItem( IDC_RESULT );
    ASSERT( pWnd );
    if( pWnd )
        pWnd->SetWindowText( szResult );
}
```

Compile and run the ComboList project. Experiment by adding new entries to the combo box, and by expanding and closing the combo box. Other messages sent to the combo box can be trapped and displayed just as CBN_EDITUPDATE was handled in Listing 19.6.

Summary

In this chapter, I discussed list-box and combo-box controls and how they are used in Windows programs. I also covered associating these controls with CListBox and CComboBox objects.

Using Image Lists and Bitmaps

In this chapter, I discuss image lists and bitmaps. Bitmaps are the most common way to store and display images in a Windows program, and most programs written for Windows make some use of bitmaps. Image lists can be used to store collections of bitmaps, making them useful when several bitmaps are needed, such as in tree-view and list-view controls. I also look at some of the advanced drawing features offered by image lists.

What Is a Bitmap?

What A bitmap is a graphical object that can be used to represent an image in programs written for Windows. Using a bitmap, an image can be easily stored, loaded, and displayed. A bitmap is only one of many graphical objects available when writing Windows programs. Other types of graphical objects include these:

- Pens, used for drawing lines and other shapes. Pens are covered in detail in Chapter 30, "Using Pens."

- Brushes, used to color large areas with a particular color or pattern. Brushes are covered in Chapter 31, "Brushes."

■ Fonts, used to provide the characteristics for displayed text in a Windows program. Fonts are discussed in Chapter 32, "Fonts."

Why Use a Bitmap?

Why Bitmaps provide a flexible way to store image data in a Windows program. The data structure used for a bitmap is straightforward and allows a wide variety in the types of bitmaps that can be stored. Although image lists (described later in this chapter) provide extra features, many times a simple bitmap is the easiest way to display an image on the screen.

How Is a Bitmap Used?

How The easiest way to create a bitmap is to use an image editor like the one that is integrated in Developer Studio. I use the image editor in this chapter to create a bitmap that is displayed in a dialog box-based program's main dialog box. I use the same editor in later chapters when we create icons and cursors.

Once you've created the bitmap using the image editor, you can manipulate it by using the MFC CBitmap class. You can load the bitmap into your program by calling the LoadBitmap member function:

```
bmpHello.LoadBitmap( IDB_HELLO );
```

Once the bitmap has been loaded, it can be displayed to any output device by using a device context. I cover more operations that can be performed with bitmaps in Chapter 33, "Icons."

Adding a Bitmap to a Project

A bitmap can be displayed in any project that handles the WM_PAINT message. As an example, create an SDI program named Bitmap, following the steps used in Chapter 13, "Using Visual C++ for Windows Programming." After you have created the project, open the resource file by clicking on the ResourceView tab in the Project Workspace menu.

Start the image editor by selecting Insert, then Resource from the main menu. The image editor is also used to edit cursor and icon resources, as I discuss in later chapters.

The image editor displays a large grid that represents the bitmap surface, as well as two dockable toolbars:

■ The Graphics toolbar consists of tools you can use to draw different shapes and text.
■ The Colors palette contains the colors that are available for drawing the bitmap.

Both toolbars can be used as either floating palettes or docked toolbars.

Select the text tool from the Graphics toolbar, and choose your favorite color from the Colors palette. Type a hello message as shown in Figure 20.1.

Figure 20.1.
The IDB_HELLO bitmap
used in the Bitmap
sample program.

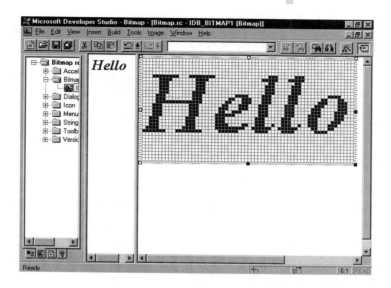

As with most resources, you can adjust the size of the bitmap by dragging the edges of the grid in the desired direction. Change the size of the bitmap so that the text fits inside the bitmap without any clipping. You can select a different font by pressing the Font button on the text tool. Feel free to add other effects by selecting other tools from the Graphics toolbar.

You can change the properties for a bitmap resource by double-clicking the edge of the bitmap grid, or by right-clicking the bitmap's edge, and selecting Properties from the pop-up menu. Change the name of the bitmap resource to IDB_HELLO. Using names that begin with IDB_ for bitmaps is a standard naming convention in Windows programming.

Loading and Displaying a Bitmap

Open the BitmapView.cpp source file, and locate the member function CBitmapView::OnDraw. The function should already contain several lines of source code, which you can replace with the function provided in Listing 20.1.

Listing 20.1. The CBitmapView::OnDraw function, used to display a bitmap.

```
void CBitmapView::OnDraw(CDC* pDC)
{
    CBitmap      bmpHello;
    bmpHello.LoadBitmap( IDB_HELLO );

    // Calculate bitmap size using a BITMAP structure.
    BITMAP       bm;
    bmpHello.GetObject( sizeof(BITMAP), &bm );

    // Create a memory DC, select the bitmap into the
    // memory DC, and BitBlt it into the view.
```

continues

Listing 20.1. continued

```
CDC          dcMem;
dcMem.CreateCompatibleDC( pDC );

CBitmap* pbmpOld = dcMem.SelectObject( &bmpHello );
pDC->BitBlt( 10,10, bm.bmWidth, bm.bmHeight,
             &dcMem, 0,0, SRCCOPY );

// Reselect the original bitmap into the memory DC.
dcMem.SelectObject( pbmpOld );
}
```

Before the bitmap is displayed in Listing 20.1, information about the bitmap is collected using the SelectObject member function, which fills a BITMAP structure with information. Two pieces of useful information the BITMAP structure can provide are the width and height of the bitmap.

When displaying a bitmap, the bitmap is first selected into a special device context known as a *memory device context*, or *memory DC*. A memory DC is just a memory location that allows for drawing images offscreen, which improves performance. The BitBlt function is used to transfer the image from the memory DC to the view's device context, passed as a parameter to OnDraw. BitBlt is an abbreviation for Bit-Block Transfer, which is the process used to move the image from the memory DC to the actual device context. I cover BitBlt in detail in Chapter 29, "Device Contexts."

When you compile and run the Bitmap project, the IDB_HELLO bitmap is displayed in the view window. Experiment by changing the size and color of the bitmap, or by combining the source code provided in Listing 20.1 with the DrawText function discussed in Chapter 13.

If you play with the Bitmap program long enough, you may discover a problem that occurs when using bitmaps. Although the background of the IDB_HELLO bitmap is white, it is not transparent. If the color of the view background was gray or another color, the bitmap would look like a white square containing text. It is possible to display a bitmap with a transparent background, although it takes a great deal of advanced graphics work. Fortunately, the image list, first introduced for Windows 95, has the ability to draw a transparent bitmap.

What Is an Image List?

An image list is similar to an array of bitmaps, just like a roll of film is an array of images. Unlike rolls of film, an image list can grow, if needed, as extra images are added to the list. Each bitmap stored in an image list is associated with an index, which can be used to retrieve a particular image.

Image lists are used by three of the new common controls introduced in Windows 95: tree views, list views, and toolbars. These controls all use image lists to store their bitmaps. Image lists can also be used outside of these new controls, and they provide an easy way to store a series of bitmaps, because you only need to handle a single image-list object instead of separate objects for each bitmap.

Why Use an Image List?

One major reason to use an image list is the new common controls available beginning with Windows 95. If you want to display bitmaps in tree views or list views, you must use an image list. If your program needs to manage several different bitmapped images, a single image list is easier to use than a series of bitmaps. Accessing and displaying multiple images from an image list is much easier than handling multiple `CBitmap` objects. In addition, there are two features offered by image lists that are difficult to duplicate with regular bitmaps:

Why

- Transparent images
- Overlaid images

A transparent image is difficult to achieve using a normal bitmap. In the simplest cases, about twice as many lines of code are required to draw a bitmap transparently as are required to draw it as an opaque image against a drawing surface. Using an image list, drawing a transparent bitmap is almost effortless, requiring little more than parameters that are set correctly.

An overlaid image is created by combining two images to form a single, combined image. This is useful when showing special attributes for items represented by images stored in an image list. For example, when a shared directory is shown in the Explorer, a server "hand" is superimposed over the directory's folder. This is an overlaid image.

How Is an Image List Used?

As for almost everything else in Windows, there is an MFC class for image lists, too. The `CImageList` class is used to create, display, and otherwise manage image lists in an MFC-based Windows program.

How

Image lists often are used with three other MFC classes: `CTreeCtrl`, `CListCtrl`, and `CToolbarCtrl`. I cover these classes in the next three chapters. However, you can also use an image list as a collection of bitmaps, which I do in this chapter. Using image lists in this way helps show off the different things you can do with image lists before they are used with the common controls.

As an example of using image lists, create an SDI project named ImageList. This project uses an image list to display a series of bitmaps in the program's client area.

Creating an Image List

The first step in creating an image list is to create a series of bitmaps, each of which is the same size. Although the images can be any size, the sample code in this section assumes the bitmaps are 32 pixels on each side. The bitmaps used in the example are shown in Figure 20.2.

Figure 20.2.
*Bitmaps used in the
ImageList example.*

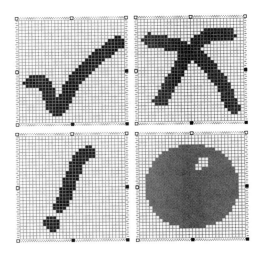

Create the four bitmaps, and name them as shown in Table 20.1.

Table 20.1. Bitmaps used in the ImageList project.

ID	Description
IDB_CROSS	Cross mark
IDB_CHECK	Check
IDB_BANG	Exclamation point
IDB_BALL	Ball

Adding a bitmap resource to an image list consists of three steps:

1. Load the bitmap.
2. Add the bitmap to the image list.
3. Delete the bitmap object.

The bitmap object is deleted because the image list makes a copy of the bitmap and stores the image internally. As a rule of thumb, any time a Windows GDI object is loaded, it should be deleted to prevent memory leaks. The steps above are handled by `AddBitmapToImageList`, a new function added to the `CImageListView` class. Add the function provided in Listing 20.2 to the ImageListView.cpp source file.

Listing 20.2. The `CImageListView::AddBitmapToImageList` function.

```
BOOL CImageListView::AddBitmapToImageList( UINT nResourceID )
{
    BOOL bReturn;
    CBitmap bmp;

    bReturn = bmp.LoadBitmap( nResourceID );
    if( bReturn != FALSE )
    {
        bReturn = m_imageList.Add( &bmp, RGB(255,255,255) );
        bmp.DeleteObject();
    }
    return bReturn;
}
```

The `AddBitmapToImageList` function is used because four bitmap resources are added to the image list. Adding the bitmaps using a new member function reduces the amount of code you must write, and helps reduce the chance of errors, because every bitmap is loaded using the same function.

After adding the member function to the ImageListView.cpp file, add the source code from Listing 20.3 to the `CImageListView` class, found in the file ImageListView.h. Add the source code in the class implementation section, which is marked by the `// Implementation` comment. After the comment, there is a `protected:` label inserted by AppWizard for user-supplied variables and functions.

Listing 20.3. Source code to be added to the `CImageListView` class.

```
protected:
    BOOL        AddBitmapToImageList( UINT nResourceID );
    CImageList  m_imageList;
```

The actual work of creating the image list is done when the view is constructed. The image list can be built at any time; however, it is costly to create an image list in terms of computing power. Creating the image list in the constructor lets you build it once, rather than each time it is used. Add the source code from Listing 20.4 to the constructor for `CImageListView`.

Listing 20.4. The `CImageListView` constructor.

```
CImageListView::CImageListView()
{
    m_imageList.Create( 32, 32, TRUE, 4, 1 );

    AddBitmapToImageList( IDB_CROSS );
    AddBitmapToImageList( IDB_CHECK );
    AddBitmapToImageList( IDB_BANG );
    AddBitmapToImageList( IDB_BALL );
}
```

The image list is created using one of the CImageList::Create functions. This version of Create is useful when an image list is used as a bitmap collection; I use other versions of Create in the following chapters. This version of Create has five parameters:

- The height of each bitmap; in this case, 32 pixels
- The width of each bitmap; in this case, 32 pixels
- Whether or not the image list can be masked for transparency; in this case, TRUE
- The number of bitmaps stored initially in the image list; in this case, four
- The "grow-by," or the number of bitmaps added when the image list is expanded; in this case, one

If the image list will be expanded, the "grow-by" parameter should be a larger number because expanding a bitmap consumes a lot of computing power.

Displaying an Image List Using the *CImageList::Draw* Function

Individual items stored in an image list can be drawn using the CImageList::Draw member function, as shown in Listing 20.5.

Listing 20.5. Using CImageList::Draw to display a bitmap from an image list.

```
void CImageListView::OnDraw(CDC* pDC)
{
    CPoint ptImage( 0, 0 );
    for( int nImage = 0; nImage < 3; nImage++ )
    {
        m_imageList.Draw( pDC, nImage, ptImage, ILD_NORMAL );
        ptImage.x += 50;
    }
}
```

The individual image bitmaps stored in an image list can also be extracted as icons using the ExtractIcon member function:

```
HICON hicon = m_imageList.ExtractIcon( nImage );
```

The only parameter needed for ExtractIcon is the image index. You can then use the icon extracted just like any icon handle. I discuss icons in Chapter 33.

Displaying a Transparent Image

There are two methods you can use to display a bitmap transparently. The easiest way is to define a background color mask for the bitmap, as done in Listing 20.2. The background color of the image list can then be adjusted to allow the background color of the drawing surface to "shine through," giving the image a transparent effect. Replace the CImageList::OnDraw function with the code provided in Listing 20.6, and then recompile and run the Bitmap program.

Listing 20.6. Using the `CImageList::Draw` function to display a bitmap transparently.

```
void CImageListView::OnDraw(CDC* pDC)
{
    m_imageList.SetBkColor( CLR_NONE );
    CPoint ptImage( 0, 0 );
    for( int nImage = 0; nImage < 3; nImage++ )
    {
        m_imageList.Draw( pDC, nImage, ptImage, ILD_TRANSPARENT );
        ptImage.x += 50;
    }
}
```

Two changes have been made to `OnDraw` in Listing 20.1 that make it possible to draw the image list transparently. First, the background color is set to `CLR_NONE` using the `CImageList::SetBkColor` function. The `CLR_NONE` parameter tells a masked image list to prepare to use the color mask when drawing any images. If nontransparent bitmaps are used, it's possible to set the image background to any color by using the `SetBkColor` function.

Second, the `ILD_TRANSPARENT` flag is used when `CImageList::Draw` is called. This tells the image list to combine the image mask with the bitmap, if a mask exists. In this case, the bitmap uses a color mask, so the background color is made transparent.

Displaying an Overlapped Image

An overlapped image is two images from the same bitmap, with one image superimposed on the other. Before using an image as an overlay, it must be defined as an overlay image. You can define up to four bitmaps per image list as overlays using the `CImageList::SetOverlayImage` function:

```
m_imageList.SetOverlayImage( 0, 1 );
```

The `SetOverlayImage` function takes two parameters: the image index used as the overlay, and the overlay index used to identify the overlay. Just to make things even easier, unlike every other index used in Windows, the overlay index starts at one instead of zero.

To use an overlaid image, the `CImageList::Draw` function is used as in previous examples, except that the `ILD_OVERLAYMASK` flag is used. The `INDEXTOOVERLAYMASK` macro is combined with `ILD_OVERLAYMASK` flag to specify the overlay image index to be combined with the base image. Listing 20.7. is a new version of `OnDraw` that displays an overlaid image using an image list.

Listing 20.7. Using `CImageList::Draw` function to display an overlapped image.

```
void CImageListView::OnDraw(CDC* pDC)
{
    m_imageList.SetBkColor( CLR_NONE );
    CPoint ptOverlay( 50, 80 );
    m_imageList.SetOverlayImage( 0, 1 );
```

continues

Listing 20.7. continued

```
m_imageList.Draw( pDC,
                  3,
                  ptOverlay,
                  ILD_OVERLAYMASK | INDEXTOOVERLAYMASK(1) );
}
```

Summary

In this chapter, I discussed bitmaps and image lists, two methods used to display images in a Windows program. I used image lists to draw a series of bitmaps that were either opaque, transparent, or overlaid with a second image.

PART VI

View Classes

21 Tree Views

22 Up-Down, Progress, and Slider Controls

23 Control Bars

24 List View Controls

25 Document/View Architecture

26 Using Form Views

27 Multiple Views

28 Split Views

Tree Views

One of the most popular controls released with Windows 95 is the tree view control. In this chapter, I present this control and use it as a main view in an SDI application and as a control in a dialog box. I look at two MFC classes that are used for tree view controls and implement a simple drag-and-drop example.

What Is a Tree View Control?

What Tree controls are similar to the list box controls discussed in Chapter 19, "Using List-Box and Combo-Box Controls," except that they display information in a tree, or hierarchy. Tree view controls are often used to display disk directories or the contents of books or other documents.

Items in a tree view control are arranged into groups, with "child" items located under "parent" items. Child items are also indented, or "nested," under a parent. The Windows Explorer is one of the applications that uses the new tree control, shown in Figure 21.1.

Figure 21.1.
The Windows Explorer is one of the many applications that use tree view controls.

You can create tree view controls with several different styles. For example, many tree view controls display a bitmap next to each item. Many also display a tree control button next to each item. This button contains a plus sign if an item can be expanded. If the button is clicked, the tree view expands to display the item's children. Once expanded, the item displays a button with a minus sign.

Tree controls are often used to contain a large amount of information. The user can control the amount of information displayed by expanding or collapsing tree items. When more horizontal or vertical room is needed, the tree control automatically displays scroll bars.

Why Use a Tree View Control?

Why The tree control is a popular control because it enables you to display a great deal of information in a hierarchy. Unlike a list box, a small amount of high-level information can be presented initially, enabling the user to decide which parts of the tree should be expanded. The tree control also enables information to be displayed so that relationships between different items in the control can be seen. For example, in the Explorer, subdirectories are nested in order to show their positions in the directory.

Tree views are popular because they offer a wide range of options. As with list view controls, which are discussed in Chapter 24, "List View Controls," tree view controls put the user in charge. As you see in an example later in this chapter, it's very easy to enable a user to perform drag-and-drop operations in a tree view control. With a few lines of code, you can also enable a user to edit the labels for individual tree view items.

How Are Tree View Controls Used?

How There are two ways to use tree controls in your MFC-based programs. When a tree control is used in a dialog box, the control is added just as buttons, list boxes, and other controls have been added in previous chapters. The MFC class CTreeCtrl is used to interact with tree controls and is associated with a tree view control using ClassWizard.

Tree view controls can also be used in a view. The CTreeView class is a specialized view that consists of a single tree control. The CTreeView class is derived from CCtrlView, which is itself derived from CView. The class inheritance tree for CTreeView is provided in Figure 21.2.

Figure 21.2.
The inheritance tree for
CTreeView.

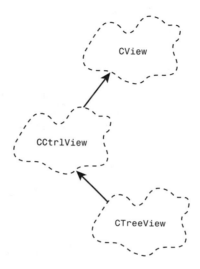

Because CTreeView is derived from CView, it can be used just like CView. For the first example in this chapter, you use CTreeView as the main view in an MFC-based application.

Using a Tree View Control as a View

For this example, create an SDI project named TreeEx using AppWizard. In the final AppWizard page, a checkered flag is displayed along with a list box containing classes that are generated for the application. Follow these steps to use a tree view as the application's main view:

1. Select the view class in the class list box, in this case, CTreeExView.
2. Select CTreeView from the Base Class combo box.
3. Click the Finish button to end the AppWizard process.

You can compile and run the TreeEx application; however, no items have been added to the tree control yet. In the next section, you see how items are added to a tree view.

Adding Items to a *CTreeView*

As discussed earlier, the CTreeView class is derived from CView and contains a tree view control that covers the entire view surface. To get access to the tree view control, you use the GetTreeControl function.

```
CTreeCtrl& tree = GetTreeCtrl();
```

Note that the return value from GetTreeCtrl is a reference to a CTreeCtrl object. This means that the return value must be assigned, or bound, to a CTreeCtrl reference variable. Once the CTreeCtrl reference variable has been assigned a value, it cannot be re-assigned.

After you have access to the tree view control, items can be added to the control in several different ways. When adding simple items to a tree control, only the label for the item must be provided:

```
HTREEITEM hItem = tree.InsertItem( "Foo" );
```

This line adds an item to the tree control at the first, or root, level. The return value from InsertItem is a handle to the new item if it was inserted successfully, or NULL if the item could not be inserted. To add an item as a child, pass the parent's handle as a parameter when inserting the item.

```
tree.InsertItem( "Bar", hItem );
```

The source code provided in Listing 21.1 uses the functions discussed previously to add eight items in the CTreeExView::OnInitialUpdate function.

Listing 21.1. Adding items to a CTreeView.

```
void CTreeExView::OnInitialUpdate()
{
    CTreeView::OnInitialUpdate();
    CTreeCtrl& tree = GetTreeCtrl();

    HTREEITEM hChapter = tree.InsertItem( "Chapter 1" );
    tree.InsertItem( "What", hChapter);
    tree.InsertItem( "Why", hChapter );
    tree.InsertItem( "How", hChapter );
    hChapter = tree.InsertItem( "Chapter 2" );
    tree.InsertItem( "What", hChapter );
    tree.InsertItem( "Why", hChapter );
    tree.InsertItem( "How", hChapter );
}
```

After you add the source code from Listing 21.1, compile and run the TreeEx project. This version of the tree view control is a minimal tree control. There are no connecting lines, no bitmaps, and no pushbuttons; in short, it's fairly boring.

In addition to other view and window styles that are available, there are four style options that you can apply specifically to a tree view control:

- TVS_HASLINES adds connecting lines between parent and child items.
- TVS_LINESATROOT adds lines for the root items in the tree control. This attribute is ignored if TVS_HASLINES is not selected.

- **TVS_HASBUTTONS** adds the plus and minus buttons for items that can be expanded.
- **TVS_EDITLABELS** enables the user to edit a tree view item label.

You usually don't need to get involved with defining the styles for a view; the default settings are good enough 99 percent of the time. For a tree view, however, you might want to select one or more of the optional styles by modifying the `CTreeExView::PreCreateWindow` function. The source code in Listing 21.2 applies all of the optional attributes except for `TVS_EDITLABELS`.

Listing 21.2. Modifying the tree view style in `PreCreateWindow`.

```
BOOL CTreeExView::PreCreateWindow(CREATESTRUCT& cs)
{
    cs.style |= ( TVS_HASLINES|TVS_LINESATROOT|TVS_HASBUTTONS );
    return CTreeView::PreCreateWindow(cs);
}
```

Compile and run the TreeEx example, and you'll see that the example now has lines and buttons. It might sound like a small addition, but it makes the control much easier to use, especially if the tree must be expanded and collapsed frequently.

Adding Tree View Controls to Dialog Boxes

For the second example in this chapter, you add a tree view control to the TreeEx About dialog box. This version of the tree view control supports drag-and-drop and also displays bitmaps for each item.

Adding a tree control to a dialog box is almost exactly like adding a list box to a dialog box. Select the ResourceView tab in the project workspace window and open the Dialog folder. Open the `IDD_ABOUTBOX` dialog box resource by double-clicking the `IDD_ABOUTBOX` icon or by right-clicking the icon and selecting Open from the pop-up menu.

Remove the current controls except for the OK button from `IDD_ABOUTBOX`. Add a tree view control to the dialog box by dragging the tree view icon onto the dialog box or by selecting a tree view control and clicking on the dialog box. The modified dialog box is shown in Figure 21.3.

As shown in Figure 21.3, the tree view control displays a simulated tree to assist in sizing the control. A tree control is often larger than a list box due to the space required for indenting the nested child items.

Figure 21.3.
*Adding a tree view
control to a dialog box.*

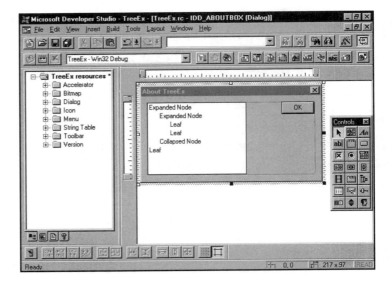

Setting Tree View Control Properties

The tree view control's properties are set using the properties dialog box. Some of the properties available for tree view controls are also available for list boxes. The tree view control property options include the following:

- ID is used for the tree view control resource ID. A default resource ID, such as IDC_TREE1, is supplied by Developer Studio.

- Visible is used to indicate that the control is initially visible. This checkbox is usually checked.

- Disabled is used to indicate that the list should be initially disabled. This checkbox is usually cleared.

- Group is used to mark the first control in a group. This checkbox is usually cleared.

- Tabstop indicates that this control can be reached by pressing Tab on the keyboard. This checkbox is usually checked.

- Help ID indicates that a context-sensitive help ID should be generated for this control.

- Has Buttons indicates that the control should be drawn with buttons. Each tree control item that can be expanded has a button drawn to the left of the item. This checkbox is usually cleared.

- Has Lines is used to indicate that lines should be drawn connecting items in the control. This checkbox is usually cleared.

- Border is used to indicate that a border should be drawn around the tree control. This checkbox is usually checked.

- Lines at Root indicates that lines should be drawn at the first, or "root," level of the control. This option is ignored if the Has Lines checkbox is not selected.

- Edit Labels enables a user to change the values of labels in the control. This checkbox is usually cleared.

- Disable Drag Drop prevents drag-and-drop for items contained in the tree view control. This item is usually cleared.

- Show Selection Always uses the system highlight colors for selected items. This item is usually cleared.

Open the properties dialog box for the tree view control and change the resource ID to IDC_TREE. All other properties should be set to their default values except for the following items, which should be checked:

- Has Lines
- Lines at Root
- Has Buttons

Using ClassWizard, associate a CTreeCtrl member variable with the new tree control, using the values from Table 21.1.

Table 21.1. Values used to add a CTreeCtrl member variable for CAboutDlg.

Control ID	Variable Name	Category	Type
IDC_TREE	m_tree	Control	CTreeCtrl

Creating an Image List Control

The version of the tree view control contained in the About dialog box displays two bitmaps next to tree view items:

- A notebook icon for root-level items
- A document page icon for second-level items

As discussed in Chapter 20, "Using Image Lists and Bitmaps," an image list can consist of a single bitmap that has one or more segments. The bitmap shown in Figure 21.4 contains both images used by the tree view control.

Use the image editor to create the bitmap in Figure 21.4. Use red as a background color for the bitmap to make it easier to draw the bitmap transparently. Use the values from Table 21.2 for the bitmap.

Figure 21.4.
Bitmaps displayed in the tree view control.

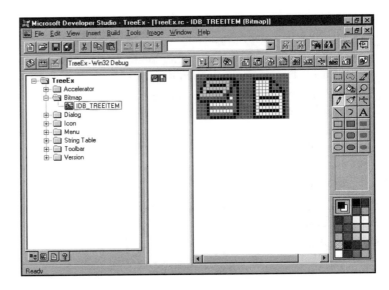

Table 21.2. Attributes for the image list bitmap used in TreeEx.

Resource ID	Height	Item Width	Total Width
IDB_TREE	14	14	28

Modifying the Dialog Box Class

The CAboutDlg class must be modified in order to handle the tree view control. You must add a total of four new member variables to the CAboutDlg class:

- A CImageList variable is used to supply the images displayed next to each item in the tree control.
- A BOOL flag is used to indicate that a drag-and-drop operation is in progress.
- An HTREEITEM variable refers to an item being dragged.
- Another HTREEITEM variable refers to the current drop target.

Add the source code provided in Listing 21.3 to the implementation section of the CAboutDlg class declaration.

Listing 21.3. Additions to the CAboutDlg class declaration.

```
// Implementation
protected:
    CImageList  m_imageList;
    BOOL        m_bIsDragging;
    HTREEITEM   m_dragItem;
    HTREEITEM   m_dragTarget;
```

The tree control is initialized when the CAboutDlg class receives the WM_INITDIALOG message. Using ClassWizard, add a message-handling function for WM_INITDIALOG and accept the suggested name of OnInitDialog. Add the source code in Listing 21.4 to the OnInitDialog member function. A little cut-and-paste editing can save you some typing here because this source code is similar to the source code used earlier in Listing 21.1.

Listing 21.4. The CAboutDlg::OnInitDialog member function.

```
BOOL CAboutDlg::OnInitDialog()
{
    CDialog::OnInitDialog();
    m_imageList.Create( IDB_TREE, 14, 1, RGB(255,0,0) );
    m_tree.SetImageList( &m_imageList, TVSIL_NORMAL );
    HTREEITEM hChapter;
    hChapter = m_tree.InsertItem( "Chapter 1", 0, 0 );
    m_tree.InsertItem( "What", 1, 1, hChapter );
    m_tree.InsertItem( "Why", 1, 1, hChapter );
    m_tree.InsertItem( "How", 1, 1, hChapter );
    hChapter = m_tree.InsertItem( "Chapter 2", 0, 0 );
    m_tree.InsertItem( "What", 1, 1, hChapter );
    m_tree.InsertItem( "Why", 1, 1, hChapter );
    m_tree.InsertItem( "How", 1, 1, hChapter );
    return TRUE;
}
```

There are a few small differences between Listing 21.1 and Listing 21.4. In Listing 21.4, an image list is first created and then associated with the tree view control by calling the SetImageList function. In addition, the InsertItem function uses two extra parameters.

```
m_tree.InsertItem( "How", 1, 1, hChapter );
```

As in the earlier example, the first parameter is the text label associated with the tree item. The second parameter is the image index associated with the item when it's not selected; the third parameter is the selected image index. This enables you to specify different images for selected and non-selected items. As before, the last parameter is a handle to the item's parent item, or it can be omitted if the item is added at the root-level.

Tree View Control Notifications

Tree controls communicate with their parent windows using notification messages. I'll look at TVN_BEGINDRAG, the message used for drag-and-drop in this section.

Adding Drag-and-Drop to a Tree View Control

In order to handle drag-and-drop inside a tree view control, you must handle the following three messages:

- TVN_BEGINDRAG notifies the tree view control's parent that a drag has been started. For this example, you only enable second level items to be dragged.

- WM_MOUSEMOVE is sent as the mouse is moved. If a drag is in progress, the drag image is moved to the new cursor position.

- WM_LBUTTONUP is sent as the left mouse button is released. If a drag is in progress, the drag is completed by moving the drag item into the new position.

Using ClassWizard, add message-handling functions for these messages to the CAboutDlg class, using the values from Table 21.3.

Table 21.3. Message-handling functions used for drag-and-drop.

Object ID	Message	Function
IDC_TREE	TVN_BEGINDRAG	OnBegindragTree
CAboutDlg	WM_MOUSEMOVE	OnMouseMove
CAboutDlg	WM_LBUTTONUP	OnLButtonUp

The source code for the three functions is provided in Listing 21.5.

Listing 21.5. Functions used to implement simple drag-and-drop.

```
void CAboutDlg::OnBegindragTree(NMHDR* pNMHDR, LRESULT* pResult)
{
    NM_TREEVIEW* pNMTreeView = (NM_TREEVIEW*)pNMHDR;
    m_dragItem = pNMTreeView->itemNew.hItem;
    if( m_tree.GetParentItem( m_dragItem ) != NULL )
    {
        CImageList* pDragImage;
        pDragImage = m_tree.CreateDragImage( m_dragItem );
        m_tree.SelectItem( m_dragItem );
        pDragImage->BeginDrag( 0, CPoint(0,0) );
        pDragImage->DragEnter( &m_tree, pNMTreeView->ptDrag );
        SetCapture();
        m_bIsDragging = TRUE;
    }
    *pResult = 0;
}
void CAboutDlg::OnMouseMove(UINT nFlags, CPoint point)
{
    if( m_bIsDragging == TRUE )
    {
        CPoint      ptTree( point );
        MapWindowPoints( &m_tree, &ptTree, 1 );
        CImageList::DragMove( ptTree );
        UINT uHitTest = TVHT_ONITEM;
        m_dragTarget = m_tree.HitTest( ptTree, &uHitTest );
    }
    CDialog::OnMouseMove(nFlags, point);
}
void CAboutDlg::OnLButtonUp(UINT nFlags, CPoint point)
{
    if( m_bIsDragging == TRUE )
    {
```

```
        CImageList::DragLeave( &m_tree );
        CImageList::EndDrag();
        ReleaseCapture();
        m_bIsDragging = FALSE;
        if( m_dragTarget != NULL )
        {
            HTREEITEM hParent;
            hParent = m_tree.GetParentItem( m_dragTarget );
            CString szLabel = m_tree.GetItemText( m_dragItem );
            if( hParent != NULL )
                m_tree.InsertItem( szLabel, 1, 1, hParent,
                                        m_dragTarget );
            else
                m_tree.InsertItem( szLabel, 1, 1, m_dragTarget,
                                        TVI_FIRST );
            m_tree.DeleteItem( m_dragItem );
        }
    }
    else
        CDialog::OnLButtonUp(nFlags, point);
}
```

The source code in Listing 21.5 is all you need to perform a minimal drag-and-drop operation. The drag sequence starts with the tree view control sending the TVN_DRAGBEGIN to the control's parent—in this case, the TreeEx About dialog box. The MFC framework translates this message into a CAboutDlg::OnBegindragTree function call. Inside this function, the handle to the drag item is stored in m_dragItem. In this example, you aren't dragging items at the root level, so GetParentItem is used to get a handle to the drag item's parent; if NULL is returned, the item is at the root level, and the drag never starts.

If m_dragItem has a parent, a temporary drag image list is created by calling the CreateDragImage function. The image list returned by this function is used to update the cursor position. The BeginDrag function associates an image index with the drag operation, and the DragEnter function "locks" the window so it can't be updated and enables the drag image to be displayed.

As the mouse is moved across the screen during the drag-and-drop, WM_MOUSEMOVE messages are sent to the dialog box. The CAboutDlg::OnMouseMove function checks to see if a drag-and-drop is in progress. If so, the drag image is moved to the new mouse position using the DragMove function. Because this is a static function, it can be called without specifying a CImageList object. A "hit test" is also performed to determine if the mouse cursor is over a tree item; if so, a handle to the tree item is stored for future use as a possible drop target. If the hit test fails, the m_dragTarget member variable is set to NULL, indicating a drop is not possible.

At some point, the user releases the left mouse button, resulting in a WM_LBUTTONUP message, which is translated into a call to the CAboutDlg::OnLButtonUp function. If a drag-and-drop is in progress, the operation is completed by calling the DragLeave and EndDrag functions. The mouse capture is released, and the m_bIsDragging flag is set to FALSE.

If the user has released the mouse button over a target, the drop target handle, m_dragTarget, is not NULL. If the drop target is a second level item, the drag item is inserted just after the drop target. If the drop target is a root-level item, the drag item is inserted as the first child item. These calls to the InsertItem function use a fourth parameter, which is a handle for the item just before the new item. This parameter can be one of three predefined values:

- TVI_FIRST inserts the item as the first child, as used in this example.
- TVI_LAST inserts the item as the last child.
- TVI_SORT sorts the item alphabetically.

After the drag item has been inserted in a new position, the old position is removed using the DeleteItem function. In order to implement a copy-drag, just eliminate the call to DeleteItem.

Summary

In this chapter, I discussed the tree view control. I discussed tree view control options and created two examples: a tree view used as an SDI main view and a tree view control in a dialog box. I also covered drag-and-drop as well as edit notifications.

Up-Down, Progress, and Slider Controls

In this chapter, I discuss three controls that were first offered in Windows 95: the up-down or spin control, the slider, and the progress control. I cover each of these controls in detail and build a dialog box-based sample program.

What Are Up-Down Controls?

What Up-down controls, often called spin controls, are a pair of small arrows that resemble the ends of a scroll bar but are smaller. Up-down controls are often used to adjust the value of another control that is associated with the up-down control. Known as a "buddy" control, this is usually an edit control.

An up-down control can also be aligned horizontally. A horizontal up-down control is not called a left-right control; it keeps its original name.

By default, clicking the up arrow decreases the value of the buddy control, and clicking the down arrow increases the value contained in the buddy control. This behavior is confusing to most people; fortunately, it's easy to change, as you see in the section, "How Is an Up-Down Control Used?"

Why Use an Up-Down Control?

Why

Up-down controls are often used with an edit control as the buddy control. The up-down control can easily run through a range of available values for the edit control. By setting a range for the up-down control, you can ensure that the user selects a value within the acceptable range for the edit control.

Up-down controls are ideal for situations where a set of values can be scrolled by a user. If the values are adjusted up or down by a few units, an up-down control is perfect because it enables the user to select a new value with a few key presses.

How Is an Up-Down Control Used?

How

An up-down control is very easy to use. To use the default functionality of the up-down control, you need to write exactly zero lines of source code! Even the most advanced uses for up-down controls require just a few lines of source code; most of the code is written by ClassWizard.

The Sample Program

For the examples created in this chapter, you use a dialog box-based project named Controls. This project starts with an up-down control; later in the chapter, you add a slider and a progress control.

To create the Controls project, use AppWizard to create a new project workspace. Select a Dialog-based project and click the Finish button.

Adding an Up-Down Control to a Dialog Box

Adding an up-down control to the Controls dialog box is just like adding other controls. Open the main dialog box in the dialog box editor by selecting the ResourceView tab in the project workspace and opening the Dialog folder. Open the IDD_CONTROLS_DIALOG by double-clicking the dialog box icon or by right-clicking the icon and selecting Open from the pop-up menu.

You can either drag and drop an up-down control from the control palette to the main dialog box, or you can select the up-down control on the tool palette using the mouse and then click the desired position in the main dialog box.

Open the properties dialog box for the up-down control by double-clicking the control and change the resource ID to IDC_SPIN. All other properties should be set to their default values.

Up-Down Control Properties

As with other controls, up-down controls have properties that you can change using the Developer Studio resource editor. The properties available for a up-down control include the following:

- ID is used for the up-down control's resource ID. A default resource ID, such as IDC_SPIN1, is supplied by Developer Studio.

- Visible is used to indicate that the control is initially visible. This checkbox is usually checked.

- Disabled is used to indicate the control should be initially disabled. This checkbox is usually cleared.

- Group is used to mark the first control in a group. This checkbox is usually cleared.

- Tabstop indicates that this control can be reached by pressing Tab on the keyboard. This checkbox is usually checked.

- Help ID indicates that a context-sensitive help ID should be generated for this control.

- Orientation indicates whether the up-down control should be vertical or horizontal. The default selection is vertical.

- Alignment specifies how the buddy control and up-down control are associated with each other. Possible values are Right, Left, and Unattached. The default value is Unattached, but in most cases, you should select Left or Right.

- Auto Buddy indicates whether the up-down control should use the previous control in the tab order as its buddy control. This checkbox is cleared by default but should be checked in most cases.

- Set Buddy Integer indicates that the up-down control should set the value of the attached buddy control. This checkbox is cleared by default but should be checked in most cases.

- No Thousands indicates that no separator should be provided for a value greater than 1,000 in the up-down control. This checkbox is usually cleared.

- Wrap indicates that the up-down control should "wrap around" after reaching its maximum value. If this option is not selected, the up-down control stops after reaching its maximum limit. This checkbox is usually cleared.

- Arrow Key indicates that the keyboard's arrow keys can be used to change the value of the up-down control. This checkbox is usually cleared.

Adding a Buddy Control

The easiest way to add a buddy control to an up-down control requires no source code; instead, you use the dialog box editor. Follow these steps to associate an edit control with an up-down control:

1. Add an edit control to the dialog box. Most users expect the up-down control to be placed against the buddy control; it helps emphasize the connection between the two controls.

2. Open the properties dialog box for the edit control and change the resource ID to IDC_EDIT. All other properties should be set to their default values.

3. Set the tab order for the edit control so that it is the control immediately before the up-down control. You can select the tab order by choosing Tab Order from the Layout menu or by pressing Ctrl+D. Each control is displayed with a small label that represents the control tab order. To change the tab order, use the mouse to click each control in the new tab order sequence.

4. Open the properties dialog box for the up-down control and set the alignment value to Right. This aligns the up-down control on the right side of the buddy control.

5. Keep the properties dialog box open and check the Auto Buddy and Set Buddy Integer checkboxes.

The IDD_CONTROLS_DIALOG with an up-down control and the buddy edit control is shown in Figure 22.1.

Figure 22.1.
The main dialog box used in the Controls sample program.

Believe it or not, that's all there is to using an up-down control. If you compile and execute the Controls project, you can use the up-down control to change the value contained in the edit control.

To set, validate, or retrieve the value of the edit control, use ClassWizard to associate a CEdit object with the edit control or use one of the other techniques discussed in Chapter 18, "Using Edit Controls."

Changing the Range of the Up-Down Control

As discussed earlier, the default behavior for an up-down control is to increment the control if the down arrow is clicked and decrement the control if the up arrow is clicked. You can change this behavior by reversing the range of the up-down control.

The MFC class CSpinButtonCtrl can be used to manage an up-down control. To change the range of an up-down control, use the CSpinButtonCtrl's SetRange function.

```
m_spin.SetRange( 100, 0 );
```

Use ClassWizard to associate the IDC_SPIN control with a CSpinButtonCtrl object, using the values from Table 22.1.

Table 22.1. Values used to add a `CSpinButtonCtrl` member variable for `CControlsDlg`.

Control ID	Variable Name	Category	Type
IDC_SPIN	m_spin	Control	CSpinButtonCtrl

To set a new range for the up-down control, add the source code from Listing 22.1 to the `CControlsDlg::OnInitDialog` member function. This source code should be added just after the `// TODO` comment.

Listing 22.1. Setting the range for an up-down control.

```
// TODO: Add extra initialization here
    m_spin.SetRange( 0, 100 );
```

Compile and execute the Controls project. The up-down control increments the edit control when its up arrow is clicked and decrements the edit control when the down arrow is clicked.

What Are Slider Controls?

What

A slider control, also known as a trackbar control, is a control that contains a slide bar that you can move between two points. A slider is used in the Display applet that is part of the Windows Control Panel. The Settings property page uses a slider to set the screen resolution.

The user moves the slide bar by dragging it with the mouse or by setting the keyboard focus to the slider and using the arrow keys on the keyboard. You can create sliders with optional tick marks that help the user to judge the position of the slide bar.

Why Use a Slider Control?

Why

Sliders are useful when a user is asked to select a value within a certain range. A slider gives the user immediate feedback about the control's current value, as well as the value's relationship to the high and low ranges.

How Is a Slider Control Used?

How

Sliders are used in the same way as most other controls. Although you can create a slider from scratch, it's much easier to add one in the Developer Studio dialog box editor.

Open the `IDD_CONTROLS_DIALOG` resource and add a slider control by dragging a slider control from the control palette and dropping it on the dialog box. Figure 22.2 shows the Controls dialog box after you add the slider control.

Figure 22.2.
The main dialog box
from the Controls project
after you add a slider.

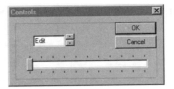

Open the properties dialog box for the slider control and change the resource ID to IDC_SLIDER. All other properties can remain set to their default values for now. In the next section, I talk about the properties offered for slider controls.

Slider Control Properties

The properties dialog box for a slider control contains many of the same options offered for up-down controls, as well as a few that are exclusive to slider controls. The available options include the following:

- ID is used for the slider's resource ID. A default resource ID, such as IDC_SLIDER1, is supplied by Developer Studio.
- Visible is used to indicate that the control is initially visible. This checkbox is usually checked.
- Disabled is used to indicate the control should be initially disabled. This checkbox is usually cleared.
- Group is used to mark the first control in a group. This checkbox is usually cleared.
- Tabstop indicates that this control can be reached by pressing Tab on the keyboard. This checkbox is usually checked.
- Help ID indicates that a context-sensitive help ID should be generated for this control.
- Orientation is used to specify if the slider is vertical or horizontal. The default value is vertical.
- Point is used to indicate the position of optional tick marks. There are three options: Top/Left, Bottom/Right, or Both. The default value is Bottom/Right.
- Tick Marks indicates that tick marks should be drawn for the slider. This checkbox is usually cleared.
- Autoticks indicates that tick marks should be drawn at intervals along the slider control. This option checkbox is usually cleared.
- Enable Selection enables the slider to be used to select a range of values. This checkbox is usually cleared.
- Border is used to specify that a border should be drawn around the control. This checkbox is usually checked.

In the next section, you use a slider to control a trackbar. To prepare for that example, open the properties dialog box and make sure the following slider properties are selected:

- `Tick Marks`
- `Autoticks`
- `Enable Selection`

What Are Progress Controls?

A progress control, also known as a progress bar, is commonly used to indicate the progress of an operation and is usually filled from left to right as the operation is completed. You can also use progress controls for indicating temperature, water level, or similar measurements. In fact, an early term for this type of control was "Gas Gauge," back in the old days when programmers had mules and most Windows programs were written in C.

What

Progress controls are used in Developer Studio to indicate the progress of saving or loading a project workspace. Progress controls are also used by Windows Explorer when copying or moving files.

Why Use Progress Controls?

Progress controls are an easy way to give feedback to the user about the status of a task. Instead of waiting an unknown length of time, the user can see what portion of a job has yet to be completed.

Why

How Are Progress Controls Used?

A progress control is added to a dialog box in the same way as the up-down and slider controls discussed earlier. Using the Developer Studio dialog box editor, add a progress control to the Controls project main dialog box. Figure 22.3 shows the main dialog box from the Controls project after the progress control has been added.

How

Figure 22.3.
The Controls dialog box after adding the progress control.

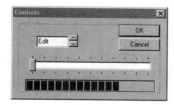

After you add the control, open the properties dialog box and change the resource ID to IDC_PROGRESS. A progress control doesn't have optional properties other than those available on all controls.

- ID is used for the progress control's resource ID. A default resource ID, such as IDC_PROGRESS1, is supplied by Developer Studio.
- Visible is used to indicate that the control is initially visible. This checkbox is usually checked.
- Disabled is used to indicate the control should be initially disabled. This checkbox is usually cleared.
- Group is used to mark the first control in a group. This checkbox is usually cleared.
- Tabstop indicates that this control can be reached by pressing Tab on the keyboard. This checkbox is usually checked.
- Help ID indicates that a context-sensitive help ID should be generated for this control.
- Border is used to specify that a border should be drawn around the control. This checkbox is usually checked.

For this example, you can set the progress control properties to their default values.

Using a Slider to Update a Progress Control

In this section, you use the IDC_SLIDER slider control to change the value displayed by the progress control. Using ClassWizard, add two new member variables associated with the slider and progress controls to the CControlsDlg class. Use the values from Table 22.2 for the new controls.

Table 22.2. Values for slider and progress control member variables.

Control ID	Variable Name	Category	Type
IDC_SLIDER	m_slider	Control	CSliderCtrl
IDC_PROGRESS	m_progress	Control	CProgressCtrl

Initializing the Slider and Progress Controls

The slider and progress controls must be initialized before you can use them. The CProgressCtrl and CSliderCtrl classes each provide a SetRange function that is used to set minimum and maximum values for their respective controls.

```
m_slider.SetRange( 0, 100 );
```

The slider also enables tick marks to be placed along the slider control if the Autoticks checkbox has been selected. Use the `SetTicFreq` function to specify the distance between each tick mark. To add tick marks every 10 positions, pass a value of ten to `SetTicFreq`.

```
m_slider.SetTicFreq( 10 );
```

Listing 22.2 contains new source code for the initialization section of `OnInitDialog`. Add this source code just after the `// TODO` comment.

Listing 22.2. Initializing the controls in `CControlsDlg::OnInitDialog`.

```
// TODO: Add extra initialization here
m_spin.SetRange( 0, 100 );
m_slider.SetRange( 0, 100 );
m_slider.SetTicFreq( 10 );
m_progress.SetRange( 0, 100 );
```

Handling Messages from the Slider

When a slider is moved, it notifies its parent using WM_SCROLL and WM_HSCROLL messages. Because the slider in this example is a horizontal slider, it sends WM_HSCROLL messages to the main dialog box. Using ClassWizard, add a message-handling function to the `CControlsDlg` class for the WM_HSCROLL message. The source code for the `OnHScroll` function is provided in Listing 22.3.

Listing 22.3. Using slider scroll messages to update the progress control.

```
void CControlsDlg::OnHScroll(UINT nSBCode, UINT nPos,
                             CScrollBar* pScrollBar )
{
    int nSliderPos = m_slider.GetPos();
    m_progress.SetPos( nSliderPos );
}
```

The code in Listing 22.3 is called whenever the trackbar position is changed. The `CSliderCtrl::GetPos` function is used to collect the current slider position, which is then used to update the progress control using the `CProgressCtrl::SetPos` function.

Summary

In this chapter, you looked at up-down, slider, and progress controls, three of the simpler controls offered by Windows. You examined the uses for each control and the MFC classes used to interact with them and created a small dialog box-based project that used all three controls.

Control Bars

Control bars are windows that are attached to a frame window, such as toolbars, dialog bars, and status bars. Creating and using these controls is discussed in this chapter, as well as the MFC classes that are used to support them. You build a sample program that demonstrates how these control bars are used.

What Are Control Bars?

What Control bars are user interface elements that are used to contain other controls or windows. There are three types of control bars.

- Status bars are the simplest type of control bar. Status bars are permanently attached to the bottom of a frame window.
- Toolbars contain buttons that are used as menu shortcuts.
- Dialog bars contain buttons and other types of controls, such as combo boxes, list boxes, or progress controls.

In an MFC-based application, control bars are owned by the main frame window. Dialog bars and control bars can be either docked on the frame window or free floating. Docked toolbars and control bars can be "torn off," or undocked. When a control bar is floating, it has a small title bar that displays the window caption.

The CtrlBar Sample Program

In this chapter, a sample program named CtrlBar is used to demonstrate how control bars are used in MFC-based applications. To create CtrlBar, follow these steps:

1. Open a new Project Workspace named CtrlBar.
2. When AppWizard appears, select the Single document option and click the Finish button.
3. When the New Project Information dialog box appears, click the OK button. AppWizard creates the files needed to generate the CtrlBar sample program.

If you compile and run the skeleton CtrlBar program generated by AppWizard, you see that there is already a large amount of control bar functionality in the program, even without any programming on your part. You get this basic functionality for free; later you see how to extend the basic toolbar and status bar provided by AppWizard.

What Are Status Bars?

What

A status bar is a control bar that is attached to the bottom edge of an application's frame window. Most status bars provide a method to hide the status bar if more screen real estate is needed. This is considered good style from a user-interface perspective, and all applications created by AppWizard enable the status bar to be hidden.

Status bars are usually split into several panes, also known as indicators. For example, the CtrlBar program has panes that are dedicated to displaying the status of the Caps Lock and Num Lock keys.

Why Use Status Bars?

Why

Status bars are a standard user interface element. Most users expect to see a status bar to provide menu prompts and other user useful information. Status bars are popular because they are less intrusive than dialog boxes or other methods used to update users.

How Are Status Bars Used?

How

In an MFC-based program, all control bars are owned and controlled by the main frame window. The main frame class, CMainFrame, includes a CStatusBar object named m_wndStatusBar. The m_wndStatusBar object is constructed with the CMainFrame object and is created and initialized during the CMainFrame::OnCreate function.

```
if (!m_wndStatusBar.Create(this) ||
    !m_wndStatusBar.SetIndicators(indicators,
    sizeof(indicators)/sizeof(UINT)))
{
```

```
        TRACE0("Failed to create status bar\n");
        return -1;        // fail to create
}
```

Before you create a status bar, you must create an array of resource IDs used for each pane of the status bar. This array of resource IDs is passed as a parameter to the `SetIndicators` function. The IDs are used to identify each status pane and the default text string for each pane. There must be a default string resource assigned for each pane added to the status bar.

The properties for a status bar pane are set by calling the `SetPaneInfo` function.

```
m_wndStatusBar.SetPaneInfo(4, ID_INDICATOR_TIME, SBPS_POPOUT, 80);
```

The `SetPaneInfo` function takes four parameters: the pane index, the pane ID, the pane style, and the pane width. The available pane styles include the following:

- `SBPS_STRETCH` indicates that this pane can stretch to fill unused space. Only one pane per status bar can have this attribute. AppWizard gives this attribute to the first pane.

- `SBPS_NOBORDERS` indicates that no 3-D border should be drawn around the pane.

- `SBPS_POPOUT` specifies that a reverse border should be drawn so that the pane "pops out."

- `SBPS_NORMAL` creates a status bar without stretch, borders, or pop-out effects.

- `SBPS_DISABLED` indicates that no text should be drawn.

Part VI

Essential Example

A Status Bar Example

For a status bar example, add an extra status bar pane that displays the current time. Adding an extra status bar pane consists of the following steps:

- Add a new ID to the indicator array.
- Add a new default text item to the string table.
- Add an update command handler for the status bar pane.

In addition, you must add a function to handle a timer message used to update the time.

Adding a New Status Bar Indicator ID

To define a new resource symbol, open the Resource Symbols dialog box by selecting Resource Symbols from the View menu. You see a list of resource symbols defined for the CtrlBar application. To add a new resource, click the New button and enter ID_INDICATOR_TIME as the new symbol name.

In the MainFrame.cpp source file is an array of UINT used to define the layout of the status bar. Edit the indicators array so that it resembles the source code provided in Listing 23.1. You have to add the last item in the array.

Listing 23.1. Changes to the `indicators` array in MainFrame.cpp.

```
static UINT indicators[] =
{
    ID_SEPARATOR,           // status line indicator
    ID_INDICATOR_CAPS,
    ID_INDICATOR_NUM,
    ID_INDICATOR_SCRL,
    ID_INDICATOR_TIME
};
```

Follow these steps to add a string table resource using the ID_INDICATOR_TIME symbol:

1. Click the ResourceView tab in the Project Workspace window.
2. Display the resource types used in the project by opening the top-level resource folder.
3. Open the String Table resource folder.

4. Open the string table for editing by double-clicking the String Table icon.

5. Insert a new item into the string table by pressing the Ins key on the keyboard. Enter a value of ID_INDICATOR_TIME as the ID and Time not set as the caption.

Defining the Timer and Pane Styles

Define a style for the new status bar item and begin a timer that expires every second in the CMainFrame::OnCreate function. Add the source code from Listing 23.2 at the end of the OnCreate function. The return statement is already included in the function by AppWizard.

Listing 23.2. Changes to the CMainFrame::Create member function.

```
// Start timer for the status bar clock
m_wndStatusBar.SetPaneInfo(4, ID_INDICATOR_TIME, SBPS_POPOUT, 80);
SetTimer( 1, 1000, NULL );
return 0;
```

Handling the Timer

Using ClassWizard, add a message-handling function for WM_TIMER to the CMainFrame class. This function is called every time that the timer set in Listing 23.2 expires—once per second. When the timer expires, the main frame should invalidate the status bar rectangle, causing it to be repainted. Add the source code in Listing 23.3 to the CMainFrame::OnTimer function.

Listing 23.3. Invalidating the status bar in the OnTimer function.

```
void CMainFrame::OnTimer(UINT nIDEvent)
{
    m_wndStatusBar.InvalidateRect( NULL );
}
```

When the status bar is invalidated, the MFC framework updates each pane using a CCmdUI handler. Although you can use ClassWizard to create CCmdUI handlers for most user-interface objects, you must create status bar pane handlers by hand. When adding message handlers manually, you must be very careful not to modify any source code located between // AFX comments because this code is reserved for ClassWizard.

Add a declaration for a CCmdUI update function to the CMainFrame class declaration, as shown in Listing 23.4. You need to add only one line of code—the declaration for OnUpdateTimer, located just above the DECLARE_MESSAGE_MAP() macro.

Listing 23.4. Changes to the `CMainFrame` class declaration.

```
// Generated message map functions
protected:
    //{{AFX_MSG(CMainFrame)
    afx_msg int OnCreate(LPCREATESTRUCT lpCreateStruct);
    afx_msg void OnTimer(UINT nIDEvent);
    //}}AFX_MSG
    afx_msg void OnUpdateTimer(CCmdUI* pCmdUI);
    DECLARE_MESSAGE_MAP()
```

Next, add the entry in the message map found in MainFrame.cpp, as shown in Listing 23.5. Again, only the `OnUpdateTimer` line must be added.

Listing 23.5. The `CMainFrame` message map after adding `OnUpdateTimer`.

```
BEGIN_MESSAGE_MAP(CMainFrame, CFrameWnd)
    //{{AFX_MSG_MAP(CMainFrame)
    ON_WM_CREATE()
    ON_WM_TIMER()
    //}}AFX_MSG_MAP
    ON_UPDATE_COMMAND_UI(ID_INDICATOR_TIME,OnUpdateTimer)
END_MESSAGE_MAP()
```

Add the `OnUpdateTimer` function, as shown in Listing 23.6.

Listing 23.6. The `OnUpdateTimer` member function.

```
void CMainFrame::OnUpdateTimer(CCmdUI* pCmdUI)
{
    pCmdUI->Enable();
    CTime    theTime = CTime::GetCurrentTime();
    CString szTime = theTime.Format( "%I:%M:%S %p" );
    pCmdUI->SetText( szTime );
}
```

Compile and run the CtrlBar example. The status bar has a new pane at its far right side that contains the current time.

What Are Dialog Bars?

What   Dialog bars are similar to modeless dialog boxes except that they can be embedded in or docked against the main frame or free-floating on the Windows workspace. This property makes dialog bars similar to toolbars except that they can contain any type of control, just like a dialog box.

Dialog bars often contain combo boxes, list boxes, and edit controls. Users can tab from control to control and can dock or float the dialog bar, if enabled by the dialog bar's properties.

Why Use Dialog Bars?

Dialog bars enable you to provide easy access to commonly used controls and commands. If the dialog bar's properties enable it, you can dock the dialog bar against any frame window edge. The major benefit of dialog bars is that they appear to be a toolbar, but they enable any sort of control to be embedded.

Why

How Are Dialog Bars Used?

The first step in using a dialog bar is defining a dialog box resource using the Developer Studio dialog box editor. If the dialog bar is docked against the top or bottom edges of the main frame, the dialog box resource is usually "stretched."

How

Unlike with the CDialog class, you usually don't need to derive your own class from CDialogBar. Messages from controls in the dialog bar are routed to the dialog bar's owner—usually CMainFrame. Unfortunately, ClassWizard does not manage these message maps for you; they must be edited by hand.

Creating a Dockable Dialog Bar

To prepare a dialog bar for docking, the CControlBar::EnableDocking member function must be called:

```
m_dlgBar.EnableDocking( CBRS_ALIGN_ANY );
```

The single parameter passed to the EnableDocking function specifies the docking alignment for the control bar. You can specify the following values for this parameter:

- CBRS_ALIGN_TOP enables docking along the top edge of the client area.
- CBRS_ALIGN_BOTTOM enables docking along the bottom edge of the client area.
- CBRS_ALIGN_LEFT enables docking along the left edge of the client area.
- CBRS_ALIGN_RIGHT enables docking along the right edge of the client area.
- CBRS_ALIGN_ANY enables docking along any edge of the client area.
- CBRS_NOALIGN specifies that the control bar is not repositioned when the parent is resized.
- CBRS_SIZE_DYNAMIC indicates that the control bar is dynamic.
- CBRS_FLOATING indicates that the control bar is floating.
- CBRS_SIZE_FIXED indicates that the control bar is fixed.
- CBRS_HIDE_INPLACE specifies that the control bar is not displayed to the user.
- CBRS_FLOAT_MULTI enables several toolbars to be docked in the same row of the frame window.

When a dockable dialog bar is created, the caption for the window should be set using SetWindowText. This gives the dialog bar a title when it is floated off the frame window.

Adding a Dialog Bar Example to the CtrlBar Project

As an example of a dialog bar, add a dialog bar to the CtrlBar sample project. The dialog bar is initially docked in the main frame window, just below the existing toolbar.

Creating the Dialog Box Resource

Using the Developer Studio dialog box editor, create a new dialog box resource, using IDD_BAR as the resource ID. Make sure that the dialog box resource has the following properties:

- Child Window
- No Frame
- Visible checkbox not checked

Add two child controls to the dialog box—a button and a combo box, as shown in Figure 23.1.

Figure 23.1.
The IDD_BAR *resource in the Developer Studio dialog box editor.*

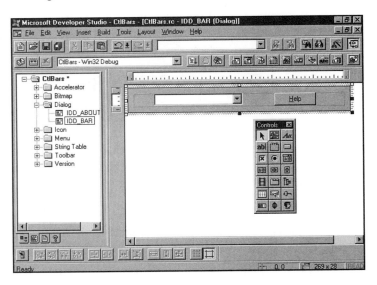

Use the values from Table 23.1 for the controls added to the dialog box resource.

Table 23.1. Controls added to the IDD_BAR dialog box.

Control	Caption	Resource ID
Button	&Help	IDC_BAR_HELP
Combo box	-	IDC_COMBO

Modifications to the *CMainFrame* Class

The new CDialogBar object is a member variable in the CMainFrame class. Add the source code provided in Listing 23.7 to the implementation section of the CMainFrame class declaration.

Listing 23.7. Additions to the `CMainFrame` class declaration.

```
protected:  // control bar embedded members
    CDialogBar  m_dlgBar;
```

The dialog bar is created and initialized in the `CMainFrame:OnCreate` function. Add the source code in Listing 23.8 to the `OnCreate` function, after the changes made earlier in Listing 23.3.

Listing 23.8. Additions to the `CMainFrame::OnCreate` function.

```
// Create a dialog bar
m_dlgBar.Create( this, IDD_BAR, CBRS_TOP, IDD_BAR );
m_dlgBar.SetWindowText( "Dialog Bar" );
m_dlgBar.EnableDocking( CBRS_ALIGN_ANY );
// Dock the control bar on the main frame window.
DockControlBar( &m_dlgBar );
```

As discussed earlier, messages from controls located in a dialog bar are routed to the parent of the dialog bar, and the message maps are not managed by ClassWizard. Edit the message map function declaration in MainFrame.h so that it resembles the source code provided in Listing 23.9. You need to add only one line of code—the line that declares the `OnBarHelp` function.

Listing 23.9. Updates to the `CMainFrame` message map declarations.

```
// Generated message map functions
protected:
    //{{AFX_MSG(CMainFrame)
    afx_msg int OnCreate(LPCREATESTRUCT lpCreateStruct);
    afx_msg void OnTimer(UINT nIDEvent);
    //}}AFX_MSG
    afx_msg void OnUpdateTimer(CCmdUI* pCmdUI);
    afx_msg void OnBarHelp();
    DECLARE_MESSAGE_MAP()
```

Next, add the entry in the message map found in MainFrame.cpp, as shown in Listing 23.10. Again, only the `OnBarHelp` line must be added.

Listing 23.10. Updates to the `CMainFrame` message map.

```
BEGIN_MESSAGE_MAP(CMainFrame, CFrameWnd)
    //{{AFX_MSG_MAP(CMainFrame)
    ON_WM_CREATE()
    //}}AFX_MSG_MAP
    ON_UPDATE_COMMAND_UI(ID_INDICATOR_TIME,OnUpdateTimer)
    ON_BN_CLICKED(IDC_BAR_HELP, OnBarHelp)
END_MESSAGE_MAP()
```

Add the `OnBarHelp` function provided in Listing 23.11 to the MainFrame.cpp source file. This function is called when the `IDC_BAR_HELP` button is clicked on the dialog bar.

Listing 23.11. The `CMainFrame::OnBarHelp` function.

```
void CMainFrame::OnBarHelp()
{
    AfxMessageBox( "Dialog bar help has been selected" );
}
```

Compile and run the new version of the CtrlBar sample program. Notice that the dialog bar can be undocked and moved around the desktop. Clicking the dialog bar's help button pops up a message box. When the dialog bar is undocked, the title is displayed.

What Are Toolbars?

What Toolbars contain buttons that are used to send commands to an application. They are usually used to provide quick and easy access to commands that are also available as menu items. The properties for toolbar items are similar to the properties for menu items. However, instead of checking a menu item, a toolbar button is pressed down to indicate that it is selected.

Toolbars are similar to dialog bars except that they only contain buttons. As with dialog bars, they can be docked against a main frame or free-floating. Unlike dialog bars, toolbars can only contain buttons.

Why Use Toolbars?

Why Toolbars provide quick access to commands that are usually available through the menu. Toolbars also enable command actions to be associated with a picture; this makes a program that uses an icon much easier to use than one that doesn't.

How Are Toolbars Used?

How You use the MFC `CToolbar` class to manage the toolbar control. The `CToolbar` object is declared as a member variable of the `CMainFrame` class, the same way `CDialogBar` objects are.

When toolbar control items use the same resource IDs as the menu items that they represent, it is very easy to add a toolbar to an MFC-based application. The menu and toolbar generate the same commands for the application and use the same message-handling functions. When the status for a menu item is updated, the status of the toolbar is also updated.

Creating the Bitmap Resource

The first step in creating a toolbar is creating a bitmap to be used for the toolbar's button faces. Each button face must be the same size; the default is 16 pixels wide and 15 pixels high.

Creating a Toolbar Control

The LoadToolbar function is used to load the toolbar bitmap. After you load the toolbar bitmap, you set the position of each button in the toolbar by calling the SetButtons member function.

```
m_toolBar.LoadBitmap( IDB_TOOLS );
m_toolBar.SetButtons( arToolButtons,
                      sizeof(arToolButtons)/sizeof(UINT) );
```

The SetButtons function has two parameters: an array of UINT containing the resource ID for each toolbar item and the number of items in the toolbar. The array is exactly like the status bar indicator array used in this chapter's first example.

A toolbar can be given floating and dockable properties in the same way a dialog bar can.

```
m_toolBar.EnableDocking( CBRS_ALIGN_ANY );
```

All of the alignment options used for dialog bars also apply for toolbars. In addition, the following control bar options are usually used only for toolbars:

- CBRS_TOOLTIPS indicates that the control bar displays tool tips when the cursor passes over a toolbar button.
- CBRS_FLYBY indicates that the status bar displays information about a button when it is selected.

Adding a Toolbar Example to the CtrlBar Project

For an example demonstrating how toolbars are used, add a second toolbar to the CtrlBar project. The new toolbar is dockable and handles the following three menu functions:

- Displaying the About dialog box
- Toggling the original toolbar on or off
- Toggling the status bar on or off

Creating a Toolbar Bitmap

Using the Developer Studio image editor, create the bitmap shown in Figure 23.2. The bitmap is 48 pixels wide and 15 pixels high. Use IDB_TOOLS as the bitmap's resource ID.

Figure 23.2.
The IDB_TOOLS bitmap in Developer Studio's image editor.

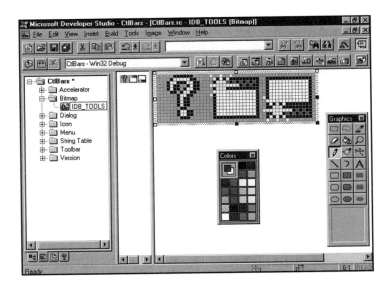

Modifications to the *CMainFrame* Class

The new CToolbar object is a member variable in the CMainFrame class. Add the declaration of m_toolBar to the CMainFrame class declaration, as shown in Listing 23.12, just after the existing declaration of m_dlgBar.

Listing 23.12. Additions to the CMainFrame class declaration.

```
protected:  // control bar embedded members
    CDialogBar  m_dlgBar;
    CToolBar    m_toolBar;
```

Every toolbar is created using an array of UINT that represents the menu ID of every toolbar item. Add the arToolButtons array shown in Listing 23.13 to the MainFrame.cpp source file, just below the other control bar arrays. Note that each array member is a menu ID. The ID_SEPARATOR value is used to create a space between adjacent toolbar items.

Listing 23.13. The resource ID array used by the new toolbar.

```
static UINT BASED_CODE arToolButtons[] =
{
    ID_APP_ABOUT,
        ID_SEPARATOR,
    ID_VIEW_TOOLBAR,
    ID_VIEW_STATUS_BAR,
};
```

Add the source code in Listing 23.14 to the CMainFrame::OnCreate member function. This source code creates a new toolbar using the IDB_TOOLS bitmap and floats the toolbar instead of docking it.

Listing 23.14. Additions to the CMainFrame::OnCreate function.

```
// Create a floating toolbar
m_toolBar.Create( this );
m_toolBar.SetWindowText( "Tools" );
m_toolBar.LoadBitmap( IDB_TOOLS );
m_toolBar.SetButtons( arToolButtons,
                      sizeof(arToolButtons)/sizeof(UINT) );
// Enable docking, even though the toolbar will float initially.
m_toolBar.EnableDocking( CBRS_ALIGN_ANY );
// Calculate the location to float the toolbar.
CRect    rc;
GetClientRect( &rc );
ClientToScreen( &rc );
FloatControlBar( &m_toolBar, rc.TopLeft() );
UINT nOldStyle = m_toolBar.GetBarStyle();
m_toolBar.SetBarStyle(nOldStyle | CBRS_TOOLTIPS | CBRS_FLYBY);
```

Compile and run the CtrlBar sample program. You can use the new toolbar to display or hide the status bar and original toolbar and also to display the CtrlBar About box.

Summary

In this chapter, I discussed control bars and the MFC classes that are used to implement status bars, dialog bars, and toolbars. You also built a small sample program that illustrates how these controls can be used.

List View Controls

List views are extremely flexible controls that were first introduced with Windows 95. In this chapter, I discuss list view controls and how they are used in MFC-based applications. You build a sample program to demonstrate how list view controls are used.

What Is a List View Control?

List views are one of the new common controls first released with Windows 95. A list view control is used to display information and an associated icon in one of four different formats:

- Icon view displays a 32×32 pixel icon next to a list item label.
- Small icon view displays a smaller 16×16 pixel icon next to a list item label.
- List view displays small icons and list items arranged in a row.
- Report view displays items and their associated icons, along with subitems that are arranged in columns.

When you use a list view control, you can provide a menu or other method to enable the user to switch between the different viewing modes.

The Windows Explorer uses a list view control and offers all four view styles. The Explorer is shown in Figure 24.1 with the contents of the C:\ directory contained in a report view.

Figure 24.1.
The Windows Explorer
uses a list view control.

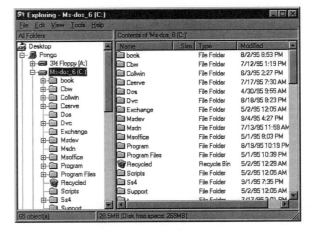

Why Use a List View Control?

Why

List views are very popular with users because they offer several different ways to display information. When you allow the user to switch between view styles, the list view control puts the user in charge of how information is displayed.

List view controls can be used to associate icons with information, as the Explorer does for file names. The user is free to select between different sized icons, or even the report view, which can display extra information about each item. List view controls also support drag-and drop operations similar to the tree view controls discussed in Chapter 21, "Tree Views."

How Is a List View Control Used?

How

As with the tree view controls discussed in Chapter 21, there are two ways to use list view controls in your MFC-based programs. The most common way to use a list view control is to embed it into a dialog box resource, as with any other control. The MFC class CListCtrl is used to interact with list view controls and is associated with a list view control using ClassWizard.

List view controls can also be used in a view. The CListView class is a specialized view that consists of a single list view control, in the same way the CTreeView class uses a CTreeCtrl object. The CListView class is derived from CCtrlView in the same way CTreeView is.

List View Control Properties

The list view control's properties are set using the properties dialog box in the same way other controls are. Some of the properties available for list view controls are also available for list boxes. The list view control property options include the following:

- ID is used for the list view control resource ID. A default resource ID, such as IDC_LIST1, is supplied by Developer Studio.

- Visible is used to indicate that the control is initially visible. This checkbox is usually checked.

- Disabled is used to indicate the list should be initially disabled. This checkbox is usually cleared.

- Group is used to mark the first control in a group. This checkbox is usually cleared.

- Tabstop indicates that this control can be reached by pressing Tab on the keyboard. This checkbox is usually checked.

- Help ID indicates that a context-sensitive help ID should be created for this control. This checkbox is normally cleared.

- View specifies the initial view used by the list view control. Possible values are Icon, Small Icon, List, or Report.

- Align specifies whether the items are aligned to the top or left sides of the control. This property only applies in the icon or small icon views.

- Sort enables items to be sorted based on their labels as they are entered into the list view control.

- Auto arrange specifies that items should be kept arranged when viewed in the icon or small icon views.

- Single selection enables a single list view item to be selected.

- Share image list indicates that image lists used by the list view control might be used by other controls and should not be destroyed automatically by the control.

- No label wrap specifies that each item label must be displayed on a single line, rather than wrapped, as is the standard behavior.

- Edit labels enables labels to be edited by the user. If this property is enabled, you must handle edit notification messages sent by the control.

- Owner draw fixed indicates that the owner of the control has responsibility for drawing the control, instead of Windows. Using owner-drawn controls is discussed in Chapter 39, "Owner-Drawn Controls."

- No scroll disables scrolling.

- No column header removes the header control that is usually included in the report view.

- No sort header disables the sorting function that is available through the header control.

- Border indicates that a border should be drawn around the control.

Associating Image Lists with a List Control

The images displayed in the list view next to each item are stored in image lists that are associated with the list view control. Constructing and managing image lists was discussed in Chapter 20, "Using Image Lists and Bitmaps." An image list is added to a list view control with the SetImageList function.

```
checkedm_listCtrl.SetImageList( &m_imageSmall, LVSIL_SMALL );
```

There are two parameters passed to the list view control: a pointer to the image list and a style parameter that indicates the type of images stored in the image list. There are three image list types:

- LVSIL_NORMAL is used for the image list used in the icon view.
- LVSIL_SMALL is used for the image list used in the small icon view.
- LVSIL_STATE is used for state images, if there are any.

Once the image list control has been added to the list view control, the list view control takes responsibility for destroying the image list.

Adding Items to a List View Control

The LV_ITEM structure is used to represent an item in a list view control. This structure is used when adding, modifying, or fetching list view items. The data members for the LV_ITEM structure include the following:

- mask is used to indicate which members are being used for the current function call. Possible values for this member are given later in this section.
- item contains the index of the item referred to by this structure.
- iSubItem contains the index of the current subitem. A "subitem" is a string that is displayed in a column to the right of an item's icon and label in the report view. All items in a list view have the same number of subitems.
- state and stateMask contain the current state of the item and the valid states of the item.
- pszText contains the address of a string that is used as the item's label. This member must be assigned the LPSTR_TEXTCALLBACK value if a callback function is used to set the item's text.
- cchTextMax specifies the size of the buffer provided in the pszText member if the structure is receiving item attributes. Otherwise, this member is not used.
- iImage contains the image list index for this item.

The LV_ITEM structure's mask member is used to indicate which parts of the structure are valid or should be filled in. It can be one or more of the following values:

- LVIF_TEXT indicates that the pszText member is valid.
- LVIF_IMAGE indicates that the iImage member is valid.

- LVIF_PARAM indicates that the lParam member is valid.
- LVIF_STATE indicates that the state member is valid.

Inserting a List View Item

The InsertItem function is used to add an item to a list view control.

```
m_listItem.InsertItem( &listItem );
```

A pointer to a LV_ITEM structure is passed as the parameter to InsertItem. LV_ITEM data members are filled with data for the new item before it is inserted.

```
listItem.mask = LVIF_TEXT;
listItem.iItem = 0;
listItem.pszText = szText;
m_listCtrl.InsertItem( &listItem );
```

Adding Column Information for the Report View

Unlike the other three list view styles, the report view displays additional information for each item contained in the list. The extra items are subitems that are arranged in columns. Each list view item must have the same number of subitems.

Subitems are added to a list view control in two steps: first the header control is initialized and then the subitems are added. List view columns are inserted using LV_COLUMN structures and the InsertColumn function. The LV_COLUMN structure has the following members:

- mask indicates the member variables that are used for the current function call. Values for the mask member variable are discussed at the end of this section.
- fmt specifies the alignment used for the column. There are three possible values: LVCFMT_LEFT, LVCFMT_RIGHT, and LVCFMT_CENTER. The first column must use the LVCFMT_LEFT value.
- cx specifies the width of the column in pixels.
- pszText points to a string containing the column text. If the structure is used to fetch information, this member holds the address of the buffer that contains the column heading text.
- cchTextMax stores the size of the buffer that is pointed to by pszText. This member is only used when receiving data.
- iSubItem specifies the column number.

The mask member variable is used to specify which member values are valid, in the same way the LV_ITEM structure's mask member variable is used. Possible values include the following:

- LVCF_FMT indicates that the fmt member is valid.
- LVCF_SUBITEM indicates that the iSubItem member is valid.
- LVCF_TEXT indicates that the pszText member is valid.
- LVCF_WIDTH indicates that the cx member is valid.

After you fill in the values for a LV_COLUMN structure, the column is added to the list view control using the InsertColumn function.

```
m_listCtrl.InsertColumn( nColumn, &listColumn );
```

Changing the Current View for a List View Control

Switching views in a list view control requires just a few lines of code. The current view style is stored in a structure maintained by Windows. This information can be retrieved using the GetWindowLong function.

```
DWORD dwOldStyle = GetWindowLong( hWndList, GWL_STYLE );
```

The GetWindowLong function has two parameters:

- A window handle to the image list control
- A GWL constant that specifies the type of information requested—in this case, GWL_STYLE

The return value from GetWindowLong contains all of the Windows style information for the image list. If you are interested in the current view, the unnecessary information should be masked off using LVS_TYPEMASK.

```
dwOldStyle &= ~LVS_TYPEMASK; // Mask off extra style info
```

After the mask has been applied, the style information is one of the following values:

- LVS_ICON
- LVS_SMALLICON
- LVS_LIST
- LVS_REPORT

To change to another view, you use the SetWindowLong function. When applying a new list view style, you must make sure that the style bits that are not associated with the list view style are left undisturbed. This is usually done in four steps:

1. Get the existing window style bit information using GetWindowLong.
2. Strip off the list view style information, leaving the other style information intact.
3. Combine a new list view style with the old style information.
4. Apply the new style information using SetWindowLong.

These steps are often combined into a few lines of code in the following way:

```
DWORD dwNewStyle = LVS_ICON;
DWORD dwOldStyle = GetWindowLong( hWndList, GWL_STYLE );
dwNewStyle |= ( dwOldStyle &= ~LVS_TYPEMASK );
SetWindowLong( hWndList, GWL_STYLE, dwNewStyle );
```

Essential Example

A List View Control Example

As an example of how list view controls are used, create a dialog box-based application. This program displays a list view control containing three items. You can use radio buttons to switch between the different view styles.

Use AppWizard to create a dialog box-based application named ListEx. Feel free to accept any of the options offered by AppWizard; this example works with any AppWizard parameters.

Adding Controls to the ListEx Dialog Box

You must add a total of five controls to the ListEx main dialog box: four radio buttons and one list view control. Add the controls to the dialog box as shown in Figure 24.2.

Figure 24.2.
The ListEx main dialog box in the dialog editor.

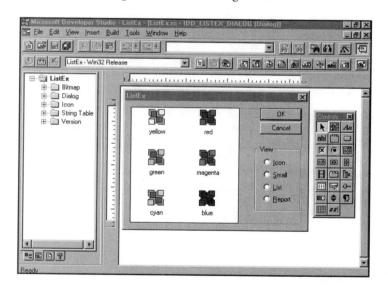

Properties for the list view and radio button controls are listed in Table 24.1. All properties that aren't listed should be set to the default values.

Table 24.1. Property values for controls in the ListEx main dialog box.

Control	Resource ID	Caption
Icon view radio	IDC_RADIO_ICON	&Icon
Small radio	IDC_RADIO_SMALL	&Small
List radio	IDC_RADIO_LIST	&List
Report radio	IDC_RADIO_REPORT	&Report
List view control	IDC_LIST	none

Use ClassWizard to associate a CListCtrl member variable with IDC_LIST, using the values from Table 24.2.

Table 24.2. Values for a new CListCtrl member variable in CListExDlg.

Control ID	Variable Name	Category	Type
IDC_LIST	m_listCtrl	Control	CListCtrl

Next, use ClassWizard to create message-handling functions that are called when the radio buttons are selected. Add a total of four member functions to the CListExDlg class, using the values from Table 24.3.

Table 24.3. Values for a new CListCtrl member variable in CListExDlg.

Object ID	Class Name	Message	Function
IDC_RADIO_ICON	CListExDlg	BN_CLICKED	OnRadioIcon
IDC_RADIO_SMALL	CListExDlg	BN_CLICKED	OnRadioSmall
IDC_RADIO_LIST	CListExDlg	BN_CLICKED	OnRadioList
IDC_RADIO_REPORT	CListExDlg	BN_CLICKED	OnRadioReport

Creating the Image Lists

You must create two bitmaps for the ListEx application. One bitmap is used for the large icon bitmap and one for the small icon bitmap. The two bitmaps are shown in Figure 24.3. Each of the bitmaps contains two balls of the same size, and each ball is a different color.

Figure 24.3.
*Bitmaps used for the
ListEx image lists.*

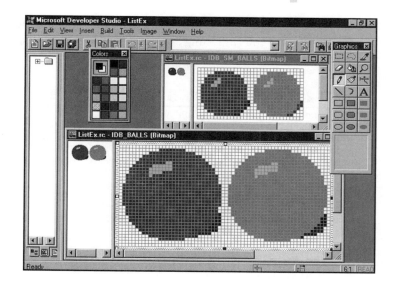

The properties for the two bitmaps are provided in Table 24.4.

Table 24.4. Properties for the ListEx image list bitmaps.

Resource ID	Width	Height	Background
IDB_BALLS	64	32	White
IDB_SM_BALLS	32	16	White

Modifications to the *CListExDlg* Class

The CListExDlg class must have two small modifications made to its class declaration:

- You must add two CImageList member variables for the list view control.
- You must add a SetListView member function. This function handles switching between different list view styles.

Add the source code provided in Listing 24.1 to the implementation section of the CListExDlg class declaration.

Listing 24.1. Changes to the CListExDlg class declaration.

```
// Implementation
protected:
    void SetListView( DWORD dwView );
    CImageList  m_imageLarge;
    CImageList  m_imageSmall;
```

The CListExDlg::OnInitDialog member function is called when the main dialog box is initialized. Add the source code in Listing 24.2 to the OnInitDialog function, just after the // TODO comment provided by AppWizard.

Listing 24.2. Changes to the CListExDlg class implementation.

```
// TODO: Add extra initialization here
    m_imageLarge.Create( IDB_BALLS, 32, 1, RGB(255,255,255) );
    m_imageSmall.Create( IDB_SM_BALLS, 16, 1, RGB(255,255,255) );
    m_listCtrl.SetImageList( &m_imageLarge, LVSIL_NORMAL );
    m_listCtrl.SetImageList( &m_imageSmall, LVSIL_SMALL );
    // Create list view columns
    LV_COLUMN    listColumn;
    LV_ITEM      listItem;
    char*        arColumns[3] = { "City", "Football", "Baseball" };
    listColumn.mask = LVCF_FMT|LVCF_WIDTH|LVCF_TEXT|LVCF_SUBITEM;
    listColumn.fmt = LVCFMT_LEFT;
    listColumn.cx = 60;
    for( int nColumn = 0; nColumn < 3; nColumn++ )
    {
        listColumn.iSubItem = nColumn;
        listColumn.pszText = arColumns[nColumn];
        m_listCtrl.InsertColumn( nColumn, &listColumn );
    }
    // Add list items
    listItem.mask = LVIF_TEXT | LVIF_IMAGE;
    listItem.iSubItem = 0;
    char* arCity[3]     = { "Oakland", "San Diego", "Seattle" };
    char* arFootball[3] = { "Raiders", "Chargers", "Seahawks" };
    char* arBaseball[3] = { "Athletics", "Padres", "Mariners" };
    for( int nItem = 0; nItem < 3; nItem++ )
    {
        listItem.iItem = nItem;
        listItem.pszText = arCity[nItem];
        listItem.iImage = nItem % 2;
        m_listCtrl.InsertItem( &listItem );
        m_listCtrl.SetItemText( nItem, 1, arFootball[nItem] );
        m_listCtrl.SetItemText( nItem, 2, arBaseball[nItem] );
    }
```

The source code provided in Listing 24.1 creates two image lists for the list view control and then creates the list view's column headers. After the columns are created, the three list items are inserted into the list view. The SetItemText function is used to add subitem text strings to each list item—in this case, the name of the professional football and baseball teams for each city.

Switching Between View Styles

The source code provided in Listing 24.3 is used to switch between list view styles. When a radio button is selected, its message-handling function is called. Each message-handling function passes a different list view style parameter to the SetListView member function. The SetListView function uses the SetWindowLong function to change the list view to the selected style.

Listing 24.3. Functions used to change the control's view style.

```
void CListExDlg::OnRadioIcon()
{
    SetListView( LVS_ICON );
}
void CListExDlg::OnRadioList()
{
    SetListView( LVS_LIST );
}
void CListExDlg::OnRadioReport()
{
    SetListView( LVS_REPORT );
}
void CListExDlg::OnRadioSmall()
{
    SetListView( LVS_SMALLICON );
}
void CListExDlg::SetListView( DWORD dwNewStyle )
{
    DWORD    dwOldStyle;
    HWND     hWndList;

    hWndList = m_listCtrl.GetSafeHwnd();

    dwOldStyle = GetWindowLong( hWndList, GWL_STYLE );

    if( (dwOldStyle & LVS_TYPEMASK) != dwNewStyle )
    {
        // Don't forget the tilde before LVS_TYPEMASK !
        dwOldStyle &= ~LVS_TYPEMASK;
        dwNewStyle |= dwOldStyle;
        SetWindowLong( hWndList, GWL_STYLE, dwNewStyle );
    }
}
```

Compile and run the ListEx sample program. The list view initially displays its contents in the icon view. Try using the radio buttons to switch between views. When the report view is displayed, use the header control to change the spacing between columns.

Summary

In this chapter, I examined the list view control and how it is used in an MFC-based program. I also discussed how this control interacts with image lists and header controls, and you built a sample application to demonstrate how a list view control is used.

Document/View Architecture

In this chapter I cover Document/View, the architecture used for programs written using AppWizard and the MFC class library. I discuss the classes used to implement Document/View, and I build a sample project that demonstrates how a view and a document interact with each other.

What Is Document/View?

What As I discussed in Chapter 13, "Using Visual C++ for Windows Programming," the Document/View architecture is used by MFC and AppWizard to organize programs written for Windows. Document/View separates the program into four main classes:

- A document class derived from CDocument
- A view class derived from CView
- A frame class derived from CFrameWnd
- An application class derived from CWinApp

Each of these classes has a specific role to play in an MFC Document/View application. The document class is responsible for the program's data. The view class handles interaction between the document and the user. The frame class contains the view and other user interface elements, such as the menu and toolbars. The application class is responsible for actually starting the program, and handling some general purpose interaction with Windows. Figure 25.1 shows the four main parts of a Document/View program.

Figure 25.1.
The document/view
architecture.

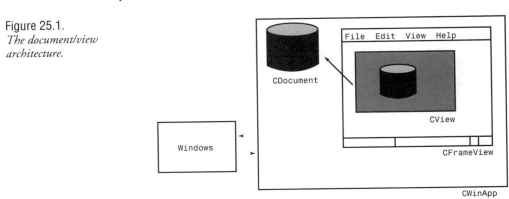

Although the name "Document/View" might seem to limit you to only word-processing applications, the architecture can be used in a wide variety of program types. There is no limitation as to the data managed by CDocument; it can be a word-processing file, a spreadsheet, or a server at the other end of a network connection providing information to your program. Likewise, there are many types of views. A view can be a simple window, as used in the simple SDI applications I've presented so far, or it can be derived from CFormView, with all the capabilities of a dialog box. I cover form views in Chapter 26, "Using Form Views."

SDI and MDI Applications

There are two basic types of Document/View programs:

- SDI, or Single Document Interface
- MDI, or Multiple Document Interface

I've used SDI applications for small examples previously, such as the ImageList example in Chapter 20. An SDI program supports a single type of document, and almost always supports only a single view. Only one document can be open at a time. An SDI application focuses on a particular task, and is normally fairly straightforward.

Several different types of documents can be used in an MDI program, with each document having one or more views. Several documents can be open at a time, and the open document often uses a customized toolbar and menus that fit the needs of that particular document.

Why Use Document/View?

Why

The first reason to use Document/View is that it provides a large amount of application code for free. You should always try to write as little new source code as possible, and that means using MFC classes and letting AppWizard and ClassWizard do a lot of the work for you. A large amount of the code that is written for you in the form of MFC classes and AppWizard code uses the Document/View architecture.

The Document/View architecture defines several main categories for classes used in a Windows program. Document/View provides a flexible framework that you can use to create almost any type of Windows program. One of the big advantages of the Document/View architecture is that it divides up the work in a Windows program into well-defined categories. Most classes fall into one of the four main class categories:

- Controls and other user-interface elements related to a specific view
- Data and data-handling classes, which belong to a document
- Work that involves handling the toolbar, status bar, and menus, usually belonging to the frame class
- Interaction between the application and Windows occurring in the class derived from `CWinApp`

Dividing work done by your program helps you to manage the design of your program more effectively. Extending programs that use the Document/View architecture is fairly simple, because the four main Document/View classes communicate with each other through well-defined interfaces. For example, to change an SDI program to an MDI program, you must write little new code. Changing the user interface for a Document/View program impacts only the view class, or classes; no changes are needed for the document, frame, or application classes.

How Is Document/View Used?

How

Developer Studio provides all the tools you need to create a Document/View application. The basic tools to create and maintain a Document/View program are AppWizard and ClassWizard. Use AppWizard to create the initial project for an SDI or MDI program. Use ClassWizard to add classes, handle messages, and add variables to classes that are included in a project.

Using AppWizard

Use AppWizard to create SDI and MDI applications. In earlier chapters I used AppWizard to create the SDI programs I used as examples. Although it is more complicated, you can create an MDI application almost as easily as an SDI using AppWizard.

The basic difference in an SDI application and an MDI application is that an MDI application must manage multiple documents and, usually, multiple views; the SDI application uses only a single document, and normally only a single view.

Both SDI and MDI applications use an object called a document template to create a relationship between a view, a document, and a frame class, as well as an identifier used for the program's menu, icon, and other resources. The CSingleDocTemplate class is used for SDI applications, and the CMultiDocTemplate class is used for MDI applications. These two classes share a common base class, CDocTemplate. Listing 25.1 is an example of a document template used for an SDI program.

Listing 25.1. How AppWizard uses a document template in an SDI application.

```
CSingleDocTemplate* pDocTemplate;
pDocTemplate = new CSingleDocTemplate( IDR_MAINFRAME,
                               RUNTIME_CLASS(CTestDoc),
                               RUNTIME_CLASS(CMainFrame),
                               RUNTIME_CLASS(CTestView));

AddDocTemplate(pDocTemplate);
```

In an MDI program, there are two types of frame windows: the main frame, which encompasses the entire client area, and the child frame, which contains each MDI child window. The different windows used in an MDI program are shown in Figure 25.2.

Figure 25.2.
The windows used in a typical MDI program.

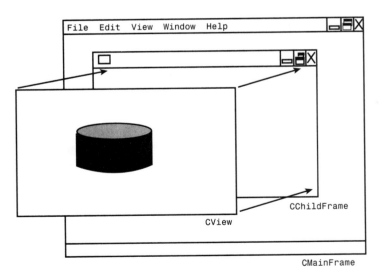

The C++ source code generated by Developer Studio for an MDI program is slightly different than the code it generates for an SDI program. Examining this code, shown in Listing 25.2, shows some of the differences between MDI objects and SDI objects.

Listing 25.2. AppWizard code that uses a document template in an MDI application.

```
CMultiDocTemplate* pDocTemplate;
pDocTemplate = new CMultiDocTemplate( IDR_TESTTYPE,
                                RUNTIME_CLASS(CTestDoc),
                                RUNTIME_CLASS(CChildFrame),
                                RUNTIME_CLASS(CTestView));
AddDocTemplate(pDocTemplate);
```

CChildFrame is a class included in every MDI project created by AppWizard, and is derived from CMDIChildFrame. The reason this class is provided is to make it easy to customize the frame to suit your needs. Every MDI child window has a frame, which owns the minimize, maximize, and close buttons and the frame around the view. Any customization you want to do to the frame is done in the CChildFrame class.

Using ClassWizard

I've used ClassWizard in previous chapters to add member variables to dialog box classes, add new classes to a project, and handle messages sent to view windows and dialog boxes. ClassWizard is also used to add interfaces defined as part of the Document/View architecture. In most cases, default behavior provided by the MFC framework is enough for simple programs.

I detail the interfaces used by the document and view classes in the next section. However, almost all of these interfaces are added using ClassWizard. Let's look at one of these interfaces, GetFirstViewPosition. A document can obtain a pointer to the first view associated with the document using this function. Normally, the framework will maintain a list of the views associated with a document, but you can keep this list yourself by overriding this function. Because the GetFirstViewPosition function is virtual, your implementation of it always is called if available.

To add an implementation for one of the Document/View interface functions, follow these steps, which are similar to the steps used to add message handling functions:

1. Open ClassWizard.
2. Select the name of the class that supplies the interface to be added; in this case, a class derived from CDocument.
3. Select the tab labeled "Message Maps."
4. Select the CDocument-derived class as the object ID.
5. Select the interface function to be added from the list box.
6. Press the button labeled "Add Function."
7. Close ClassWizard.

You can use ClassWizard to override all of the interfaces defined for programs using the Document/View architecture. Interfaces such as GetFirstViewPosition are rarely overridden, except when debugging. If you provide a new version of GetFirstViewPosition, you probably should override the related function `GetNextView` as well. I discuss the most commonly used Document/View interfaces in the next section.

What Are the Document/View Interfaces?

What The most commonly used interfaces in a Document/View program handle communication between the document and view objects, and between Windows and the document and view objects. I discuss the major interfaces in this section; others are discussed in later chapters. For example, I present interfaces related to printing in Chapter 35, "Printing."

Each of these interfaces has a particular purpose. Some are always overridden in the classes you include in your project; many are only overridden when needed. These are three of the major interfaces used in a Document/View program:

- `GetDocument`, a `CView` member function used to retrieve a pointer to its document
- `UpdateAllViews`, a `CDocument` member function used to update views associated with a document
- `OnNewDocument`, a `CDocument` member function that is used to initialize the document's member data

Remember, this list is just an overview of the major interfaces. The list does not cover all of the interfaces required in an SDI or MDI program. Your mileage may vary; after using the Document/View architecture for a while, you may have another set of favorite interfaces.

Why Use the Document/View Interfaces?

Why The interfaces defined by the Document/View architecture represent guarantees about how each of the MFC classes that make up an application behave with regard to each other. For example, the MFC framework always calls the `CDocument::OnNewDocument` function when a new document is created. The MFC framework, and other classes that may be part of an MFC-based program, expect the new document to be initialized after this function has been called.

Using well-defined interfaces like `CDocument::OnNewDocument` to perform specific tasks enables you to modify only the functions where you need to take special action; you can let the MFC framework handle most functions and interfaces if you want the default behavior.

The Document/View architecture also makes it easy to separate work. For example, data belongs only to the document; a view calls the `GetDocument` function to collect a document pointer, then uses member functions to collect or update data.

How Are the Document/View Interfaces Used?

Each of the interfaces I discussed earlier has a specific role. For the remaining examples in this chapter, I use an MDI program named DVTest to demonstrate how you can use each of these interfaces.

To create the DVTest example, use AppWizard to create a default MDI program. Name the program DVTest. Feel free to accept or change any of the default parameters offered by AppWizard, as they have no impact on these examples. When finished, DVTest displays a collection of names stored by the document class.

Creating a Data Model

As a first step, add a `CArray` template object to the document class, as a private data member. Add the source code from Listing 25.3 to the `CDVTestDoc` class header, found in the DVTestDoc.h file. Add the source code to the attributes section of the class declaration, which begins with the `// Attributes` comment generated by AppWizard.

Listing 25.3. Changes to the `CDVTestDoc` class declaration.

```
// Attributes
public:
    CString GetName( int nIndex ) const;
    int     AddName( const CString& szName );
    int     GetCount() const;

private:
    CArray<CString, CString>    m_arNames;
```

Since the `CDVTestDoc` class contains a `CArray` member variable, the template collection declarations must be included into the project. Add an `#include` statement to the bottom of the StdAfx.h file.

```
#include "afxtempl.h"
```

The next step is to implement the functions described in the `CDVTestDoc` class interface. These functions provide access to the data stored in the document. Add the source code in Listing 25.4 to the DVTestDoc.cpp file.

Listing 25.4. New functions added to the `CDVTestDoc` class.

```
CString CDVTestDoc::GetName( int nIndex ) const
{
    ASSERT( nIndex < m_arNames.GetSize() );
    return m_arNames[nIndex];
```

continues

Listing 25.4. continued

```
}

int CDVTestDoc::AddName( const CString& szName )
{
    return m_arNames.Add( szName );
}

int CDVTestDoc::GetCount() const
{
    return m_arNames.GetSize();
}
```

Every document class must specify some access functions to add and retrieve data. The three functions in Listing 25.4 are typical access functions in that they do not just expose the CArray template. The data could also be stored in another type of collection. Storing the data in a CArray object is an implementation detail that should not be of interest to users of the CDVTestDoc class. This allows the internal implementation of CDVTestDoc to be changed in the future, if necessary.

Initializing a Document's Contents

You create and initialize document objects in two different ways, depending on the type of application using the document:

- A new MDI document object is created for every new document opened by the program.
- SDI programs create a single document object, which is reinitialized each time a new document is opened.

In most cases, the best place to perform any initialization is in the CDocument::OnNewDocument member function. This function is provided with some default code inserted by AppWizard. Edit the OnNewDocument function so it looks like the code provided in Listing 25.5.

Listing 25.5. Changes to the CDVTestDoc::OnNewDocument member function.

```
BOOL CDVTestDoc::OnNewDocument()
{
    TRACE( "CDVTest::OnNewDocument" );
    if (!CDocument::OnNewDocument())
        return FALSE;

    m_arNames.RemoveAll();
    m_arNames.Add( "Curly" );
    m_arNames.Add( "Moe" );
    m_arNames.Add( "Shemp" );
    return TRUE;
}
```

Listing 25.5 clears the contents of the m_arNames collection and adds three new names. The TRACE macro sends an output message to the compiler's debug window, which displays useful information as the program executes.

Getting the Document Pointer

Every view is associated with one, and only one, document. When a view must communicate with its associated document, the GetDocument function is used. If the view is created by AppWizard, as CDVTestView is, the GetDocument function returns a pointer to the proper document type. Listing 25.6 is a version of OnDraw that uses GetDocument to retrieve a pointer to the CDVTestDoc class, then uses the pointer to collect the names contained in the document.

Listing 25.6. Using GetDocument to fetch the document pointer.

```
void CDVTestView::OnDraw(CDC* pDC)
{
    CDVTestDoc* pDoc = GetDocument();
    ASSERT_VALID(pDoc);

    // Calculate the space required for a single
    // line of text, including the inter-line area.
    TEXTMETRIC  tm;
    pDC->GetTextMetrics( &tm );
    int nLineHeight = tm.tmHeight + tm.tmExternalLeading;

    CPoint  ptText( 0, 0 );
    for( int nIndex = 0; nIndex < pDoc->GetCount(); nIndex++ )
    {
        CString szName = pDoc->GetName( nIndex );
        pDC->TextOut( ptText.x, ptText.y, szName );
        ptText.y += nLineHeight;
    }
}
```

There are three main parts to Listing 25.6:

- In the first part, the document pointer is retrieved using GetDocument. The pointer value is validated using the ASSERT_VALID macro. You should always use this macro after an old-style cast to ensure that the pointer is accurate.

- In second part, the size of a line of text is calculated using the CDC::GetTextMetrics function. This function fills the TEXTMETRICS structure with information about the current font used by the device context. The tmHeight member is the maximum height of a character, and the tmExternalLeading member is the spacing between character lines. Adding these two values together results in a good spacing value between displayed rows of text.

- Finally, the third part collects each name in turn from the document, using the functions added earlier to the document class. After each line of text is displayed, the ptText.x value is increased by the line spacing value calculated earlier.

Summary

In this chapter I've discussed the basic Document/View architecture used in most MFC programs. I covered using the AppWizard and ClassWizard and created a sample program demonstrating the use of Document/View.

Using Form Views

In this chapter I cover form views, which are a convenient way to use controls in your views. I create a form view and use it to insert and retrieve data from a document.

What Is a Form View?

What A form view is a view that can contain controls, just like a dialog box. You normally add controls to a form view using a dialog resource, the same way you build dialog boxes. However, unlike dialog boxes, a form view is never modal; in fact, several form views may be open simultaneously, just like other views.

The CFormView class is just one of the view classes included in the MFC class library. Figure 26.1 presents a class diagram showing the classes derived from CView.

Figure 26.1.
The MFC view classes.

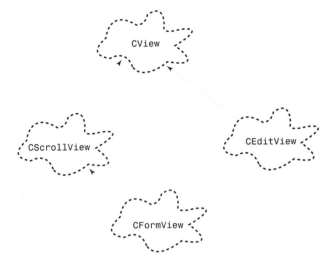

Each view class shown in Figure 26.1 has a specific purpose. Because form view classes are so versatile and easy to use, I'll concentrate on them for many of the examples in this book. However, I also discuss the other types of views from time to time, such as scroll and edit views.

What Are the Other Types of Views?

What A *scroll view* is a view that can be larger than its visible area. The invisible part of the view can be made visible using scroll bars associated with the view. An easy way to visualize how scrolling works is to imagine a large virtual view, hidden except for a small window used as a viewport, as shown in Figure 26.2.

Figure 26.2.
Scrolling a view using
`CScrollView.`

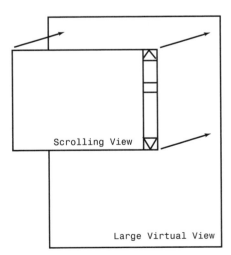

Only a portion of the entire view is visible in Figure 26.2. The view window "scrolls" in order to move to a different part of the document; the underlying large view retains its original position. Although you can implement scrolling yourself for any class derived from CView, much of the work is done for you if you use CScrollView. I discuss scrolling in more detail in Chapter 28, "Split Views."

Use the edit view to create a view that consists of an edit control. The edit view automatically supports printing, using the clipboard cut, paste, and copy functions, and Find and Replace. The edit view is supported by the CEditView class, so it can be associated with a document just like any other view.

The edit view does not support true what-you-see-is-what-you-get (WYSIWYG) editing; only one font is supported for the entire view, and the display is not always 100 percent accurate with regard to a printed page. For more sophisticated editing, you can use an RTF control, as I discuss in Chapter 37, "Rich Edit Controls."

Why Use a Form View?

Why

The most common reason to use a form view is that it's an easy-to-use view that looks like a dialog box. With practice, you can create a form view in a few minutes. You can add controls used in a form view to the form view's dialog resource, just as you add controls to a resource used by a normal dialog box. After you add the controls, you can associate them with MFC objects and class member variables, just as you associate controls with dialog boxes.

Using form views enables you to easily adapt the DDX and DDV routines used by dialog boxes to a view. Unlike a modal dialog box, several different form views can be open at once, making your program much more flexible. Like other views, a form view has access to all of the Document/View interfaces, giving it direct access to the document class.

It's common for a form view to be one of several possible views for a document. In an MDI application, it's common to have more than one view for each document type. For example, a form view can be used as a data entry view, and another type of view can be used for display purposes.

How Is a Form View Used?

How

Using a form view requires only a few more steps than using a dialog box. All of the hard work is handled by the framework and the MFC CFormView class. Using ClassWizard, you can add a form view to a project using 30 or 40 lines of your own code.

Adding a Form View to the DVTest Project

To illustrate how form views are used, add a form view to a project that was built using AppWizard. To reduce the amount of code that must be entered, you can reuse the DVTest project built in Chapter 25, "Document/View Architecture."

To recap, the DVTest project stored a collection of names in its document class. In this chapter, I associate a form view with the document, and use it to display and input names into the program. For now, the form view is the only view associated with the document; I discuss multiple views in the next chapter.

Creating a Dialog Resource for a Form View

Although a form view uses a dialog resource to lay out its controls, a form view isn't really a dialog box; rather, a form view uses the dialog resource as a template when the view is created. For this reason, the CFormView class has special requirements for the dialog resources it uses. Use the properties shown in Table 26.1 for dialog resources used for form views.

Table 26.1. Properties for dialog resources used by form views.

Property	Value
Style	Child
Border	None
Visible	Unchecked
Titlebar	Unchecked

Other than the values listed in Table 26.1, there are no other limitations for dialog box properties or controls. Any controls you can add to a dialog box can be used in a form view. As an example, add a dialog resource to the DVTest project. This dialog resource will be used in a form view, as shown in Figure 26.3.

Figure 26.3.
The dialog resource used as a form view in the CDVTest sample project.

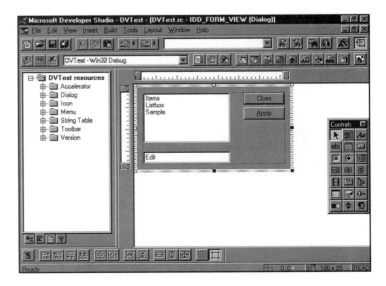

Set the dialog resource and control resource IDs as listed in Table 26.2. The list box should not be automatically sorted by Windows for this example, so clear the Sort attribute for the list box control. Use default properties for all other controls.

Table 26.2. Properties for the CDVTest form view dialog resource.

Property	ID
Dialog	IDD_FORM_VIEW
Edit Control	IDC_EDIT
List Control	IDC_LIST
Close Button	IDC_CLOSE
Apply Button	IDC_APPLY

Adding a Form View Class to a Project

Use ClassWizard to add a form view class to a project, much as you would add a dialog box class to a project. After creating the dialog resource, add the form view class using the following steps:

1. Open ClassWizard. Because ClassWizard knows that a new resource has been added, a dialog box prompts you to choose between three options for the new dialog resource. Select the option labeled "Create a new class."
2. Fill in the Add Class dialog box, using the values from Table 26.3, then press the button labeled "Create."

Table 26.3. Sample values for the Add Class dialog box.

Control	Value
Name	CFormTest
Base Class	CFormView
File	FormTest.cpp
Dialog ID	IDD_FORM_VIEW
OLE Automation	None
Component Gallery	Cleared

Use ClassWizard to add two member variables to the CFormTest class, as shown in Table 26.4.

Table 26.4. Control variables added to the `CFormTest` class.

Control ID	Control Type	Variable Type	Variable Name
IDC_LIST	Control	CListCtrl	m_lbNames
IDC_EDIT	Control	CEdit	m_edNames

Using *CFormView* Instead of *CView*

Because `CFormView` is a subclass derived from `CView`, you can substitute it for `CView` in most cases. As I discussed in Chapter 25, a document class is associated with a view class using a `CMultiDocTemplate` object in MDI programs. The view associated with a particular document can be changed by editing the parameters used when the `CMultiDocTemplate` object is constructed.

Listing 26.1 associates the `CFormTest` view class with the `CDVTestDoc` document class. Update the code that creates the document template in the `CDVTestApp::InitInstance` function, found in the CDVTestView.cpp source file. You have to change only the fourth parameter to the constructor, as shown by the comment.

Listing 26.1. Constructing a `CMultiDocTemplate` object that associates `CDVTestDoc` and `CFormTest`.

```
CMultiDocTemplate* pDocTemplate;
    pDocTemplate = new CMultiDocTemplate(
        IDR_FORMVITYPE,
        RUNTIME_CLASS(CDVTestDoc),
        RUNTIME_CLASS(CChildFrame),
        RUNTIME_CLASS(CFormTest));   // Change this line
    AddDocTemplate(pDocTemplate);
```

Because `CFormTest` is now used, the class declaration for `CFormTest` must be included into the DVTest.cpp source file. Add the following line after all other `#include` directives at the top of the DVTest.cpp source file:

```
#include "FormTest.h"
```

Handling Events and Messages in the Form View Class

A form view must handle a wide variety of messages. Just like any view, it must support a number of interfaces as part of the Document/View architecture. However, unlike other views, a form view must also handle any controls contained by the view.

For example, there are two events generated by controls that must be handled in the `CFormTest` class:

- When the button labeled "Apply" is pressed, the view should update the document and prepare for a new entry.
- When the button labeled "Close" is pressed, the view should be closed.

Use ClassWizard to add two message handling functions for these events, using the values from Table 26.5.

Table 26.5. Message-handling events added to the CFormTest class.

Control ID	Message	Function Name
IDC_APPLY	BN_CLICKED	OnApply
IDC_CLOSE	BN_CLICKED	OnClose

The code to handle control events is fairly straightforward. Edit the new functions added to the CFormTest class so that they look like the code in Listing 26.2.

Listing 26.2. CFormTest functions used to handle control messages.

```
void CFormTest::OnApply()
{
    CDVTestDoc* pDoc;
    pDoc = (CDVTestDoc*)GetDocument();
    ASSERT_VALID( pDoc );

    CString szName;
    m_edNames.GetWindowText( szName );
    m_edNames.SetWindowText( "" );
    m_edNames.SetFocus();

    if( szName.GetLength() > 0 )
    {
        int nIndex = pDoc->AddName( szName );
        m_lbNames.InsertString( nIndex, szName );
        m_lbNames.SetCurSel( nIndex );
    }
}

void CFormTest::OnClose()
{
    PostMessage( WM_COMMAND, ID_FILE_CLOSE );
}
```

You must manually add an #include statement for the document class. At the top of the FormView.cpp file, add the following line just after all the other #include directives:

```
#include "DVTestDoc.h"
```

The OnApply function is split into three main parts:

- The document pointer is retrieved and verified, as in the OnDraw function discussed in Chapter 25.
- The contents of the edit control are collected and stored in a CString object. After the string is collected, the control is cleared, and the input focus is returned to the edit control. This allows a new entry to be made immediately by the user.
- If a string was entered, szName will have a length greater than zero. If so, the name is added to the document and the list box is updated. The SetCurSel function is used to scroll to the new list box item.

The OnClose member function uses the PostMessage function to send an ID_FILE_CLOSE message to the application. This has the same effect as selecting Close from the File menu.

Handling *OnInitialUpdate*

When using a form view, update it during OnInitialUpdate, as the view is initially displayed. In Chapter 25, CDVTestView used OnDraw to retrieve the document's contents and display the items in the view. The OnInitialUpdate function uses code that is similar, as shown in Listing 26.3. Before editing the code, add the OnInitialUpdate function to the CFormTest class using ClassWizard.

Listing 26.3 Using OnInitialUpdate to retrieve data from the document.

```
void CFormTest::OnInitialUpdate()
{
    CFormView::OnInitialUpdate();

    CDVTestDoc* pDoc = (CDVTestDoc*)GetDocument();
    ASSERT_VALID(pDoc);

    for( int nIndex = 0; nIndex < pDoc->GetCount(); nIndex++ )
    {
        CString szName = pDoc->GetName( nIndex );
        m_lbNames.AddString( szName );
    }
}
```

Sizing a Form View to a Dialog Resource

When a dialog box is displayed, the dialog resource is used to size the dialog box's window. A form view is not automatically sized this way, which leads to an unexpected display if you aren't aware of this behavior. However, you can resize the view to the exact dimensions of the dialog resource by using the ResizeParentToFit function. Add the following two lines of code to the CFormTest::OnInitialUpdate member function:

```
ResizeParentToFit( FALSE );
ResizeParentToFit();
```

Nope, it's not a typo; you must call `ResizeParentToFit` twice to make sure that the size is calculated correctly. The first call allows the view to expand, while the second call shrinks the view to fit the dialog resource.

Preventing a View Class from Being Resized

Like all views, you can resize a form view in three ways:

- By dragging the view's frame with the mouse
- By pressing the minimize icon
- By pressing the maximize icon

Although the minimize button is handy, the other sizing methods are a problem for form views. Because a form view looks like a dialog box, and the control layout is specified in the dialog resource, it's a good idea to prevent resizing by a user.

The form view class doesn't actually have any control over the minimize and maximize buttons—they belong to the frame, which also controls the ability to change the size of the view by dragging it with a mouse. The `CChildFrame` class is the frame used by default in MDI applications, although you can change the frame class by using a different class name when the document template is created.

To remove the sizable frame and minimize button from the frame class, add two lines of code to the frame class `PreCreateWindow` member function. The `PreCreateWindow` function is called just before the window is created. This enables you to change the style of the window, as shown in Listing 26.4.

Listing 26.4. Using the `PreCreateWindow` function to change `CChildFrame` style attributes.

```
BOOL CChildFrame::PreCreateWindow(CREATESTRUCT& cs)
{
    // Mask away the thickframe and maximize button style bits.
    cs.style &= ~WS_THICKFRAME;
    cs.style &= ~WS_MAXIMIZEBOX;
    return CMDIChildWnd::PreCreateWindow(cs);
}
```

The &= operator is the C++ bitwise and operator, and is used to clear or remove a bit that is set in a particular value. The tilde (~) is the C++ inversion operator, used to "flip" the individual bits of a particular value. These two operators are commonly used together to mask off attributes that have been set using the bitwise or operator. In Listing 26.4, the WS_THICKFRAME and WS_MAXIMIZEBOX attributes are cleared from the cs.style variable.

Summary

In this chapter I discussed using form views in place of dialog boxes or standard views. Form views enable you to easily use controls in a view, just as they are used in dialog boxes. I also modified the DVTest project built in Chapter 25 to use a form view.

Multiple Views

In this chapter I discuss offering more than one view for a single document. Associating a second view with a document enables you to present the data contained in a document in another way. In this chapter, you modify the DVTest project from the previous chapter by adding a second view that lists all the names found in the document's database.

What Are Multiple Views?

What Programs written for Windows sometimes offer multiple views for their data. For example, many word processors offer print preview and layout views of a document, in addition to the normal WYSIWYG view that's used most of the time. Providing multiple views for a single document is a different issue from allowing several different documents to be open at the same time; each view actually is connected to a single document, as shown in Figure 27.1.

Figure 27.1.
Multiple views
connected to a single
document in an MDI
application.

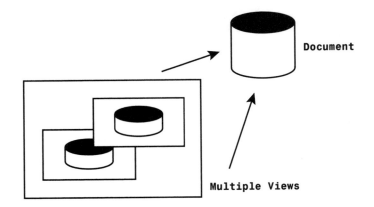

Because each of these views is connected to a single document, there must be some way to update the views when needed to keep them synchronized. When one of the views changes the document, all views must immediately be updated.

Why Use Multiple Views?

Why The most common reason to use multiple views is that there are different ways of looking at information contained in a document. For example, a form view often is used to give detailed information about a particular item in a database; another view might be used for data entry; still another type of view might be used to provide a summary of all items in the same database. Offering several views at the same time provides maximum flexibility for users of the program.

Using multiple views allows each view to be specialized for a particular purpose. If only a single view were allowed, that view would have to be extremely flexible to suit the needs of every user of your program. Creating specialized views for particular purposes allows each of these views to do a single job for which it is well suited.

How Are Multiple Views Used?

How Using multiple views in an MDI application is easy because the Document/View architecture keeps the document and view classes separate from each other. The document class is mainly passive; it notifies the framework when views should be updated, but otherwise relies on the view classes to change or request data stored in the document.

A new view is easily associated with an existing document. Once a document class has been modified to work with multiple views, any number of view classes can be added to the program without further modifications to the document class. Here are the steps required to modify an MDI program to use multiple views:

■ Create a new view class, in addition to any existing view associated with the document.

- Create shared resources, if needed for the new view class.
- Add code to the view classes to properly handle the `OnInitialUpdate` and `OnUpdate` virtual functions.
- Modify the document class to call `UpdateAllViews` when the data contained in the document changes.
- Modify the application class so that it stores pointers to document templates it creates.
- Add code to the main frame class to handle menu selections that select a particular view.

I cover each of these steps in the following sections. Because the Document/View architecture is designed to support multiple views, you can rely on ClassWizard to write much of the code for you. To reduce the amount of typing needed, continue to modify the DVTest program from the previous chapter.

Creating a New View

The first step in adding a new view to an existing document is to define the view by creating a view class. Any type of view can be added to an existing MDI program. In this set of examples, the new view displays the names contained in the document class. The existing form view is used to add names to the `DVTestDoc` document.

The new view class, `CDisplayView`, is derived directly from `CView`. Because `CDisplayView` only displays information, it only has to support two new interfaces:

- `OnInitialUpdate`, called when the view is first created
- `OnUpdate`, called when the document updates its views

To create a new view to add to the CDVTest project, follow these steps:

1. Open ClassWizard.
2. Press the button labeled Add Class and select the New option from the drop-down menu.
3. Use the values from Table 27.1 to fill in the Add Class dialog box.
4. Press the button labeled Create, and close ClassWizard.

Table 27.1. Values used to add the `CDisplayView` class.

Control	Value
Name	`CDisplayView`
Base Class	`CView`
OLE Automation	None
Add to Component Gallery	Unchecked

ClassWizard adds the new view to the project and creates some default initialization functions. However, the view class isn't useful until you do some additional work to associate it with the document class and define how it displays information.

When you create a new view using ClassWizard, you must add functions to handle the Document/View interfaces; they aren't automatically created as they are for views created by AppWizard when a new project is created. Using ClassWizard, add two message-handling functions to the CDisplayView class by following these steps:

1. Select CDisplayView as the class name.
2. Press the tab labeled Message Maps.
3. Select CDisplayView as the Object ID.
4. Select OnInitialUpdate as the message type.
5. Press the button labeled Add Function.
6. Repeat Steps 1 through 5, adding a message-handling function for OnUpdate.

Modifying the *OnDraw* Function

As I discussed earlier, when you finish the CDisplayView class, it will list the names contained in the CDVTestDoc document class. Like other OnDraw functions, CDisplayView::OnDraw retrieves a pointer to the document class and collects information about the items to be displayed in the view. The source code for CDisplayView::OnDraw is provided in Listing 27.1. Because the OnDraw function must access the CDVTestDoc class, add this #include directive for the CDVTestDoc class:

```
#include "DVTestDoc.h"
```

Add this include statement after the other include statements near the beginning of the DisplayView.cpp source file.

Listing 27.1. Source code for CDisplayView::OnDraw.

```
void CDisplayView::OnDraw(CDC* pDC)
{
    CDVTestDoc* pDoc = (CDVTestDoc*)GetDocument();
    ASSERT_VALID(pDoc);

    // Calculate the space required for a single
    // line of text, including the inter-line area.
    TEXTMETRIC  tm;
    pDC->GetTextMetrics( &tm );
    int nLineHeight = tm.tmHeight + tm.tmExternalLeading;

    CPoint  ptText( 0, 0 );
    for( int nIndex = 0; nIndex < pDoc->GetCount(); nIndex++ )
    {
        CString szName = pDoc->GetName( nIndex );
        pDC->TextOut( ptText.x, ptText.y, szName );
```

```
        ptText.y += nLineHeight;
    }
}
```

Notice that the OnDraw function used in CDisplayView is the same as the CDVTestView::OnDraw function in Listing 25.6. Although that view had exclusive access to its document, the same source code works when the document is shared by multiple views. You add the code for the OnInitialUpdate and OnUpdate member functions later in the section titled "Adding the OnInitialUpdate and OnUpdate Member Functions."

Creating and Maintaining Multiple Document Templates

When a single view and document are associated with each other, a CMultiDocTemplate is passed to the MFC framework, and the application never sees it again. When multiple views are created, the application class must keep track of the document templates used for the document and view associations. The application class stores these pointers and provides them to the CMainFrame class when needed. Add the source code in Listing 27.2 to the implementation section of the CDVTestApp class declaration. These additions declare two member variables that are used to cache pointers to the document templates and two member functions used to get access to the pointers.

Listing 27.2. Changes to the CDVTestApp class declaration.

```
public:
    CDocTemplate* GetDisplayTemplate() const;
    CDocTemplate* GetFormTemplate() const;
private:
    CDocTemplate* m_pDisplayTemplate;
    CDocTemplate* m_pFormTemplate;
```

The two document template pointers are set during the CDVTestApp::InitInstance member function. Instead of creating a CMultiDocTemplate object and passing it immediately to the AddDocTemplate function, CMultiDocTemplate objects are created, and their pointers are stored in the new member variables. Replace the current code used to create the document templates in CDVTestApp::InitInstance with the source code provided in Listing 27.3.

Listing 27.3. Changes to CDVTestApp::InitInstance creating two document templates.

```
m_pFormTemplate = new CMultiDocTemplate(
                            IDR_DVTESTTYPE,
                            RUNTIME_CLASS(CDVTestDoc),
                            RUNTIME_CLASS(CChildFrame),
                            RUNTIME_CLASS(CFormTest) );
m_pDisplayTemplate = new CMultiDocTemplate(
```

continues

Listing 27.3. continued

```
                                     IDR_DISPLAYTYPE,
                                     RUNTIME_CLASS(CDVTestDoc),
                                     RUNTIME_CLASS(CChildFrame),
                                     RUNTIME_CLASS(CDisplayView) );

AddDocTemplate( m_pFormTemplate );
```

Each of the document templates created in Listing 27.3 describes views associated with the CDVTestDoc class. One of the document templates uses the CFormTest class from Chapter 26, "Using Form Views," while the other template uses the CDisplayView class. Because this class is new to the DVTest.cpp file, add an #include directive for the CDisplayView class:

```
#include "DisplayView.h"
```

Listing 27.4 contains the source for the new CDVTestApp functions that return pointers to the CDocTemplate pointers created during CDVTest::OnInitInstance. The CMainFrame class uses these pointers when creating new views.

Listing 27.4. CDVTestApp functions used to return pointers to the document templates.

```
CDocTemplate* CDVTestApp::GetDisplayTemplate() const
{
    return m_pDisplayTemplate;
}

CDocTemplate* CDVTestApp::GetFormTemplate() const
{
    return m_pFormTemplate;
}
```

Adding Shared Resource

One of the parameters used when creating a document template is the *shared-resource identifier*. This resource ID is used to identify several different resources used by the view:

- A resource string; specify the file type, file extension, and document name for the document template
- An icon for the view
- A menu used when the view is active

Each of these resources must be created for a new view. Although it's possible to just share an existing resource ID, it's a much better practice to provide at least a customized icon for the new view.

Creating a Menu for the New View

Click the IDR_DVTESTTYPE menu item, and use Copy and Paste to create a new menu item. Rename the item by right-clicking the icon and selecting Properties from the pop-up menu.

Creating an Icon for the New View

Create an IDR_DISPLAYTYPE icon by opening the Icon folder on the resource tree. Create a copy of the existing IDR_DVTESTTYPE icon by using the Edit menu to copy and paste the icon, or by pressing Ctrl+C, then Ctrl+V.

Using a Resource String

The resource string for each document template is stored in the String Table section of the project's rc file. Open the rc file and click the String Table icon. In the DVTest project, the resource string for the current document template is stored under the name IDR_DVTESTTYPE. You can add a new string to the String Table by pressing the Insert key on the keyboard. Create a new string resource named IDR_DISPLAYTYPE with the string value shown below:

```
\nDVTest\n\n\n\nDVTest.Document\nDVTest Document
```

The contents of the resource string are split into seven sections, with each section separated by \n. Each of the seven sections has a particular purpose, as shown in Table 27.2.

Table 27.2. Values for subsections of resource strings used in DVTest.

Section	IDR_DVTEST	IDR_DISPLAYTYPE
Title		
Document Name	DVTest	DVTest
New File Name	DVTest	
Filter Name		
Filter Extension		
Type ID	DVTest.Document	DVTest.Document
Type Name	DVTest Document	DVTest Document

The new resource string is almost the same as the original string. The only difference is that there is no entry for the section marked New File Name. This is a clue to the MFC framework that this document template is not used to create new documents; rather, it is used only to open a new view on an existing document.

You don't have to worry too much about the purpose for each segment. The MFC framework uses these segments when registering your application with Windows, and when opening new views and documents. In Chapter 42, "Serialization and Document/View," you see how to use resource strings to help specify the type of file that stores the contents of a document.

Adding Menu Items for New Views

You add new views by selecting a menu item from the Windows menu. Add the menu items using the Developer Studio resource editor, as I discussed in Chapter 15, "Menus." Use the values from Table 27.3 to add the menu items to the IDR_DISPLAYTYPE and IDR_DVTESTTYPE menus and to add message-handling functions to the CMainFrame class.

Table 27.3. New member functions for the CMainFrame class.

Menu ID	Caption	Event	Function Name
ID_WINDOW_DISPLAY	&Display View	COMMAND	OnWindowDisplay
ID_WINDOW_FORM	&Form View	COMMAND	OnWindowForm

Listing 27.5 provides the source code for the message-handling functions.

Listing 27.5. CMainFrame member functions used to create new views.

```
void CMainFrame::OnWindowForm()
{
    CMDIChildWnd* pActiveChild = MDIGetActive();
    if( pActiveChild != 0 )
    {
        CDocument*  pDocument = pActiveChild->GetActiveDocument();
        if( pDocument != 0 )
        {
            CDVTestApp*     pApp = (CDVTestApp*)AfxGetApp();
            CDocTemplate*   pTemp;
            CFrameWnd*      pFrame;
            pTemp = pApp->GetFormTemplate();
            pFrame = pTemp->CreateNewFrame(pDocument,pActiveChild);
            if( pFrame != 0 )
            {
                pTemp->InitialUpdateFrame(pFrame, pDocument);
            }
        }
    }
}

void CMainFrame::OnWindowDisplay()
{
    CMDIChildWnd* pActiveChild = MDIGetActive();
    if( pActiveChild != 0 )
    {
        CDocument*  pDocument = pActiveChild->GetActiveDocument();
        if( pDocument != 0 )
        {
            CDVTestApp*     pApp = (CDVTestApp*)AfxGetApp();
            CDocTemplate*   pTemp;
            CFrameWnd*      pFrame;
            pTemp = pApp->GetDisplayTemplate();
```

```
            pFrame = pTemp->CreateNewFrame(pDocument,pActiveChild);
            if( pFrame != 0 )
            {
                pTemp->InitialUpdateFrame(pFrame, pDocument);
            }
        }
    }
}
```

These functions are nearly identical: the only difference between them is the call to either GetDisplayTemplate or GetFormTemplate. The functions provided in Listing 27.5 follow these steps when creating a new view:

1. Get a pointer to the active child window.
2. Get a pointer to the active document.
3. Get a pointer to the application.
4. Using the application pointer, get the document template for the new view.
5. Using the document template, create a new frame associated with the active frame from step one and the document pointer from step two.
6. Update the frame.

These basic steps can be followed no matter what classes are involved or how many views and documents are being managed by the application.

Updating Multiple Views

One of the most important issues when a document has more than one view is ensuring that each view is accurate. If one view changes data loaded in the document, all views must be notified about the change; otherwise, they will present information that is out of date. The mechanism used by Document/View applications to keep documents and views synchronized is shown in Figure 27.2.

Figure 27.2.
The document class controls the updating of all views.

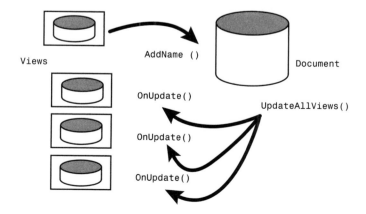

Views

AddName ()

Document

OnUpdate()

UpdateAllViews()

OnUpdate()

OnUpdate()

Every document should provide updates to its associated views by calling the UpdateAllViews function when data contained by the document has been changed. To update all views associated with a document, you can use a line like this:

```
UpdateAllViews( NULL );
```

The default implementation of UpdateAllViews notifies every view that the document has been changed by calling each view object's OnUpdate member function. The NULL parameter causes all views to be updated. If a view pointer is passed as a parameter, that view is not updated. Listing 27.6 provides the new source code for the CDVTestDoc::AddName function.

Listing 27.6. A new version of CDVTestDoc::AddName that causes views to be updated.

```
int CDVTestDoc::AddName( const CString& szName )
{
    TRACE("CDVTestDoc::AddName, string = %s\n", (LPCSTR)szName);
    int nPosition = m_arNames.Add( szName );
    UpdateAllViews( NULL );
    return nPosition;
}
```

Adding the *OnInitialUpdate* and *OnUpdate* Member Functions

The OnInitialUpdate and OnUpdate member functions for CDisplayView invalidate the view area, causing the view to be repainted. When Windows sends a WM_PAINT message to the view, the OnDraw member function is called, redrawing the view with the new contents. Edit the OnInitialUpdate and OnUpdate functions as shown in Listing 27.7.

Listing 27.7. Source code for the CDisplayView update functions.

```
void CDisplayView::OnInitialUpdate()
{
    CView::OnInitialUpdate();
    InvalidateRect( NULL );
}

void CDisplayView::OnUpdate(CView* pSender, LPARAM lHint,
                            CObject* pHint)
{
    InvalidateRect( NULL );
}
```

All view classes should provide OnUpdate member functions that are called by the MFC framework after the document class calls UpdateAllViews. Note that the entire view is redrawn whenever the document has been updated. In Chapter 28, "Split Views," I discuss some ways to optimize updating a view.

The current view, CFormTest, must also support OnUpdate. Add the OnUpdate function to the CFormTest class using ClassWizard. Listing 27.8 provides the source code for the CFormTest::OnUpdate function.

Listing 27.8. Source code for the CFormTest::OnUpdate function.

```
void CFormTest::OnUpdate(CView* pSender, LPARAM lHint,
                         CObject* pHint)
{
    CDVTestDoc* pDoc = (CDVTestDoc*)GetDocument();
    ASSERT_VALID(pDoc);

    m_lbNames.ResetContent();
    for( int nIndex = 0; nIndex < pDoc->GetCount(); nIndex++ )
    {
        CString szName = pDoc->GetName( nIndex );
        m_lbNames.AddString( szName );
    }
}
```

The solution provided in Listing 27.8 is not very efficient, because the list box is always completely emptied and refilled whenever the document is updated. I present a more efficient method for updating views in Chapter 28.

Now that you have implemented OnUpdate, change the OnInitialUpdate member function so that it performs only work that needs to be done when the view is initially displayed. Remove source code from CFormTest::OnInitialUpdate so it looks like the function provided in Listing 27.9.

Listing 27.9. CFormTest::OnInitialUpdate after removing unnecessary code.

```
void CFormTest::OnInitialUpdate()
{
    CFormView::OnInitialUpdate();
    ResizeParentToFit( FALSE );
    ResizeParentToFit();
}
```

Because OnUpdate handles inserting new items into the list box, you should change the OnApply member function so that it does not add strings to the list box. Edit the OnApply member function so it looks like the code in Listing 27.10.

Listing 27.10. CFormTest::OnApply after removing list box AddString code.

```
void CFormTest::OnUpdate(CView* pSender, LPARAM lHint,
                         CObject* pHint)
{
    CDVTestDoc* pDoc = (CDVTestDoc*)GetDocument();
    ASSERT_VALID(pDoc);
```

continues

Listing 27.10. continued

```
CString szName;
m_edNames.GetWindowText( szName );
m_edNames.SetWindowText( "" );
m_edNames.SetFocus();
if( szName.GetLength() > 0 )
{
    pDoc->AddName( szName );
}
m_lbNames.ResetContent();
for( int nIndex = 0; nIndex < pDoc->GetCount(); nIndex++ )
{
    CString szName = pDoc->GetName( nIndex );
    m_lbNames.AddString( szName );
}
}
```

Summary

In this chapter I discussed adding multiple views for a document class. I also covered the methods used for creating multiple view classes, as well as updating multiple documents.

Split Views

In this chapter I talk about split views, which are used to provide two views in a single frame. Split views can be either dynamic or static; you create both types in this chapter.

What Are Split Views?

What Split views are frames that contain a *split bar* that divides the window into two or more *panes*, or subwindows. The split bar can usually be adjusted to make one pane larger or smaller. Often, the split view includes a scroll bar that can be used to scroll inside the pane.

The panes included in a split view are normally derived from CView or one of its subclasses. However, with a little work any window can be used as a pane in a split view.

There are two basic types of split views:

- *Static split views*, which are created as split views, with all panes initially visible. Although the dividing boundary between the panes can be adjusted, there are always a fixed number of panes visible in the view.

■ *Dynamic split views*, in which a view is initially displayed without any split panes. The user can open a split view at any time by dragging a split-bar control located in the corner of the view. Developer Studio uses this scheme in its editor window: by dragging the flat bar on top of the scroll bar, the user can split the editor view into two views.

The choice of split bar type depends on the application. In editing and view windows, a dynamic split bar is a natural enhancement to scroll bars. If the purpose of the split view is to show two or more different types of views, a static split view is a better choice. In this chapter you create both types of split views.

Why Use Split Views?

Why

Like scroll bars, split views offer a way to easily view documents that are larger than the available screen area. A scroll bar enables you to traverse the document, while a split view enables you to look at two different parts of the document simultaneously, as shown in Figure 28.1.

Figure 28.1.
A split view displaying two different parts of a larger view.

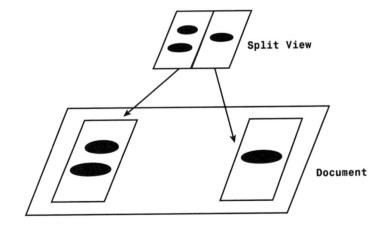

Split views are also used to integrate two different views into one easy-to-use frame. For example, a form view can be integrated with another view that displays the document in a completely different way.

How Are Split Views Used?

How

You can add a dynamic split view to an existing project with just a few lines of code, if you use ClassWizard to add the necessary classes and message-handling functions. Static split views require slightly more code; however, it's strictly "boilerplate" code, which is similar for all projects. In addition, the amount of code added is a good bargain in light of the extra functionality added to your program.

Chapter 28

The split-view functionality is actually a feature handled by the frame window, rather than by any of the views included in the split view. The actual work of maintaining the split bar and the view panes is handled by the `CSplitterWnd` class, with almost no work required in most cases.

Creating a Scrolling, Dynamic Split View

For the examples in this chapter, continue to use the DVTest project used in Chapter 26, "Using Form Views," and Chapter 27, "Multiple Views." The first split view you create is a dynamic splitter associated with a view class derived from `CScrollView`. This is a common way to use splitters, and one that's easy to implement. Later in this chapter you create a static split view that provides form and display views at the same time.

Creating a Scroll View

The first step in creating your dynamic split view is to create a scrolling view that works much like the `CDisplayView` class from Chapter 26. Although a scrolling view isn't necessary for a split view, it's convenient to use one because the split view reduces the amount of each pane that is visible at any given time.

To create a scroll view for an existing project using ClassWizard, follow these steps:

1. Open ClassWizard.
2. Press the button labeled Add Class, and select New from the drop-down menu.
3. Use the values from Table 28.1 to fill in the Add Class dialog.

Table 28.1. Values for a new scroll view for the DVTest project.

Control	Value
Name	CScrollDisplay
BaseClass	CScrollView
File	ScrollDisplay.cpp
OLE Automation	None
Add to Component Gallery	Unchecked

4. Press the button labeled Create, and close ClassWizard.

As in Chapter 27, you must add functions to handle the Document/View interfaces. However, you can copy the source code for these functions directly from the existing `CDisplayView` class. Using ClassWizard, add the `OnUpdate` message-handling function to the `CScrollDisplay` class by following these steps:

1. Select `CScrollDisplay` as the class name.
2. Press the tab labeled Message Maps.

3. Select `CScrollDisplay` as the Object ID.

4. Select `OnUpdate` as the message type.

5. Press the button labeled Add Function.

You must edit three `CScrollDisplay` member functions:

- `OnIntialUpdate`

- `OnUpdate`

- `OnDraw`

The source code for each of these functions is provided in Listing 28.1. All of this source code can be copied from the same functions that are part of the `CDisplayView` class.

Listing 28.1. Source code for the `CDisplayScroll` member functions.

```
void CScrollDisplay::OnInitialUpdate()
{
    CScrollView::OnInitialUpdate();
    CSize sizeTotal;
    sizeTotal.cx = sizeTotal.cy = 100;
    SetScrollSizes(MM_TEXT, sizeTotal);

    InvalidateRect( NULL );
}
void CScrollDisplay::OnDraw(CDC* pDC)
{
    CDVTestDoc* pDoc = (CDVTestDoc*)GetDocument();
    ASSERT_VALID(pDoc);

    // Calculate the space required for a single
    // line of text, including the inter-line area.
    TEXTMETRIC  tm;
    pDC->GetTextMetrics( &tm );
    int nLineHeight = tm.tmHeight + tm.tmExternalLeading;

    CPoint  ptText( 0, 0 );
    for( int nIndex = 0; nIndex < pDoc->GetCount(); nIndex++ )
    {
        CString szName = pDoc->GetName( nIndex );
        pDC->TextOut( ptText.x, ptText.y, szName );
        ptText.y += nLineHeight;
    }
}
void CScrollDisplay::OnUpdate(CView* pSender, LPARAM lHint,
                              CObject* pHint)
{
    InvalidateRect( NULL );
}
```

The `CDisplayScroll` class must have access to the `CDVTestDoc` class declaration. Add the following #include statement just after the other include statements at the beginning of the ScrollDisplay.cpp source file:

```
#include "DVTestDoc.h"
```

These are all of the changes required to create a scroll view for an existing project. To use this new scroll view in place of an existing view, just edit the document template constructor in the application's OnInitInstance function so that CScrollDisplay is used instead of the existing class. However, for the example in this chapter, you also are creating a split view frame. In the next step, you create a new MDI child frame window for the view that allows a scroll bar to be used.

Creating a Dynamic Split Frame Class

As I discussed earlier in this chapter, the split-view functionality actually is handled by the frame class. To create a split view, you must create a new frame class derived from CMDIChildWnd, and include a CSplitterWnd member variable. The CSplitterWnd object actually creates and maintains the split views for the child window frame. Adding a split view to an SDI program is similar, except that the new frame class is derived from CFrameWnd.

Creating a new split-view frame class requires the same steps as creating any other MFC-based class. To create a new frame class for an existing project using ClassWizard, follow these steps:

1. Open ClassWizard.
2. Press the button labeled Add Class and select New from the drop-down menu.
3. Use the values from Table 28.2 to fill in the Add Class dialog.
4. Press the button labeled Create, and close ClassWizard.

Table 28.2. Values for a new scroll view for the DVTest project.

Control	Value
Name	CScrollSplit
BaseClass	CMDIChildFrame
File	ScrollSplit.cpp
OLE Automation	None
Add to Component Gallery	Unchecked

The CScrollSplit class must have one new member variable: m_wndSplit, a CWndSplitter object. The m_wndSplit variable is added as a private member of the CScrollSplit class, in the attributes section of the class declaration, as shown in Listing 28.2. Remember, the attributes section begins with the // Attributes comment.

Listing 28.2. Adding a CSplitterWnd member variable to the CScrollSplit class.

```
// Attributes
private:
    CSplitterWnd    m_wndSplit;
```

Use ClassWizard to add one message-handling function for the `CScrollSplit` class, `OnCreateClient`, which is called when the frame creates the contents of its client area. Listing 28.3 provides the source code for the `CScrollSplit::OnCreateClient` member function.

Listing 28.3. The source code for `CScrollSplit::OnCreateClient`.

```
BOOL CScrollSplit::OnCreateClient(LPCREATESTRUCT lpcs,
                                  CCreateContext* pContext)
{
    CSize   size( 10, 10 );
    return m_wndSplit.Create( this, 2, 2, size, pContext );
}
```

The `OnCreateClient` member function delegates all of its work to the `CWndSplitter::Create` function, which automatically creates a dynamic split view for the `CScrollSplit` frame class. These parameters are passed to the `m_wndSplit.Create` function:

- The parent window, which is the `CScrollSplit` object, or the `this` pointer
- The maximum number of rows in the split window; in this case, two
- The maximum number of columns in the split view; in this case, two
- The minimum size of the split view
- The `CCreateContext` pointer

Using the New Split View Classes in DVTest

To use the new scrolling version of the display class instead of the current display class, just change the statement in which a `CMultiDocTemplate` object is created and assigned to `m_pDisplayTemplate` in `CDVTestApp::OnInitInstance`. Listing 28.4 contains the new source code.

Listing 28.4. Creating a new document template that uses a split view.

```
// New version of the display document template that includes
// a splitter view.
m_pDisplayTemplate = new CMultiDocTemplate(
                             IDR_DISPLAYTYPE,
                             RUNTIME_CLASS(CDVTestDoc),
                             RUNTIME_CLASS(CScrollSplit),
                             RUNTIME_CLASS(CScrollDisplay));
```

The code in Listing 28.4. causes two things to happen:

- When the view is created, `CScrollDisplay` is used instead of `CDisplayView`. This view has scrolling capabilities built-in, so more items can be added than fit on a single screen.

■ Dynamic split controls are added by the `CScrollSplit` frame class, allowing the view to be split into separate panes on demand.

Compile the project and try out the new split view. In the next section, you add a static split view class.

Creating a Static Split View

In this section you add a static split bar to the DVTest project. Unlike the dynamic split view you created earlier, you must add some source code to the `OnCreateClient` member function. Although it requires more code, the static split view is more useful than a dynamic split view in cases where a form view shares a frame with another type of view, such as a scrolling view.

Creating a Static Split View Class

The first step in creating a static split view is exactly like creating a dynamic split view. Create the `CSplitFrame` class using ClassWizard, just as you created `CScrollSplit` in the previous section. Use the values from Table 28.3 to fill in the Add Class dialog.

Table 28.3. Values for the `CSplitFrame` class.

Control	Value
Name	CSplitFrame
BaseClass	CMDIChildFrame
File	SplitFrame.cpp
OLE Automation	None
Add to Component Gallery	Unchecked

Like the `CScrollSplit` class I discussed earlier, the `CSplitFrame` class must have a `CWndSplitter` object as a member variable. As shown in Listing 28.5, add `m_wndSplit` as a private member variable.

Listing 28.5. Adding a `CSplitterWnd` member variable to the `CSplitForm` class.

```
// Attributes
private:
    CSplitterWnd    m_wndSplit;
```

Use ClassWizard to add the `CSplitForm::OnCreateClient` function, which is called when the frame creates the contents of its client area. This is the same function you added earlier in this chapter for the `CScrollSplit` class. Listing 28.6 provides the source code for the `OnCreateClient` member function.

Listing 28.6. Source code for the `CSplitFrame::OnCreateClient` function.

```
BOOL CSplitFrame::OnCreateClient(LPCREATESTRUCT lpcs, CCreateContext* pContext)
{
    if( m_wndSplit.CreateStatic(this, 2, 1) == FALSE )
    {
        TRACE0("Failed to CreateStaticSplitter\n");
        return FALSE;
    }
    BOOL bCreated = m_wndSplit.CreateView( 0,
                                           0,
                                           pContext->m_pNewViewClass,
                                           CSize(100, 115),
                                           pContext );
    if( bCreated == FALSE )
    {
        TRACE0("Failed to create first pane\n");
        return FALSE;
    }
    // add the second splitter pane
    bCreated = m_wndSplit.CreateView( 1,
                                      0,
                                      RUNTIME_CLASS(CFormTest),
                                      CSize(0, 0),
                                      pContext);
    if( bCreated == FALSE )
    {
        TRACE0("Failed to create second pane\n");
        return FALSE;
    }
    // activate the input view
    SetActiveView((CView*)m_wndSplit.GetPane(0,0));
    return TRUE;
}
```

The new code in Listing 28.6 uses the `CFormTest` class. Add an `#include` for `"FormTest.h"` at the top of the SplitFrame.cpp file, just after the other include statements:

```
#include "FormTest.h"
```

Listing 28.6 is by far the largest function required in this chapter. Most of the code is due to the fact that both views contained in the view are created inside the `OnCreateClient` function. Note that each of the views is created through `m_wndSplitter`, the `CSplitterWnd` object. This is because the `CWndSplitter` class is responsible for managing the split views after they are created.

The first two parameters in the call to `CreateView` specify the *pane*, or window position this view will have in the splitter window. The first parameter is the row position; the second parameter is the column position. Position 0,0 is the upper-left pane, while position 1,0 is the pane under 0,0.

The `GetPane` function takes the pane position as an argument and returns a pointer to the window contained in the pane. After getting a pointer to the upper-left pane, that view is made active by calling `SetActiveView`.

Using the Static Split View in DVTest

Making use of this new static split view in the DVTest program only takes a few lines of code. You can copy most of it from similar functions added earlier in this chapter, or in Chapter 27.

The first step is to create a new document template variable in the CDVTestApp class. As shown in Listing 28.7, add a new function named GetSplitTemplate, and a CDocTemplate pointer named m_pSplitTemplate to the CDVTestApp class declaration.

Listing 28.7. Additions to the CDVTestApp class declaration.

```
public:
    CDocTemplate* GetDisplayTemplate() const;
    CDocTemplate* GetFormTemplate() const;
    CDocTemplate* GetSplitTemplate() const;
    ~CDVTestApp();
private:
    CDocTemplate* m_pDisplayTemplate;
    CDocTemplate* m_pFormTemplate;
    CDocTemplate* m_pSplitTemplate;
```

Listing 28.8 contains the source for the new CDVTestApp function that returns a pointer to the new document template.

Listing 28.8. A CDVTestApp function used to return a pointer to the new document template.

```
CDocTemplate* CDVTestApp::GetSplitTemplate() const
{
    return m_pSplitTemplate;
}
```

As I discussed in Chapter 27, all document templates that aren't added to the applications template list must be deleted in the CDVTestApp destructor. The code in Listing 28.9 adds a line that deletes the m_pSplitTemplate pointer.

Listing 28.9. The new version of the CDVTestApp destructor.

```
CDVTestApp::~CDVTestApp()
{
    delete m_pDisplayTemplate;
    delete m_pSplitTemplate;
}
```

To create the new document template used for the static split view, add the code in Listing 28.10 to the CDVTestApp::OnInitInstance member function. Add this code just after the other document templates have been created.

Listing 28.10. Additional code added to `CDVTestApp::OnInitInstance`.

```
m_pSplitTemplate = new CMultiDocTemplate(
                            IDR_DISPLAYTYPE,
                            RUNTIME_CLASS(CDVTestDoc),
                            RUNTIME_CLASS(CSplitFrame),
                            RUNTIME_CLASS(CScrollDisplay));
```

The new code in Listing 28.10 uses the `CSplitFrame` class. Add an `#include` for `"SplitFrame.h"` at the top of the CDVTest.cpp file, just after the other include statements:

```
#include "SplitFrame.h"
```

Adding a New Menu Item

The new static split view is displayed by selecting a menu item from the Window menu, as was done in Chapter 27. Use the values from Table 28.4 to add the menu items to the `IDR_DISPLAYTYPE` and `IDR_DVTESTTYPE` menus and to add message-handling functions to the `CMainFrame` class.

Table 28.4. New member functions for the `CMainFrame` class.

Menu ID	Caption	Event	Function Name
ID_WINDOW_SPLIT	Split View	COMMAND	OnWindowSplit

The source code for the message-handling function is provided in Listing 28.11.

Listing 28.11. `CMainFrame` member functions used to create the new split view.

```
void CMainFrame::OnWindowSplit()
{
    CMDIChildWnd* pActiveChild = MDIGetActive();
    if( pActiveChild != 0 )
    {
        CDocument*  pDocument = pActiveChild->GetActiveDocument();
        if( pDocument != 0 )
        {
            CDVTestApp*     pApp = (CDVTestApp*)AfxGetApp();
            CDocTemplate*   pTemp;
            CFrameWnd*      pFrame;
            pTemp = pApp->GetSplitTemplate();
            pFrame = pTemp->CreateNewFrame(pDocument,pActiveChild);
            if( pFrame != 0 )
            {
                pTemp->InitialUpdateFrame(pFrame, pDocument);
            }
        }
    }
}
```

The source code provided in Listing 28.11 is almost identical to the code provided in Chapter 27 when you added multiple views. The only difference is in line 12, where `pApp->GetSplitTemplate` is called.

Summary

In this chapter I discussed adding split views to an MDI application. You added both dynamic and static split views to the DVTest project, and created a new scrolling view class for DVTest.

PART VII

The Graphics Interface

29 Device Contexts

30 Using Pens

31 Brushes

32 Fonts

33 Icons

34 Cursors

Device Contexts

In this chapter I discuss device contexts. All output in a program written for Windows must be done using a device context. I present the MFC device context classes, and you build a sample program that demonstrates how a device context is used with text output.

What Are Device Contexts?

What A device context is an important part of the Windows Graphics Device Interface, or GDI. A device context, often abbreviated as *DC*, is a structure that stores information needed when a program written for Windows must display output to a device. Device contexts are maintained by Windows. The device context stores information about the drawing surface and its capabilities. Before using any of the GDI output functions, you must create a device context.

A GDI object can be selected into a device context in order to provide specific drawing capabilities for the DC. Each GDI object can be used to create a different sort of output. For example, a GDI pen object can be used to draw lines, while brush objects are used to fill screen areas. The GDI objects most commonly used with device contexts are listed in Table 29.1.

Table 29.1. Commonly used GDI objects in Windows programs.

Object	Purpose
Pen	Drawing lines
Brush	Filling regions
Bitmap	Displaying images
Font	Setting typeface characteristics

Because of the way device contexts insulate a program written for Windows from the actual device hardware, output is often said to be "written to a device context." This independence from hardware makes it easy to send output to a printer that looks very much like screen output. I discuss printing in detail in Chapter 35, "Printing."

Types of Device Contexts

Windows and the MFC class library provide the following four different basic types of device contexts. Although you use these device contexts in different situations, the basic rules for their use are consistent.

- Display DCs, used to display information to a standard video terminal. These are the most commonly used device contexts in a Windows program.

- Printer DCs, used to display output on a printer or plotter.

- Memory DCs, sometimes called *compatible device contexts*, used to perform drawing operations on a bitmap.

- Information DCs, used to collect information on a device. These DCs cannot be used for actual output. However, they are extremely fast and have little overhead, and therefore are ideal for use when information is being collected.

With the exception of the information device contexts, each of the different DC types is used for creating a different sort of output. In addition, the MFC class library offers several different types of display device contexts, which I cover in the section "How to Use Device Contexts."

Why Use Device Contexts?

The simplest reason to use device contexts is that they are required; there's simply no other way to perform output in a Windows program without them. However, using a device context is the first step toward using many of the GDI features that are available under Windows. Understanding how device contexts work can also help make your Windows programs more efficient.

The goal behind using device contexts is to give programs written for Windows hardware independence. With a little care, your program can run on any display or printer that's supported by a Windows hardware driver. Most new output devices supply a driver if Windows doesn't currently provide automatic support. This means that programs you write today will work with display devices that have not been developed yet.

In order to achieve true hardware-independence, you must take a few precautions:

- Don't hard-code any dimensions into your program. Larger or smaller screens or printers will cause hard-coded dimensions to look skewed or distorted.

- Don't assume that Windows is running on a display with a particular resolution. Making assumptions about video monitors, in particular, is a bad idea. It's a sure bet that most people don't use your screen resolution or dimensions.

- Don't assume that a certain set of colors are available, or are appropriate in all cases. For example, don't assume the workspace background is always white. There are a large number of Windows users with laptops that simulate VGA displays. Other users often change the available color scheme. The selection of colors used is strictly up to the user.

Device contexts can help by providing much of the information you need to stay hardware-independent.

How Are Device Contexts Used?

When using Developer Studio, you almost always use an MFC class to gain access to a device context. The MFC class library offers not just one, but *four* different device context classes that can help make your life easier, at least when displaying output in a Windows program:

How

- CDC, the base class for all of the device context classes

- CPaintDC, which performs some useful housekeeping functions that are needed when a window responds to WM_PAINT

- CClientDC, used when a device context will be used only for output to a window's client area

- CWindowDC, used when the entire window may be drawn on

There are more MFC device context classes, but they are used for specialized purposes, and will be discussed elsewhere in the book. For example, the CPrinterDC class will be discussed in Chapter 35.

Wizard Support for Device Contexts

When you create a class using ClassWizard or AppWizard, often code that uses or creates a device context is provided automatically. For example, the OnDraw function for a typical view class is provided in Listing 29.1.

Listing 29.1. A typical `OnDraw` function.

```
void CDisplayView::OnDraw(CDC* pDC)
{
    CDocument* pDoc = GetDocument();
    // TODO: add draw code here
}
```

The device context used for the `OnDraw` function is created by the MFC framework before the `OnDraw` function is called. Because every `OnDraw` function must display some output, the device context is provided for you automatically, without the need for you to write any code.

Most functions that need a device context have one provided as a parameter, just like `OnDraw`. This is one of the ways MFC helps make your code easier to write, and more reliable at the same time.

Selecting an Object

One of the most common mistakes made when using device contexts occurs when selecting a GDI object into a DC. When a device context is created, it contains a set of default GDI objects, as shown in Figure 29.1.

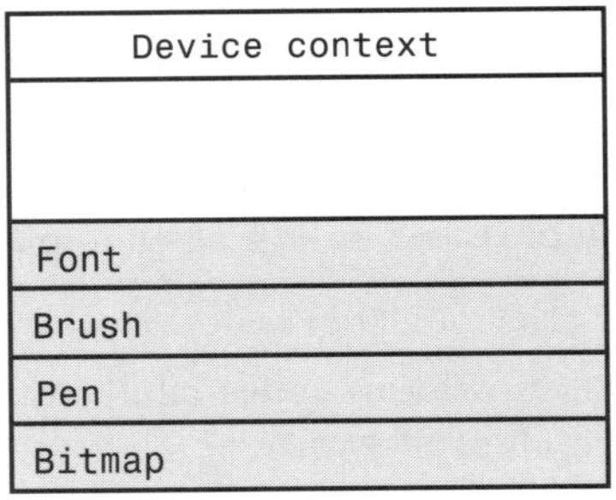

Figure 29.1.
A device context created with a collection of default GDI objects.

Device context
Font
Brush
Pen
Bitmap

When a new GDI object—for example, a bitmap—is selected into a device context, the default GDI bitmap is passed as a return value to the caller. This return value must be saved so that it can be returned to the device context later. Listing 29.2 is an example of selecting a new bitmap into a DC and returning the original GDI object at the end of the function.

Listing 29.2. Selecting and restoring a GDI object.

```
CBitmap     bmpHello;
bmpHello.LoadBitmap( IDB_HELLO );
CBitmap* pbmpOld = dcMem.SelectObject( &bmpHello );
if( pbmpOld != NULL )
{
    //
    // Use the bitmap...
    //
    dcMem.SelectObject( pbmpOld );
}
```

Notice that the pbmpOld value is checked to make sure that it isn't NULL. If the call to SelectObject fails, the original bitmap is not returned. In that case, there's no need to return the original bitmap to the DC, because a new one was never selected.

Collecting Information

The CDC class has two member functions that are commonly used to collect information:

- GetDeviceCaps, used to return information about the physical device that is associated with a device context.
- GetTextMetrics, used to retrieve information about the currently selected font.

Both of these functions receive a pointer to a structure as a parameter. After the function returns, the structure is filled with the requested information. Later in this chapter, you use these functions in a sample program.

Setting Mapping Modes

In Windows, you use *mapping modes* to define the size and direction of units used in drawing functions. As a Windows programmer, there are several different coordinate systems available to you. Mapping modes can use physical or logical dimensions, and they can start at the top, at the bottom, or at an arbitrary point on the screen.

There are a total of eight different mapping modes available in Windows. You can retrieve the current mapping mode used by a device context using the GetMapMode function, and set a new mapping mode using SetMapMode. Here are the available mapping modes:

- MM_ANISOTROPIC, which uses a viewport to scale the logical units to an application-defined value. The SetWindowExt and SetViewportExt member functions are used to change the units, orientation, and scaling.
- MM_HIENGLISH, where each logical unit is converted to a physical value of 0.001 inch. Positive x is to the right; positive y is up.
- MM_HIMETRIC, where each logical unit is converted to a physical value of 0.01 millimeter. Positive x is to the right; positive y is up.
- MM_ISOTROPIC, similar to MM_ANISOTROPIC, where logical units are converted to arbitrary units with equally scaled axes. This means that 1 unit on the x-axis is always equal to 1 unit on the y-axis. Use the SetWindowExt and SetViewportExt member functions to specify the desired units and orientation of the axes.
- MM_LOENGLISH, where each logical unit is converted to a physical value of 0.01 inch. Positive x is to the right; positive y is up.
- MM_LOMETRIC, where each logical unit is converted to a physical value of 0.1 millimeter. Positive x is to the right; positive y is up.
- MM_TEXT, where each logical unit is converted to 1 device pixel. Positive x is to the right; positive y is down.

■ MM_TWIPS, where each logical unit is converted to 1/20 of a point. Because a point is 1/72 inch, a *twip* is 1/1440 inch. This mapping mode is useful when sending output to a printer. Positive x is to the right; positive y is up.

Essential Example

Device Context Example

To demonstrate some basic ideas about how device contexts can be used, create a sample SDI program named DCTest. To help reduce the amount of typing required for examples, I use the DCTest program for the remaining GDI chapters, through Chapter 34, "Cursors."

The DCTest Program

DCTest is an SDI program that displays some information about the current device context, its map mode, and information about the default font. It will be possible to change the view's map mode using a dialog box.

To begin building the DCTest example, create an SDI program named DCTest using AppWizard. Feel free to experiment with options offered by AppWizard, as none of the options will affect the sample project.

Creating the Map Mode Dialog Box

Using Figure 29.2 as a guide, create a dialog box that changes the map mode for the view display. Give the dialog box a resource ID of IDD_MAP_MODE.

Figure 29.2.
The IDD_MAP_MODE
dialog box in the
resource editor.

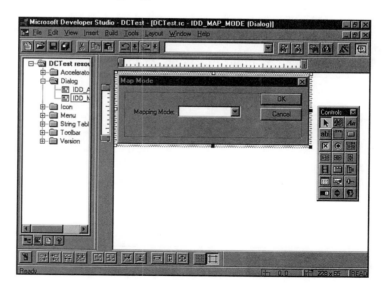

The dialog box contains one control, a drop-list combo box with a resource ID of IDC_COMBO. You can set the contents of the combo box in the resource editor, just as you set other combo-box attributes. Because this combo box contains a fixed list of items, it's easier to add them in the resource editor than in `OnInitDialog`. Add the items from the list below to the combo box:

```
MM_ANISOTROPIC
MM_HIENGLISH
MM_HIMETRIC
MM_ISOTROPIC
MM_LOENGLISH
MM_LOMETRIC
MM_TEXT
MM_TWIPS
```

Using ClassWizard, add a class named `CMapModeDlg` to handle the `IDD_MAP_MODE` dialog box. Add a `CString` variable to the class as shown in Table 29.2.

Table 29.2. New `CString` member variable for the `CMapModeDlg` class.

Resource ID	Name	Category	Variable Type
IDC_COMBO	m_szCombo	Value	CString

Adding a Menu Item

Use the values from Table 29.3 to add a menu item and a message-handling function to the `CDCTestView` class. Unlike menu-handling functions you have seen earlier, the view class must handle this menu selection because the dialog box changes data that is interesting only for the view class.

Table 29.3. New member functions for the `CDCTestView` class.

Menu ID	Caption	Event	Function Name
ID_VIEW_MAP_MODE	MapMode...	COMMAND	OnViewMapMode

Listing 29.3 contains the source code for the `OnViewMapMode` function, which handles the message sent when the new menu item is selected. If the OK button is pressed, the new map mode is calculated, based on the value contained in the combo box. The view rectangle is invalidated, which causes the view to be redrawn.

Listing 29.3. The `CDCTestView::OnViewMapMode` function.

```
void CDCTestView::OnViewMapMode()
{
    CMapModeDlg dlg;

    if( dlg.DoModal() == IDOK )
    {
        POSITION     pos;
```

```
        pos = m_map.GetStartPosition();
        while( pos != NULL )
        {
            CString szMapMode;
            int     nMapMode;
            m_map.GetNextAssoc( pos, nMapMode, szMapMode  );
            if( szMapMode == dlg.m_szCombo )
            {
                m_nMapMode = nMapMode;
                break;
            }
        }
        InvalidateRect( NULL );
    }
}
```

Add an #include statement to the DCTestView.cpp file so the CDCTestView class can have access to the CMapModeDlg class declaration. Add the following line near the top of the DCTestView.cpp file, just after the other #include statements:

```
#include "MapModeDlg.h"
```

Modifying the *CDCTestView* Class

In order to display information about the current map mode, you must first create a collection based on CMap, one of the template collection classes discussed in Chapter 11, "Collection Classes." The CMap variable, m_map, associates an integer map-mode value with a CString object that describes the map mode. As shown in Listing 29.4, add two new variables to the CDCTestView class declaration in the attributes section.

Listing 29.4. New member variables added to the CDCTestView class declaration.

```
// Attributes
private:
    CMap< int, int, CString, CString > m_map;
    int     m_nMapMode;
```

When using one of the MFC collection classes in a project, you should always add an #include statement to the stdafx.h file in the project directory:

```
#include "afxtempl.h"
```

This #include directive adds the MFC template declarations to the project's precompiled header, reducing project build time.

The source code for CDCTestView::OnDraw is provided in Listing 29.5. The current map mode is displayed, along with text and device metrics. The text metrics vary depending on the current logical mapping mode, while the device measurements remain constant. Some of the mapping modes will display the information from top to bottom, while some of the modes cause the information to be displayed from bottom to top.

Listing 29.5. The `CDCTestView::OnDraw` function.

```
void CDCTestView::OnDraw(CDC* pDC)
{
    pDC->SetMapMode( m_nMapMode );
    CRect    rcClient;
    GetClientRect( rcClient );
    pDC->DPtoLP( rcClient );
    int x = 0;
    int y = rcClient.bottom/2;

    CString szOut;
    m_map.Lookup( m_nMapMode, szOut );
    pDC->TextOut( x, y, szOut );

    TEXTMETRIC  tm;
    pDC->GetTextMetrics( &tm );
    int nCyInterval = tm.tmHeight + tm.tmExternalLeading;

    y += nCyInterval;
    szOut.Format( "Character height - %d units", tm.tmHeight );
    pDC->TextOut( x, y, szOut );

    y += nCyInterval;
    szOut.Format( "Average width - %d units", tm.tmAveCharWidth );
    pDC->TextOut( x, y, szOut );

    y += nCyInterval;
    szOut.Format( "Descent space - %d units", tm.tmDescent );
    pDC->TextOut( x, y, szOut );

    y += nCyInterval;
    szOut.Format( "Ascent space - %d units", tm.tmAscent );
    pDC->TextOut( x, y, szOut );

    int cxLog = pDC->GetDeviceCaps( LOGPIXELSX );
    y += nCyInterval;
    szOut.Format( "%d pixels per logical horiz. inch", cxLog );
    pDC->TextOut( x, y, szOut );

    int cyLog = pDC->GetDeviceCaps( LOGPIXELSY );
    y += nCyInterval;
    szOut.Format( "%d pixels per logical vert. inch", cyLog );
    pDC->TextOut( x, y, szOut );
}
```

Summary

In this chapter I started out with a discussion of the Graphics Device Interface, or GDI. I covered the basics of the device context, as well as some of the MFC classes that are used to manage them. You built a sample program that allows you to change and display information about an output device and its map mode.

Using Pens

In this chapter you get a look at pens. Pens are versatile GDI objects that are used to draw lines and geometric shapes in a Windows program. I discuss the more common attributes for pens and examine the MFC CPen class, and you build a sample program that uses pens to draw three different types of lines.

What Is a Pen?

What A pen is a Windows GDI object used to draw lines and figures. Think of a Windows pen as being like an ink pen at your desk. A Windows pen object has three attributes:

- *Width*, normally one pixel wide, although a pen can be as wide as you like
- *Style*, which can be any of the pen styles I discuss in a moment
- *Color*, which can be any Windows color packed into a COLORREF structure, and which I discuss in the section "Using Color Values with Pens."

Programs written for Windows use two types of pens:

- *Cosmetic pens*, which are always drawn in device units, regardless of the current mapping mode.
- *Geometric pens*, which are drawn in logical units and are affected by the current mapping mode. Geometric pens have more style and drawing options than cosmetic pens.

A cosmetic pen is used when lines must always be drawn with a fixed size. For example, rulers and grid lines are often drawn using cosmetic pens. Geometric pens are used when lines should reflect the scaling provided by the current mapping mode.

Why Use a Pen?

Why　A pen is perfect in situations where you must draw a geometric shape or line. Although you might use a bitmap for complicated images, you easily can draw squares, rectangles, circles, and other basic shapes using GDI objects.

You can create and use pens with a variety of styles. Cosmetic pens are extremely quick, and are mapped directly into device units. This makes them useful for drawing things like frames, borders, grid lines, and other screen objects that should not be affected by the current device context-mapping mode. Geometric pens require more CPU power, but offer more styles. You can manipulate geometric pens using any of the available mapping modes.

Pens are also useful for drawing three-dimensional highlighting or other effects. It's not uncommon for pens and other GDI objects to be used to simulate controls in Windows; before Windows 95 was released, early versions of property pages used pens to draw simulated "tabs."

How Are Pens Used?

How　Like other GDI objects, a pen normally is used by creating an MFC object. Use the CPen class to create and manage both cosmetic and geometric pens. When creating a pen, you must specify at least three things:

- The pen's style
- The pen's width
- The pen's color

The number of styles available for geometric pens is much larger than for cosmetic pens. However, cosmetic pens have much less overhead. You should use cosmetic pens whenever possible. The next few sections discuss the various options available for cosmetic and geometric pens.

Using Cosmetic Pens

Cosmetic pens are not affected by the current mapping mode's scaling factor, as they are always drawn in device units. This makes them useful for work where a line must overlay another view that may be scaled. These basic styles are available for cosmetic pens:

- PS_SOLID, which creates a solid pen.
- PS_DASH, used to creates a dashed pen. If the pen width is greater than one, the pen is drawn as PS_SOLID.
- PS_DOT, which creates a dotted pen. This style is also only valid for pens with a width of one. Wider pens are drawn as PS_SOLID.
- PS_DASHDOT, which creates a pen with alternating dashes and dots. If the pen width is greater than one, a solid pen is drawn instead.
- PS_DASHDOTDOT, which creates a pen with alternating dashes and double dots. If the pen width is greater than one, a solid pen is drawn instead.
- PS_NULL, which creates a null pen; this pen doesn't draw at all.
- PS_INSIDEFRAME, which creates a pen that draws a line inside the frame of closed shapes produced by GDI functions, such as the Ellipse and Rectangle functions.
- PS_ALTERNATE, which can be applied only to cosmetic pens, and which creates a pen that sets every other pixel.

Figure 30.1 shows examples of each of the above pen styles.

Figure 30.1.
Examples of the styles available for pens.

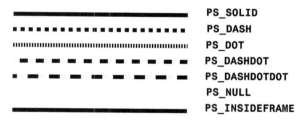

PS_SOLID
PS_DASH
PS_DOT
PS_DASHDOT
PS_DASHDOTDOT
PS_NULL
PS_INSIDEFRAME

Using Geometric Pens

Geometric pens can use all of the styles available for cosmetic pens except for the PS_ALTERNATE style, and they also have access to four additional attributes:

- A pattern used to draw the pen
- A hatch style used for some types of patterns
- The type of endcap used for terminating a line
- A joining style, used when two lines intersect

Defining Pattern Styles for Pens

In addition to the other styles shared with cosmetic pens, a geometric pen can be associated with a brush style by passing a LOGBRUSH, or *logical brush structure*, as a parameter when the pen is created. Using a LOGBRUSH structure enables you to specify patterns and hatching styles for a pen, just like a brush. I discuss using the LOGBRUSH structure in Chapter 31, "Brushes."

Defining Endcap Styles

When a line drawn with a pen terminates, an *endcap* is drawn. If the line is drawn with a geometric pen, you can specify the style of the endcap. The following endcap styles are available:

- PS_ENDCAP_ROUND, which draws rounded endcaps after the line's end point
- PS_ENDCAP_SQUARE, which draws a square box extending slightly past the line's end point as an endcap
- PS_ENDCAP_FLAT, which draws a line that ends exactly on the end point, with a flat endcap

These three styles are shown in Figure 30.2. The square and round endcaps actually extend past the end of the line drawn by the pen. The flat endcap style extends only to the end of the line.

Figure 30.2.
Endcap styles available
for geometric pens.

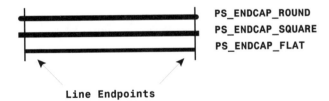

PS_ENDCAP_ROUND
PS_ENDCAP_SQUARE
PS_ENDCAP_FLAT

Line Endpoints

Defining Joining Styles

A *joining style* is used to determine how the intersection of two lines should be drawn. This attribute is only used for geometric pens; cosmetic pens are simply joined at right angles to each other. The join can be one of the following styles:

- PS_JOIN_BEVEL, which specifies a beveled join
- PS_JOIN_MITER, which specifies a miter join, but only if the join is within limits set by ::SetMiterLimit; if the join exceeds this limit, it is drawn as a beveled join
- PS_JOIN_ROUND, which specifies a rounded join

Examples of each join type are shown in Figure 30.3.

Figure 30.3.
Join styles available for
geometric pens.

PS_JOIN_MITER

PS_JOIN_ROUND

PS_JOIN_BEVEL

Using Color with Pens

All pens are given a color by passing a COLORREF structure as a parameter when they are created. A COLORREF structure is commonly used to pass color information as a parameter in Windows programs. A COLORREF is a 32-bit value, made up of four bytes (where each byte contains eight bits). Three of the bytes specify the relative intensities of red, green, and blue for a particular color, and the fourth byte is left unused.

A COLORREF is created using the RGB macro, which takes three parameters, each ranging from 0 to 255, with 255 signifying that the maximum amount of that color should be included in the COLORREF. For example, to create a COLORREF with a white value, the definition would look like this:

```
COLORREF clrWhite = RGB(255,255,255);
```

For black, the definition would look like this:

```
COLORREF clrBlack = RGB(0,0,0);
```

I use the COLORREF structure and RGB macro in examples later in this chapter.

Using the *CPen* Class

The CPen class is simple, as there are really only a few things that can be done to a pen object; most of the fun occurs when the pen object is selected into a device context. The CPen class provides three constructors: two simple constructors primarily for cosmetic pens, and another extremely flexible constructor primarily for geometric pens.

The first constructor has no arguments:

```
CPen      aGreenPen;
aGreenPen.Create( PS_SOLID, 1, RGB(0,255,0);
```

If you use this constructor, use the Create member function to actually create the pen and make it ready for use.

The second constructor provided for CPen also is used for cosmetic pens:

```
CPen    penDottedAndRed( PS_DOT, 1, RGB(255,0,0) );
```

This version of the constructor accepts three parameters: the pen style, width, and pen color.

The third constructor used for CPen objects allows any sort of pen to be created. It also uses more parameters, as shown in Listing 30.1.

Listing 30.1. Creating a brush using a LOGBRUSH structure.

```
LOGBRUSH    lbrGrnHatch;

lbrGrnHatch.lbStyle = BS_HATCHED;
lbrGrnHatch.lbColor = RGB(0,255,0);
lbrGrnHatch.lbHatch = HS_DIAGCROSS;

CPen    penGeometric( PS_DOT ¦ PS_GEOMETRIC ¦ PS_ENDCAPROUND,
                      50,
                      &lbrGrnHatch,
                      0,
                      NULL );
```

The constructor's first parameter is the pen's style, with the or operator used to combine all styles that are applied to the pen. The second parameter for the constructor is the width; if the pen is cosmetic, it must be set to one. The third parameter is a pointer to a LOGBRUSH structure. In Listing 30.1, lbrGrnHatch is defined as a diagonally cross-hatched green brush.

The last two parameters are rarely used; they define a user-supplied pattern for the pen. These two parameters are used only if the pen is created with the PS_USERSTYLE attribute. The fourth parameter is the number of elements in the style array, while the fifth parameter is an array of DWORD values, each used to define the length of a dash or space in the pen's pattern.

Using Stock Pens

The simplest pens to use are known as *stock objects*. Each type of GDI object has a certain number of stock objects which belong to the operating systems and are easy to use because they don't have to be constructed or deleted. There are three stock pens provided by Windows:

- BLACK_PEN, which, oddly enough, provides a black pen
- WHITE_PEN, which provides a white pen
- NULL_PEN, which provides a NULL pen, and is exactly the same as creating a pen with the PS_NULL style

Each of these pens is exactly one unit wide. If you need a wider pen, you must create one using the CPen class. These pens are used through a CDC object by calling the SelectStockObject function, passing the stock object as a parameter, as follows:

```
CPen* pOldPen = pDC->SelectStockObject( BLACK_PEN );
```

As with other GDI objects, it's a good idea to maintain the pattern of storing the first GDI object returned from a SelectObject function so that it can be returned to the operating system.

Drawing with Pens

Pens are just one of the GDI objects that you can use with a device context. After a pen has been selected into a device context, there are several different drawing functions that can be performed with the device context. The CDC class used to represent device contexts, as I discussed in Chapter 29, "Device Contexts," includes these drawing functions often used with pens:

- Ellipse, used to draw an ellipse. This function is also used to draw circles, as a circle is just a special type of ellipse.

- Arc, used to draw a portion of an ellipse.

- LineTo and MoveTo, used to draw lines. Together they are often used to draw highlighting, squares, rectangles, and other types of figures.

Part VII

Essential Example

A GDI Example Using Pens

As an example using pens, you can modify the DCTest program you created in the previous chapter. The changes use three pens to draw three figures in the view window, in a variety of styles and colors.

Modifying the existing project also gives you a chance to see how different mapping modes affect the figures drawn using pens. Although some of the listings may look long, most of them only require a few changes in the source code that is already present.

Modifying the Mapping-Mode Dialog Box

As the first step in the sample program, modify the mapping-mode dialog box and the CMapModeDlg class to support extra options that are used when drawing with pens. The new version of the IDD_MAP_MODE dialog box is shown in Figure 30.4.

Figure 30.4.
*The new version of
the mapping-mode
dialog box.*

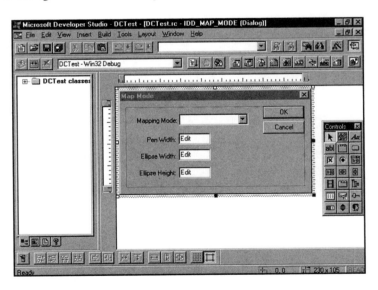

Use the values from Table 30.1 for the new controls you add to the mapping-mode dialog box, using ClassWizard to add member variables to the CMapModeDlg class. All existing controls should remain as they are.

Table 30.1. Values for new edit controls you add to the mapping-mode dialog box.

Edit Control	Resource ID	Variable Name	Type
Pen Width	IDC_WIDTH	m_nPenWidth	int
Ellipse Width	IDC_CXELLIPSE	m_cxEllipse	int
Ellipse Height	IDC_CYELLIPSE	m_cyEllipse	int

Modifying the *CDCTestView* Class

You must modify the CDCTestView class slightly to add three new member variables to store the pen height and the ellipse variables you just added to the dialog box class. Add three new member variables to the attributes section of the CDVTestView class declaration, as is shown in Listing 30.2.

Listing 30.2. New member variables added to the CDCTestView class.

```
// Attributes
private:
    // Variables added for Chapter 29
    CMap< int, int, CString, CString > m_map;
    int     m_nMapMode;
    // Variables added for Chapter 30
    int     m_cxEllipse;
    int     m_cyEllipse;
    int     m_nPenWidth;
```

Do not modify the declarations for existing member variables.

Modifying the *CDCTestView* Member Functions

You must modify three CDCTestView member functions:

- The CDCTestView constructor
- The CDCTestView::OnViewMapMode menu handler
- The CDCTestView::OnDraw member function

Each of these views is modified in the following sections. None of these member functions are new; they are all used in the current DCTest project.

Add three new lines to the CDCTestView constructor to initialize the new variables added to the CDCTestView class. Listing 30.3 is the new version of the CDCTestView constructor. Most of the function should already be entered; you need only to add the last three lines.

Listing 30.3. The new version of the CDCTestView constructor.

```
CDCTestView::CDCTestView()
{
    m_nMapMode = MM_TEXT;
    m_map.SetAt( MM_ANISOTROPIC, "MM_ANISOTROPIC" );
    m_map.SetAt( MM_HIENGLISH, "MM_HIENGLISH" );
    m_map.SetAt( MM_HIMETRIC, "MM_HIMETRIC" );
    m_map.SetAt( MM_ISOTROPIC, "MM_ISOTROPIC" );
    m_map.SetAt( MM_LOENGLISH, "MM_LOENGLISH" );
    m_map.SetAt( MM_LOMETRIC, "MM_LOMETRIC" );
    m_map.SetAt( MM_TEXT, "MM_TEXT" );
    m_map.SetAt( MM_TWIPS, "MM_TWIPS" );
    m_nPenWidth = 1;
    m_cxEllipse = 100;
    m_cyEllipse = 200;
}
```

Modify the CDCTestView::OnViewMapMode function to handle the changes in the Map Mode dialog box. Listing 30.4 provides the source code for the new version of OnViewMapMode. There are a total of six new source code lines, each marked with a comment. You should need only to add these six lines; the rest of the function should have been created already.

Listing 30.4. The new version of the CDCTestView::OnViewMapMode function.

```
void CDCTestView::OnViewMapMode()
{
    CMapModeDlg dlg;
    // The next three lines are added for Chapter 30
    dlg.m_nPenWidth = m_nPenWidth;  // 1
    dlg.m_cxEllipse = m_cxEllipse;  // 2
    dlg.m_cyEllipse = m_cyEllipse;  // 3
    if( dlg.DoModal() == IDOK )
    {
        // The next three lines are added for Chapter 30
        m_nPenWidth = dlg.m_nPenWidth;  // 4
        m_cxEllipse = dlg.m_cxEllipse;  // 5
        m_cyEllipse = dlg.m_cyEllipse;  // 6
        POSITION    pos;
        pos = m_map.GetStartPosition();
        while( pos != NULL )
        {
            CString szMapMode;
            int     nMapMode;
            m_map.GetNextAssoc( pos, nMapMode, szMapMode );
            if( szMapMode == dlg.m_szCombo )
            {
                m_nMapMode = nMapMode;
                break;
            }
        }
        InvalidateRect( NULL );
    }
}
```

Last but not least, you must create a new version of the OnDraw function. Almost all of this version of OnDraw is new because you are now drawing with pens. Use the source code provided in Listing 30.5 for the new version of CDCTestView::OnDraw.

Listing 30.5. The new version of CDCTestView::OnDraw.

```
void CDCTestView::OnDraw(CDC* pDC)
{
    pDC->SetMapMode( m_nMapMode );
    // Draw an ellipse based on the current map-mode and values
    // supplied by the user.
    CRect   rcClient;
    GetClientRect( rcClient );
    pDC->DPtoLP( rcClient );      // Covert device units to logical
    CPoint  ptCenter( rcClient.Width()/2, rcClient.Height()/2 );
    CRect   rcEllipse( ptCenter.x - ( m_cxEllipse/2 ),
                       ptCenter.y - ( m_cyEllipse/2 ),
                       ptCenter.x + ( m_cxEllipse/2 ),
                       ptCenter.y + ( m_cyEllipse/2 ) );
    CPen    penRed( PS_SOLID, m_nPenWidth, RGB(255,0,0) );
    CPen*   pOldPen = pDC->SelectObject( &penRed );
    pDC->Ellipse( rcEllipse );
    // Draw a black box around the ellipse, using one of the stock
    // pens.
    pDC->SelectStockObject( BLACK_PEN );
    pDC->MoveTo( rcEllipse.TopLeft() );
    pDC->LineTo( rcEllipse.right, rcEllipse.top );
    pDC->LineTo( rcEllipse.BottomRight() );
    pDC->LineTo( rcEllipse.left, rcEllipse.bottom );
    pDC->LineTo( rcEllipse.left, rcEllipse.top );
    // Draw an arc using the client area as a bounding rectangle.
    // Clip the arc so that only the lower-left half is displayed.
    CPen    penDottedAndGreen( PS_DOT, 1, RGB(0,255,0) );
    pDC->SelectObject( &penDottedAndGreen );
    pDC->Arc(rcClient, rcClient.TopLeft(),rcClient.BottomRight());
    pDC->SelectObject( &pOldPen );
}
```

Summary

In this chapter I examined pens and the MFC class CPen. You also created an example that used device contexts to perform simple drawing, and you set device-mapping modes.

Brushes

In this chapter I discuss using another GDI object known as a *brush*. A brush is similar to a pen, except that it's used to fill an area with a color or pattern. In this chapter, you get a look at using the MFC CBrush class, and you modify the DCTest sample program to use brushes.

What Are Brushes?

A brush is a GDI object used to fill a control, window, or other area when programming for Windows. A brush is much like a pen; you select it the same way, some of the attributes are similar, and there are a series of stock objects that you can use without much overhead. However, you use a brush to fill an area rather than draw a line or a figure. A common use for brushes is to color windows, controls, or dialog boxes.

Every brush has several attributes:

- *Color*, used to specify the brush color. You use a COLORREF value, just as when you specify a pen color.
- *Pattern*, used to define the pattern used by the brush.
- *Hatching style*, used when a hatch pattern is specified.

By choosing different values for attributes given to a brush, you can achieve a wide variety of effects.

Why Use a Brush?

Why

A brush is the only way to fill in an area in a program written for Windows. Any time you fill an area with a color or pattern, you use a brush.

Brushes can be used for small areas, such as controls, or areas as large as the entire desktop. In an example later in this chapter, you use a brush to change the color of a dialog box's background.

How Are Brushes Used?

How

In a program you write with Visual C++, you normally create and use CBrush objects the way you create and use CPen objects. Every brush has a set of attributes that defines how it appears and behaves; and, just as with pens, Windows stores a number of *stock brushes* that are available by calling the SelectStockObject function.

Your Windows program can create four basic types of brushes:

- *Solid brushes*, which are similar to solid pens, except they are used to fill areas instead of drawing lines. You normally give these brushes a color when you use a COLORREF to create them.
- *Stock brushes*, which are predefined brushes stored and maintained by Windows, much like the stock pens discussed in Chapter 30, "Using Pens."
- *Hatch brushes*, which fill an area with a predefined hatch pattern, as shown in Figure 31.1. These brushes can also be colored when they are created.
- *Pattern brushes*, which fill an area with a pattern supplied in an 8×8 bitmap, as shown in Figure 31.1.

Figure 31.1.
Examples of styles available for brushes.

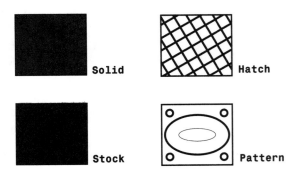

You create each of these brush types using a different function call. For example, a solid brush is created using CreateSolidBrush, while a hatched brush is created using CreateHatchBrush. When using the CBrush class, it's also possible to call a specialized CBrush constructor to construct the CBrush object in the desired style. I discuss using the CBrush class later in this chapter.

You can create solid and hatch brushes with a color attribute that specifies the color used when the brush fills an area. In the case of a hatched brush, the color specifies the color of the hatching lines.

Hatch Styles for Brushes

There are six hatch styles available for hatch brushes. You create a hatch style by passing one of the styles below as a parameter when you create the brush:

- `HS_BDIAGONAL`, which creates a brush with a downward hatch pattern. The lines used in the hatch pattern run from left to right, at 45 degrees.
- `HS_CROSS`, which creates a hatch pattern with vertical and horizontal intersecting lines.
- `HS_DIAGCROSS`, which creates a cross-hatch pattern with each line angled at 45 degrees.
- `HS_FDIAGONAL`, which creates a brush with an upward hatch pattern. The lines used in the hatch pattern run from left to right, at 45 degrees.
- `HS_HORIZONTAL`, which creates a horizontal hatch pattern.
- `HS_VERTICAL`, which creates a vertical hatch pattern.

Figure 31.2 shows examples of these six hatching styles.

Figure 31.2.
Examples of brush hatching styles.

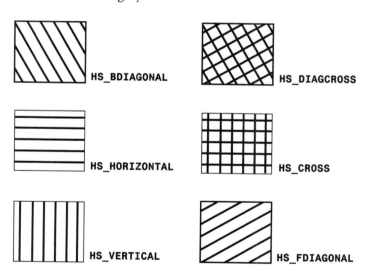

Using the *CBrush* Class

To use a brush in an MFC program, create a `CBrush` object and select it into a device context. You can create the brush using single-step construction, like this:

```
CBrush    brBlack( RGB(0,0,0) );
```

Alternatively, use two-step construction, where the brush object is constructed and then explicitly created, like this:

```
CBrush    brBlack();
brBlack.CreateSolidBrush( RGB(0,0,0) );
```

The advantage of using two-step construction is that the function used to create a brush returns FALSE if the function fails. If single-step construction fails, a CResourceException is thrown.

Unlike pens, which used style bits to determine the type of pen to be created, separate functions are used for different brush types. When using two-step construction, there are three functions you can use to create a brush after you construct the CBrush object:

- CreateSolidBrush
- CreateHatchBrush
- CreatePatternBrush

There are four different constructors provided for CBrush. In addition to the default constructor, three constructors can be used to create a specific type of brush in one step. The second constructor is used to create a solid brush, and takes one COLORREF parameter, indicating the color used for the brush:

```
CBrush    brGreen( RGB(0,0,255) );
```

Using this brush is equivalent to using the default constructor, then calling CreateSolidBrush.

The third form of the CBrush constructor is used to create a hatched brush, and takes the hatching style and hatch color as parameters:

```
CBrush    brGray( HS_CROSS, RGB(192,192,192) );
```

This constructor is equivalent to using the default constructor, then calling CreateHatchBrush.

Use the fourth and final constructor for CBrush to create brushes that have bitmap patterns. The constructor takes a pointer to a CBitmap object as a parameter:

```
CBrush    brArrow( &bmpArrow );
```

The CBitmap object must be at least eight pixels by eight pixels. If the bitmap is larger, only the upper-left eight pixel squares are used for the brush pattern.

Logical Brushes

Logical brushes are defined using the LOGBRUSH structure. A logical brush often is used when specifying how a brush should be constructed. For example, in Chapter 30, you used a LOGBRUSH structure to specify the characteristics of a geometric pen. Think of a LOGBRUSH as a recipe for a brush that might be created: it's not a brush yet, but it may help build a brush in the future.

The LOGBRUSH structure has three data members:

- lbrStyle, which contains the brush style.
- lbrColor, which stores a COLORREF value for the brush.
- lbrHatch, which stores a hatch style if needed.

Each of the three LOGBRUSH data members corresponds to one of the style attributes available for brushes discussed earlier in this chapter. To create a logical brush, just assign values to the three data members, as with any structure. Listing 31.1 uses a logical brush to create a red, hatched brush.

Listing 31.1. Filling a LOGBRUSH structure.

```
LOGBRUSH      lbrRed;
CBrush        theRedBrush;
lbrRed.lbrStyle = BS_HATCH;
lbrRed.lbrColor = RGB(255,0,0);
lbrRed.lbrHatch = HS_CROSS;
theRedBrush.CreateBrushIndirect( &lbrRed );
```

Using the Common Color Dialog Box

The Windows operating system includes a series of dialog boxes as part of the operating system. These dialog boxes are guaranteed to be present, and using them requires just a few lines of code. Use these dialog boxes for common operations where it's beneficial for all Windows programs to have a similar look and feel. The common dialog boxes shipped with Windows can help you to:

- Select a file to be opened.
- Choose a font.
- Choose a color.
- Create a standard Find and Replace dialog box.
- Choose Options and print to a supported printer.

To use the common color dialog box, just create a CColorDialog object and call DoModal, just as with any other dialog box:

```
CColorDialog    dlgColor;
if( dlgColor.DoModal() )
{ //....
```

If IDOK is returned from the dialog box, the CColorDialog::GetColor function gets the selected color value. The example in the next section uses the color dialog box to choose a brush color. I cover using other common dialog boxes in later chapters. (For example, I cover using the font-selection dialog box in Chapter 32, "Fonts.")

Essential Example

A GDI Example Using Brushes

As an example of how to use brushes, modify the DCTest project that you've been using for the last two chapters. The new version of the project displays a colored ellipse on a gray view background. Both the ellipse and background color are filled using CBrush objects. You can change the color of the ellipse using the common color dialog box; and, as a bonus, the mapping-mode dialog box color changes to match the ellipse.

Changing the Mapping-Mode Dialog Box and *CMapModeDlg* Class

Modify the mapping-mode dialog box to allow the user to choose a color for the dialog box and a brush used for the view. The CMapModeDlg class needs two new variables: a COLORREF for the currently selected color, and a CBrush object that has been created using the current color. Listing 31.2 contains the changes to the CMapModeDlg class declaration. Add the new code in the Dialog Data section, just after the AFX_DATA comments.

Listing 31.2. Changes to the CMapModeDlg class declaration.

```
// Dialog Data
    //{{AFX_DATA(CMapModeDlg)
    enum { IDD = IDD_MAP_MODE };
    CString    m_szCombo;
    int        m_cyEllipse;
    int        m_cxEllipse;
    int        m_nPenWidth;
    //}}AFX_DATA
    // Variable added in Chapter 31
public:
    COLORREF m_clrChoice;
private:
    CBrush    m_brControl;
```

You must change the mapping-mode dialog box slightly for this example. Remove the pen-width edit control and add a pushbutton control, as shown in Figure 31.3. Use ClassWizard to remove the m_nPenWidth member variable from the CMapModeDlg class.

Figure 31.3.
The new version of
the mapping-mode
dialog box.

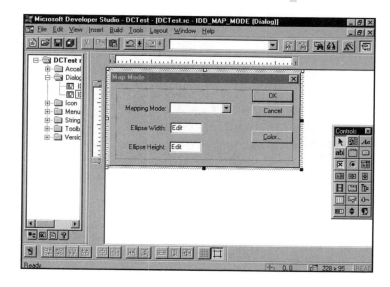

Use the values from Table 31.1. for the new button control.

Table 31.1. Values for the new Color button.

Resource ID	Caption	Function
IDC_COLOR	&Color...	CMapModeDlg::OnColor

Using ClassWizard, add a new message-handling function to the CMapModeDlg class named
CMapModeDlg::OnColor. The source code for OnColor is provided in Listing 31.3.

Listing 31.3. The CMapModeDlg::OnColor member function.

```
void CMapModeDlg::OnColor()
{
    CColorDialog    dlgColor;
    if( dlgColor.DoModal() == IDOK )
    {
        m_clrChoice = dlgColor.GetColor();
        // If the brush already exists, delete the current
        // GDI object before calling CreateSolidBrush
        if( m_brControl.Detach() )
            m_brControl.DeleteObject();
        m_brControl.CreateSolidBrush( m_clrChoice );
        InvalidateRect( NULL );
    }
}
```

The `OnColor` function creates a common color dialog box, and displays it using `DoModal`. If the user selects a new color, the color is collected, and the brush is updated. If the brush has previously been created, the `Detach` and `DeleteObject` functions must be called to destroy the current brush before creating a new brush.

Handling the *WM_CTLCOLOR* Message

Before displaying any control or dialog box, Windows asks for the control's color by sending a `WM_CTLCOLOR` message to the owner of the control. To specify a color to be used for the control or dialog box, return a solid brush containing the color in response to this message, as shown in Listing 31.4. The `m_brControl` brush is a class member variable because it must survive for the life of the control.

Listing 31.4. Changing the color of a dialog box by handling `WM_CTLCOLOR`.

```
HBRUSH CMapModeDlg::OnCtlColor(CDC* pDC,CWnd* pWnd,UINT nCtlColor)
{
    if( nCtlColor == CTLCOLOR_DLG || nCtlColor == CTLCOLOR_STATIC )
    {
        pDC->SetBkMode( TRANSPARENT );
        return (HBRUSH)m_brControl.GetSafeHandle();
    }
    else
        return CDialog::OnCtlColor(pDC, pWnd, nCtlColor);
}
```

The easiest way to deal with colored dialog boxes is shown in Listing 31.4, where the text-drawing mode is set to transparent by calling `SetBkMode`. If this line is commented out, you will see that the static text has colored areas around each color. By setting the drawing mode to transparent, the text is drawn without including the text background color, allowing the dialog box color to show through.

The `GetSafeHandle` function is used with all GDI objects to return a handle to the underlying object. A `CBrush` object returns an `HBRUSH` handle; a `CPen` object returns an `HPEN`, and so on.

The `WM_CTLCOLOR` message is sent for every control type found in the dialog box. It's possible to set different colors for each control type by testing for the values found in Table 31.2. If a brush is not returned, determine the return value by calling `CDialog::OnCtlColor`.

Table 31.2. Control-type message return value.

Control Message Value	Control Type
CTLCOLOR_BTN	Button control
CTLCOLOR_DLG	Dialog box
CTLCOLOR_EDIT	Edit control

Control Message Value	Control Type
CTLCOLOR_LISTBOX	List box control
CTLCOLOR_MSGBOX	Message box
CTLCOLOR_SCROLLBAR	Scroll bar control
CTLCOLOR_STATIC	Static control

Updating the *CDCTestView* Class

The CDCTestView class must store the color and brush selected by the user to color the ellipse and mapping-mode dialog box. There is one new variable added to the attributes section of the CDCTestView class, as shown in Listing 31.5: the m_clrChoice variable stores the currently selected color for the ellipse.

Listing 31.5. Changes to the CDCTestView class declaration.

```
// Attributes
private:
    // Variables added for Chapter 29
    CMap< int, int, CString, CString > m_map;
    int      m_nMapMode;
    // Variables added for Chapter 30
    int      m_cxEllipse;
    int      m_cyEllipse;
    // Variable added for Chapter 31
    COLORREF m_clrChoice;
```

Changes to *CDCTestView* Member Functions

To update the DCTest project to use brushes instead of pens, you must make four basic changes to the CDCTestView member functions:

- All references to m_nPenWidths must be removed.
- The new variable, m_clrChoice, must be initialized in the constructor.
- The OnViewMapMode function must update the m_clrChoice variable if the user changes the color.
- The OnDraw function must be changed to use brushes instead of pens.

Edit the constructor for CDCTestView so it looks like the source code provided in Listing 31.6. The m_nPenWidth variable has been removed, and one line has been added to initialize the m_clrChoice variable.

Listing 31.6. The CDCTestView constructor.

```
CDCTestView::CDCTestView()
{
    m_nMapMode = MM_TEXT;
    m_map.SetAt( MM_ANISOTROPIC, "MM_ANISOTROPIC" );
    m_map.SetAt( MM_HIENGLISH, "MM_HIENGLISH" );
    m_map.SetAt( MM_HIMETRIC, "MM_HIMETRIC" );
    m_map.SetAt( MM_ISOTROPIC, "MM_ISOTROPIC" );
    m_map.SetAt( MM_LOENGLISH, "MM_LOENGLISH" );
    m_map.SetAt( MM_LOMETRIC, "MM_LOMETRIC" );
    m_map.SetAt( MM_TEXT, "MM_TEXT" );
    m_map.SetAt( MM_TWIPS, "MM_TWIPS" );
    m_cxEllipse = 100;
    m_cyEllipse = 200;
    // The next line is added for Chapter 31
    m_clrChoice = RGB(0,0,0);
}
```

Modify the CDCTestView::OnViewMapMode function as shown in Listing 31.7. The code in this listing removes all references to the m_nPenWidth variable, and the function now tracks the color selected by the user. A total of two lines have been removed and one line added to the existing function.

Listing 31.7. The OnViewMapMode function.

```
void CDCTestView::OnViewMapMode()
{
    CMapModeDlg dlg;
    // The next three lines are added for Chapter 30
    dlg.m_cxEllipse = m_cxEllipse;
    dlg.m_cyEllipse = m_cyEllipse;
    // The next line is added for Chapter 31
    dlg.m_clrChoice = m_clrChoice;
    if( dlg.DoModal() == IDOK )
    {
        // The next three lines are added for Chapter 30
        m_cxEllipse = dlg.m_cxEllipse;
        m_cyEllipse = dlg.m_cyEllipse;
        // The next line is added for Chapter 31
        m_clrChoice = dlg.m_clrChoice;
        POSITION    pos;
        pos = m_map.GetStartPosition();
        while( pos != NULL )
        {
            CString szMapMode;
            int     nMapMode;
            m_map.GetNextAssoc( pos, nMapMode, szMapMode );
            if( szMapMode == dlg.m_szCombo )
            {
                m_nMapMode = nMapMode;
                break;
            }
        }
        InvalidateRect( NULL );
    }
}
```

Modify the CDCTestView::OnDraw function as shown in Listing 31.8. The new version of OnDraw uses a CBrush object to fill the view window with a red brush. Another CBrush object is used to draw an ellipse in the center of the view using a user-defined color to fill the figure.

Listing 31.8. The OnDraw member function modified to use brushes.

```
void CDCTestView::OnDraw(CDC* pDC)
{
    CRect rcClient;
    GetClientRect( rcClient );
    pDC->DPtoLP( rcClient );
    CBrush  brRed( RGB( 255, 0, 0 ) );
    pDC->FillRect( rcClient, &brRed );
    CPoint  ptCenter( rcClient.Width()/2, rcClient.Height()/2 );
    CRect   rcEllipse( ptCenter.x - ( m_cxEllipse/2 ),
                       ptCenter.y - ( m_cyEllipse/2 ),
                       ptCenter.x + ( m_cxEllipse/2 ),
                       ptCenter.y + ( m_cyEllipse/2 ) );
    CBrush  brEllipse( m_clrChoice );
    CBrush* pOldBrush = pDC->SelectObject( &brEllipse );
    pDC->Ellipse( rcEllipse );
    pDC->SelectObject( &pOldBrush );
}
```

Summary

In this chapter I discussed using brushes to fill areas in Windows and using the CBrush object in several different ways. You modified the DCTest project to use brushes to draw GDI figures. I also discussed using the color common dialog box.

Fonts

In this chapter I discuss fonts. Fonts define the symbols and characters used to display text in a Windows program. I present the basic attributes that are available for fonts, as well as how to use the common font dialog box provided as part of Windows, which greatly simplifies selecting a font. At the end of the chapter, there's some sample code that shows how fonts are used in a Windows program.

What Are Fonts?

What Fonts are GDI objects, much like the pens and brushes I discussed in the previous two chapters, and are used to define the characters used for output in a Windows program. A collection of characters and other symbols that share the same attributes are called a *font*.

In this chapter you see some terms that are unique to programming with fonts:

- A *glyph* is an individual character.
- *Font pitch* refers to the width of individual characters; *fixed pitch* means that each character has the same width, *variable pitch* means that some characters will be wider than others.

- A *serif* is the small cross at the ends of some characters. A font with a serif has short crosses at the ends of lines making up the font; Times New Roman is such a *serif font*. A font without serifs is often called a *sans serif font*. Figure 32.1 shows examples of a sans serif and a serif font.

Figure 32.1.
Sans serif and serif fonts.

Fonts are maintained by Windows. Information about each currently installed font is stored in a system table known as the *font table*.

There are three different types of fonts; each type has different capabilities:

- *Raster fonts* are created from bitmaps, and are stored in resource files with a .FON extension. Each bitmap is created for a specific screen resolution and is used by windows to map out exactly how the glyph will look when it is displayed.

- *Vector fonts* consist of a series of endpoints that are connected together to create each glyph and also are found in files with a .FON extension. Unlike raster fonts, vector fonts are device-independent, but they are the slowest of the three font types.

- *TrueType* fonts are the most flexible of all Windows fonts. First introduced in Windows 3.1, TrueType fonts consist of line and curve information, as well as hints about each glyph. Each TrueType font is stored in two files: one with a .FOT extension, the other with a .TTF extension.

Fonts are also arranged into six families that define the general attributes of the font. Fonts in the same family share similar strokes, serifs, or pitch.

The six font families are these:

- *Decorative*, which specifies novelty fonts such as Old English.

- *Dontcare*, which specifies a generic group of fonts; either the information doesn't exist, or is unimportant.

- *Modern*, which specifies fonts that have fixed pitch, and may or may not have serifs. Courier New is an example of a modern font.

- *Roman*, which specifies fonts that have variable pitch and have serifs, such as Times New Roman.

- *Script*, which specifies fonts that are similar to handwriting.

- *Swiss*, which specifies a font that is fixed pitch and does not have serifs, such as Arial.

Chapter 32

Why Use Fonts?

Strictly speaking, fonts are not necessary for most programs written for Windows. A default font is selected into every device context automatically, and it may work just fine for most applications. However, almost every program can benefit from using fonts that have been selected to suit its specific needs.

Why

Scaleable fonts that can display text in italic, bold, or underlined give a program an extra amount of usability. Most printers supported by Windows also allow TrueType fonts to be displayed on a printer exactly as they are on a video screen; this is an extra advantage, as it greatly simplifies the work required for printing.

Finally, once you decide to use fonts is your programs, it's trivial to allow users to select their own fonts. Later in this chapter I cover using the common font dialog box for selecting fonts.

How Are Fonts Used?

Like other GDI objects, the easiest way to use a font is to use the MFC class library. Like other GDI objects, fonts must be used with a device context and are influenced by the current state of the device context, such as mapping mode and color definitions. When you're working with text output, the CFont class helps make using a font easy.

How

There are two basic ways to use a font in your program:

- You can specify exactly what sort of font should be used.
- You can specify font general attributes and let Windows select a font for you.

Font Attributes

In addition to the font families I discussed earlier in this chapter, there are other general attributes you can use to specify a font. There are several font attributes, mainly because there are many different ways to display characters in a program written for Windows. Don't worry; after you've used fonts a few times, you'll be able to create fonts with no trouble at all. Later in the chapter, I use examples to demonstrate how you can use these attributes.

The Font Height and Width

You can specify the height of the font using one of these methods:

- If a height greater than zero is specified, Windows tries to match the requested height with one of the available fonts, and the font is mapped using logical units.
- If a font height of zero is specified, a reasonable default font is used. In this case, "reasonable" is defined by Windows.
- If the specified height is a negative number, the font is mapped using hardware units. Windows searches for a font that matches the absolute value of the size provided.

Logical units normally are used for screen display, and physical units are normally used for printing. In Chapter 35, "Printing," you use MM_TWIPS to create fonts based on device units.

The width of a font normally is set to zero, which tells Windows to select an appropriate default width. However, in some cases you may want to specify your own font width to display compressed or elongated text.

The Font Character Set

Every font is made up of a large number of characters and other symbols that can be displayed. The actual symbols that are contained in a font depend on the character set supported by that font. These three character sets are available:

- ANSI_CHARSET, used for most output when programming in Windows. This is the character set you're most likely to use. The symbol ANSI_CHARSET is defined as equal to zero, which makes it easy to use as a default parameter.

- OEM_CHARSET, used mainly for console mode programs, is almost identical to the ANSI character set. This character set is system-dependent, and can't be used reliably for every machine capable of running Windows. Some of the low and high-numbered characters are different, but these are rarely used in Windows.

- SYMBOL_CHARSET, used to display symbols such as the ones used in math formulas.

Attributes that Affect Font Output

Three parameters specify output attributes of the selected font: *output precision*, *clipping precision*, and *output quality*.

Output precision is used to specify how closely the font returned by Windows must match the requested font. A range of options is available, from allowing Windows to select a reasonable match to requiring an exact match:

- OUT_DEFAULT_PRECIS, used when Windows can choose a "reasonable" font. This is the most often-selected option and is equivalent to using zero as a parameter.

- OUT_STRING_PRECIS, used to specify that the font chosen by Windows must match the requested font's size.

- OUT_CHARACTER_PRECIS, used to specify that the font must match all requested attributes except orientation and escapement.

- OUT_STROKE_PRECIS, used to specify that the font chosen must exactly match the requested font.

Clipping precision is used to specify how characters are treated when they lie on a clipping boundary. There are three options:

- CLIP_DEFAULT_PRECIS, which allows Windows to select a "reasonable" font. This is the most often selected option and is equal to zero.

- CLIP_CHARACTER_PRECIS, which requires Windows to select a font that allows individual characters to be clipped if any part of the character lies outside the clipping region.

- CLIP_STROKE_PRECIS, which requires Windows to choose a font that allows portions of an individual character to be clipped if a character falls on the clipping boundary.

The output quality of the font refers to the degree to which GDI routines must match logical font attributes to the physical representation of the font. Here, again, there are three options:

- DEFAULT_QUALITY, where appearance doesn't matter; Windows is free to provide a "reasonable" font. This is a commonly selected option and is equivalent to using zero as a parameter.

- DRAFT_QUALITY, where fast output is given higher priority over print quality. Some effects, such as strikethrough, bold, italic, and underlined characters, are synthesized by GDI routines if necessary.

- PROOF_QUALITY, where the output quality is given higher priority than output speed. The quality of the font is more important than exact matching of the logical-font attributes. Some effects, such as strikethrough, bold, italic, and underlined characters, are synthesized by GDI routines if necessary.

Font Pitch and Family Attributes

As I discussed earlier, all fonts have a certain pitch. When requesting a font from Windows, there are three different choices for the pitch:

- DEFAULT_PITCH, where Windows selects a reasonable font based on other specified attributes.

- FIXED_PITCH, where the font created by Windows must have a fixed pitch.

- VARIABLE_PITCH, where the font is specified to have a variable pitch.

As I discussed earlier, the font family describes general characteristics for a type of font and can be used when a specific font may not be available on all machines. Here are the values for font families:

- FF_DECORATIVE

- FF_DONTCARE

- FF_MODERN

- FF_ROMAN

- FF_SCRIPT

- FF_SWISS

The pitch attribute can be combined with a font family attribute using the bitwise or operator, like this:

```
lfHeading.lfPitchAndFamily = DEFAULT_PITCH ¦ FF_SWISS;
```

It isn't necessary to combine the pitch and family attributes. For example, in the above example it's possible to specify just FF_SWISS.

Font Weights

You can specify the relative weight of a font, based on a scale from zero to 1,000. A weight of 400 describes a "normal" font, while 700 is used for a "bold" font. If you use zero, Windows uses a reasonable default weight for the font. Each of the weight options between 0 and 900 have symbolic names, as shown in Table 32.1.

Table 32.1. Symbolic names for font weights.

Symbol	Weight
FW_DONTCARE	0
FW_THIN	100
FW_EXTRALIGHT	200
FW_ULTRALIGHT	200
FW_LIGHT	300
FW_NORMAL	400
FW_REGULAR	400
FW_MEDIUM	500
FW_SEMIBOLD	600
FW_DEMIBOLD	600
FW_BOLD	700
FW_EXTRABOLD	800
FW_ULTRABOLD	800
FW_BLACK	900
FW_HEAVY	900

Although not every weight is available for every font, Windows tries to select a font weight close to the requested value.

Other Font Attributes

It's possible to define the escapement and orientation of a font. The *escapement* is the angle, in tenths of a degree, formed by a line of text in relation to the bottom of the page. For example, an escapement of 900 describes a font where each line of text is rotated 90 degrees counterclockwise. The *orientation* of a font is similar to the escapement but applies to each character rather than to an entire line of text.

Italic, underline, or strikethrough effects are assigned by specifying TRUE or FALSE for each of these attributes.

Finally, you can specify the typeface name. This is the name of a font that should be a good match for the parameters specified in other parts of the font description. If this parameter is set to NULL, Windows uses the other parameters when searching for a font. If you specify a name, that name is used to search for a font. If a font with that name is found, it is used.

Creating a Font Using *CFont*

The first time you consider creating a CFont object, you may be intimidated by the large number of parameters it takes. Don't worry; most of the parameters can actually be set to default values, or zero, and the Windows font mapper selects a font for you.

For example, Listing 32.1 creates two fonts. One font, fntArial, uses zero for all of the parameters, and specifies a font name. The other font, fntBoldSwiss, specifies many of the characteristics of a desired font, and the font mapper determines a reasonable font. Add the source code from Listing 32.1 to the CDCTestView::OnDraw function in the DCTest project. The DCTest project was created in Chapter 31.

Listing 32.1. Two different ways to create a CFont object.

```
void CDCTestView::OnDraw(CDC* pDC)
{
    CRect rcClient;
    GetClientRect( rcClient );
    pDC->DPtoLP( rcClient );
    COLORREF clrOld = pDC->SetTextColor( m_clrChoice );
    int nOldMode = pDC->SetBkMode( TRANSPARENT );
    CFont    fntArial, fntBoldSwiss;
    fntArial.CreateFont( 0, 0, 0, 0, 0, 0, 0, 0,
                         0, 0, 0, 0, 0, "Arial" );
    fntBoldSwiss.CreateFont( rcClient.Height()/20, 0, 0, 0,
                    FW_BOLD, TRUE, FALSE, 0, ANSI_CHARSET,
                    OUT_TT_PRECIS, CLIP_DEFAULT_PRECIS,
                    DEFAULT_QUALITY, DEFAULT_PITCH | FF_SWISS,
                    NULL );
    CString szMsg = "Hello! Change the color and mapping mode";
    CFont* pOldFont = pDC->SelectObject( &fntArial );
    pDC->TextOut( 0, rcClient.Height()/4, szMsg );
    pDC->SelectObject( &fntBoldSwiss );
    pDC->TextOut( 0, rcClient.Height()/2, szMsg );
    // Restore the old GDI objects
    pDC->SelectObject( pOldFont );
    pDC->SetTextColor( clrOld );
    pDC->SetBkMode( nOldMode );
}
```

Creating a Font Using a *LOGFONT* Structure

The LOGFONT structure is often used to describe a font. Just as the LOGBRUSH structure I discussed in Chapter 31 was used to describe a particular brush, the LOGFONT structure is used to describe a particular font. A LOGFONT isn't a font; it's just a description, so it contains members for all of the attributes available for a font.

Using a LOGFONT simplifies creating fonts, because many of the attributes for a series of fonts can be shared. Listing 32.2 is a version of CDCTestView::OnDraw that uses a LOGFONT structure to create several different fonts.

Listing 32.2. Using a LOGFONT structure to create fonts.

```
void CDCTestView::OnDraw(CDC* pDC)
{
    CRect rcClient;
    GetClientRect( rcClient );
    pDC->DPtoLP( rcClient );
    COLORREF clrOld = pDC->SetTextColor( m_clrChoice );
    int nOldMode = pDC->SetBkMode( TRANSPARENT );
    CString szMsg = "Hello! I'm an Arial font";
    CFont   fntArial;
    LOGFONT lf;
    memset( &lf, 0, sizeof(LOGFONT) );
    lstrcpy( lf.lfFaceName, "Arial" );
    fntArial.CreateFontIndirect( &lf );
    CFont* pOldFont = pDC->SelectObject( &fntArial );
    pDC->TextOut( rcClient.Width()/2, rcClient.Height()/2, szMsg );
    pDC->SelectObject( pOldFont );
    pDC->SetTextColor( clrOld );
    pDC->SetBkMode( nOldMode );
}
```

Most of the earlier version of OnDraw can remain in place; only the middle part of the function has changed between Listings 32.1 and 32.2. The first eight and the last five lines are the same in both versions.

Using the Common Font Dialog Box

Like the other common dialog boxes, the common font dialog box enables you, as a programmer, to easily use a commonly used dialog box in your Windows programs. The common font dialog box is extremely flexible from a user's point of view; the user can change the color, style, typeface, and size of the font in a single dialog box. In this section, you use the common font dialog box to select a font to be used in the view window.

The font is represented by a LOGFONT variable that is a member of the CDCTestView class. After selecting a new font with the common dialog box, the LOGFONT variable is updated and the view redrawn.

There are five steps involved in adding support for the common font dialog box:

- Add a new LOGFONT variable to the CDCTestView class.
- Modify the CDCTestView constructor.
- Create a new menu item for changing the font.
- Create a function in the CDCTestView class to handle the new menu item.
- Modify the CDCTestView::OnDraw member function so that the new LOGFONT variable is used when creating a font.

Just to make things interesting, you modify the OnDraw function to display the text rotated around the center of the view.

Add a *LOGFONT* Variable to the *CDCTestView* Class

The first step is to add a LOGFONT variable to the CDCTestView class. Although the font is created and destroyed every time the OnDraw member function is called, the LOGFONT variable stores the current attributes for the font selected for the view. Add this line to the attributes section of the CDCTestView class declaration:

```
LOGFONT     m_logFont;
```

The CDCTestView class constructor must initialize this variable to a known value. Listing 32.3 contains the source code for the new version of the CDCTestView constructor. Only the last two lines of the source code have been added since the previous version.

Listing 32.3. Source code to initialize the m_logFont variable.

```
CDCTestView::CDCTestView()
{
    m_nMapMode = MM_TEXT;
    m_map.SetAt( MM_ANISOTROPIC, "MM_ANISOTROPIC" );
    m_map.SetAt( MM_HIENGLISH, "MM_HIENGLISH" );
    m_map.SetAt( MM_HIMETRIC, "MM_HIMETRIC" );
    m_map.SetAt( MM_ISOTROPIC, "MM_ISOTROPIC" );
    m_map.SetAt( MM_LOENGLISH, "MM_LOENGLISH" );
    m_map.SetAt( MM_LOMETRIC, "MM_LOMETRIC" );
    m_map.SetAt( MM_TEXT, "MM_TEXT" );
    m_map.SetAt( MM_TWIPS, "MM_TWIPS" );
    m_cxEllipse = 100;
    m_cyEllipse = 200;
    // The next line is added for Chapter 31
    m_clrChoice = RGB(0,0,0);
    // the next two lines added for Chapter 32
    memset( &m_logFont, 0, sizeof(LOGFONT) );
    lstrcpy( m_logFont.lfFaceName, "Arial" );
}
```

Add a New Menu Item

Using the Developer Studio resource editor, add a new menu item to the View menu, using the values from Table 32.2.

Table 32.2. Values used for the Font menu item.

Resource ID	Caption	Member Function
ID_VIEW_FONT	&Font...	CDCTestView::OnViewFont

Use ClassWizard to add a message-handling function to the CDCTestView class for the new menu item, using the default name of OnViewFont. The source code for OnViewFont is shown in Listing 32.4.

Listing 32.4. The CDCTestView::OnViewFont member function.

```
void CDCTestView::OnViewFont()
{
    CFontDialog dlgFont( &m_logFont );
    dlgFont.DoModal();
    m_clrChoice = dlgFont.GetColor();
    InvalidateRect( NULL );
}
```

The source code in Listing 32.4 is the heart of this example. The current LOGFONT is passed to the common font dialog box during construction, which uses it as a starting point when the dialog box is initially displayed. After the user dismisses the dialog box, the LOGFONT will contain any modifications done by the user. Because the LOGFONT structure doesn't store the text color, the GetColor function is called to update any color selections made in the common dialog box.

Modify the *OnDraw* Member Function

The final step in this example is to use the selected font to draw a rotating text message in the view. The lfEscapement field from the LOGFONT structure is used to specify the angle of text line. The source code in Listing 32.5 updates the font's escapement in a for loop, causing the text to rotate.

Listing 32.5. Displaying a rotating text message using a LOGFONT.

```
void CDCTestView::OnDraw(CDC* pDC)
{
    CRect rcClient;
    GetClientRect( rcClient );
    pDC->DPtoLP( rcClient );
    COLORREF clrOld = pDC->SetTextColor( m_clrChoice );
    int nOldMode = pDC->SetBkMode( TRANSPARENT );
```

```
        CString szMsg = "  ...Help! I'm Spinning and I can't get up!";
        CFont   fntRotate;
        for( int nDegrees = 0; nDegrees < 3600; nDegrees += 200 )
        {
            m_logFont.lfEscapement = nDegrees;
            fntRotate.CreateFontIndirect( &m_logFont );
            CFont* pOldFont = pDC->SelectObject( &fntRotate );
            pDC->TextOut( rcClient.Width()/2,
                          rcClient.Height()/2,
                          szMsg );
            pDC->SelectObject( pOldFont );
            fntRotate.DeleteObject();
        }
        pDC->SetTextColor( clrOld );
        pDC->SetBkMode( nOldMode );
    }
```

The text will rotate around the center of the view, as shown in Figure 32.2. The font and color are updated when a new selection is made in the font dialog box.

Figure 32.2.
Displaying rotating text using font escapement.

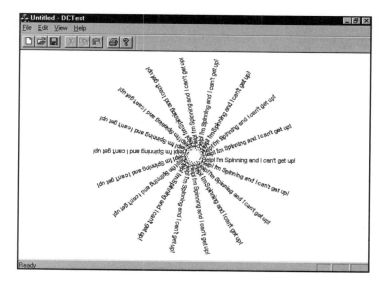

Summary

In this chapter I discussed using fonts in Windows programs, as well as how to use the CFont and CFontDialog classes. Sample programs illustrated the use of the LOGFONT structure, the use of the common font dialog box, and rotating fonts.

Icons

In this chapter I discuss another type of GDI resource: the icon. Icons are most often used to represent other objects, such as minimized programs or child windows. In this chapter I discuss how to use icons in your application, and you use a sample program that draws a pair of icons on top of two button controls in a dialog box.

What Is an Icon?

What An icon is a small bitmap that represents another object in a Windows program. For example, icons are used to represent minimized child windows in an MDI application. Icons also are widely used by Windows itself. When a program is minimized, its icon is displayed in the Windows 95 taskbar. When you're using the Explorer, the icon representing an application associated with each file is displayed next to the file's name. Windows displays the program's icon in the upper-left corner of the main window title bar.

Icons also are used in dialog boxes. For example, the message box dialog boxes discussed in Chapter 16 use icons to indicate the type of message conveyed. It's also common practice to include an application's icon in the About dialog box.

There are several different types of icon resources. In Chapter 24, "List View Controls," I discussed large and small icons. There are four different types of icons available:

- Large icons, used for most programs written for Windows prior to the release of Windows 95. These icons are 32 pixels on each side, and support 16 colors.
- Small icons, first introduced with Windows 95. These smaller icons are usually a smaller version of a program's large icon.
- 256-color icons, which support more than the standard 16 colors available to other types of icons. These icons are 48 pixels on each side, and are never displayed as a program's icon when the window is minimized.
- Monochrome icons support only two colors, and are 32 pixels on each side.

Why Use an Icon?

Why

Icons are similar to bitmaps, which I covered in Chapter 20, "Using Image Lists and Bitmaps." However, the code required to use an icon is so simple, there's not even an MFC class name CIcon dedicated to making using icons easier.

The Windows 95 Explorer uses the icon resources associated with your program when determining which icons to display. If large and small icons are available, the Explorer uses the icon resources from your application's EXE file. However, if you provide only a large icon, the Explorer synthesizes a small icon, which usually results in a small, distorted icon.

Icons can also be used with image lists. As I discussed in Chapter 20, an image list is ideal for collecting images. Any image stored in an image list can be converted into an icon using the ExtractIcon member function.

How Are Icons Used?

How

Because icons are resources, you add them to a program's resource file just as you do bitmaps, menus, and dialog boxes. You create new icons using the resource editor, much as you created bitmaps in Chapter 20.

Creating Icons Using the Image Editor

When creating a new project, AppWizard creates a set of default icons for your project automatically. The Developer Studio image editor can be used to edit or create new icons for your project.

To open the image editor, open the resource view in the project workspace and then open the Icon folder. Double-click any icon resource contained in the folder to open the editor. In an MDI application created by AppWizard, there will be two icon resources defined for a new project:

- `IDR_MAINFRAME`, an icon that is associated with the application; this is the "MFC cube" icon by default.

- `IDR_MYAPPTYPE`, where MyApp is the name of the project. This icon is used to represent the MDI child window. By default, this icon is the standard MFC "Doc" icon.

You can change these icon resources to represent the application you are working with. The color and tool palettes work just as they did when you edited bitmaps in Chapter 20, except that there are two new items in the color palette:

- The "transparent" color, which lets the background show through the icon
- The "reverse video" color, which lets the background show through after reversing the video

You can find the transparent and reverse video colors on the upper-right corner of the color palette. Switch to the transparent color by clicking the small video display icon with a green screen, and switch to the reverse video color by clicking the small video display with the red screen.

Inserting a New Icon Resource

To insert a new icon resource into an existing project, select Resource from the Insert menu, and select Icon from the resource type dialog box. You can also right-click the Icon folder in the resource view, and select Insert Icon from the pop-up menu; either of these actions opens the image editor with a blank icon, ready for editing. You can change attributes for icon resources, as with all resources, by double-clicking the edge of the icon resource, choosing Properties from the Edit menu, or by pressing Alt+Enter on the keyboard.

Loading an Icon

Once you have added an icon to a project, loading and displaying it requires three lines of code. To load an icon and prepare it for display, use the `LoadIcon` function:

```
HICON hico = AfxGetApp()->LoadIcon( IDI_LOGO );
```

Because `LoadIcon` is a `CWinApp` member function, a pointer to the application's `CWinApp` object must be fetched using the `AfxGetApp` function.

After the icon has been loaded, display it by calling `DrawIcon`:

```
pDC->DrawIcon( 0,0, hIcon );
```

The `DrawIcon` function is a member of the `CDC` class. The coordinates and icon handle must be passed as parameters.

After using `LoadIcon`, release the icon resource by calling the `DestroyIcon` function:

```
DestroyIcon( hIcon );
```

If you forget to call `DestroyIcon`, the memory allocated for the icon is not released.

Changing a Program's Icon

The icon used for a program is created by AppWizard when you initially create the project. To change this icon, open the image editor by double-clicking the application's icon in the resource view Icon folder.

After opening the icon, use the image editor tools to modify the icon as desired. Every application written for Windows can have its icon displayed in large and small formats. If you edit one of the icon formats, make sure you make corresponding changes in all formats supported by the icon. To display and edit all of the available formats, click the drop-down combo box above the image editor, which displays all of the supported formats for the icon. Selecting a new format loads that version of the icon into the image editor.

Every child window type also has a unique icon. You can edit that icon just as you do the program's main icon. As I discussed earlier in this chapter, the child window icon is named with a shared resource identifier in the form IDR_MYAPPTYPE, where the application is named MyApp.

Retrieving Icons from Image Lists

When an image is stored in an image list, the image list often draws the item directly, using the MFC CImageList::Draw member function. However, you also can have the image list create an icon based on an individual image. The CImageList::ExtractIcon member function is used to create such an icon:

```
HICON hIcon = m_imageList.ExtractIcon( 2 );
```

Using this member function is useful when several icons must be stored together. As I discussed in Chapter 20, an image list makes a convenient collection for all types of bitmapped images.

Displaying an Icon on a Button

Another useful way to use an icon is to display it in a button. Beginning with Windows 95, it's possible to display an icon in a button almost as easily as displaying a text string. Use the CButton member function SetIcon to set a button's icon. The icon must be loaded before it is used, and must be destroyed after the button is destroyed.

Adding New Icon Resources

For this example, add two buttons to the DCTest About dialog box. These two "stoplight" buttons work just like the traditional OK and Cancel buttons. Figure 33.1 shows the IDI_RED icon; although you can't tell from the figure, this icon consists of a red circle surrounded by the transparent color. Also, create a similar icon named IDI_GREEN, using a green circle surrounded by the transparent color.

Figure 33.1.
*The new icons used in
the DCTest example.*

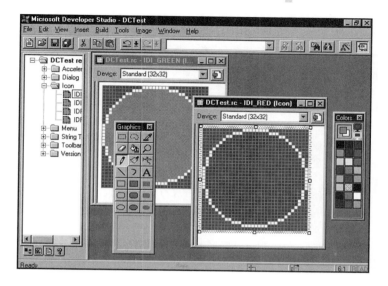

Use the two icons created earlier to label buttons in the DCTest About dialog box. Modify the
IDD_ABOUT dialog box by adding an extra button to it, as shown in Figure 33.2.

Figure 33.2.
*The About dialog box
used in the Icon
example.*

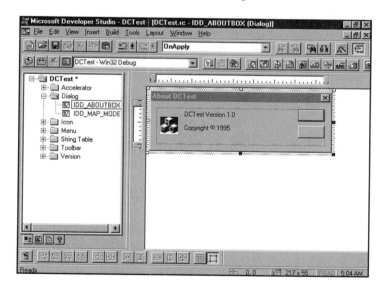

Use the values from Table 33.1 to set the attributes for the two buttons in the About dialog
box. Use ClassWizard to add the two buttons to the CAboutDlg class as CButton variables.

Table 33.1. Values used for button controls in the DCTest About dialog box.

ID	Variable Name	Control Type	Attributes
IDOK	m_btnOkay	CButton	Visible, Tabstop, Icon, Default
IDCANCEL	m_btnCancel	CButton	Visible, Tabstop, Icon

Buttons that have icon labels instead of text must have the DCTest attribute set. Review each button's properties dialog box, under the tab labeled "Settings," and make sure the Icon option is checked.

Changes to the *CAboutDlg* Class

Add two new variables to the CAboutDlg class. These variables are used to store the handles to icons displayed on the dialog box buttons. Add the source code from Listing 33.1 to the Implementation section of the CAboutDlg project. Also, add a declaration for a destructor for the CAboutDlg class just after the constructor declaration.

Listing 33.1. Additions to the CAboutDlg class declaration.

```
// Implementation
public:
    ~CAboutDlg();
protected:
    HICON    m_hIconOkay;
    HICON    m_hIconCancel;
```

The icons are added to the dialog box's buttons when the dialog box receives the WM_INITDIALOG message. Using ClassWizard, add a message-handling function for WM_INITDIALOG to the CAboutDlg class. Use the default name provided by ClassWizard, OnInitDialog. Edit the OnInitDialog member function so it looks like the code provided in Listing 33.2.

Listing 33.2. The AboutDlg::OnInitDialog member function.

```
BOOL CAboutDlg::OnInitDialog()
{
    CDialog::OnInitDialog();
    CWinApp* pApp = AfxGetApp();
    if( pApp != 0 )
    {
        m_hIconOkay = pApp->LoadIcon( IDI_GREEN );
        m_hIconCancel = pApp->LoadIcon( IDI_RED );
        m_btnOkay.SetIcon( m_hIconOkay );
        m_btnCancel.SetIcon( m_hIconCancel );
    }
    return TRUE;
}
```

The source code in Listing 33.2 loads the two "stoplight" icons created earlier. After the icons are loaded, the icon handles are passed to SetIcon function for each of the buttons contained in the dialog box.

When an icon is drawn on a button, the icon is clipped if necessary. The icon is not scaled to fit inside the button; it is displayed "actual size." This may mean that you must experiment with the relative sizes of the icon and the button.

As the dialog box is destroyed, the icons previously loaded using LoadIcon must be destroyed. Use the source code from Listing 33.3 to create the CAboutDlg class destructor.

Listing 33.3. Using the CAboutDlg class destructor to destroy the previously loaded icons.

```
CAboutDlg::~CAboutDlg()
{
    DestroyIcon( m_hIconOkay );
    DestroyIcon( m_hIconCancel );
}
```

Summary

In this chapter I discussed icons and how to use them in Windows programs. I covered changing the main program icon, as well as child icons. You used a sample program to demonstrate the functions used to load, draw, and destroy icon resources.

Cursors

In this chapter I discuss using cursors when programming for Windows.
You create a cursor as an application resource that is used in the example's
dialog box. You also build several short sample programs that demonstrate changing the cursor to an hourglass, clipping the cursor to a particular rectangle, and other topics.

What Is a Cursor?

A cursor is the little bitmap that moves around the screen providing
feedback about the current mouse position. The cursor also provides other
types of feedback:

- If the application is busy and won't accept input, most applications change the regular cursor to the hourglass cursor.

- If the cursor is over a window or control that accepts text input,
  most applications change the regular cursor to the "I-beam"
  cursor.

The most commonly used cursors are supplied by Windows. The hourglass, I-beam, and arrow cursors are three of the more popular standard
cursors. In addition, each program can define cursors that you add to the
application just as you do other resources.

Why Use a Cursor?

Why

The cursor is an important part of the feedback supplied to a user of a Windows program. Changing the style of cursor is an easy way to alert the user that a change of some type has occurred. Many times, changing the cursor is the only type of feedback required.

When a user sees the hourglass cursor after asking for work to be done in a dialog box, the user knows that the program is busy performing the task and can't be interrupted until the arrow cursor replaces the hourglass.

How Is a Cursor Used?

How

Most window classes have a cursor assigned to the class. In almost all cases, it's the standard arrow cursor. This means that for most default behavior, you don't have to do anything to use a cursor; Windows provides it free of charge. However, there are some situations where you must take control over the cursor yourself. For the examples in this chapter, you create an SDI project named Cursor.

Creating a Cursor Resource

A cursor image is created using the Developer Studio image editor, much like bitmaps and icons have been created in earlier chapters. Figure 34.1 shows the cursor used in later examples ready for editing in the image editor.

Figure 34.1.
The IDC_BANG cursor inside the Developer Studio image editor.

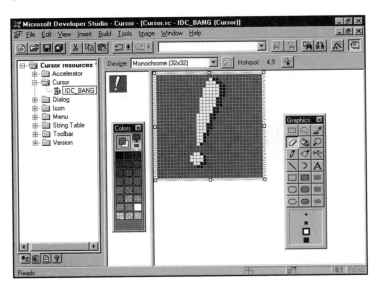

Create the cursor shown in Figure 34.1 and name it IDC_BANG. To create a cursor resource, select Resource from the Insert menu and select Icon from the resource type dialog box, or right-click the cursor folder in the resource view window. The editing tools you use to create a cursor are the same ones you used to create icons in the previous chapter. The standard Windows naming convention is for cursors to have names beginning with IDC_.

Adding a Hotspot to a Cursor

Every cursor has a *hotspot*, which is the actual point that determines the current cursor position. The hotspot for the arrow cursor is located at the end of the arrow. The default hotspot for a cursor is the upper-left corner of the cursor. The cursor image editor enables you to move the hotspot to a position that is reasonable for the cursor image.

For example, the IDC_BANG cursor you created in the previous section will not work properly if a new hotspot is not defined. Because the current hotspot is part of the background, this cursor won't work so well for operations where the mouse clicks must be accurate. One solution, as shown in Figure 34.2, is to modify the cursor to add a well-defined hotspot to the cursor; in this case a "bull's-eye," or target in the upper-left corner of the cursor bitmap.

Figure 34.2.
The new version of the
IDC_BANG, with a
hotspot and a bull's-eye.

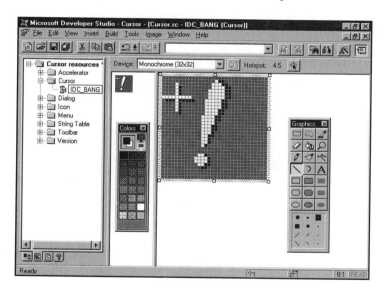

The hotspot control is a button located above the edited image. Click the hotspot button, then click the new hotspot pixel. For IDC_BANG, create a new hotspot in the center of the bull's-eye.

Changing a Cursor

Changing the current mouse cursor is probably the most common cursor-related activity in Windows programming. The operating system sends a WM_SETCURSOR message to a window as the mouse cursor passes over it. You can use this message to change the cursor, or you can let Windows choose the cursor that was defined for the window when it was registered.

To change the current cursor for a window, you handle the WM_SETCURSOR message. Using ClassWizard, add a message-handling function for WM_SETCURSOR to the CAboutDlg class. Listing 34.1 contains source code for the OnSetCursor that changes the cursor to IDC_BANG.

Listing 34.1. Changing the cursor during WM_SETCURSOR.

```
BOOL CAboutDlg::OnSetCursor(CWnd* pWnd, UINT nHitTest,
                           UINT message)
{
    // Load and set the new cursor. Return TRUE to stop
    // further processing of this message.
    CWinApp* pApp = AfxGetApp();
    HICON hIconBang = pApp->LoadCursor( IDC_BANG );
    SetCursor( hIconBang );
    return TRUE;
}
```

Conditionally Changing a Cursor

It's often convenient to change a cursor conditionally; for example, based on the cursor's location. Listing 34.2 is a new version of OnSetCursor that restores the arrow cursor when the cursor is over the dialog box's OK button.

Listing 34.2. Conditionally changing the cursor during WM_SETCURSOR.

```
BOOL CAboutDlg::OnSetCursor(CWnd* pWnd, UINT nHitTest,
                           UINT message)
{
    BOOL    bReturn;
    CRect   rcBtn;
    CPoint  ptCursor;
    //
    // Calculate the current cursor position, and change the
    // cursor if we're not over the OK button.
    //
    CWnd*   pBtn = GetDlgItem( IDOK );
    pBtn->GetWindowRect( rcBtn );
    GetCursorPos( &ptCursor );
    if( rcBtn.PtInRect( ptCursor ) == FALSE )
    {
        // Load and set the new cursor. Return TRUE to stop
        // further processing of this message.
        CWinApp* pApp = AfxGetApp();
        HICON hIconBang = pApp->LoadCursor( IDC_BANG );
        SetCursor( hIconBang );
        bReturn = TRUE;
    }
    else
    {
        // We're over the OK button, use the default cursor.
        bReturn = CDialog::OnSetCursor(pWnd, nHitTest, message);
    }
    return bReturn;
}
```

Using the Standard Cursors

Windows provides 19 standard cursors for use in your programs. These cursors often are used by Windows. For example, the IDC_APPSTARTING cursor is displayed when an application is launched by Windows. Table 34.1 lists the names and descriptions of the 19 standard cursors.

Table 34.1. The standard cursors provided by Windows.

Cursor Name	Description
IDC_ARROW	Arrow cursor
IDC_IBEAM	I-beam cursor
IDC_WAIT	Hourglass cursor
IDC_CROSS	Crosshair cursor
IDC_UPARROW	Up-arrow cursor
IDC_SIZENWSE	Sizing cursor, points northwest and southeast
IDC_SIZENESW	Sizing cursor, points northeast and southwest
IDC_SIZEWE	Sizing cursor, points west and east
IDC_SIZENS	Sizing cursor, points north and south
IDC_SIZEALL	Sizing cursor, points north, south, east, and west
IDC_NO	"No" cursor
IDC_APPSTARTING	Application-starting cursor
IDC_HELP	Help cursor
IDI_APPLICATION	Application icon
IDI_HAND	Stop sign icon
IDI_QUESTION	Question mark icon
IDI_EXCLAMATION	Exclamation point icon
IDI_ASTERISK	Asterisk or information icon
IDI_WINLOGO	Windows logo icon

Using these cursors is similar to using stock objects. Listing 34.3 uses the IDC_UPARROW cursor in response to WM_SETCURSOR.

Listing 34.3. Using a standard Windows cursor.

```
BOOL CAboutDlg::OnSetCursor(CWnd* pWnd, UINT nHitTest,
                            UINT message)
{
    // Load and set the new cursor. Return TRUE to stop
    // further processing of this message.
    CWinApp* pApp = AfxGetApp();
```

continues

Listing 34.3. continued

```
    HICON hIconBang = pApp->LoadStandardCursor( IDC_UPARROW );
    SetCursor( hIconBang );
    return TRUE;
}
```

A cursor set in response to the WM_SETCURSOR message will interfere with the remaining examples in the chapter. After you are finished with this example, remove the OnSetCursor function using ClassWizard.

Changing the Cursor to the Hourglass

When a large amount of processing is performed, it's common to ignore input from the user. It's considered good manners for a Windows program to change the cursor to an hourglass when user input won't be acknowledged.

A common place to ignore user input is during long initialization routines. It's not uncommon to display a user interface, but disregard user input, until the initialization is complete. It may take several seconds before an application is ready for input, particularly in applications that work with large amounts of data that must be initialized. In these cases, the BeginWaitCursor and EndWaitCursor functions should be used.

To demonstrate how these functions are used, add two message-handling functions to the CAboutDlg class using ClassWizard. Add a message-handling function for WM_INITDIALOG and WM_TIMER, and accept the default function names provided by ClassWizard. Listing 34.4 contains the source code for the OnInitDialog and OnTimer functions.

Listing 34.4. Modifying OnInitDialog and OnTimer to use the hourglass cursor.

```
BOOL CAboutDlg::OnInitDialog()
{
    CDialog::OnInitDialog();

    SetCapture();
    BeginWaitCursor();
    SetTimer( 1, 15000, NULL );

    return TRUE;
}

void CAboutDlg::OnTimer(UINT nIDEvent)
{
    ReleaseCapture();
    EndWaitCursor();
    KillTimer( 1 );
}
```

In Listing 34.4, the OnInitDialog function simulates the beginning of a long processing period. The SetCapture and BeginWaitCursor functions are called to change the cursor to an hourglass. While changed, the cursor cannot be used to interact with any controls. A five second timer is started, which calls the OnTimer function when the timer expires. The OnTimer function restores the cursor and kills the timer.

The order of the statements in OnInitDialog is important. Before calling BeginWaitCursor, the mouse must be captured using SetCapture; otherwise, the hourglass cursor immediately reverts to the arrow cursor.

Clipping a Cursor

There are times when it is convenient to restrict a cursor to a single window. This is usually the case when working with error messages, or in other situations where you would like to force the user to make a selection. Forcing a cursor to stay with the boundaries of a single window is known as "clipping the cursor."

As an example, force the cursor to stay over the Cursor project's About dialog box. Using ClassWizard, add message-handling functions for the WM_DESTROY and WM_MOVE to the CAboutDlg class. Add the source code in Listing 34.5 to the CAbout::OnMove and CAbout::OnDestroy member functions.

Listing 34.5. Source code used to form a clipping region for the cursor.

```
void CAboutDlg::OnMove(int x, int y)
{
    CDialog::OnMove(x, y);

    CRect    rcCursor;
    GetWindowRect( rcCursor );
    ClipCursor( &rcCursor );
}

void CAboutDlg::OnDestroy()
{
    ClipCursor( NULL );
    CDialog::OnDestroy();
}
```

When the MFC framework creates the About dialog box and moves it to the center of the view window, the WM_MOVE message is sent to the CAboutDlg class. Inside the OnMove function, the dialog box's screen coordinates are used to set the clipping rectangle for the cursor. When the dialog box is destroyed, the WM_DESTROY message is handled by the CAboutDlg::OnDestroy function, and the clipping rectangle is reset.

It is important to reset the cursor clipping region by calling ClipCursor(NULL) when the window is destroyed, or when the clipping region is no longer needed. If this function is not called, the cursor will be restricted to the requested rectangle even after the window has disappeared.

Part VII

Summary

In this chapter I discussed using cursors when programming for Windows. I provided several different examples showing how to capture the mouse, set the hourglass cursor, and conditionally change a cursor inside a dialog box.

PART VIII

Miscellaneous Topics

35 Printing

36 Using Property Pages and Property Sheets

37 Rich Edit Controls

38 Subclassing and Superclassing Controls

39 Owner-Drawn Controls

40 Using OLE Controls

41 Serialization

42 Serialization and Document/View

Printing

In this chapter I cover the support provided for printing using the Document/View architecture. Printing using the MFC class library is much simpler than printing in a straight SDK and C environment, and you create a small sample program at the end of this chapter to demonstrate how printing is done for a Document/View application.

What Is Printing in a Windows Program?

What Programs written for Windows should be hardware-independent. This extends to the printer, where all output is performed through device contexts, much as displays to the screen are done.

Many programs written for Windows need no hardcopy output. However, many programs can benefit by providing reports or other information in a printout. The Document/View architecture and MFC class library provide standard printing functionality to all SDI and MDI applications.

Part VIII

Why Use the MFC Printing Support?

Why Historically, printing in a program written for Windows has been a nightmare. Using the traditional SDK approach, it seems like there are dozens of function calls and structures that must be used to display output to a printer. Because Windows supports literally hundreds of printers, it can be difficult to ensure that printed output is printed correctly.

The Document/View architecture and the MFC class library help make it much easier to create hardcopy printouts in a Windows program. You can use the common print dialog box, and reuse view functions that are used for displaying information to the screen.

How Is the Printer in an MFC Program Used?

How Printing in an MFC program is almost effortless. If your program uses the Document/View architecture, and does all of its drawing in the OnDraw function, you may not need to do anything to get basic printing to work. The source code provided in Listing 35.1 is an example of a simple OnDraw function that can be used for screen and printer output.

Listing 35.1. A simple OnDraw function that works for the screen and printer.

```
void CPrintView::OnDraw(CDC* pDC)
{
    CString szMsg = "Hello printer and view example.";

    pDC->TextOut( 0, 50, szMsg );
}
```

Using the view's OnDraw member function is an easy way to take advantage of the hardware independence offered by Windows. If your code is portable enough to run on a variety of screen displays, you probably will get an acceptable printout using most printers available for Windows.

On the other hand, there are many cases where you may want to get more involved in the printing. For example, if your view is not WYSIWYG, the printed output may not be suitable. If your view is a form view, for example, you may want to print your document's data in another form, such as a list of items in the entire document, or detailed information about an item in the current form.

When you customize the view functions that are responsible for printing, you can also offer nice user interface elements such as headers, footers, page numbers, or special fonts.

Understanding the MFC Printing Routines

If you want to get involved in printing, here are the CView routines that are used to print a view:

- OnPreparePrinting, called before the common print dialog box is displayed
- OnBeginPrinting, where GDI resources specific to using the printer should be allocated
- OnPrepareDC, called once per page, just before the printout begins
- OnPrint, called to actually draw to the printer's DC
- OnEndPrinting, called once after all pages have been printed, or after the job is canceled; this is where GDI resources specific to using the printer are released

These member functions are called by the MFC framework as the print routine progresses. The relationship between these routines is shown in Figure 35.1.

Figure 35.1.
CView member functions called while printing a document.

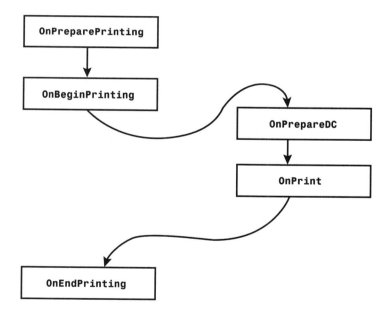

As shown in Figure 35.1, only the OnPrepareDC and OnPrint member functions are called for every page sent to the printer. The other functions are used to initiate variables in preparation of the printout, or to clean up and free resources after the printout has been completed.

When AppWizard creates a view class for your program, the OnPreparePrinting, OnBeginPrinting, and OnEndPrinting functions are automatically provided for you. You can add the other member functions with ClassWizard if you need to override the basic functionality.

Part VIII

Exploring the *CPrintInfo* Class

The CPrintInfo class is used to store information about the current state of a printout. A pointer to a CPrintInfo object is passed as a parameter to functions involved in the printout. You can access attributes of the CPrintInfo object for information about the printout, or in some cases you can change the attributes to customize the printout. Here are the most commonly used CPrintInfo members:

- m_bPreview, a flag that is set to TRUE if the document is being previewed
- m_bContinuePrinting, a flag that is set to FALSE to stop the print loop
- m_nCurPage, which contains the currently printing page number
- m_rectDraw, which contains the current printout rectangle
- SetMinPage, which sets the document's first page number
- SetMaxPage, which sets the document's last page number
- GetMinPage, which returns the value previously set as the document's first page number
- GetMaxPage, which returns the value previously set as the document's last page number
- GetFromPage, which returns the number of the first page being printed
- GetToPage, which returns the number of the last page being printed

Some of these members are used in a particular function. As I discuss each function in the next few sections, I also cover commonly used CPrintInfo members.

Using the *OnPreparePrinting* Function

The OnPreparePrinting function is generated by AppWizard for a project's initial view class. This function is called before the common print dialog box is displayed, and it gives you an opportunity to change the values displayed in the print dialog box.

If your document has more than one page, you should calculate the number of pages, if possible. This allows the maximum number of pages to be displayed in the print dialog box. You can set the number of pages by calling the CPrintInfo::SetMaxPages function:

```
pInfo->SetMaxPages( 2 );
```

You should not allocate any resources in this function, as you are not notified if the user cancels the print dialog box. I discuss allocating resources for printing in the next section.

Using the *OnBeginPrinting* Function

The OnBeginPrinting function is called after the user has pressed OK in the print dialog box in order to start the printout. This function is the proper place to allocate resources such as fonts, brushes, and pens that may be needed for the printout. In the example I present later, this function is used to create two CFont objects.

This function is called only once for each printout. If this function is called, the OnEndPrinting function is called after the printout is finished in order to give you a chance to free resources allocated in the OnBeginPrinting function.

Using the *OnPrepareDC* Function

The OnPrepareDC function is called just prior to a page being printed or displayed in the view. If OnPrepareDC is called with the CPrintInfo pointer set to NULL, the document is not being printed.

This function often is overridden for multiple-page documents, in order to continue the printout over multiple pages. To print another page, set the CPrintInfo::m_bContinue member variable to TRUE:

```
pInfo->m_bContinuePrinting = TRUE;
```

Using the *OnPrint* Function

The OnPrint function is the printing counterpart to OnDraw. In fact, many programs can just use the default version of OnPrint, which calls OnDraw. However, most printouts can benefit from providing page numbers, headers, footers, or special fonts that aren't displayed in the view.

When printing, the MM_TWIPS mapping mode is used. A *twip* is one-twentieth of a point, which is, in turn, almost exactly 1/72 of an inch. If you need help on the math, that's about 1,440 twips per inch. The really odd thing about MM_TWIPS is that the mapping mode begins with the upper-left corner at (0,0) and runs in a negative direction down the page, making the point one inch below the origin (0,-1440). Like other modes, the mapping mode extends in a positive direction to the right side of the page.

The OnPrint function is called once for every page. If you're printing data that is arranged so that the page number can easily be determined, it's a good idea to use the CPrintInfo parameter to determine the current page number. Remember, the user may ask for a range of pages to be printed, not just the entire document.

Using the *OnEndPrinting* Function

The OnEndPrinting function is called after the printout is finished. This function may be called because the job was completed successfully, or because it has failed; you don't really know. The purpose of this function is to release any resources that were allocated in the OnBeginPrinting function.

Essential Example

A Printing Example

As an example of the MFC print functions, create a small program that displays information to the screen and the printer. To begin, create an SDI or MDI project named Print using ClassWizard. Use the source code provided earlier, in Listing 35.1, for the CView::OnDraw function.

Using ClassWizard, add two message-handling functions for the CPrintView class: OnPrepareDC and OnPrint. The other printing functions have already been included in the CPrintView class by AppWizard.

Add two new member variables to the attributes section of the CPrintView class, as shown in Listing 35.2.

Listing 35.2. New CPrintView member variables.

```
protected:
    CFont*   m_pFntNormal;
    CFont*   m_pFntBanner;
```

The two new member variables are used for fonts created and used during the printout.

The *OnBeginPrinting* Function

As I discussed earlier, the OnBeginPrinting function is called just before printing begins. Add the source code provided in Listing 35.3 to the OnBeginPrinting function. This version of OnBeginPrinting creates two new fonts that are used in the printout. (I discussed creating fonts in Chapter 32.)

Listing 35.3. Allocating new fonts in the OnBeginPrinting function.

```
void CPrintView::OnBeginPrinting(CDC* pDC, CPrintInfo* pInfo)
{
    m_pFntNormal = new CFont;
    m_pFntBanner = new CFont;

    LOGFONT lf;
    memset( &lf, 0, sizeof(LOGFONT) );
    lstrcpy( lf.lfFaceName, "Arial" );
    m_pFntNormal->CreateFontIndirect( &lf );

    lf.lfItalic = TRUE;
    lf.lfWeight = FW_BOLD;
    m_pFntBanner->CreateFontIndirect( &lf );
}
```

The *OnEndPrinting* Function

Use the OnEndPrinting function to release the resource allocated in OnBeginPrinting. Add the source code from Listing 35.4 to the OnEndPrinting function.

Listing 35.4. Releasing resources in the OnEndPrinting function.

```
void CPrintView::OnEndPrinting(CDC* pDC, CPrintInfo* pInfo)
{
    delete m_pFntBanner;
    delete m_pFntNormal;
}
```

The *OnPrint* Function

The default implementation of OnPrint calls the OnDraw member function. For this example, add the source code from Listing 35.5 to OnPrint, which sends a header followed by several rows of text to the printer.

Listing 35.5. Printing a header and text using the OnPrint function.

```
void CPrintView::OnPrint(CDC* pDC, CPrintInfo* pInfo)
{
    CString     szHeader = "Essential Visual C++ Programming";
    CString     szMsg    = "Hardcopy Printout Example";
    CPoint      pt( 0, 0 );
    int         nOldMode = pDC->SetMapMode( MM_TWIPS );
    // Print header
    CFont*      pOldFont = pDC->SelectObject( m_pFntBanner );
    TEXTMETRIC  tm;
    pDC->GetTextMetrics( &tm );
    int         cyText = tm.tmHeight + tm.tmExternalLeading;
    pDC->TextOut( pt.x, pt.y, szHeader );
    // Move down one line, and print an underline bar using a
    // stock black pen.
    CPen* pOldPen = (CPen*)pDC->SelectStockObject( BLACK_PEN );
    pt.y -= cyText;
    pDC->MoveTo( pt );
    pDC->LineTo( 10000, pt.y );
    pt.y -= cyText;
    // Recalculate the text metrics based on a new font, and
    // print main text message until the end of the page.
    pDC->SelectObject( m_pFntNormal );
    pDC->GetTextMetrics( &tm );
    cyText = tm.tmHeight + tm.tmExternalLeading;
    // Add Listing 35.7 here for page-size independence.
    int nLength = (int)(pDC->GetDeviceCaps(VERTSIZE)/25.4) * -1440;
    nLength += 1440;
    for( pt.y -= cyText; pt.y > nLength; pt.y -= cyText )
    {
        pDC->TextOut( pt.x, pt.y, szMsg );
    }
    pt.y -= cyText;
```

Listing 35.5. continued

```
    pDC->MoveTo( pt );
    pDC->LineTo( 10000, pt.y );
    // Restore old GDI objects to prevent resource leaks.
    pDC->SelectObject( pOldFont );
    pDC->SelectObject( pOldPen );
    pDC->SetMapMode( nOldMode );
}
```

The *OnPrepareDC* Function

The OnPrepareDC function is called just before each page is printed. The default version of this function allows one page to be printed. By modifying the bContinuePrinting flag, you can use this function to cause the printout to continue. Add the source code provided in Listing 35.6 to the OnPrepareDC function.

Listing 35.6. The OnPrepareDC function.

```
void CPrintView::OnPrepareDC(CDC* pDC, CPrintInfo* pInfo)
{
    CView::OnPrepareDC(pDC, pInfo);
    if( pInfo )
    {
        if( pInfo->m_nCurPage < 3 )
            pInfo->m_bContinuePrinting = TRUE;
        else
            pInfo->m_bContinuePrinting = FALSE;
    }
}
```

Compile and run the Print project, and send the output to the printer, using either the File menu or the toolbar icon. Send two sample printout pages to the printer.

Summary

In this chapter I discussed the print functions and support offered by MFC and the Document/View architecture. You also created a small sample program that sent two pages of text to the printer.

Using Property Pages and Property Sheets

This chapter covers property sheets and property pages, also known as tabbed dialog boxes. I discuss the MFC classes that are used in property sheets and property pages, as well as the functions used to maintain them. A small sample program is built at the end of the chapter to illustrate the steps required to build a property sheet.

What Are Property Pages and Property Sheets?

What Property sheets and property pages are one of the hottest new user interface elements in Windows programs. A property sheet looks like a normal modal dialog box but instead contains one or more views, called property sheet pages, with only one page visible at a time. Property sheets are often called tabbed dialog boxes, due to the tabs that are used to switch between the property sheet pages. A property sheet consists of three parts:

- A tab control is used to switch between the property sheet pages.

- One or more property sheet pages are associated with one tab each in the tab control. Only one of the property pages is visible. Property sheet pages contain controls in the same way as dialog boxes.

- A property sheet object is similar to a dialog box, containing the tab control and one or more property sheet pages. You never see an empty property sheet; there must always be at least one property sheet page.

Property sheets are everywhere in Windows 95 and Developer Studio. For example, properties for the Windows 95 taskbar are accessed with a property sheet. In Developer Studio, selecting Options from the Tools menu displays a large property sheet.

Why Use Property Pages and Property Sheets?

Why

Property sheets are an easy way to group a large number of controls into a single dialog box. Instead of requiring a user to navigate through a series of cascading dialog boxes, you can use several pages, each with a specific purpose.

It's also possible to combine several dialog boxes into a single property sheet and its associated property sheet pages. Figure 36.1 shows how several related dialog boxes can be combined into a single property sheet.

Figure 36.1.
Several related dialog boxes can often be combined into a single property sheet.

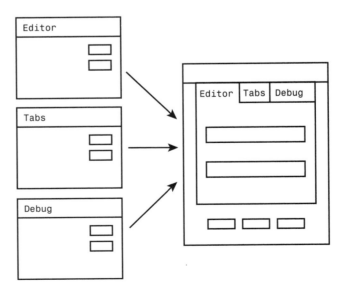

The property sheet used to set options for Developer Studio is an example of a property sheet that replaces several traditional dialog boxes. A single property sheet enables a user to have access to all of the Developer Studio options without dealing with a separate dialog box for each type of option.

How Are Property Pages and Property Sheets Used?

Property sheets and property sheet pages are used almost exactly in the same way dialog boxes are. The MFC CPropertySheet and CPropertyPage classes are used as base classes instead of the CDialog class. In general, the following steps create a property sheet: **How**

1. Create a CPropertySheet object.
2. Create one or more property page objects and add them to the property sheet.
3. Call the property sheet's DoModal member function.
4. Update property sheet data exactly as you would for modal dialog boxes.

Each of these four steps is discussed in the next few sections. The steps involved are fairly simple and very much like the steps used to add dialog boxes to an application using ClassWizard and the CDialog class.

Creating a *CPropertySheet* Object

The CPropertySheet class serves as a container for property sheet pages. In most cases, such as the example that is presented here, the default behavior offered by CPropertySheet is sufficient, and a CPropertySheet object can be created directly—usually with a single parameter specifying the caption for the property sheet.

```
CPropertySheet    nameSheet( "Names" );
```

Creating a Property Page

In contrast to the CPropertySheet class, each page class must be a new class derived from CPropertyPage, as discussed in a section later in this chapter. There must be at least one property page contained by the property sheet; if the last page is removed, the property sheet is automatically closed.

Before adding a property page class to your project, you must create the dialog resource for the property page. Use ClassWizard to add a class derived from CPropertyPage to the project for each property page.

Creating a Dialog Resource for a Property Page

Every property page must have a dialog resource created for it. The property page uses this dialog resource to lay out controls in the property page, much in the same way a form view uses a dialog resource to determine how to lay out controls.

Every dialog resource used as a property page must follow these guidelines:

- It must have a caption because the dialog box caption labels the "tab" associated with the property page.
- The window style must be set to Child.
- The frame style must be set to Thin.
- The Disabled and Titlebar options must be selected.

In addition, the first property page added to the property sheet is used to determine the size for the sheet and all pages added to the dialog box. For this reason, you should add your largest property page first or coordinate the sizes of the property pages.

Deriving a Class from *CPropertyPage* Using ClassWizard

After you create the dialog resource, you must add a class derived from CPropertyPage to the project. Open ClassWizard and add the new class to the project using the Add Class dialog box. This step is exactly the same as adding a class based on CDialog except that the base class is CPropertyPage. Two classes derived from CPropertyPage are created in the example later in this chapter.

Adding Message-Handling Functions to *CPropertyPage*

There are two message-handling functions often used by property pages:

- OnApply is called for each property page when a user clicks the Apply Now button. The default version of OnApply calls the OnOk member function and validates any input that has been made so far. You can use ClassWizard to add your own version of the OnApply function if you want to perform additional work when the user clicks the Apply Now button.
- OnKillActive is called as a user changes to a new property page. This is a good place to verify input. If the page should not be changed, you can keep the current tab active by returning FALSE from this function.

Other message-handling functions have default implementations that you don't usually need to override in simple property sheets. These other member functions include the following:

- OnQueryCancel is called by the MFC framework when the property sheet's Cancel button is clicked but before the cancel has taken place. This gives each page a chance to veto the cancellation.

- OnCancel is called by the MFC framework when the property sheet's Cancel button is clicked and after all property pages have acknowledged the OnQueryCancel function.
- OnOK is called by the MFC framework when the property sheet's OK, Apply Now, or Close buttons are clicked.
- OnSetActive is called by the MFC framework as the property page becomes the active page.
- OnReset is called by the MFC framework when the property sheet's Reset button is clicked.

Calling the Property Sheet's *DoModal* Function

You can use the DoModal and Create member functions to create modal and modeless property sheets. To display a modal property sheet, call the DoModal member function, but to display a modeless property sheet, use the Create member function. You can test the return value from DoModal to determine if the dialog box was closed or canceled.

```
if( nameSheet.DoModal() != IDCANCEL )
{
    // Update data
}
```

Exchanging Data with Property Sheets and Property Sheet Pages

Data is exchanged with a property sheet much as it is with a dialog box. However, the data contained in a property sheet is actually member data that belongs to the individual property sheet pages. Therefore, the simplest way to exchange data with a property sheet is to interact with each page individually.

Each CPropertyPage object handling a property sheet page can have class member variables that are associated with dialog box controls using ClassWizard. This is exactly the same process discussed in Chapter 16, "Dialog Boxes." After the property sheet has been dismissed, you can update the property sheet page member variables, as with CDialog member variables.

Essential Example

The Cool Property Sheet Example

As a property sheet example, use a project that contains a property sheet with two pages: The first page contains a name and address, and the second page stores hobby information.

To get started on this example, use AppWizard to create an SDI project named TabExample. Alternatively, you can use an existing project as a starting point because this example focuses on the property sheet, rather than the application around it.

Creating the Dialog Resources

As discussed earlier in this chapter, every property sheet page needs a dialog resource. When creating dialog resources for the property pages, remember to apply the styles provided in the section "Creating a Dialog Resource for a Property Page" earlier in this chapter. Also, the first property sheet page is used to determine the size for the entire property sheet and subsequent pages. Make sure that the dialog resource used for the first page is the largest page or that all the pages are the same size.

Creating the Name Page

The first dialog box is used to store a name and address, as shown in Figure 36.2.

Figure 36.2.
The dialog resource used for the Name property sheet page.

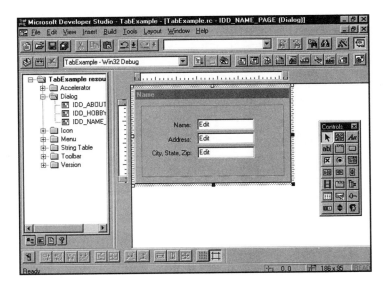

Use the resource ID IDD_NAME_PAGE for the dialog box. Use the values from Table 36.1 for the dialog box's attributes.

Table 36.1. Attributes for the `IDD_NAME_PAGE` dialog box.

Name	Value
Window style	Child
Frame style	Thin
Disabled	Checked
System Menu	Unchecked
Titlebar	Checked
Caption	Name

Use the values from Table 36.2 for edit controls added to the dialog box.

Table 36.2. Values used for the `IDD_NAME_PAGE` dialog resource.

Edit Control	Resource ID	Category	Type	Member Variable
Name	`IDC_EDIT_NAME`	Value	CString	`m_szName`
Address	`IDC_EDIT_ADDRESS`	Value	CString	`m_szAddress`
City, State, Zip	`IDC_EDIT_CITY`	Value	CString	`m_szCity`

Use ClassWizard to create a new class to handle the `IDD_NAME_PAGE` property page. Use the values from Table 36.3 for the Add Class dialog box. Note that the base class for the `CNamePage` class is `CPropertyPage`, rather than `CDialog`.

Table 36.3. Values used for the Add Class dialog box.

Control	Value
Name	`CNamePage`
Base Class	`CPropertyPage`
File	NamePage.cpp
Dialog ID	`IDD_NAME_PAGE`
OLE Automation	None
Component Gallery	Cleared

Click the Create button. The `CNamePage` class is generated and added to your project. Change to the Member Variables tab and add control member variables to the `CNamePage` class, using the values from Table 36.2.

Creating the Hobby Page

The second dialog resource is used to collect information about hobbies, as shown in Figure 36.3. Create this dialog resource using the same attributes that were used for the previous dialog box, but instead make the dialog box caption "Hobbies" and its resource ID IDD_HOBBY_PAGE.

Figure 36.3.
The hobby page resource ID in the Developer Studio dialog editor.

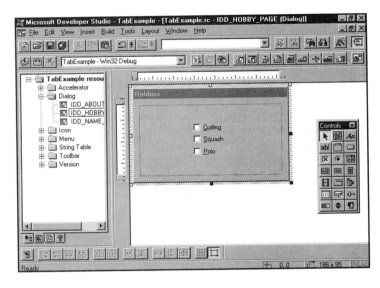

Use the values from Table 36.4 for the checkboxes added to the IDD_HOBBY_PAGE dialog resource.

Table 36.4. Values used for the IDD_HOBBY_PAGE dialog resource.

Checkbox	Resource ID
Curling	IDC_CHECK_CURLING
Squash	IDC_CHECK_SQUASH
Polo	IDC_CHECK_POLO

Use ClassWizard to create a new class to handle the IDD_HOBBY_PAGE property page, using the values from Table 36.5.

Table 36.5. Values used for the Add Class dialog box.

Control	Value
Name	CHobbyPage
Base Class	CPropertyPage
File	HobbyPage.cpp

Control	Value
Dialog ID	IDD_HOBBY_PAGE
OLE Automation	None
Component Gallery	Cleared

Click the Create button to add the CHobbyPage class to your project. Unlike the name page, the hobby page has no member variables.

Creating the Property Sheet

In this example, the CMainFrame class handles a menu item that creates the property sheet. Create a new menu item under the View menu, using the values from Table 36.6 for the menu item and its message-handling function. Use ClassWizard to add a message-handling function for the new menu item.

Table 36.6. New member functions for the CMainFrame class.

Menu ID	Caption	Event	Function Name
ID_VIEW_NAMES	&Names...	COMMAND	OnViewNames

Listing 36.1 contains the source code for the OnViewNames function, which handles the message sent when the Names menu item is selected.

Listing 36.1. Creating a property sheet in the CMainFrame::OnViewNames function.

```
void CMainFrame::OnViewNames()
{
    CPropertySheet   nameSheet( "Hobby List" );

    CNamePage        pgName;
    CHobbyPage       pgHobby;

    nameSheet.AddPage( &pgName );
    nameSheet.AddPage( &pgHobby );

    nameSheet.DoModal();
}
```

The CNamePage and CHobbyPage class declarations must be included into the source file. Add the #include statements from Listing 36.2 to the MainFrm.cpp source file after the other #include statements.

Listing 36.2. Additional `#include` statements for MainFrm.cpp.

```
#include "NamePage.h"
#include "HobbyPage.h"
```

Compile and run the project. The property sheet is displayed when you select Names from the View menu.

Handling the Apply Button

The current property page example works fine, but the Apply button is disabled. The button remains disabled unless a property page explicitly enables it by calling the `SetModified` function.

Enabling the Apply Now Button

The best place to call `SetModifed` is after a control has been changed. For example, the `CNamePage` class can call `SetModified` after an edit control has been updated. Using ClassWizard, add a message-handling function for the `EN_CHANGE` message sent from the `IDC_EDIT_NAME` edit control. The source code for the `CNamePage::OnChangeEditName` function is provided in Listing 36.3.

Listing 36.3. Handling edit control updates in the `CNamePage` class.

```
void CNamePage::OnChangeEditName()
{
    SetModified();
}
```

In our example, once the user updates the edit control used to collect the name, the Apply button is enabled. You can also have more complicated requirements for enabling the button, such as verifying input or requiring that more than one control has valid input.

For the hobby property page, the Apply button should be enabled after the user changes any of the checkboxes. Using ClassWizard, add message-handling functions for `BN_CLICKED` for every checkbox, accepting the default names suggested by ClassWizard. The source code for these functions is provided in Listing 36.4.

Listing 36.4. Handling check button updates in the `CHobbyPage` class.

```
void CHobbyPage::OnCheckCurling()
{
    SetModified();
}

void CHobbyPage::OnCheckPolo()
{
    SetModified();
}
```

```
void CHobbyPage::OnCheckSquash()
{
    SetModified();
}
```

Receiving Messages from the Apply Button

Clicking the Apply button calls the OnApply function for every loaded property page. Property pages that have not been loaded are not called because they haven't had any data changed yet. An example of an OnApply function is provided in Listing 36.5. This function displays a message box when the Apply button is clicked.

Listing 36.5. The CHobbyPage::OnApply member function.

```
BOOL CHobbyPage::OnApply()
{
    AfxMessageBox( "Hobby Page Applied" );
    return CPropertyPage::OnApply();
}
```

Summary

In this chapter, I discussed property sheets and property pages, as well as the MFC classes that are used to create them. For an example, you created a small property sheet that contains two property pages.

Rich Edit Controls

The rich edit control is one of the most interesting controls released with Windows 95. In this chapter, I discuss the basic functions that are available when using the rich edit control, as well as the MFC classes that are used to support it. At the end of the chapter, there is a short example that demonstrates how character formatting can be performed using a rich edit control.

What Is the Rich Edit Control?

What The rich edit control is an edit control that uses a subset of the rich text format (RTF) to store text contained in the control. The rich edit control is almost like having a complete word processor in a single control.

The edit control uses the RTF format to store its text while keeping the low-level details about RTF hidden from the user of the control. Although the rich edit control does not support the entire RTF specification, it supports the most commonly used parts, and it simply ignores any input that it can't handle.

What Is Rich Text Format (RTF)?

What

The rich text format is a specification that defines how applications can embed formatting information inside a document. Unlike a proprietary formatting scheme that is supported by a single application, the RTF specification is used by many applications to store data. This is important for situations where a document must be shared on different types of computers or by different applications. For example, an RTF document created by FrameMaker on a UNIX machine can be used by Word for Windows without losing formatting information.

If you are interested in the details about RTF, the specification is available from Microsoft and can be downloaded from the MSWORD forum. You can visit the MSWORD forum by entering GO MSWORD at any ! prompt. Version 1.3 of the specification is 92 pages long and contains a sample application that demonstrates how RTF is used if you don't have a rich edit control.

If you're not concerned with the details of RTF, don't worry; the rich edit control handles all the difficult work for you.

Why Use the Rich Edit Control?

Why

The rich edit control enables you to have edit controls that are capable of displaying multiple formats in a single control window. When you use a standard edit control, the font, color, and other formatting options must be consistent for all text contained in the control. Using the rich edit control enables you to be flexible; every character can have its own formatting style.

The rich edit control also enables you to specify paragraph styles—something that is not possible using a standard edit control. You can independently specify tab positions, indentations, and paragraph alignment styles for each paragraph.

Even with all of the extra functionality offered by a rich edit control, it is still compatible with the original edit control. All messages and functions that you use for standard edit controls can be used with rich edit controls.

How Is the Rich Text Control Used?

How

The rich edit control can be used in two ways. It can replace a standard edit control in a dialog box to collect and display user input. The MFC CRichEditCtrl class is used to wrap the edit control and provide access to its advanced functions, much in the same way the CEdit class provides easy access to the standard edit control.

The rich edit control can also be integrated into the MFC Document/View architecture, using the CRichEditView and CRichEditDoc classes.

Using the Rich Edit Document/View Classes

The rich edit Document/View classes help simplify the creation of simple word processing applications. There are three rich edit classes that work together for Document/View integration:

- CRichEditView actually contains the rich edit control and is responsible for all of the interaction with the control for user input and formatting.

- CRichEditDoc is used to serialize the data in the control to and from storage.

- CRichEditCntrItem handles the OLE interface for items embedded in the rich edit control.

The CRichEditView class contains a CRichEditCtrl object. This MFC class is discussed in the next section and provides access to the actual rich edit control. To retrieve a reference to the CRichEditCtrl object, use the GetRichEditCtrl function.

```
CRichEditCtrl&  rtfEdit = GetRichEditCtrl();
```

Using the *CRichEditCtrl* Class

The MFC CRichEditCtrl class is used to interact with a rich edit control. This class is similar to the CEdit class, but there are many more options available for formatting text.

Controlling Character Formatting

The CRichEditCtrl class offers two functions for controlling character formatting: GetSelectionCharFormat and SetSelectionCharFormat. These functions work for individual characters or with the currently selected text area. The GetSelectionCharFormat function is used to collect information about a character's format.

```
CHARFORMAT    chFormat;
DWORD dwSel = rtfEdit.GetSelectionCharFormat( chFormat );
```

The SetSelectionCharFormat function is used to set the format attributes for a character.

```
rtfEdit.SetSelectionCharFormat( chFormat );
```

The CHARFORMAT structure contains information about the character selection and is used for retrieving or setting character format information. The return value from GetSelectionCharFormat is a mask that represents which CHARFORMAT structure members are valid for the entire selection. The members of the CHARFORMAT structure include the following:

- cbSize specifies the size of this CHARFORMAT structure. You must fill in this value if you create the structure. If the structure is returned as a result from Windows, this value should not be changed, even if you pass it as a parameter in a later function call.

- dwMask is used to determine the valid members of the structure. This member is discussed in detail at the end of this list.

- dwEffects specifies the effects that are applied to the selection. The possible values for this member are discussed after this list.
- yHeight specifies the character height in twips. Twips are one twentieth of a point. Since there are approximately 72 points in an inch, each twip is about 1/1440 of an inch.
- yOffset specifies the character's offset relative to the baseline. If this value is positive, the character is a superscript; if negative, it is a subscript.
- crTextColor specifies the character text color. This value is only used if the CFE_AUTOCOLOR flag is not set in the dwEffects member.
- bCharSet can be any of the values allowed by the LOGFONT structure's lfCharSet member variable. Using the LOGFONT structure is discussed in Chapter 32, "Fonts."
- bPitchAndFamily specifies the font family and pitch. This member supports the same values as the LOGFONT structure's lfPitchAndFamily member variable.
- szFaceName is a null-terminated string that specifies the font face used by the character.

Using the *dwMask* and *dwEffects* Flags

The dwMask member is used to specify which structure members contain valid data. More than one of the values for dwMask can be combined by using ¦, the bitwise OR operator. The values for dwMask include the following:

- CFM_FACE indicates the szFaceName value is valid.
- CFM_SIZE indicates the yHeight value is valid.
- CFM_OFFSET indicates the yOffset value is valid.
- CFM_BOLD indicates the state of the dwEffects CFE_BOLD flag is valid.
- CFM_COLOR indicates the crTextColor value, as well as the dwEffects CFE_AUTOCOLOR flag, is valid.
- CFM_ITALIC indicates the dwEffects CFE_ITALIC flag is valid.
- CFM_PROTECTED indicates the dwEffects CFE_PROTECTED flag is valid.
- CFM_STRIKEOUT indicates the dwEffects CFE_STRIKEOUT flag is valid.
- CFM_UNDERLINE indicates the dwEffects CFE_UNDERLINE flag is valid.

The dwEffects member contains the formatting flags for the character selection. Before using any information from dwEffects, test dwMask to make sure the data is valid. The dwEffects members are provided in Table 37.1.

Table 37.1. Formatting flags in the CHARFORMAT dwEffects member.

Flag	Indicates the Character Is
CFE_AUTOCOLOR	Default Color
CFE_BOLD	Bold
CFE_ITALIC	Italic
CFE_STRIKEOUT	Struck Out
CFE_UNDERLINE	Underlined
CFE_PROTECTED	Protected

When the CFE_AUTOCOLOR flag is set, the default color can be obtained by calling the GetSysColor function.

```
GetSysColor( COLOR_WINDOWTEXT );
```

As with the flags and attributes from other Windows structures that use combined values, the dwMask and dwEffects member variables are used with the C++ ¦ (bitwise OR) and & (bitwise AND) operators. To determine if a flag is set, use the bitwise AND operator.

```
if( chFormat.dwMask & CFM_BOLD > 0 )
```

To set a flag, use the bitwise OR operator; you can use the form that combines the OR and assignment operators.

```
chFormat.dwEffects ¦= CFE_BOLD;
```

To clear a flag, use the bitwise AND operator with the negation operator.

```
chFormat.dwEffects &= ~CFE_BOLD;
```

Controlling Paragraph Formatting

In addition to offering character formatting, the CRichEditCtrl class offers two functions for controlling paragraph formatting: GetParaFormat and SetParaFormat. These functions work for individual paragraphs or with multiple paragraphs in a text selection area. Use the GetParaFormat function to retrieve paragraph information.

```
PARAFORMAT    parFormat;
DWORD dwSel = rtfEdit.GetParaFormat( parFormat );
```

Use the SetParaFormat function to set the format attributes for a paragraph.

```
rtfEdit.SetParaFormat( parFormat );
```

Like the CHARFORMAT structure, the PARAFORMAT structure contains information about the paragraph and is used for retrieving or setting paragraph format information. The members of the PARAFORMAT structure include the following:

- cbSize specifies the size of this PARAFORMAT structure. You must fill in this value if you create the structure. If the structure is returned as a result from Windows, this value should not be changed, even if you pass it as a parameter in a later function call.

- dwMask is used to determine the valid members of the structure. This member is discussed in detail at the end of this list.

- wNumbering is used to specify the paragraph's numbering and bulleting options. This member can be zero or PFN_BULLET.

- dxStartIndent specifies the first line indentation for the paragraph. If dwMask includes the PFM_OFFSETINDENT style bit, this member refers to the relative offset that is added to the starting indentation of the paragraph.

- dxRightIndent specifies the right indentation, relative to the right margin.

- dxOffset specifies the indentation for lines after the first line. This value is relative to the first line's starting indentation. If dxOffset is negative, the first line of the paragraph is indented. If dxOffset is positive, the first line is outdented.

- wAlignment specifies how the paragraph text is aligned. For left alignment, use PFA_LEFT; for right alignment, use PFA_RIGHT; for paragraphs that are centered, use PFA_CENTER.

- rgxTabs is an array that contains tab stop positions for the paragraph. The maximum number of tab positions is defined as MAX_TAB_STOPS.

- cTabCount contains the number of tab positions stored in the rgxTabs array.

The PARAFORMAT structure's dwMask member variable is used in the same way as the dwMask member variable found in the CHARFORMAT structure. In both cases, dwMask specifies which member variables can be used. Of course, the PARAFORMAT's dwMask member variable has different flags.

- PFM_ALIGNMENT indicates the wAlignment value is valid.

- PFM_NUMBERING indicates the wNumbering value is valid.

- PFM_OFFSET indicates the dxOffset value is valid.

- PFM_RIGHTINDENT indicates the dxRightIndent value is valid.

- PFM_STARTINDENT indicates the dxStartIndent value is valid and contains an absolute indentation value.

- PFM_OFFSETINDENT indicates the dxStartIndent is valid and specifies a relative offset.

- PFM_TABSTOPS indicates the cTabStops and rgxTabStops values are valid.

It's possible to specify both PFM_STARTINDENT and PFM_OFFSETINDENT. If that happens, PFM_STARTINDENT takes precedence.

Essential Example

A Rich Edit Control Example

For this example, create an SDI project named RichText using AppWizard. In the final AppWizard page, a checkered flag is displayed along with a list box containing classes that are generated for the application. Follow these steps to use the rich edit Document/View classes:

1. Select the view class in the class list box—in this case, CRichTextView.

2. Select CRichEditView from the Base combo box.

3. Click the Finish button to complete the AppWizard process.

AppWizard might display a message box notifying you of new options that will be added to your project. Accept any suggested changes. You can compile and run the RichText application; however, no character formatting options have been added to the project. In the next section, you see how character formatting is performed.

Creating a Format Dialog Box

Using Figure 37.1 as a guide, create a character format dialog box. This dialog box is used to display or change character formatting for text in the RichText application. Give the dialog box a resource ID of IDD_FORMAT.

Figure 37.1.
The character format-
ting dialog box from the
RichText example.

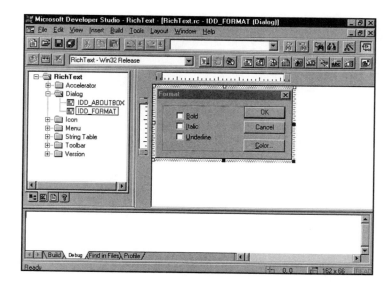

The dialog box contains four new controls: three checkboxes and one pushbutton. The checkboxes are used to set or clear character formatting flags, and the pushbutton displays a common color dialog box that can be used to select the text color. The resource IDs for each of these controls is provided in Table 37.2.

Table 37.2. Control properties from the Format dialog box.

Control	Resource ID
Bold checkbox	IDC_BOLD
Italic checkbox	IDC_ITALIC
Underline checkbox	IDC_UNDERLINE
Color pushbutton	IDC_COLOR

Creating the *CFormatDlg* Class

Use ClassWizard to create a new class to handle the Format dialog box, using the values from Table 37.3 for ClassWizard's Add Class dialog box.

Table 37.3. Values for the Add Class dialog box.

Control	Value
Name	CFormatDlg
Base Class	CDialog
File	FormatDlg.cpp
Dialog ID	IDD_FORMAT
OLE Automation	None
Add to Component Gallery	Cleared

Next, associate CFormatDlg member variables with the controls included in the Format dialog box, using ClassWizard and the values listed in Table 37.4. These variables are used to report and set formatting flags in the rich edit control.

Table 37.4. Values used to add member variables for CFormatDlg.

Control ID	Variable Name	Category	Type
IDC_BOLD	m_bBold	Value	BOOL
IDC_ITALIC	m_bItalic	Value	BOOL
IDC_UNDERLINE	m_bUnderline	Value	BOOL

Add a message-handling function for the IDC_COLOR button using ClassWizard and the values listed in Table 37.5. This function is used to display the common color dialog box in order to select the current text color.

Table 37.5. Adding a message-handling function for the Format dialog box.

Object ID	Message	Class	Function
IDC_COLOR	BN_CLICKED	CFormatDlg	OnColor

The source code for the OnColor function is provided in Listing 37.1.

Listing 37.1. The CFormatDlg::OnColor member function.

```
void CFormatDlg::OnColor()
{
    CColorDialog   dlg;
    dlg.m_cc.rgbResult = m_clrText;
    if( dlg.DoModal() )
    {
        m_clrText = dlg.GetColor();
    }
}
```

When the OnColor function is called, the common color dialog box is displayed. If the color dialog box is dismissed with the OK button, the selected color is stored in the m_clrText member variable.

Add a declaration for the m_clrText member variable to the CFormatDlg class declaration. Add the declaration of m_clrText in the implementation section under a public label, as shown in Listing 37.2.

Listing 37.2. Changes to the CFormatDlg class declaration.

```
// Implementation
public:
    BOOL    m_clrText;
```

Changes to the *CRichTextView* Class

The Format dialog box is displayed when a user clicks the right mouse button inside the view window. Add a message-handling function for WM_RBUTTONUP to the CRichTextView class, using the values from Table 37.6.

Table 37.6. Values for the new `CRichTextView` message-handling function.

Object ID	Message	Class	Function
CRichTextView	WM_RBUTTONUP	CRichTextView	OnRButtonUp

The source code for the OnRButtonUp function is provided in Listing 37.3.

Listing 37.3. The `CRichTextView::OnRButtonUp` member function.

```
void CRichTextView::OnRButtonUp(UINT nFlags, CPoint point)
{
    CRichEditView::OnRButtonUp(nFlags, point);
    CRichEditCtrl&  rtfEdit = GetRichEditCtrl();
    WORD wSelType = rtfEdit.GetSelectionType();
    if( wSelType & SEL_TEXT )
    {
        CFormatDlg  dlg;
        CHARFORMAT  chFormat;
        DWORD dwSel = rtfEdit.GetSelectionCharFormat( chFormat );
        if( dwSel & CFM_BOLD )
            dlg.m_bBold = chFormat.dwEffects & CFE_BOLD;
        if( dwSel & CFM_ITALIC )
            dlg.m_bItalic = chFormat.dwEffects & CFE_ITALIC;
        if( dwSel & CFM_UNDERLINE )
            dlg.m_bUnderline = chFormat.dwEffects & CFE_UNDERLINE;
        if( dwSel & CFM_COLOR )
            dlg.m_clrText = chFormat.crTextColor;

        if( dlg.DoModal() == IDOK )
        {
            if( dlg.m_bBold == TRUE )
                chFormat.dwEffects |= CFE_BOLD;
            else
                chFormat.dwEffects &= ~CFE_BOLD;
            if( dlg.m_bItalic )
                chFormat.dwEffects |= CFE_ITALIC;
            else
                chFormat.dwEffects &= ~CFE_ITALIC;
            if( dlg.m_bUnderline )
                chFormat.dwEffects |= CFE_UNDERLINE;
            else
                chFormat.dwEffects &= ~CFE_UNDERLINE;
            chFormat.crTextColor = dlg.m_clrText;
            rtfEdit.SetSelectionCharFormat( chFormat );
        }
    }
    else
    {
        AfxMessageBox( "Please select some text" );
    }
}
```

Add an #include statement in RichTextView.cpp that includes the class definition for CFormatDlg, found in FormatDlg.h. Add the following line just above the #include statement for RichTextView.h:

```
#include "FormatDlg.h"
```

Compile and run the RichText example. You can select a block of text using the mouse and change the format of the characters by right-clicking anywhere in the view window.

Summary

In this chapter, I discussed the rich edit control, along with the MFC classes that are used with it. You created a sample program that used the CRichEditView class to demonstrate how the rich edit control functions are used.

Subclassing and Superclassing Controls

In this chapter, I discuss subclassing and superclassing controls, two techniques that enable you to provide extra functionality to existing Windows controls. I discuss the support provided for subclassing included in the MFC class library, as well as how subclassed controls are used.

What Is Subclassing and Superclassing?

What Superclassing and subclassing are two techniques that change the behavior of a window. These techniques are most often used on controls. Subclassing and superclassing enable you to add new functionality to a window or control without recreating the window from scratch.

When a window is created, messages are sent from the Windows operating system to a window procedure associated with that window. As discussed in Chapter 14, "Messages and Event-Driven Programming," most of the work involved with window procedures is hidden from you when using Visual C++ and the MFC class library. Messages sent to a window created as part of your application are routed through the MFC framework and translated into function calls, such as WM_PAINT, as shown in Figure 38.1.

Figure 38.1.
In an MFC program, messages to a window procedure are translated into function calls.

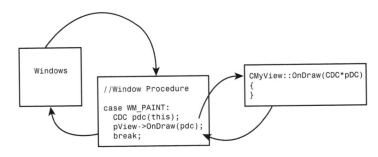

Although you never see the window procedures in an MFC program, every window created in a program written for Windows has a window procedure somewhere. Although controls also have window procedures, they're maintained by Windows, and most of the time you never deal with them.

About Subclassing

Subclassing a window involves replacing the current window procedure with a procedure provided by you. This window procedure has access to every message sent to the window or control after it is created. Figure 38.2 is a representation of message routing after a control has been subclassed.

Figure 38.2.
Messages sent to a subclassed control are redirected to the subclass window procedure.

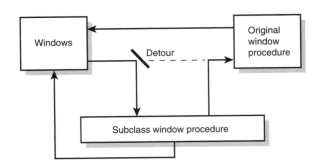

When a subclass window procedure receives a message, it can do one of three things.

- It can do nothing and "eats" the message, preventing it from reaching the original window procedure.
- It can pass the message to the original window procedure.

■ It can perform some processing on the message and either pass it on or eat it and prevent it from reaching the original window procedure.

About Superclassing

The drawback to subclassing a window procedure is that the window or control is already constructed before any messages are intercepted. If you need access to a control before it is created, you must superclass the control.

When a control is superclassed, a new type of window is registered and created that is based on an existing window. The new superclass is responsible for creating the new control and passing the necessary messages to the original window procedure.

Unlike subclassing, superclassing is not directly supported by the MFC class library. Superclassing a window requires a great deal of work, which I'm not going to discuss in detail here. In most cases, subclassing a window gives you all of the functionality you need.

Why Use Subclassing?

Subclassing a control or window enables you to add functionality to a control or window without creating it from scratch. Subclassing is most often used with controls. Any time that a control offers almost all the functionality you need, consider subclassing the control.

Why

For example, list boxes do not usually respond to the Enter key. However, by subclassing a list box, you can easily detect and process the Enter key. Edit controls are also frequently subclassed. The Microsoft Developer Network CD contains an elaborate subclassed edit control called CPicEdit that uses a "picture" parameter to specify how data must be entered into the control.

It would take a substantial amount of work to implement a list box or edit control from scratch in order to add a small amount of extra functionality. In our example in the next section, you subclass a control using just a few lines of code.

How Is a Control Subclassed?

When you're using SDK functions and straight C, subclassing a window involves substituting a new window procedure for an existing one, rerouting messages, and involving lots of pointers and several bottles of antacid. However, the MFC class library makes subclassing very easy. All windows in an MFC program are derived from the CWnd class. The CWnd::SubclassDlgItem function handles all the messy details of subclassing for you, resulting in a painless procedure.

How

As an example, let's subclass an edit control so that it accepts only digits, rejecting any other input. Using AppWizard, create a new SDI or MDI project named Subclass. You can also use an existing project because this example focuses on the edit control rather than the entire project.

Subclassing an Edit Control

For our example, you intercept the WM_CHAR message sent to the edit control because that is the message that carries character input. When you're subclassing a control, it can be helpful to use a flow chart to map how different messages are handled by the subclass.

Creating a New Edit Control Class

The first step in creating a subclassed edit control is creating a new class derived from the MFC CEdit class. The new edit control class handles messages received by the edit control in the following way:

- If any message except WM_CHAR is received, the message is passed on to the original edit control window procedure unchanged.

- If the WM_CHAR message is received with a numeric character, the message is sent to the original window procedure.

- If WM_CHAR is received with a character that isn't allowed, the message is eaten, and the original edit control window procedure never sees it.

The only message that is actually handled by the new class is WM_CHAR. All other messages not handled by the new edit control class are passed to the original edit control's window procedure. Using ClassWizard, create a new class named CNumericEdit. Use the values from Table 38.1 for the Add Class dialog box.

Table 38.1. Values used to create the CNumericEdit class.

Control	Value
Name	CNumericEdit
Base Class	CEdit
File	NumericEdit.cpp
Dialog ID	Disabled
OLE Automation	None
Component Gallery	Cleared

Using ClassWizard, add a message-handling function for WM_CHAR to the CNumericEdit class. Accept the default function name of OnChar and use the source code from Listing 38.1 to implement the function.

Listing 38.1. The `CNumericEdit::OnChar` function.

```
void CNumericEdit::OnChar(UINT nChar, UINT nRepCnt, UINT nFlags)
{
    // Allow only numbers and the backspace character.
    if( (nChar >= '0' && nChar <= '9')||(nChar == VK_BACK) )
        CEdit::OnChar(nChar, nRepCnt, nFlags);
    else
        MessageBeep( MB_ICONASTERISK );
}
```

Using a Subclassed Edit Control

As an example showing the use of a subclassed edit control, let's add a dialog box to the Subclass project. The first step is to create a dialog box that uses at least one edit control, such as the dialog box shown in Figure 38.3.

Figure 38.3.
*The subclass sample
dialog box.*

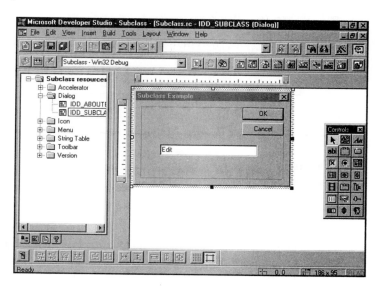

Use the values from Table 38.2 for the edit control and dialog box attributes.

Table 38.2. Attributes for the dialog box and edit control.

Name	Resource ID	Caption
Dialog	IDD_SUBCLASS_DLG	Subclass Example
Edit control	IDC_EDIT_NUMERIC	

Using ClassWizard, create a new class for the dialog box, using the values from Table 38.3.

Table 38.3. Values used to create the CSubclassDlg class.

Control	Value
Name	CSubclassDlg
Base Class	CDialog
File	SubclassDlg.cpp
Dialog ID	IDD_SUBCLASS_DLG
OLE Automation	None
Component Gallery	Cleared

The CSubclassDlg class uses a CNumericEdit object to handle the edit control instead of a CEdit object. Add a CNumericEdit variable named m_editNumeric to the implementation section of the CSubclassDlg class declaration, using the source code provided in Listing 38.2.

Listing 38.2. Adding a CNumericEdit member variable to CSubclassDlg.

```
// Implementation
protected:
    CNumericEdit    m_editNumeric;
```

Add an #include statement to the top of the SubclassDlg.h file to include the class declaration for CNumericEdit.

```
#include "NumericEdit.h"
```

When subclassing a dialog box control, you must create the edit control before it can be subclassed. The best place to subclass the edit control is when the dialog box receives the WM_INITDIALOG message. Using ClassWizard, add a message-handling function for WM_INITDIALOG to the CSubclassDlg class and accept the default name of OnInitDialog. The source code for OnInitDialog is provided in Listing 38.3.

Listing 38.3. Subclassing an edit control in OnInitDialog.

```
BOOL CSubclassDlg::OnInitDialog()
{
    CDialog::OnInitDialog();

    m_editNumeric.SubclassDlgItem( IDC_EDIT_NUMERIC, this );
    return TRUE;
}
```

As with most of the dialog boxes created for examples in this book, this dialog box is created by selecting a menu item. Add a menu item to the View menu and handle the function in `CMainFrame`, using the values from Table 38.4.

Table 38.4. New member functions for the `CMainFrame` class.

Menu ID	Caption	Event	Function Name
ID_VIEW_SUBCLASS	Numbers Only...	COMMAND	OnViewSubclass

Listing 38.4 contains the source code for the `OnViewSubclass` function, which handles the message sent when the new menu item is selected.

Listing 38.4. Creating a `CSubclassDlg` object.

```
void CMainFrame::OnViewSubclass()
{
    CSubclassDlg    dlg;

    dlg.DoModal();
}
```

Before you compile, add an `#include` statement to the top of the MainFrame.cpp source file.

```
#include "SubclassDlg.h"
```

Compile and run the Subclass project. The subclassed edit control accepts only numbers or backspaces; no other characters are accepted. Try modifying the `CNumericEdit::OnChar` function to accept only characters or values within certain ranges.

Summary

In this chapter, I discussed control superclassing and subclassing, as well as the MFC support provided for subclassing controls. As an example, you created a subclass of the edit control so that only numbers could be entered.

Owner-Drawn Controls

In this chapter I cover creating and using owner-drawn controls. I discuss the basic steps involved in creating an owner-drawn control, and the MFC support provided for these controls. At the end of the chapter, you create an owner-drawn list box control that displays a checkbox next to the items contained in the control.

What Are Owner-Drawn Controls?

What Owner-drawn controls are drawn by the owner of the control; usually, a view or dialog box. This is unlike most controls, which are drawn by Windows. Owner-drawn controls often add bitmaps, figures, or other visual effects, and sometimes offer extra functionality. For example, Developer Studio uses an owner-drawn list box to display icons for the various types of projects that can be created by AppWizard.

Five types of controls can be owner-drawn:

- Buttons
- List boxes
- Combo boxes
- Menus
- List views

What Are Self-Drawn Controls?

What

Self-drawn controls are similar to owner-drawn controls, except that they are controlled by a reusable C++ class that is used to handle drawing the control. This places the responsibility of drawing the control on the C++ class instead of on the control's parent. This leads to more reusable code because the drawing routines aren't duplicated every time the control is used.

Self-drawn controls have the same features as owner-drawn controls; the only difference is in the way the control is actually implemented. A self-drawn control class is derived from an MFC control class, such as CList box or CComboBox, and handles all of the owner-drawn messages inside that class.

Why Use Owner-Drawn Controls?

Why

Owner-drawn controls give you a chance to add extra functionality to standard controls, without the need to completely recreate the control from scratch. Using owner-drawn controls to extend the control's functions is similar to subclassing a window, as I described in Chapter 38.

Both subclassing and using the owner-drawn functions enable you to leverage the existing control so that you only have to be concerned with the extra functionality added by your code. For example, many early versions of tree controls used owner-drawn list boxes to display their information.

Your owner-drawn controls probably won't be as complex as the File Manager, especially now that the tree view control is available. However, understanding how an owner-drawn control works can help you easily add extra features to your programs.

How Are Owner-Drawn Controls Used?

How

In order for an owner-drawn control to work, the owner of the control and Windows use four messages to exchange information about the control:

- WM_DRAWITEM, handled by the OnDrawItem function
- WM_MEASUREITEM, handled by the OnMeasureItem function

- WM_COMPAREITEM, handled by the OnCompareItem function
- WM_DELETEITEM, handled by the OnDeleteItem function

It's not necessary for every type of control to handle every message. Table 39.1 lists the message-handling functions that should be implemented for each type of owner-drawn control.

Table 39.1. Functions that must be implemented for owner-drawn controls.

Function	Button	Menu	Combo Box	List Box	List View
OnDrawItem	Yes	Yes	Yes	Yes	Yes
OnMeasureItem	No	Yes	Yes	Yes	Yes
OnCompareItem	No	No	Yes	Yes	Yes
OnDeleteItem	No	No	Yes	Yes	Yes

Each of these functions pass a structure as a parameter that is used for information purposes. In some cases, the structure should be updated by the function. For example, during OnCompareItem, the COMPAREITEMSTRUCT is updated with the results of a comparison of two list items.

Handling the *WM_DRAWITEM* Message

When an owner-drawn control must be drawn, Windows sends a WM_DRAWITEM message to the control's owner. The MFC framework translates this message into an OnDrawItem function call. When processing OnDrawItem, your program is expected to draw all aspects of the control, including the control's selection state and focus states.

The OnDrawItem function is called with two parameters: a pointer to a DRAWITEMSTRUCT structure, and a resource ID for the control being drawn. The DRAWITEMSTRUCT structure contains everything you need to draw the control. Here are the most commonly used members of a DRAWITEMSTRUCT:

- itemID, which contains the menu item ID for a menu item or the index of an item in a list box or combo box. For an empty list box or combo box, this member can be -1, meaning that the entire control should be drawn as having the focus.
- hDC, which identifies the device context. The device context must be used when drawing the control. For MFC applications, this device context usually is attached to a CDC object.
- rcItem, which defines the boundaries of the control to be drawn.
- itemData, which contains the item value associated with the item.
- itemAction, which indicates the type of drawing to be done. The actual value for itemAction can be a combination of the values listed in Table 39.2.
- itemState, which indicates the new state of the item. The value of this member can be a combination of the values provided in Table 39.3.

Part VIII

Table 39.2. Possible values for `itemAction`.

Value	Description
ODA_DRAWENTIRE	The entire control must be drawn.
ODA_FOCUS	The control's focus state must be updated.
ODA_SELECT	The control's selection state must be updated.

Table 39.3. Possible values for `itemState`.

Value	Description
ODS_DEFAULT	Draw as the default item
ODS_DISABLED	Draw as disabled
ODS_FOCUS	Draw with the keyboard focus
ODS_COMBOBOXEDIT	Draw in the edit control of a combo box
ODS_CHECKED	The menu item is to be checked
ODS_GRAYED	The menu item is to be grayed
ODS_SELECTED	The menu item is selected

If the owner-drawn control is a list box or combo box, the `OnDrawItem` function is called once for every item that must be drawn. For example, if eight items are visible in an owner-drawn list box, `OnDrawItem` is called at least eight times when the list box is initially displayed.

Handling the *WM_MEASUREITEM* Message

Before asking for an item to be drawn, Windows sends an owner-drawn control the `WM_MEASUREITEM` message to determine the size of the item. The MFC framework translates this message into an `OnMeasureItem` function call. If the control is a variable-size list box, one message is sent before every item is drawn; for fixed-size list boxes, the message is sent only once.

The `OnMeasureItem` function has one parameter: a pointer to a `MEASUREITEMSTRUCT` structure. This structure must be updated so that Windows provides enough room for the control to be drawn. Here are the most commonly used `MEASUREITEMSTRUCT` members:

- `itemID`, which contains the menu item ID for a menu item or the index of an item in a list box or combo box. For an empty list box or combo box, this member can be -1, meaning that the entire control should be drawn as having the focus.
- `itemWidth`, which specifies the width of the control, in pixels. This member should be filled in before the function returns.
- `itemHeight`, which specifies the height of the control, in pixels. This member should be filled in before the function returns.
- `itemData`, containing the item value associated with the item.

If you create a dialog resource that contains an owner-drawn control, the control is constructed before it is attached to any MFC control variables. This means that you never see a WM_MEASUREITEM message for fixed list boxes contained in a dialog box. There are two options:

- Live with the default size, as in this chapter's example. One problem with this approach is that your control may not be drawn properly. If you require a certain size of list box, use the next option.

- Send a message to the control to set its size. The MFC class for each control type has a member function that simplifies setting the size for an owner-drawn control. For example, the CList box class provides a SetItemHeight function.

Handling the *WM_COMPAREITEM* Message

The list box and combo box controls provide lists of items that can be sorted. For owner-drawn list boxes and combo boxes that are sorted, the owner of the control must sort the items contained in the control. Windows sends the control's owner a WM_COMPAREITEM message to request that two items contained in the control be compared. The MFC framework translates this message into an OnCompareItem function call.

The OnCompareItem function has one parameter: a pointer to a COMPAREITEMSTRUCT structure. This structure must be updated so that Windows can determine the relative position of items contained in the control. Here are the most commonly used COMPAREITEMSTRUCT members:

- itemID1, which contains the index of the first item being compared
- itemData1, containing the item value associated with the first item being compared
- itemID2, which contains the index of the second item being compared
- itemData2, containing the item value associated with the second item being compared

The OnCompareItem function must determine the relative order of the two items, and return one of the values from Table 39.4. If sorting order is not important, the control should be given an unsorted attribute, which results in this function never being called.

Table 39.4. Return values from OnCompareItem.

Value	Description
-1	Item 1 should be placed before item 2.
0	Item 1 and item 2 sort the same.
1	Item 1 should be placed after item 2.

Handling the *WM_DELETEITEM* Message

Owner-drawn list boxes and combo boxes normally contain pointers to dynamically allocated objects. When the control that contains the items is deleted, Windows sends a WM_DELETEITEM message for each item contained in the control. Like the other messages associated with owner-drawn controls, the MFC framework translates the message into a function call; in this case, OnDeleteItem.

The OnDeleteItem function has one parameter: a pointer to a DELETEITEMSTRUCT structure. This structure is used to identify the item to be deleted. The most commonly used DELETEITEMSTRUCT member is the itemData member, containing the item value associated with the item being deleted.

An Owner-Drawn List Box

As an example of using owner-drawn controls, in this section you create a dialog-based project that contains an owner-drawn list box. To get started, create a dialog-based project named OwnDraw using AppWizard.

Modifying the Dialog Resource

Add a list box to IDD_OWNDRAW_DIALOG, the main dialog box used by the OwnDraw application. Use the values from Table 39.5 for the list-box attributes.

Table 39.5. List-box attributes for the OwnDraw application.

Control	Value
Resource ID	IDC_LIST
OwnerDraw	Fixed
Sort	Unchecked

Figure 39.1 shows the main dialog box used by the OwnDraw application in the dialog editor.

Figure 39.1.
The main dialog box
for the OwnDraw
application.

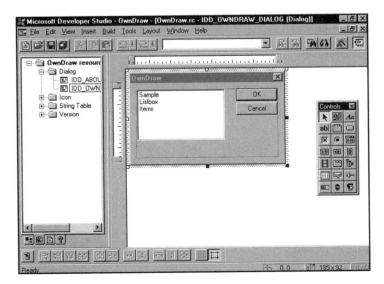

Using ClassWizard, add a member variable associated with the list-box control for the COwnDrawDlg class. Use the values from Table 39.6.

Table 39.6. Values used for the IDC_LIST variable.

Resource ID	Category	Type	Member Variable
IDC_LIST	Control	CListBox	m_lbOwnDraw

Creating the *CListItem* Structure

Simple list boxes that are drawn by Windows normally store a string for each item contained in the list box. Almost all owner-drawn list boxes and combo boxes store pointers to objects that represent each item in the list box. This pointer is passed back to the control's owner as part of the structure parameter in the owner-drawn messages discussed earlier.

The OwnDraw application uses a simple structure named CListItem to represent each item in the list box. Add the source code provided in Listing 39.1 to the top of the OwnDrawDlg.cpp source file, just after the #include statements.

Listing 39.1. The CListItem structure.

```
struct CListItem
{
    CListItem( const CString& szItem, BOOL bChecked )
    {
        m_szItem = szItem;
        m_bChecked = bChecked;
    }
    CString m_szItem;
    BOOL    m_bChecked;
};
```

The CListItem structure has two members: m_szItem, which is a string that will be displayed in the list box, and m_bChecked, which is TRUE if a checkmark should be placed next to the item.

Adding Items to the List Box

For this example, three CListItem objects are created when the main dialog box receives the WM_INITDIALOG message. Add the source code provided in Listing 39.2 to the COwnDrawDlg::OnInitDialog function, after the // TODO comment. Because these object are created using new, you must use delete to destroy them later.

Listing 39.2. Additions to the COwnDrawDlg::OnInitDialog function.

```
    // TODO: Add extra initialization here
    CListItem* pMoe = new CListItem( "Moe", TRUE );
    CListItem* pShep = new CListItem( "Shep", TRUE );
```

continues

Listing 39.2. continued

```
CListItem* pZaphod = new CListItem( "Zaphod", FALSE );
m_lbOwnDraw.AddString( (LPCSTR)pMoe );
m_lbOwnDraw.AddString( (LPCSTR)pShep );
m_lbOwnDraw.AddString( (LPCSTR)pZaphod );
```

In a more elaborate example, a new CListObject might be created after a user pressed a button labeled Add.

Handling the Owner-Drawn Messages

Using ClassWizard, add message-handling functions to the COwnDrawDlg class. Use the values from Table 39.7.

Table 39.7. Owner-drawn messages sent to the COwnDrawDlg class.

Message	Function
WM_COMPAREITEM	OnCompareItem
WM_DELETEITEM	OnDeleteItem
WM_DRAWITEM	OnDrawItem
WM_MEASUREITEM	OnMeasureItem

Drawing the List-Box Items

The OnDrawItem function is called whenever an owner-drawn control must be repainted. In this example, there's only one owner-drawn control in the dialog box; if there were more, the nIDCtl parameter would be used to determine which control was being drawn. Add the source code provided in Listing 39.3 to the COwnDrawDlg::OnDrawItem function.

Listing 39.3. The COwnDrawDlg::OnDrawItem function.

```
void COwnDrawDlg::OnDrawItem(int nIDCtl, LPDRAWITEMSTRUCT lpdis)
{
    CRect rc = lpdis->rcItem;
    CDC *pdcTmp = CDC::FromHandle( lpdis->hDC );
    if( nIDCtl != -1 )
    {
        COLORREF        clrBkgrnd;
        COLORREF        clrTxt;
        if( lpdis->itemAction & (ODA_DRAWENTIRE | ODA_SELECT) )
        {
            // If we are gaining or losing the selection status,
            // choose the proper color for the background.
```

```
        if( lpdis->itemState & ODS_SELECTED )
        {
            clrBkgrnd = GetSysColor(COLOR_HIGHLIGHT );
            clrTxt = GetSysColor(COLOR_HIGHLIGHTTEXT );
        }
        else
        {
            clrBkgrnd = GetSysColor( COLOR_WINDOW);
            clrTxt = GetSysColor( COLOR_WINDOWTEXT);
        }
        //   - Draw the checkbox for the item, and move the
        //   rect to the right so the checkbox isn't covered.
        CListItem* pItem = (CListItem*)lpdis->itemData;
        DrawCheckBox( rc, pdcTmp, pItem->m_bChecked );
        rc.left += rc.Height();
        //   - Fill the item's rectangle with the selected
        //   color.
        CBrush brHighlight( clrBkgrnd );
        CBrush* pbrOld = pdcTmp->SelectObject( &brHighlight );
        COLORREF clrOldBk = pdcTmp->SetBkColor( clrBkgrnd );
        COLORREF clrOldTxt = pdcTmp->SetTextColor( clrTxt );
        pdcTmp->FillRect( rc, &brHighlight );
        //   - Draw the text on top of the rectangle.
        pdcTmp->TextOut( rc.left, rc.top, pItem->m_szItem );
        pdcTmp->SetBkColor( clrOldBk );
        pdcTmp->SetTextColor( clrOldTxt );
        pdcTmp->SelectObject( pbrOld );
    }
}
// Handle the focus rectangle
if( lpdis->itemAction & ODA_FOCUS )
{
    pdcTmp->DrawFocusRect( rc );
}
}
```

This is by far the longest source code example in the book, but it's actually handling several simple tasks. Although the source code is used for this example, the basic tasks performed in this OnDraw function are similar for all owner-drawn controls:

- Checking the value of itemID
- Selecting the current control colors
- Calling a function to draw special effects; in this case, a checkbox
- Filling the control with the current color
- Drawing the item text
- Setting the focus rectangle

These steps are applied to the list-box item in several layers, as shown in Figure 39.2. The background color, checkbox, text, and focus rectangle are applied on top of each other.

Figure 39.2.
The steps involved in drawing a list-box item.

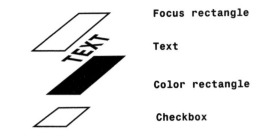

Focus rectangle

Text

Color rectangle

Checkbox

The first, most important step in a list box is to check the DRAWITEMSTRUCT to determine whether the itemID value is -1. If it is, the function is being called to draw the focus state for the entire control, not a single item.

The next step is to draw the selection state of the list box item if the selection state of the item is changing, or if the entire item is being drawn. The itemAction member is used to determine what drawing function is needed, while the itemState member is tested to determine the state of the control. In this case, the GetSysColor functions are used to get the colors selected by the user for the current color scheme.

The next step is to draw the checkbox. This is handled by the DrawCheckBox function, which I discuss in the next section.

After drawing the checkbox, the control rectangle is adjusted so its left edge begins after the checkbox. This is an easy trick used to keep the checkbox undisturbed. The CDC::FillRect function is called to fill the remaining rectangle with the control color you selected previously.

The next steps are to draw the text and restore the old background colors and brush. It's important to return the device context to its original condition.

The focus rectangle is drawn as a separate step, because the focus rectangle must be kept synchronized. The focus rectangle works like an exclusive "or": the rectangle is either on or off. If it's off, calling DrawFocusRect turns it on; if it's off, DrawFocusRect removes it. Using the basic algorithm from Listing 39.3 keeps the focus rectangle consistent.

Drawing the Checkbox

This function is completely optional; if your fingers are sore from the previous listing, you can skip this step, and the list box won't display any checkboxes. However, assuming that you would like to display a checkbox, add a declaration for a protected function named DrawCheckBox to the COwnDrawDlg class declaration. Add this new function declaration in the implementation section:

```
// Implementation
protected:
    void  DrawCheckBox( CRect& rc, CDC *pdc, BOOL bChecked );
```

The `DrawCheckBox` function is used to draw a small checkbox next to each item in the list box. Add the source code provided in Listing 39.4 to the OwnDrawDlg.cpp source file.

Listing 39.4. The `COwnDrawDlg::DrawCheckBox` function.

```
void  COwnDrawDlg::DrawCheckBox(  CRect&          rc,
                                  CDC             *pdc,
                                  BOOL            bChecked )
{
    CDC    dcMem;
    CRect rcBox( rc.TopLeft(), CSize(rc.Height(),rc.Height()) );
    rcBox.DeflateRect( 2, 2 );
    pdc->SelectStockObject( BLACK_PEN );
    pdc->MoveTo( rcBox.TopLeft() );
    pdc->LineTo( rcBox.right, rcBox.top );
    pdc->LineTo( rcBox.BottomRight() );
    pdc->LineTo( rcBox.left, rcBox.bottom );
    pdc->LineTo( rcBox.TopLeft() );
    if( bChecked )
    {
        pdc->LineTo( rcBox.BottomRight() );
        pdc->MoveTo( rcBox.left, rcBox.bottom );
        pdc->LineTo( rcBox.right, rcBox.top );
    }
}
```

The `DrawCheckBox` function selects the stock black pen and draws a checkbox around a rectangle on the left side of the control. Using the `LineTo` and `MoveTo` functions is similar to playing connect-the-dots: first the square box is drawn, then the "X" is drawn if the item should have a checkmark.

Handling Other Owner-Drawn Messages

The source code for the `OnDeleteItem` function is provided in Listing 39.5. The `OnDeleteItem` function casts the `itemData` member to a pointer to `CListItem`, then deletes that pointer. If you skip this step, memory leaks will result because the memory allocated to objects placed into the list box won't be released.

Listing 39.5. The `OnDeleteItem` member function.

```
void COwnDrawDlg::OnDeleteItem(int nIDCtl, LPDELETEITEMSTRUCT lpdis)
{
    if( (nIDCtl != -1)&&(lpdis != 0) )
    {
        CListItem* pItem = (CListItem*)lpdis->itemData;
        delete pItem;
    }
}
```

The `OnCompareItem` and `OnMeasureItem` functions use the default versions that are supplied by ClassWizard in this example.

Summary

In this chapter I discussed owner-drawn controls, and the support offered for them by the MFC class library. You also created an owner-drawn list box that displays a checkbox next to each item.

Using OLE Controls

OLE controls enable you to reuse custom controls written for Windows. In this chapter, I discuss OLE controls and how they are used. There is also a small example at the end of the chapter that uses one of the OLE controls included with Visual C++.

What Is an OLE Control?

What An OLE control is a reusable control that is packaged and available for use in your applications. As the name suggests, OLE controls use OLE, or Object Linking and Embedding, interfaces for communication to and from the control.

In many ways, OLE controls replace VBX controls. The VBX control specification was originally designed for use in the Visual Basic programming environment. The VBX soon proved to be very popular—so much so that an entire industry has sprung up, specializing in supplying reusable controls to Windows developers.

The VBX specification could not be extended to 32-bit systems, such as Windows 95 or Windows NT. Instead, Microsoft has developed OLE controls, sometimes called OCX controls. Unlike VBX controls, OLE controls can be developed for both the 16- and 32-bit versions of Windows. In addition, they have features that make them more attractive for distribution, such as support for licensing and localization into different languages.

A wide range of OLE controls is available. Later in this chapter, you can follow the steps required to use the OLE grid control, which enables you to write simple spreadsheet applications.

Why Use an OLE Control?

Why

OLE controls are easy to use in your MFC-based applications because they have been designed for reuse. Developer Studio includes the Component Gallery, a tool that helps you to easily integrate OLE controls into your MFC programs.

Because OLE controls use a standard interface that is not specific to any particular programming language, OLE controls can be used by a variety of development tools. The OLE controls that you use today in a Visual C++ program can also be used with other tools, such as Access 95, Visual FoxPro, and Visual Basic 4.0.

OLE controls offer more functionality than is available with standard controls offered by Windows. For example, before the release of Windows 95, many VBX vendors offered VBX controls that were similar to tree view controls; these vendors are now offering OLE controls with features that are not available when using standard controls.

How Is an OLE Control Used?

How

An OLE control always communicates with an OLE control container. These objects understand the OLE control interfaces, as shown in Figure 40.1. The OLE control sends messages to the OLE container when an event occurs inside the control. In OLE-speak, this is known as firing an event. Mouse clicks, pressed buttons, and expiring timers are examples of events.

Figure 40.1.
Messages sent to and from OLE controls in an MFC program.

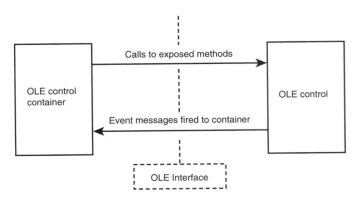

When an OLE control container needs to communicate with an OLE control, it interacts with a set of properties and methods that are exposed by the OLE control. An example of an OLE property is the font or background color used by a control. A method is just another word for a function call that is used to collect information about the control.

Every class derived from CWnd in an MFC application can be used as an OLE control container. The MFC class COleControl is used as a base class for all OLE controls created using MFC.

Using the Component Gallery

The Developer Studio Component Gallery is used to store reusable components that can be used in your MFC-based Windows projects. Whenever you add a class using ClassWizard, you can add the class to the Component Gallery by selecting the Add to Component Gallery checkbox.

The most important components stored in the Component Gallery are OLE controls. To display all the OLE controls available on your machine, select Components from the Insert menu. After the Component Gallery dialog box is displayed, select the OLE Controls tab; this displays all of the available OLE controls, as shown in Figure 40.2.

Figure 40.2.
Displaying available
OLE controls in the
Component Gallery.

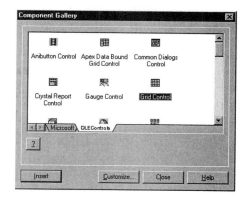

Adding an OLE Control to the Dialog Editor

Before using an OLE control in a dialog box, you must insert the control into the dialog editor's control palette. To add an OLE control to the dialog editor, follow these steps:

1. Select one of the displayed OLE control icons.
2. From the Component Gallery dialog box, click the Insert button.
3. A list box containing classes that will be added to your project is displayed inside the Confirm Classes dialog box. Click the OK button to add the classes to your project.
4. Click the Close button to dismiss the Component Gallery dialog box.

The OLE control you selected is now included in the dialog editor's control palette. Open a dialog box for editing, and you see the new control palette, including the new OLE control.

You can use the new OLE control as you would any other control. To add it to a dialog box resource, drag and drop the control on the dialog box, or select the OLE control's icon and click on the dialog box resource.

Using ClassWizard to Configure an OLE Control

Before you can use the OLE control, it must be integrated into your project. As with any other control added to a dialog box, use ClassWizard to add message-handling functions and associate the control with an MFC object.

When adding a member variable associated with an OLE control, you can use ClassWizard as you would if the control were a button, list box, or another standard Windows control. Unlike standard Windows controls, each OLE control has a large number of variable types. In addition to the object used to interact with the control, every property exposed by the control can be associated with a variable.

Essential Example

An Example Using an OLE Custom Control

As an example of using an OLE control in an MFC-based project, I show how the OLE grid control is used in a dialog box-based program created with AppWizard. The grid control is used to create a small spreadsheet in the main dialog box.

To get started with the sample project, use AppWizard to create a dialog box-based application named CustomCtrl. In contrast to most of the book's other AppWizard examples, for this project you must select one of the options offered by the wizard. On the second AppWizard page, select the OLE Control's checkbox. Selecting this option causes AppWizard to configure the project to be OLE control-ready.

What Is a Grid Control?

A grid control is a popular reusable component that is similar to a spreadsheet. Many suppliers of Visual Basic controls offer grid controls, and Microsoft includes an OLE grid control with Developer Studio.

What

As you can probably guess by its name, a grid control is divided into a series of rectangles, or grids. Vertical lines separate the controls into columns, and horizontal lines divide the control into rows. The intersection of a row and column is known as a cell.

A grid control can contain a mixture of images and text. In most cases, text is used. You cannot directly edit the individual cells in a grid control. The grid control is strictly a read-only window, although there are ways to simulate cell editing that are discussed later in this chapter.

Why Use a Grid Control?

The most common use for a grid control is creating a small spreadsheet. If you want to display a small budget or other information, a grid control is ideal. In addition, you can use a grid control whenever you need to arrange information into rows and columns. For example, a calendar dialog box might use a grid control to provide access to the individual days of the month.

Why

A grid control spares you the work of creating and maintaining a large number of smaller controls. The grid control tracks the active cell, as well as the size and contents of each cell. When you need access to a particular cell, the grid control can provide that information through a function call. At a minimum, grid controls enable you to do the following:

- Retrieve current row, cell, and column information.
- Set attributes for the current cell, such as font, size, and contents.
- Retrieve the attributes of the current cell.

Adding a Grid OCX to the Dialog Editor

To add a grid OLE control to the CustomCtrl project's main dialog box, you must first add the grid control to the dialog editor's control palette by following these steps:

1. Open the Component Gallery by selecting Component from the Insert menu.
2. Display the available OLE controls by clicking the OLE Controls tab.
3. Select the Grid icon and then click the Insert button.
4. Accept the list of classes that will be added to the project by clicking the OK button.
5. Close the Component Gallery dialog box.

Adding a Grid Control to the Main Dialog Box

Before adding the grid control to the main dialog box, you must first load the dialog box resource into the dialog editor. Open the ResourceView in the project workspace. Then open the dialog box resource folder and double-click the IDD_CUSTOMCTRL_DIALOG icon. This opens the dialog box resource inside the Developer Studio dialog editor.

To add a grid control, drag and drop the grid control from the control palette to the dialog box resource. For this example, you must also add an edit control with a resource ID of IDC_EDIT and a pushbutton control with an ID of IDC_CALC to the dialog box. The finished main dialog box resource is shown in Figure 40.3.

Figure 40.3.
The main dialog box resource for the CustomCtrl project.

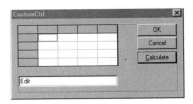

The properties for the OLE grid control are provided in Table 40.1. Use the default properties for the edit control.

Table 40.1. Properties used for the OLE grid control.

Property	Value
ID	IDC_GRID
Rows	5
Cols	5

Property	Value
FixedRows	1
FixedCols	1
ScrollBars	None

Initializing the Grid Control

Before adding the source code used to initialize the grid control, add member variables to the CCustomCtrlDlg class associated with the grid and edit controls. Using ClassWizard, add the member variables using the values from Table 40.2.

Table 40.2. Values used for the grid and edit control member variables.

Resource ID	Category	Type	Variable Name
IDC_EDIT	Control	CEdit	m_edit
IDC_GRID	Control	CGridCtrl	m_grid

Due to the way that the Developer Studio tools are integrated, ClassWizard knows all about the OLE grid control and understands that the CGridCtrl class is used to interact with the control.

The main dialog box class, CCustomCtrlDlg, uses three new member variables to interact with the grid control.

- m_nRow is used to store the current cell row when a cell is being edited.
- m_nCol is used to store the current cell column when a cell is being edited.
- m_bEditing is set to TRUE when a cell is being edited and FALSE otherwise.

Add the declarations for these variables to the CCustomCtrlDlg class, as shown in Listing 40.1. Then add the source code to the implementation section, just after the // Implementation comment.

Listing 40.1. Modifications to the CCustomCtrlDlg class declaration.

```
// Implementation
protected:
    BOOL    m_bEditing;
    int     m_nRow;
    int     m_nCol;
```

The grid control must be initialized during the main dialog box's OnInitDialog member function. Add the source code from Listing 40.2 to the CCustomCtrlDlg::OnInitDialog member function, just after the //TODO comment.

Listing 40.2. Initializing the OLE grid control in `OnInitDialog`.

```
// TODO: Add extra initialization here
m_bEditing = FALSE;
m_nRow = 1;
m_nCol = 1;
char*   arCols[4] = { "Jan", "Feb", "Mar", "Apr" };
char*   arRows[4] = { "Gas", "Phone", "MSN", "Total" };
m_grid.SetRow( 0 );
for( int nCol = 0; nCol < 4; nCol++ )
{
    m_grid.SetCol( nCol + 1 );
    m_grid.SetText( arCols[nCol] );
}
m_grid.SetCol( 0 );
for( int nRow = 0; nRow < 4; nRow++ )
{
    m_grid.SetRow( nRow + 1 );
    m_grid.SetText( arRows[nRow] );
}
```

The source code added to the `OnInitDialog` function first initializes the new member variables added in Listing 40.1. The remaining code initializes the grid control.

The first `for` loop in Listing 40.2 sets the column headings to the first four months of the year. The next `for` loop sets the text used as row titles in the grid control. This short snippet of code shows how a grid control is typically used: select a cell and then set or retrieve the text stored in that cell.

Detecting Grid Control Events

When an event occurs in the grid control, the control fires an event message to its container. The MFC framework translates this event message into a function call. To define the Click event message that is handled by the main dialog box, you use ClassWizard to add a message-handling function for the message, as shown in Table 40.3.

Table 40.3. OLE event messages handled by the `CCustomCtrlDlg` class.

Object ID	Class Name	Message	Function
IDC_GRID	CCustomCtrlDlg	Click	OnClickGrid

Add the source code for the `CCustomCtrlDlg::OnClickGrid` function provided in Listing 40.3.

Listing 40.3. Handling a mouse click event from the OLE grid control.

```
void CCustomCtrlDlg::OnClickGrid()
{
    CString szText = m_grid.GetText();
    if( m_bEditing == FALSE )
    {
        // Save the current grid position and set the edit flag.
        m_nRow = m_grid.GetRow();
```

```
        m_nCol = m_grid.GetCol();
        m_bEditing = TRUE;
        // Get the current grid text, and display it in the edit
        // control.
        szText = m_grid.GetText();
        m_edit.SetWindowText( szText );
        m_edit.ShowWindow( SW_SHOW );
        m_edit.SetFocus();
        m_edit.SetSel( 0, -1 );
    }
    else
    {
        // Roll up the edit control, and update the previous
        // grid position. You must save the current position,
        // go back to the old position, and then return to the
        // current position.
        int nCurrentRow = m_grid.GetRow();
        int nCurrentCol = m_grid.GetCol();
        m_grid.SetRow( m_nRow );
        m_grid.SetCol( m_nCol );
        m_grid.SetFocus();

        CString szEntry;
        m_edit.GetWindowText( szText );
        szEntry.Format("%01.2f", atof(szText) );

        m_edit.ShowWindow( SW_HIDE );
        m_grid.SetText( szEntry );
        m_bEditing = FALSE;
        m_grid.SetRow( nCurrentRow );
        m_grid.SetCol( nCurrentCol );
    }
}
```

If the program receives a Click event, the m_bEditing flag is checked to see if a cell is currently being edited. If not, the current row and column are collected from the grid control. This information is used later when the editing job is finished. The text stored in the current grid cell is retrieved and displayed in the edit control. Finally, the edit control text is selected, which makes it easy for a user to overwrite the current contents.

If there is a cell being edited, the text contained in the edit control is stored in the grid. However, it must be stored in the cell that was originally clicked to open the edit control. This cell position was stored when the edit control was opened and is now used to reset the current row and column. The edit control text is reformatted into a standard dollars-and-cents format and stored in the original cell position.

The GetRow and GetCol functions provided by CGridCtrl are examples of OLE control methods that are exposed by the grid control. For a complete list of exposed methods, open the project workspace view and click the ClassView tab. Open the CGridCtrl class icon, and you see a list of the available member functions.

Recalculating the Grid Control Contents

Each column in the spreadsheet is recalculated when you click the Calculate button. Add a message-handling function to the CCustomCtrlDlg class that handles messages from the Calculate button, using the values from Table 40.4.

Table 40.4. Messages handled by the CCustomCtrlDlg class.

Object ID	Class Name	Message	Function
IDC_CALC	CCustomCtrlDlg	BN_CLICKED	OnCalc

Add the source code in Listing 40.4 to the CCustomCtrlDlg::OnCalc member function.

Listing 40.4. Recalculating the contents of the OLE grid control.

```
void CCustomCtrlDlg::OnCalc()
{
    // Close current editing job, if any.
    if( m_bEditing != FALSE )
    {
        CString szEntry, szText;
        m_edit.GetWindowText( szText );
        szEntry.Format("%01.2f", atof(szText) );
        m_edit.ShowWindow( SW_HIDE );
        m_grid.SetText( szEntry );
        m_bEditing = FALSE;
    }
    for( int nCol = 1; nCol < 5; nCol++ )
    {
        double  dTotal = 0.0;
        m_grid.SetCol( nCol );
        for( int nRow = 1; nRow < 4; nRow++ )
        {
            m_grid.SetRow( nRow );
            CString szCell = m_grid.GetText();
            dTotal += atof( szCell );
        }
        CString szTotal;
        szTotal.Format( "%01.2f", dTotal );
        m_grid.SetRow( 4 );
        m_grid.SetText( szTotal );
    }
}
```

Compile and run the CustomCtrl example. The grid control is initially empty. Clicking on a cell displays the edit control, which enables you to enter or change the cell's contents. Clicking the Calculate button totals each column in the grid control.

Chapter 48

Summary

In this chapter, I discussed OLE controls and the Developer Studio tools that are used with them. As part of the discussion, you created an example that used an OLE grid control as a small spreadsheet.

Serialization

In this chapter, I discuss serialization, the method used to store an object to a file or another type of storage. You create an example of a class that can be serialized in this chapter. This class is used as a starting point for the next chapter, where it is used in a Document/View serialization example.

What Is Serialization?

What Serialization is the way that classes derived from CDocument store and retrieve data from an archive, which is usually a file. Serialization is the process of storing the state of an object for the purpose of loading it at another time. The property of an object to be stored and loaded is sometimes called persistence, which is also defined as the capability of an object to remember its state between executions. Figure 41.1 shows the interaction between a serialized object and an archive.

Figure 41.1.
Serializing an object to and from an archive.

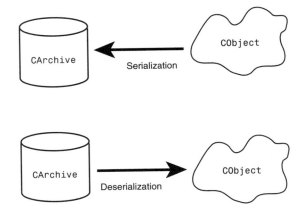

When an object is serialized, information about the type of object is written to the storage along with information and data about the object. When an object is deserialized, the same process happens in reverse, and the object is loaded and created from the input stream.

Why Use Serialization?

Why

The goal behind serialization is to make the storage of complex objects as simple and reliable as the storage of the basic data types available in C++. You can store a basic type, such as an int, in a file in the following way:

```
int nFoo = 5;
fileStream << nFoo;
```

If a file contains an int value, it can be read from the stream in the following way:

```
fileStream >> nFoo;
```

A persistent object can be serialized and deserialized using a similar syntax, no matter how complicated the object's internal structure. The alternative is to create routines that understand how every object is implemented and handle the process of storing and retrieving data from files.

Using serialization to store objects is much more flexible than writing specialized functions that store data in a fixed format. Objects that are persistent are capable of storing themselves, instead of relying on an external function to read and write them to disk. This makes a persistent object much easier to reuse because the object is more self-contained.

Persistent objects also help you easily write programs that are saved to storage. An object that is serialized might be made up of many smaller objects that are also serialized. Because individual objects are often stored in a collection, serializing the collection also serializes all objects contained in the collection.

How Is Serialization Used?

In Part II, "The C++ Language," I used the insertion operator, or <<, to output a value to the screen. This operator is actually the C++ left shift operator, but it is overloaded so that whenever an output object and variable are separated by a <<, as in the following code line, the variable is written to the output object.

How

```
file_object << data
```

In a similar way, whenever input is performed and the objects are separated by a >>, as in the following code line, a new value for the variable is retrieved from the input object.

```
file_object >> data
```

In C++, unlike some other languages, input and output is controlled by the interaction between file and variable objects. The exact process used for input and output is controlled by the way that the classes implement the >> and << operators.

For an example for the topics in this chapter, you create a persistent class named CUser, along with the helper functions required to serialize a collection of CUser objects. Each CUser object contains a customer name and e-mail address. The source code provided in this chapter is used in Chapter 42, "Serialization and Document/View," to demonstrate using serialization in an actual Windows project.

The MFC Classes Used for Serialization

There are two MFC classes that you use to serialize objects:

- CArchive is almost always a file and is the object that other persistent objects are serialized to or from.

- CObject defines all of the interfaces used to serialize objects to or from a CArchive object.

Objects are serialized in one of two ways. As a rule of thumb, if an object is derived from CObject, that object's Serialize member function is called in the following way:

```
myObject.Serialize( ar );
```

If the object is not derived from CObject—such as a CRect object, for example—you should use the insertion operator in the following way:

```
ar << rcWnd;
```

This insertion operator is overloaded in the same way it is for cout, cin, and cerr, which were used extensively in the first part of this book for console mode input and output.

Using the *CObject* Class

You must use the CObject class for all classes that make use of the MFC class library's built-in support for serialization. The CObject class contains virtual functions that are used during serialization; in addition, the CArchive class is declared as a "friend" class for CObject, providing it access to private and protected member variables.

The most commonly used virtual function in CObject is Serialize, which is called to serialize or deserialize the object from a CArchive object. This function is declared as virtual so that any persistent object can be called through a pointer to CObject in the following way:

```
CObject* pObj = GetNextObject();
pObj->Serialize( ar );
```

As discussed later in the section "Using the Serialization Macros," when you're deriving a persistent class from CObject, you must use two macros to help implement the serialization functions.

The *CArchive* Class

The CArchive class is used to model a generic storage object. In most cases, a CArchive object is attached to a disk file. In some cases, however, the object might be connected to an object that only seems to be a file, like a memory location or another type of storage.

When a CArchive object is created, it is defined as used for either input or output but never both. You can use the IsStoring and IsLoading functions to determine if a CArchive object is used for input or output, as shown in Listing 41.1.

Listing 41.1. Using the CArchive::IsStoring function to determine the serialization direction.

```
CMyObject:Serialize( CArchive& ar )
{
    if( ar.IsStoring() )
        // Write object state to ar
    else
        // Read object state from ar
}
```

Using the Insertion and Extraction Operators

The MFC class library overloads the insertion and extraction operators for many commonly used class and basic types. You often use the insertion operator, <<, to serialize, or store, data to the CArchive object. You use the extraction operator, >>, to deserialize, or load, data from a CArchive object.

These operators are defined for all basic C++ types, as well as a few commonly used classes not derived from CObject, such as the CString, CRect, and CTime classes. The insertion and extraction operators return a reference to a CArchive object, enabling them to be chained together in the following way:

```
archive << m_nFoo << m_rcClient << m_szName;
```

When used with classes that are derived from CObject, the insertion and extraction operators allocate the memory storage required to contain an object and then call the object's Serialize member function. If you do not need to allocate storage, you should call the Serialize member function directly.

As a rule of thumb, if you know the type of the object when it is deserialized, call the Serialize function directly. In addition, you must always call Serialize exclusively. If you use Serialize to load or store an object, you must not use the insertion and extraction operators at any other time with that object.

Using the Serialization Macros

There are two macros that you must use when creating a persistent class based on CObject. Use the DECLARE_SERIAL macro in the class declaration file and the IMPLEMENT_SERIAL macro in the class implementation file.

Declaring a Persistent Class

The DECLARE_SERIAL macro takes a single parameter: the name of the class to be serialized. A good place to put this macro is on the first line of the class declaration, where it serves as a reminder that the class can be serialized. An example of a class that can be serialized is provided in Listing 41.2. Save this source code in a file named Users.h.

Listing 41.2. The CUser class declaration.

```
#ifndef CUSER
#define CUSER
class CUser : public CObject
{
    DECLARE_SERIAL(CUser);
public:
    // Constructors
    CUser();
    CUser( const CString& szName, const CString& szAddr );
    // Attributes
    void Set( const CString& szName, const CString& szAddr );
    CString GetName() const;
    CString GetAddr() const;
    // Operations
    virtual void Serialize( CArchive& ar );
    // Implementation
private:
    // The user's name
    CString m_szName;
    // The user's e-mail address
    CString m_szAddr;
};
#endif CUSER
```

Defining a Persistent Class

The IMPLEMENT_SERIAL macro takes three parameters and is usually placed before any member functions are defined for a persistent class. The parameters for IMPLEMENT_SERIAL are the following:

- The class to be serialized
- The immediate base class of the class being serialized
- The schema, or version number

The schema number is a version number for the class layout used when you're serializing and deserializing objects. If the schema number of the data being loaded does not match the schema number of the object reading the file, the program throws an exception. The schema number should be incremented when changes are made that affect serialization, such as adding a class member or changing the serialization order.

The member functions for the CUser class, including the IMPLEMENT_SERIAL macro, are provided in Listing 41.3. Save this source code in a file named Users.cpp because you use it in the next chapter.

Listing 41.3. The CUser member functions.

```
#include "stdafx.h"
#include "Users.h"

IMPLEMENT_SERIAL( CUser, CObject, 1 );
CUser::CUser() { }
CUser::CUser( const CString& szName, const CString& szAddr )
{
    Set( szName, szAddr );
}
void CUser::Set( const CString& szName, const CString& szAddr )
{
    m_szName = szName;
    m_szAddr = szAddr;
}
CString CUser::GetName() const
{
    return m_szName;
}
CString CUser::GetAddr() const
{
    return m_szAddr;
}
```

Overriding the *Serialize* Function

Every persistent class must implement a Serialize member function, which is called in order to serialize or deserialize an object. The single parameter for Serialize is the CArchive object used for loading or storing the object. The version of Serialize used by the CUser class is shown in Listing 41.4; add this function to the Users.cpp source file.

Listing 41.4. The `CUser::Serialize` member function.

```
void CUser::Serialize( CArchive& ar )
{
    if( ar.IsLoading() )
    {
        ar >> m_szName >> m_szAddr;
    }
    else
    {
        ar << m_szName << m_szAddr;
    }
}
```

Creating a Serialized Collection

You can serialize most MFC collection classes, enabling large amounts of information to be stored and retrieved easily. For example, you can serialize a `CArray` collection by calling its `Serialize` member function. As with the other MFC template-based collection classes, you cannot use the insertion and extraction operators with `CArray`.

By default, the template-based collection classes perform a bitwise write when serializing a collection and a bitwise read when deserializing an archive. This means that the data stored in the collection is literally written, bit by bit, to the archive.

Bitwise serialization is a problem when you use collections to store pointers to objects. For example, the project in Chapter 42 uses the `CArray` class to store a collection of `CUser` objects. The declaration of the `CArray` member is as follows:

```
CArray<CUser*, CUser*&>    m_setOfUsers;
```

Because the `m_setOfUsers` collection stores `CUser` pointers, storing the collection using a bitwise write would only store the current addresses of the contained objects. This information would become useless when the archive is deserialized.

Most of the time, you need to implement a helper function to assist in serializing a template-based collection. Helper functions do not belong to a class; they are global functions that are overloaded based on the function signature. The helper function used when serializing a template is `SerializeElements`. Figure 41.2 shows how you call the `SerializeElements` function to help serialize items stored in a collection.

A version of `SerializeElements` used with collections of `CUser` objects is provided in Listing 41.5. This function is used in the next chapter.

Figure 41.2.
The
SerializeElements
helper function.

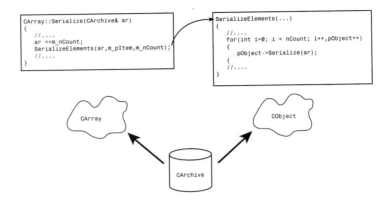

Listing 41.5. The `SerializeElements` function.

```
void AFXAPI SerializeElements( CArchive&    ar,
                               CUser**      pUser,
                               int          nCount )
{
    for( int i = 0; i < nCount; i++, pUser++ )
    {
        if( ar.IsStoring() )
        {
            (*pUser)->Serialize(ar);
        }
        else
        {
            CUser* pNewUser = new CUser;
            pNewUser->Serialize(ar);
            *pUser = pNewUser;
        }
    }
}
```

The `SerializeObjects` function has three parameters:

- A pointer to a `CArchive` object, as with `Serialize`.
- The address of an object stored in the collection. In this example, pointers to `CUser` are stored in a `CArray`, so the parameter is a pointer to a `CUser` pointer.
- The number of elements to be serialized.

In this example, when you're serializing objects to the archive, each `CUser` object is individually written to the archive. When you're deserializing objects, a new `CUser` object is created, and that object is deserialized from the archive. The collection stores a pointer to the new object.

Summary

In this chapter, I discussed serialization and persistence, as well as the `CObject` and `CArchive` MFC classes. You created an example of serializable classes that is also used in the next chapter.

Serialization and Document/View

In the previous chapter, I discussed serialization and creating persistent classes. In this chapter, I cover how serialization fits into the Document/View architecture. You also create an example that uses the persistent classes from Chapter 41, "Serialization," in a Document/View application.

What Is Document/View Serialization?

What The Document/View architecture uses serialization to save or open documents. When a document is saved or loaded, the MFC framework in cooperation with the application's document class creates a CArchive object and serializes the document to or from storage.

The CDocument member functions required to perform serialization in a Document/View application are mapped onto the New, Open, Save, and Save As commands available from the File menu. These member functions take care of creating or opening a document, tracking the modification status of a document, and serializing it to storage.

When documents are loaded, a CArchive object is created for reading, and the archive is deserialized into the document. When documents are saved, a CArchive object is created for writing, and the document is written to the archive. At other times, the CDocument class tracks the current modification status of the document's data. If the document has been updated, the user is prompted to save the document before closing it.

Why Use Document/View Serialization?

Why

The Document/View support for serialization greatly simplifies the work required to save and load documents in a Windows program. For a typical program that uses persistent objects, such as the ones created in Chapter 41, you need to supply only a few lines of source code to get basic support for serialization in a Document/View program. This chapter has about a page or so of source code; most of it is for handling input and output required for the example.

The routines used by CArchive for reading and writing to storage are highly optimized and have excellent performance, even when you're serializing many small data objects. In most cases, it is difficult to match both the performance and ease of use that you get from using the built-in serialization support offered for Document/View applications.

How Are Document/View Applications Serialized?

How

As discussed in Chapter 25, "Document/View Architecture," data stored in a Document/View application is contained by a class derived from CDocument. This class also has responsibility for controlling the serialization of all data contained by the document class. This includes tracking modifications to the document so that the program can display a warning before the user closes an unsaved document.

There are five phases in a document's life cycle:

- Creating a new document
- Modifying the document
- Storing, or serializing the document
- Closing the document
- Loading, or deserializing the document

Most of these phases were discussed in earlier chapters. In this chapter, I focus on how each phase affects serialization of the document.

Creating a New Document

As discussed in Chapter 25, you create MDI and SDI documents differently. An MDI application creates a new CDocument class for every open document, whereas an SDI program reuses a single document.

Both SDI and MDI applications call the OnNewDocument function to initialize a document object. The default version of OnNewDocument calls the DeleteContents function to reset any data contained by the document. AppWizard supplies a DeleteContents function for your document class when a project is created. Most applications can just add code to DeleteContents instead of overriding OnNewDocument.

Tracking Modifications to a Document

In order to determine if a document object can be closed, the MFC framework calls IsModified, a virtual function that is part of the CDocument class. If the document has unsaved changes, the IsDocument function returns TRUE. Although this function can be overridden in any class derived from CDocument, you should usually use the default behavior.

You can use the IsModified function yourself to test whether a document has been serialized.

```
if( IsModified() == TRUE )
{
    AfxMessageBox( "Save File Now?" );
}
```

The IsModified function tests the value of a modification flag, or "dirty bit," which is set when changes are made to the document and cleared when the document is saved or loaded. Classes that are derived from CDocument must update the status of the modification flag when the data contained by the document changes. You use the SetModifiedFlag function to clear or set the modification status of a document.

```
SetModifiedFlag( FALSE );
```

The SetModifiedFlag function has a single parameter: pass TRUE to mark the document as dirty, or changed, and FALSE to mark the document as clean, or unchanged. The parameter has a default value of TRUE, so to mark the document as changed, you can call the function with no parameters.

```
SetModifiedFlag();
```

In most cases, you only call SetModifiedFlag when marking a document as changed. The MFC Document/View framework takes care of resetting the modification flag after the document is serialized.

Storing a Document

When the user saves a document by selecting Save from the File menu, the CWinApp::OnFileSave function is called. This function is almost never overridden; it's a good idea to leave it alone because it calls the CDocument::OnOpenDocument function to serialize the document's data. The default version of OnOpenDocument creates a CArchive object and passes it to the document's Serialize member function. Usually, you serialize the data contained in the document in the same way that other member data was serialized in Chapter 41. After the document's data has been serialized, the dirty bit is cleared, marking the document as unmodified. The steps involved in storing a document are shown in Figure 42.1.

Figure 42.1.
The major functions
called when you store a
document.

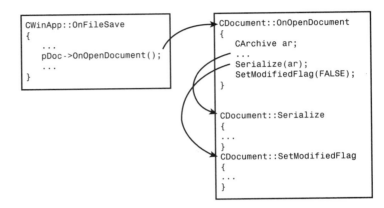

The default version of OnOpenDocument is sufficient for most applications. However, if your application stores data in a different way—for example, in several smaller files or in a database—you should override OnOpenDocument.

When the user selects Save As from the File menu, a common file dialog box collects filename information. After the user selects a filename, the program calls the same CDocument functions, and the serialization process works as described previously.

Closing a Document

When the user closes a document, the MFC Document/View framework calls the document object's OnCloseDocument member function, as shown in Figure 42.2. The default version of this function checks the document to make sure that no unsaved changes are lost by calling the IsModified function. If the user did not modify the document object, DeleteContents is called to free the data stored by the document, and all views for the document are closed.

If the user made changes to the document, the program displays a message box that asks the user if the document's unsaved changes should be saved. If the user elects to save the document, the Serialize function is called. The document is then closed by calling DeleteContents and closing all views for the document.

Figure 42.2.
*The major functions
called when you close a
document.*

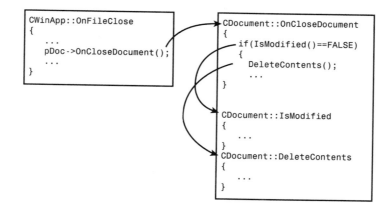

Loading a Document

When you're loading a document, the MFC framework calls the document object's
OnOpenDocument function. The default version of this function calls the DeleteContents mem-
ber function and then calls Serialize to load, or deserialize, the archive. The default version of
OnOpenDocument, shown in Figure 42.3, is sufficient for almost any application.

Figure 42.3.
*The major functions
called when you open a
document.*

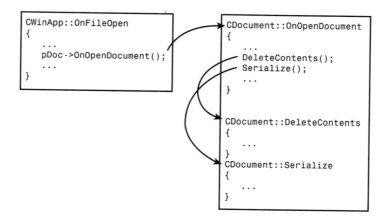

Essential Example

A Document/View Serialization Example

For an example of how to use the Document/View serialization, create a small example using the persistent classes created in the previous chapter.

Using AppWizard, create an MDI project named Customers. This project uses serialization to store a very simple list of customer names and e-mail addresses, using the persistent CUser class created in Chapter 41. Copy the source files created in Chapter 41, Users.cpp and Users.h, into the project directory and add Users.cpp to the project.

Modifying the Document Class

The document class has one new data member, a CArray object that stores a collection of CUser pointers representing a customer list. The document class also has two member functions used to get access to the array of CUser pointers. Add declarations for m_setOfUsers and two member functions to the CCustomersDoc class, as shown in Listing 42.1.

Listing 42.1. Adding a CArray member variable to the CCustomersDoc class.

```
// Attributes
public:
    int    GetCount() const;
    CUser* GetUser( int nUser ) const;
protected:
    CArray<CUser*, CUser*&> m_setOfUsers;
```

There are two other changes that you should make to the CustomersDoc.h header file. First, because the CArray template m_setOfUsers is declared in terms of CUser pointers, you must add an #include statement for the Users.h file. Second, you use a version of the SerializeElements helper function so you need a declaration of that global function. Add the source code provided in Listing 42.2 to the top of CustomersDoc.h.

Listing 42.2. Changes to the CustomersDoc.h header file.

```
#include "Users.h"
void AFXAPI SerializeElements( CArchive& ar,
                               CUser**   pUser,
                               int       nCount );
```

Since the CCustomerDoc class contains a CArray member variable, the template collection declarations must be included into the project. Add an #include statement to the bottom of the StdAfx.h file.

```
#include "afxtempl.h"
```

Creating a Dialog Box

The dialog box used to enter data for the Customers example is similar to dialog boxes created for previous examples. Create a dialog box that contains two edit controls, as shown in Figure 42.4.

Figure 42.4.
The dialog box used in the Customers sample project.

Give the new dialog box a resource ID of IDD_USER_DLG. The two edit controls are used to add user names and e-mail addresses to a document contained by the CCustomerDoc class. Use the values from Table 42.1 for the two edit controls.

Table 42.1. Edit controls contained in the IDD_USER_DLG dialog box.

Edit Control	Resource ID
Name	IDC_EDIT_NAME
Address	IDC_EDIT_ADDR

Using ClassWizard, add a class named CUsersDlg to handle the new dialog box. Add two CString variables to the class using the values from Table 42.2.

Table 42.2. New CString member variables for the CUsersDlg class.

Resource ID	Name	Category	Variable Type
IDC_EDIT_NAME	m_szName	Value	CString
IDC_EDIT_ADDR	m_szAddr	Value	CString

Adding a Menu Item

Use the values from Table 42.3 to add a menu item and message-handling function to the CCustomersDoc class. Add the new menu item, labeled Add User..., to the Edit menu. In order to reduce the amount of source code required for this example, handle the menu item directly with the document class. However, the dialog box could also be handled by a view class or CMainFrame.

Table 42.3. New member functions for the CCustomersDoc class.

Menu ID	Caption	Event	Function Name
ID_EDIT_USER	Add User...	COMMAND	OnEditUser

Listing 42.3 contains the complete source code for the OnEditUser function, which handles the message sent when the user selects the new menu item. If the user clicks the OK button, the contents of the dialog box are used to create a new CUser object, and a pointer to the new object is added to the m_setOfUsers collection. The SetModifiedFlag function is called to mark the document as changed. Add the source code provided in Listing 42.3 to the CCustomersDoc::OnEditUser member function.

Listing 42.3. Adding a new CUser object to the document class.

```
void CCustomersDoc::OnEditUser()
{
    CUsersDlg      dlg;

    if( dlg.DoModal() == IDOK )
    {
        CUser*  pUser = new CUser( dlg.m_szName, dlg.m_szAddr );

        m_setOfUsers.Add( pUser );
        UpdateAllViews( NULL );
        SetModifiedFlag();
    }
}
```

Add the source code provided in Listing 42.4 to the CustomersDoc.cpp source file. These functions provide access to the data contained by the document. The view class, CCustomerView, calls the two CCustomersDoc member functions provided in Listing 42.4 when updating the view window.

Listing 42.4. Document class member functions used for data access.

```
int CCustomersDoc::GetCount() const
{
    return m_setOfUsers.GetSize();
}

CUser* CCustomersDoc::GetUser( int nUser ) const
{
    CUser* pUser = 0;
    if( nUser < m_setOfUsers.GetSize() )
        pUser = m_setOfUsers.GetAt( nUser );
    return pUser;
}
```

Every document needs a `Serialize` member function. The `CCustomersDoc` class has only one data member so its `Serialize` function only deals with `m_setOfUsers`, as shown in Listing 42.5. Add this source code to the `CCustomersDoc::Serialize` member function.

Listing 42.5. Serializing the contents of the document class.

```
void CCustomersDoc::Serialize(CArchive& ar)
{
    m_setOfUsers.Serialize( ar );
}
```

As I discussed in Chapter 41, the `CArray` class uses the `SerializeElements` helper function when the collection is serialized. Add the `SerializeElements` function that was provided in the previous chapter in Listing 41.5 to the CustomersDoc.cpp source file.

Add an `#include` statement to the CustomersDoc.cpp file so that the `CCustomersDoc` class can have access to declarations of classes used by `CCustomersDoc`. Add the source code from Listing 42.6 near the top of the CustomersDoc.cpp file, just after the other `#include` statements.

Listing 42.6. `#include` statements used by the `CCustomersDoc` class.

```
#include "Users.h"
#include "UsersDlg.h"
```

Modifying the View

The view class, `CCustomersView`, displays the current contents of the document. When the document is updated, the view is repainted and displays the updated contents. You must update two functions in the `CCustomersView` class: `OnDraw` and `OnUpdate`.

AppWizard creates a skeleton version of the `CCustomersView::OnDraw` function. Add the source code from Listing 42.7 to `OnDraw` so that the current document contents are displayed in the view. Because this is not a scrolling view, a limited number of items from the document can be displayed. To display more information, you could use a scrolling or split view, as discussed in Chapter 28, "Split Views."

Listing 42.7. Using `OnDraw` to display the current document's contents.

```
void CCustomersView::OnDraw(CDC* pDC)
{
    CCustomersDoc* pDoc = GetDocument();
    ASSERT_VALID(pDoc);
    // Calculate the space required for a single
    // line of text, including the inter-line area.
    TEXTMETRIC  tm;
    pDC->GetTextMetrics( &tm );
    int nLineHeight = tm.tmHeight + tm.tmExternalLeading;
    CPoint  ptText( 0, 0 );
```

continues

Listing 42.7. continued

```
for( int nIndex = 0; nIndex < pDoc->GetCount(); nIndex++ )
{
    CString szOut;
    CUser* pUser = pDoc->GetUser( nIndex );
    szOut.Format( "User = %s, email = %s",
                  pUser->GetName(),
                  pUser->GetAddr() );
    pDC->TextOut( ptText.x, ptText.y, szOut );
    ptText.y += nLineHeight;
}
}
```

As with most documents, the CCustomersDoc class calls UpdateAllViews when it is updated. The MFC framework then calls the OnUpdate function for each view connected to the document.

Add a message-handling function for CCustomersView::OnUpdate and add the source code from Listing 42.8 to it. The OnUpdate function invalidates the view, resulting in the view being redrawn with the updated contents.

Listing 42.8. Invalidating the view during OnUpdate.

```
void CCustomersView::OnUpdate( CView* pSender,
                               LPARAM lHint,
                               CObject* pHint)
{
    InvalidateRect( NULL );
}
```

Add an #include statement to the CustomersView.cpp file so that the view can use the CUser class. Add the #include statement beneath the other #include statements in CustomersView.cpp.

```
#include "Users.h"
```

Summary

In this chapter, I discussed how serialization is used in a Document/View application. I covered the CDocument functions used for serialization and created a small Document/View serialization example.

Index

SYMBOLS

! (not operator), 30
!= (not equal to operator), 30
& operator
  address-of, 83
  reference, 85
&= (bitwise AND operator), 310
() (parentheses), 30
* operator
  indirection, 83-85
  multiplication, 29
+ (addition operator), 29
- (subtraction operator), 29
... (ellipsis), 139, 168
/ (division operator), 29
; (semicolons), 27-28
< (less than operator), 30
<< (insertion operator), 27, 467-469
<= (less than or equal to operator), 30
= (assignment operator), 29, 43
= = (equality operator), 30, 51
> (greater than operator), 30
>= (greater than or equal to operator), 30
>> (extraction operator), 27, 467-469
{} (curly braces), 27
| (bitwise OR operator), 181
~ (tilde), 60, 310
256-color icons, 384

A

abstract base classes, 100
adapters, 118
AddBitmapToImageList function, 236-237
addition operator (+), 29
address-of operator (&), 83
addresses (memory), 82
AddString function, 221-222, 225
algorithms, 118, 121
ancestor classes, 95

Application Architecture (MFC classes), 5
application class, 292
applications, *see* programs
Apply button, 199, 418-419
AppWizard, 5, 18-20, 144, 149-153
   creating dialog box-based projects, 195-196
   device contexts, 339-340
   Document/View architecture, 293-295
arrays, 63-67
   CArray collection class, 128-130
   collections, 126
   dynamic arrays, 87-88
ASSERT macro, 108
ASSERT_VALID macro, 108
assignment operator (=), 29, 43
associative containers, 119
attributes of fonts, 373-377

B

base classes, 93, 97-98, 103-111
BASIC, compared to Visual C++, 22
begin function, 120
BitBlt function, 234
bitmaps, 182, 231-240
   creating
      for list view controls, 286-287
      for toolbars, 275
      for tree view controls, 249-250
   icons, 383-389
bitwise AND operator (&=), 310
bitwise OR operator (|), 181
block scope, 77
blocks (compound statements), 51
Booch notation, 94
Books Online, 15

bool data type, 40
Boolean variables, 30
break statements, 53
brushes, 359-369
buddy controls, adding to up-down controls, 257-258
Build button (toolbar), 26, 33
Build menu commands
   Build, 33
   Debugger, 110
   Execute, 20, 147
   Settings, 33
building
   executable programs, 22-23
   programs (outline), 10
   SDI test projects, 207
button arrangements (message boxes), 180
button controls, 193-204
button events, adding to dialog box classes, 200-201
buttons, 193-194, 199
   displaying icons, 386-389
   see also icons; toolbar icons

C

C++ programming language
   arrays, 63-67
   building programs, 22-23
   character strings, 68-70
   classes, 57-60
   execution flow, 49-56
   expressions, 27-31
   functions, 43-47
   identifiers, 42, 80-81
   pointers, 82-88
   polymorphism, 72
   scope, 75-79
   statements, 27-28
   structures, 56-57
   variables, 37-43
CAboutDlg class, modifying, 250-251, 388-389
calling
   constructors/destructors, 60
   functions, 46-47
Cancel button, 199

CArchive class (serialization), 468
CArray collection class, 128-130
case labels (switch statements), 53
case sensitivity (variable names), 42
casting pointers (RTTI), 133-136
catch keyword, 138
categories (classes), 95
CBrush class, 361-362
CClientDC (device context class), 339
CComboBox class, 226-229
CDC (device context class), 339
CDCTestView class, 344-346, 379-380
   modifying, 355-357, 367-369
CDialog class, 186-187
CDocument class (serialization), 474-478
CEdit class, 206, 210
cells, 457
CFont class, 373, 377
CFormatDlg class, creating, 428-429
CFormView class, 306
char data type, 40
character formatting, 423-424, 427-428
character sets (font attributes), 374
character strings, 68-70
checkboxes, 193-194
CHelloApp class, 148
CHelloWnd class, 147
CImageList class, 235
class libraries (MFC classes), 5-6
classes, 57-60, 93
   abstract base classes, 100
   adapters, 118
   application class, 292
   base classes, 93, 97-98, 103-111

CAboutDlg, modifying, 250-251, 388-389
CArchive (serialization), 468
categories, 95
CBrush, 361-362
CComboBox, 226-229
CDCTestView, 344-346, 355-357, 367, 379-380
CDialog, 186-187
CEdit, 206
CFont, 373, 377
CFormatDlg, 428-429
CFormView, 306
CHelloApp, 148
CHelloWnd, 147
CImageList, 235
CListBox, 220-223
CListCtrl, 280
CListExDlg, 287-288
CListView, 280
CMainFrame, 266-267, 272-277
CMapModeDlg, 364-366
CMouseTstView, 162-164
CObject (serialization), 468
collections, 125-131
constructors, 60
CPen, 348, 351-352
CPrintInfo, 404
CPropertyPage, 412
CPropertySheet, 411
creating dialog boxes, 479
CRect, 148
CRichEdit classes, 423
CRichTextView, 429-431
CSpinButtonCtrl, 258-259
CStack template, 114-117
CString, 70-71
CTreeCtrl, 244
CTreeView, 245-247
declaring, 58, 93
derived classes, 95-96
destructors, 60
document classes, 292, 478-481
Document/View architecture, 150-151, 291-299, 423

dynamic split frame classes, creating, 327-328
edit control classes, creating, 436-437
form views, 301-302, 305-306
frame class, 292
hierarchies, 93-94
implementing, 93
inheritance, 95-96
member functions, 58-59
MFC class library, 103-111, 145-149, 339
persistent classes, 469-470
pure virtual functions, 99-100
serialization, 465-478
scope, 78-79
static class members, 79, 329-330
subclasses, 95
templates, 113-117
view class, 292
virtual destructors, 100-102
virtual functions, 98-99
ClassView tab (Project Workspace window), 19
ClassWizard, 5, 144, 160-164
configuring OLE controls, 456
device contexts, 339-340
Document/View architecture, 295-296
clipping cursors, 397
clipping precision (font attributes), 374-375
CList collection class, 127-128
CListBox class, 220-223
CListCtrl class, 280
CListExDlg class, 287-288
CListItem structure, 447
CListView class, 280
Close button, 199
Close command (File menu), 13
closing documents (serialization), 476
CMainFrame class, 266-267, 272-277

CMap collection class, 130-131
CMapModeDlg class, 364-366
CMouseTstView class, 162-164
CObject class, 104-110, 468
collecting
data from combo boxes, 226
device context data, 341
text from edit controls, 210-211
collections, 6, 118-120, 125-131, 471-472
colors
common color dialog box, 363
pens, 351
WM_CTLCOLOR message, 366-367
columns, report view (list view controls), 283-284
combo boxes, 223-229
commands
Build menu
Build, 33
Debugger, 110
Execute, 20, 147
Settings, 33
edit control editing commands, 206
File menu, 12-14
New, 12, 24-25, 33
Help menu, 14, 17
Insert menu
Components, 455
Files into Project, 25
Resource, 173, 232, 385
keyboard shortcuts, 14
Layout menu (Tab Order), 204
View menu (Project Workspace), 25
common dialog boxes, 178-179, 363, 378-381
compiling projects via AppWizard, 19-20
Component Gallery, 455
compound assignment operators, 66

compound statements, 51
conditional statements, 30
conditionally changing
   cursors, 394
configuring OLE controls via
   ClassWizard, 456
console mode programs, 21-27
const function parameters, 86
constructors, 60
   CMouseTstView class, 163
   exception handling, 139-140
containers, 118-120, 454-455
contents pane (InfoViewer),
   17-18
context-sensitive help, 16-17
control bars, 265-277
controls, 5
   button controls, 193-204
   combo boxes, 223-229
   dialog bars, 265, 270-274
   edit controls, 205-215
   form views, 301-310
   list boxes, 217-223
   list view controls, 279-289
   OLE controls, 453-462
   owner-drawn controls,
      441-452
   progress controls, 261-263
   rich edit controls, 421-431
   self-drawn controls, 442
   slider controls, 259-261
   static text controls, 185-186
   status bars, 265-268
   subclassing, 433-439
   superclassing, 433, 435
   toolbars, 265, 274-277
   tree view controls, 243-254
   up-down controls, 255-259
   VBX control specification,
      453-454
coordinate systems, mapping
   modes, 341-342
Copy command (keyboard
   shortcuts), 14
copying character strings,
   69-70
cosmetic pens, 348-349
cout, 27

CPaintDC (device context
   class), 339
CPen class, 348, 351-352
CPrintInfo class, 404
CPropertyPage class, 412
CPropertySheet class, 411
creating
   bitmaps, 232, 275
   brushes, 361-362
   CFormatDlg class, 428-429
   cursors, 392-393
   data models, 297-298
   dialog box classes, 186-187
   dialog box resources,
      182-183, 272, 304-305,
      412, 414-417
   dialog box-based projects,
      195-196
   dialog boxes, 427-428, 479
   dockable dialog bars, 271
   documents (serialization), 475
   dynamic split views, 325-329
   edit control classes, 436-437
   fonts, 377-378
   Hobby page (property sheet
      sample project), 416-417
   icons, 317, 384-385
   image lists, 235-238,
      249-250, 286-287
   map mode dialog boxes,
      343-344
   menu resources, 173-174
   menus for views, 317
   multiple document tem-
      plates, 315-316
   multiple views, 313-314
   Name page (property sheet
      sample project), 414-415
   objects at runtime, 107-108
   owner-drawn list boxes,
      446-452
   pop-up menus, 173-176
   projects, 18-19, 23-25
   property pages, 411-413
   property sheets, 411,
      417-418
   scrolling views, 325-327

SDI (Single Document
   Interface) applications via
   AppWizard, 151-152
source files, 25-26
static split views, 329-333
toolbars, 275
Windows application
   projects, 147
CRect class, 148
CRichEdit classes, 423
CRichTextView class, 429-431
CSpinButtonCtrl class,
   258-259
CStack template class,
   114-117
CString class, 70-71
CTreeCtrl class, 244
CTreeView class, 245-247
CtrlBar sample program, 266,
   272-277
curly braces ({ }), 27
current selection (combo
   boxes), 227
cursors, 182, 391-398
customizing
   AppWizard programs,
      152-153
   dialog box properties,
      184-188
Cut command (keyboard
   shortcuts), 14
CWindowDC (device context
   class), 339
CWnd base class, 104-105,
   110-111

D

data collection, 226, 341
data exchange, 211-215, 413
data models, creating, 297-298
data types, 38, 40-41,
   56-57, 63
data validation, 211-215
DC, see device contexts
DCTest program, 343-346
   brushes, 364-369
   icons, 386-388
   pens, 354-357

DDV (Dialog Data Validation) routines, 211-215
DDX (Dialog Data Exchange) routines, 211-215
Debugger command (Build menu), 110
debuggers (Developer Studio), 4, 20, 108-110
DECLARE macros, 105-107, 469
declaring
arrays, 64
character strings, 68
classes, 58, 93
function prototypes, 44-45
persistent classes, 469
pointers, 84
variables, 28, 38
Decorative font family, 372
default labels (switch statements), 53
default text, adding to edit controls, 211
defining
arrays, 64
functions, 45
geometric pen styles, 350
persistent classes, 470
styles for status bars, 269
variables, 38
delete operator, 86-88
DeleteContents function, 475-476
DeleteString function, 222
deleting text strings from list boxes, 222
derived classes, 95-96
derived types, 63
descendant classes, 95
designing object-oriented programs, 91-102
DestroyIcon function, 385
destroying objects, exception handling, 139
destructors, 60, 100-102
Developer Studio, 4-6
AppWizard, 5, 18-20, 149-153, 293-295

ClassWizard, 5, 160-162, 295-296
Component Gallery, 455
creating dialog box resources, 183
dockable windows, 16
editors, 4, 11-14
InfoViewer, 15-18
integrating with other tools, 9-10
RTTI (Run Time Type Information), 133-136
starting, 9
device contexts, 148-149, 337-346, 353
diagnostic features (MFC class library), 108
dialog bars, 265, 270-274
dialog box resources, creating, 272
dialog box-based projects, 195-203
dialog boxes, 5, 177-189
adding
buttons, 196-201
edit controls, 207-208
grid controls, 458-459
icons, 386-388
list boxes, 218-219
list view controls, 285-286
message-handling functions, 187-189
owner-drawn list boxes, 446-447
slider controls, 259-260
static text controls, 185-186
subclassed edit controls, 437-439
tree view controls, 247
up-down controls, 256
advantages of property sheets, 410-411
button controls, 193-204
CAboutDlg class, 250-251
CDialog class, 186-187
CFormatDlg class, 428-429
common dialog boxes, 178-179, 363, 378-381

creating, 182-183, 427-428, 479
dialog box editor, 196-198
edit controls, 211-215
map mode dialog boxes, 343-344, 354-355, 364-366
message boxes, 178-180
modal dialog boxes, 177, 179
modeless dialog boxes, 179
properties, 184-188
standard pushbutton layouts, 199
user input, 178-179
dialog editors, 455-458
dialog resources
creating, 304-305, 412, 414-417
sizing form views, 308-309
directories, organizing projects, 23
disabling/enabling button controls, 202
disk space requirements, installing Visual C++ 4, 8
display device contexts, 338
division operator (/), 29
do-while loops, 55
dockable control bars, 265, 271
dockable windows, 16
document classes, 292, 478-481
document templates, 293-295
adding split views, 328-332
resource strings, 317
Document/View architecture, 150-151, 291-299
printing functions, 401-408
rich edit controls, 423
serialization, 473-478
documentation for Visual C++, 7, 15
documents
adding views, 313-314
initializing objects, 298-299
modifying views, 481-482
multiple views, 311-322
serialization, 475-477

DoDataExchange function,
212-213
DoModal function, 413
Dontcare font family, 372
double data type, 40
down-casting, 135
drag-and-drop, tree view
controls, 251-254
Draw function, 238
DrawCheckBox function,
450-451
DrawIcon function, 385
drawing functions (pens), 353
DrawText function, 149
drop-down combo/list
boxes, 224
Dump function, 108-109
dynamic arrays, 87-88
dynamic lifetimes (variables),
86-87
dynamic split views, 324-329
dynamic_cast operator,
135-136
dynamically creating objects,
107-108

E

edit controls, 205-215
adding to up-down controls,
257-258
creating classes, 436-437
subclassing, 436-439
edit views, 303
editing
menu resources, 171-172
program icons, 386
source files, 12-13
editors, 4
Developer Studio, 11-14
dialog editor, 196-198,
455-458
image editor, 232, 384-385,
392-393
elements of arrays, 65-66
ellipsis (...), 139, 168
else statements, 51-52

EnableDocking function, 271
EnableWindow function, 202
enabling/disabling
Apply button (property sheet
sample project), 418-419
button controls, 202
RTTI, 136
end function, 120
endcap styles (geometric
pens), 350
equality operator (= =), 30, 51
error detection, 137-140
escapement (font
attributes), 376
events (Windows), 144, 148,
155-159
adding button events to
dialog box classes, 200-201
firing, 454
MouseTst program, 162-165
exception handling, 5,
136-140
exchanging data, 211-215, 413
executable programs, building,
22-23
Execute command (Build
menu), 20, 147
executing
MouseTst program, 165
programs, 26
projects, 20
execution flow, 49-56
Explorer icons, 384
expressions, 27-31
ExtractIcon function, 238
extraction operator (>>),
468-469

F

F1 key (context-sensitive
help), 16-17
families (font attributes),
375-376
File menu commands, 12-14
New, 12, 24-25, 33
file scope, 77

Files into Project command
(Insert menu), 25
FileView tab (Project
Workspace window), 19
Find member function, 71
firing events, 454
fixed pitch fonts, 371
float data type, 40
floating control bars, 265
floating pop-up menus, *see*
pop-up menus
focus (button controls), 203
fonts, 371-381
for loops, 55-56
form views, 301-310
formatting (rich edit controls),
423-428
frame classes, 292, 327-330
function objects, 118, 121
function prototype scope, 77
function scope, 77-78
function templates, 117
functions, 43-47
AddBitmapToImageList,
236-237
AddString, 221-222, 225
advantages, 43
arrays as parameters, 66-67
base classes compared to
derived classes, 97-98
begin, 120
BitBlt, 234
calling, 46-47
const function parameters, 86
CString class functions,
70-71
CWnd base class functions,
110-111
DDX functions, 214-215
declaring prototypes, 44-45
defining, 45
DeleteContents, 475-476
DeleteString, 222
DestroyIcon, 385
DoDataExchange, 212-213
DoModal, 413
Draw, 238
DrawCheckBox, 450-451

DrawIcon, 385
drawing functions (pens), 353
DrawText, 149
Dump, 108-109
EnableDocking, 271
EnableWindow, 202
end, 120
ExtractIcon, 238
Find, 71
GetCount, 226
GetCurSel, 223
GetDeviceCaps, 341
GetDocument, 296, 299
GetFont, 111
GetLength, 71
GetParaFormat, 425-426
GetSelectionCharFormat, 423-424
GetTextMetrics, 341
GetTreeControl, 245
GetWindowLong, 284
GetWindowText, 110
InsertItem, 246, 283
InsertString, 221-222, 225
IsModified, 475
library functions, 44
LoadBitmap, 232
LoadIcon, 385
LoadToolbar, 275
lstrlen, 69
main function, 26-27, 44
MoveWindow, 110
OnApply, 412, 419
OnBeginPrinting, 403-406
OnCancel, 413
OnCompareItem, 445
OnDeleteItem, 445-446, 451-452
OnDraw, 314-315, 340, 380-381, 402, 481-482
OnDrawItem, 443-444, 448-450
OnEditUser, 480
OnEndPrinting, 403, 405, 407
OnInitialUpdate, 308, 320-322
OnKillActive, 412

OnMeasureItem, 444-445
OnNewDocument, 296, 475
OnOK, 413
OnOpenDocument, 475-477
OnPrepareDC, 403, 405, 408
OnPreparePrinting, 403-404
OnPrint, 403, 405, 407-408
OnQueryCancel, 412
OnReset, 413
OnSetActive, 413
OnUpdate, 320-322, 482
OnUpdateTimer, 270
OnViewMapMode, 368
polymorphism, 72
pure virtual functions, 99-100
rbegin, 121
rend, 121
ResetContent, 222
return values, 47
Serialize, 470-471
SetAt, 71
SetButtons, 275
SetFont, 111
SetImageList, 282
SetModifed, 418-419
SetOverlayImage, 239
SetPaneInfo, 267
SetParaFormat, 425-426
SetRange, 258
SetSelectionCharFormat, 423-424
SetWindowLong, 284
SetWindowText, 110, 201-202
ShowWindow, 110, 202-203
string functions, 68-70
terminate, 139
testing return values, 137
UpdateAllViews, 296
variable values, changing, 85
virtual functions, 98-99
window procedures, 158

G

GDI (Graphics Device Interface) objects, 337-338
  brushes, 359-369
  fonts, 371-381
  icons, 383-389
  pens, 347-357
  selecting for device contexts, 340-341
geometric pens, 348-350
GetCount function, 226
GetCurSel function, 223
GetDeviceCaps function, 341
GetDocument function, 296, 299
GetFont function, 111
GetLength function, 71
GetParaFormat function, 425-426
GetSelectionCharFormat function, 423-424
GetTextMetrics function, 341
GetTreeControl function, 245
GetWindowLong function, 284
GetWindowText function, 110
glyphs, 371
Go button (toolbar), 110
goto statements, 78
Graphical Objects (MFC classes), 5
graphics, *see* images
greater than operator (>), 30
greater than or equal to operator (>=), 30
grid controls (custom OLE), 457-462
group boxes, 194

H

handling messages (Windows), 157-159
  ClassWizard, 160-162
  combo boxes, 227-229
  dialog boxes, 187-189
  edit control class, 436-437
  form views, 306-308

grid controls, 460-461
list boxes, 222-223
menu items, 172-173
menus, 169-170
MouseTst program, 162
owner-drawn controls, 442-452
pop-up menus, 174-176
property pages, 412-413
slider controls, 263
status bar timers, 269-270
tree view controls, 251-254
WM_CTLCOLOR message, 366-367

hardware independence (device contexts), 338-339
hatch brushes, 360-361
header files, 45
height/width (font attributes), 373-374
Hello World program, 25-27, 31-33
hello.mak, 152
hello.rc, 152
Help button, 199
Help menu commands, 14, 17
help systems, 15-18
hiding button controls, 202-203
hierarchies (classes), 93-94
Hobby page (property sheet sample project), creating, 416-417
hotspots, adding to cursors, 393
hourglass cursors, switching to, 396-397
Hungarian notation, 42-43

I

icons, 182, 383-389
creating, 317, 384-385
message boxes, 179-180
see also toolbar icons
IDE (Integrated Development Environment), 4
identifiers, 42, 75-81

if statements, 31, 50-52
image editor, creating bitmaps, 232, 384-385, 392-393
image lists, 234-240
associating with list view controls, 282
creating, 235-238, 249-250, 286-287
icons, 384
retrieving icons, 386
images
bitmaps, 231-234
cursors, 391-398
overlaid images, 235, 239-240
transparent images, 235, 238-239
IMPLEMENT macros, 105-107, 470
#include statement, 26, 119
indexes (list boxes), 218
indicators, 266
indirection operator (*), 83-85
information device contexts, 338
InfoViewer, 15-18
inheritance (classes), 95-96
initializing
arrays, 65
document objects, 298-299
grid controls, 459-460
progress/slider controls, 262-263
input operator (>>), 27, 467
Insert menu commands
Components, 455
Files into Project, 25
Resource, 173, 232, 385
insertion operator (<<), 468-469
InsertItem function, 246, 283
InsertString function, 221-222, 225
installing Visual C++ 4, 7-9
InstallShield, 9
int data type, 40
integrated editors (Developer Studio), 4

integrating Developer Studio with other tools, 9-10
interfaces (Document/View architecture), 296-299
inversion operator (~), 310
iostream library, 27
iostream.h, 45
IS-A relationships, 95
IsModified function, 475
iterations, 54-56
iterators, 118, 120-121

J–K

joining styles (geometric pens), 350

Keyboard command (Help menu), 14
keyboard layout, installing Visual C++, 8
keyboard shortcuts, editor commands, 14
keyword searching (InfoViewer), 17
keywords
catch, 138
private, 58
protected, 96
public, 58
this, 149
try, 138
typedef, 114
virtual, 98

L

labels, 77-78, 201-202
language-independence of messages, 156
large icons, 384
Layout menu commands (Tab Order), 204
length of strings, 68-71
less than operator (<), 30
less than or equal to operator (<=), 30

libraries
  functions, 44
  iostream library, 27
  MFC class library, 105, 108,
    145-149
  Standard Template Library
    (STL), 118-122
lifetime (identifiers), 80-81
**LineCut command (keyboard
  shortcuts), 14**
**Liskov Substitution
  Principle, 95**
list boxes, 217-223, 446-452
list view controls, 279-289
listings
  2.1. A minimal C++
    program, 13
  2.2. A simple C++ class
    declaration, 13
  2.3. Testing InfoViewer's
    context- sensitive help, 17
  3.1. A simple C++ console
    mode program, 25
  3.2. A C++ program that
    assigns a value to a
    variable, 29
  3.3. Testing the value of
    input data with an if
    statement, 31
  3.4. A simple Windows
    program written using C++
    and MFC, 32
  4.1. Compiler-caught
    problems, 39
  4.2. A corrected version of
    the previous example, 39
  4.3. Using sizeof to deter-
    mine the amount of storage
    required for different
    fundamental types, 41
  4.4. Some examples of good
    and bad variable names, 42
  4.5. Math functions included
    in the standard library, 44
  4.6. A function that displays
    a welcome message for a
    console mode program, 45

  4.7. An attempt to call a
    function incorrectly will be
    caught by the compiler, 47
  4.8. Storing a function's
    return value in a
    variable, 47
  5.1. A function that returns
    true if a positive number is
    passed to it, 50
  5.2. Compound
    statements, 51
  5.3. A function that uses the
    if and else statements, 52
  5.4. A menu-selection
    function, 52-53
  5.5. Using the switch
    statement, 53
  5.6. A program that executes
    a while loop 10 times, 54
  5.7. Using the do-while loop
    to test for user input in a
    console mode program, 55
  5.8. Using a for loop to print
    10 lines to the screen, 55
  5.9. Using a structure to
    calculate a weekly salary, 57
  5.10. A declaration for a
    weekly pay record class, 58
  5.11. CWeeklyPayRecord
    class, 59
  5.12. Calling constructors
    and destructors, 60
  6.1. Using arrays to track a
    baseball score, 65-66
  6.2. Using arrays as param-
    eters in function calls, 67
  6.3. Using strlen to calculate
    the length of a string, 69
  6.4. Using strcpy to copy
    character array-based
    strings, 69
  6.5. MFC CString class, 70
  6.6. Determining the
    number of characters in a
    CString object, 71
  6.7. Searching for a newline
    inside a CString object, 71

  6.8. Using overloaded
    functions, 72
  7.1. Local block scope, 77
  7.2. Function scope, 77-78
  7.3. Class scope, 79
  7.4. A variable out of scope
    but not destroyed, 80-81
  7.5. A static object in a
    function, destroyed when
    the program ends, 81
  7.6. Using sizeof with class
    types, 83
  7.7. Using a pointer variable
    with the indirection
    operator, 83-84
  7.8. Using a pointer and a
    function to change a
    variable's value, 85
  7.9. Using references to
    change the value of a
    variable, 86
  7.10. Using new and delete
    for fundamental types, 87
  7.11. Using new[] to create a
    dynamic array, 87
  8.1. Class declarations for
    geometric shapes, without
    using inheritance, 93-94
  8.2. Declarations for
    geometric shape classes,
    using a base class and
    inheritance, 96
  8.3. An example of calling
    the wrong function through
    a base-class pointer, 97
  8.4. An example of virtual
    functions and reliable base-
    class pointer use, 98-99
  8.5. Using a pure virtual
    function in a base class,
    99-100
  8.6. Deleting an object
    without a virtual destructor,
    100-101
  8.7. Correct destructor
    chosen at runtime, 101-102

9.1. The CMyObject class declaration, using CObject as a base class, 106

9.2. Member functions for the CMyObject class, 107

9.3. Creating an object at runtime using CRuntimeClass, 107

9.4. Adding a Dump function to the CMyObject declaration, 109

9.5. Adding the implementation of Dump to CMyObject, 109

9.6. Disabling and enabling a control using a CWnd pointer, 110

10.1. Using typedef to simplify template declarations, 114

10.2. The CStack template class, 115-116

10.3. CStack template, 116-117

10.4. Function template that exchanges its parameters, 117

10.5. Using ArgSwap to exchange the contents of two CString objects, 117

10.6. Standard Template Library, 122

11.1. Using the CList collection class to create a waiting list, 127-128

11.2. Using the CArray collection to store a hand of cards, 129

11.3. A customer list that uses the CMap class, 130-131

12.1. Using the dynamic_cast operator, 135-136

12.2. The traditional way to detect errors: test function return values, 137

12.3. Simple exception handling, 138

12.4. A single try block that throws two different types of expressions, 138-139

12.5. Throwing and catching errors during construction, 140

13.1. A simple MFC Windows program, written without AppWizard, 146-147

13.2. CHelloView::OnDraw function for the SDI version of Hello World!, 152

14.1. Handling mouse and WM_PAINT messages using a window procedure written in C, 158-159

14.2. The OnLButtonDown function created by ClassWizard, 160

14.3. A message map for the CMyView class, 161

14.4. New member variables for the CMouseTstView class, 163

14.5. The contructor for CMouseTstView, 163

14.6. The four mouse-handling functions for CMouseTstView, 164

14.7. The OnDraw member function for CMouseTstView, 164

15.1. The CMainFrame:: OnFileHello message-handling function, 173

15.2. New member variables for the CMenuView class, 174

15.3. The CMenuView:: OnDraw member function, 174

15.4. Popping up a menu when a right mouse click is detected, 175

15.5. Message-handling functions for floating menu items, 176

16.1. A typical resource definition for a dialog box, 182

16.2. The CHelloDlg:: OnInitDialog function, 188

16.3. The message-handling function for the Hello menu item, 188

17.1. The CButtonDlg:: OnBtnTest member function, 201

17.2. Changing the label for several buttons, 201

17.3. Using CWnd::EnableWindow to disable a dialog box control, 202

17.4. Using CWnd::ShowWindow to hide a dialog box control, 203

18.1. Handling a menu-item selection for EditTest, 207

18.2. Collecting input from an edit control using CEdit, 210

18.3. Adding default text to an edit control, 211

18.4. Using member variables to exchange information with an edit control, 214-215

19.1. Using AddString to add strings to a list box, 222

19.2. Handling a list-box notification message, 223

19.3. The CComboListDlg:: OnInitDialog function, 227

19.4. The CComboListDlg:: OnOk function, 227

19.5. The CComboListDlg:: OnCloseupCombo function, 227-228

19.6. The CComboListDlg::
OnEditupdateCombo
function, 228-229

20.1. The CBitmapView::
OnDraw function, used to
display a bitmap, 233-234

20.2. The CImageListView::
AddBitmapToImageList
function, 237

20.3. CImageListView
class, 237

20.4. The CImageListView
constructor, 237

20.5. Using
CImageList::Draw to
display a bitmap from an
image list, 238

20.6. Using the
CImageList::Draw function
to display a bitmap
transparently, 239

20.7. Using
CImageList::Draw function
to diaplay an overlapped
image, 239-240

21.1. Adding items to a
CTreeView, 246

21.2. Modifying the tree
view style in
PreCreateWindow, 247

21.3. Additions to the
CAboutDlg class declara-
tion, 250

21.4. The CAboutDlg::
OnInitDialog member
function, 251

21.5. Functions used to
implement simple drag-
and-drop, 252-253

22.1. Setting the range for an
up-down control, 259

22.2. Initializing the controls
in CControlsDlg::
OnInitDialog, 263

22.3. Using slider scroll
messages to update the
progress control, 263

23.1. Changes to the
indicators array in
MainFrame.cpp, 268

23.2. Changes to the
CMainFrame::Create
member function, 269

23.3. Invalidating the status
bar in the OnTimer
function, 269

23.4. Changes to the
CMainFrame class
declaration, 270

23.5. The CMainFrame
message map after adding
OnUpdateTimer, 270

23.6. The OnUpdateTimer
member function, 270

23.7. Additions to the
CMainFrame class
declaration, 273

23.8. Additions to the
CMainFrame::OnCreate
function, 273

23.9. Updates to the
CMainFrame message map
declarations, 273

23.10. Updates to the
CMainFrame message
map, 273

23.11. The CMainFrame::
OnBarHelp function, 274

23.12. Additions to the
CMainFrame class
declaration, 276

23.13. The resource ID
array used by the new
toolbar, 276

23.14. Additions to the
CMainFrame::OnCreate
function, 277

24.1. Changes to the
CListExDlg class declara-
tion, 287

24.2. Changes to the
CListExDlg class imple-
mentation, 288

24.3. Functions used to
change the control's view
style, 289

25.1. How AppWizard uses a
document template in an
SDI application, 294

25.2. AppWizard code that
uses a document template
in an MDI application, 295

25.3. Changes to the
CDVTestDoc class
declaration, 297

25.4. New functions added
to the CDVTestDoc class,
297-298

25.5. Changes to the
CDVTestDoc::OnNew
Document member
function, 298

25.6. Using GetDocument
to fetch the document
pointer, 299

26.1. Constructing a
CMultiDocTemplate
object that associates
CDVTestDoc and
CFormTest, 306

26.2. CFormTest functions
used to handle control
messages, 307

26.3. Using OnInitialUpdate
to retrieve data from the
document, 308

26.4. Using the
PreCreateWindow function
to change CChildFrame
style attributes, 309

27.1. CDisplayView::
OnDraw, 314-315

27.2. Changes to the
CDVTestApp class
declaration, 315

27.3. Changes to
CDVTestApp::InitInstance
creating two document
templates, 315-316

27.4. CDVTestApp
functions used to return
pointers to the document
templates, 316

27.5. CMainFrame member functions used to create new views, 318-319

27.6. A new version of CDVTestDoc::AddName that causes views to be updated, 320

27.7. CDisplayView update functions, 320

27.8. CFormTest::OnUpdate function, 321

27.9. CFormTest:: OnInitialUpdate after removing unnecessary code, 321

27.10. CFormTest::OnApply after removing list box AddString code, 321-322

28.1. CDisplayScroll member functions, 326

28.2. Adding a CSplitterWnd member variable to the CScrollSplit class, 327

28.3. CScrollSplit:: OnCreateClient, 328

28.4. Creating a new document template that uses a split view, 328

28.5. Adding a CSplitterWnd member variable to the CSplitForm class, 329

28.6. CSplitFrame:: OnCreateClient function, 330

28.7. Additions to the CDVTestApp class declaration, 331

28.8. A CDVTestApp function used to return a pointer to the new document template, 331

28.9. The new version of the CDVTestApp destructor, 331

28.10. Additional code added to CDVTestApp:: OnInitInstance, 332

28.11. CMainFrame member functions used to create the new split view, 332

29.1. A typical OnDraw function, 340

29.2. Selecting and restoring a GDI object, 340

29.3. The CDCTestView:: OnViewMapMode function, 344-345

29.4. New member variables added to the CDCTestView class declaration, 345

29.5. The CDCTestView:: OnDraw function, 346

30.1. Creating a brush using a LOGBRUSH structure, 352

30.2. New member variable added to the CDCTestView class, 355

30.3. The new version of the CDCTestView constructor, 356

30.4. The new version of the CDCTestView:: OnViewMapMode function, 356

30.5. The new version of CDCTestView::OnDraw, 357

31.1. Filling a LOGBRUSH structure, 363

31.2. Changes to the CMapModeDlg class declaration, 364

31.3. The CMapModeDlg:: OnColor member function, 365

31.4. Changing the color of a dialog box by handling WM_CTLCOLOR, 366

31.5. Changes to the CDCTestView class declaration, 367

31.6. The CDCTestView constructor, 368

31.7. OnViewMapMode function, 368

31.8. The OnDraw member function modified to use brushes, 369

32.1. Two different ways to create a CFont object, 377

32.2. Using a LOGFONT structure to create fonts, 378

32.3. Initialize the m_logFont variable, 379

32.4. The CDCTestView:: OnViewFont member function, 380

32.5. Displaying a rotating text message using a LOGFONT, 380-381

33.1. Additions to the CAboutDlg class declaration, 388

33.2. The AboutDlg:: OnInitDialog member function, 388

33.3. Using the CAboutDlg class destructor to destroy the previously loaded icons, 389

34.1. Changing the cursor during WM_SETCURSOR, 394

34.2 Conditionally changing the cursor during WM_SETCURSOR, 394

34.3. Using a standard Windows cursor, 395-396

34.4. Modifying OnInitDialog and OnTimer to use the hourglass cursor, 396

34.5. Source code used to form a clipping region for the cursor, 397

35.1. A simple OnDraw function that works for the screen and printer, 402

35.2. New CPrintView member variables, 406

35.3. Allocating new fonts in the OnBeginPrinting function, 406

35.4. Releasing resources in the OnEndPrinting function, 407

35.5. Printing a header and text using the OnPrint function, 407-408

35.6. The OnPrepareDC function, 408

36.1. Creating a property sheet in the CMainFrame::OnViewNames function, 417

36.2. Additional #include statements for MainFrm.cpp, 418

36.3. Handling edit control updates in the CNamePage class, 418

36.4. Handling check button updates in the CHobbyPage class, 418-419

36.5. The CHobbyPage:: OnApply member function, 419

37.1. The CFormatDlg:: OnColor member function, 429

37.2. Changes to the CFormatDlg class declaration, 429

37.3. The CRichTextView:: OnRButtonUp member function, 430

38.1. The CNumericEdit:: OnChar function, 437

38.2. Adding a CNumericEdit member variable to CSubclassDlg, 438

38.3. Subclassing an edit control in OnInitDialog, 438

38.4. Creating a CSubclassDlg object, 439

39.1. The CListItem structure, 447

39.2. Additions to the COwnDrawDlg:: OnInitDialog function, 447-448

39.3. The COwnDrawDlg:: OnDrawItem function, 448-449

39.4. The COwnDrawDlg:: DrawCheckBox function, 451

39.5. The OnDeleteItem member function, 451

40.1. Modifications to the CCustomCtrlDlg class declaration, 459

40.2. Initializing the OLE grid control in OnInitDialog, 460

40.3. Handling a mouse click event from the OLE grid control, 460-461

40.4. Recalculating the contents of the OLE grid control, 462

41.1. Using the CArchive::IsStoring function to determine the serialization direction, 468

41.2. The CUser class declaration, 469

41.3. The CUser member functions, 470

41.4. The CUser::Serialize member function, 471

41.5. The SerializeElements function, 472

42.1. Adding a CArray member variable to the CCustomersDoc class, 478

42.2. Changes to the CustomersDoc.h header file, 478

42.3. Adding a new CUser object to the document class, 480

42.4. Document class member functions used for data access, 480

42.5. Serializing the contents of the document class, 481

42.6. #include statements used by the CCustomersDoc class, 481

42.7. Using OnDraw to display the current document's contents, 481-482

42.8. Invalidating the view during OnUpdate, 482

lists, 126-128

LoadBitmap function, 232-234

LoadIcon function, 385

loading documents (serialization), 477

LoadToolbar function, 275

local scope, 76-77

LOGFONT structure, 378-379

logical brushes, 362-363

long double data type, 40

long int data type, 40

loops, 54-56

lstrlen function, 69

M

macros, 105-108, 469-470

main function, 26-27, 44

manually creating dialog box resources, 182

map mode dialog boxes, 343-344, 354-355, 364-366

MAPI (Messaging Application Programming Interface), 6

mapping modes, device contexts, 341-342

maps (collections), 126, 130-131

math.h, 45

mathematical operators, 29-30

MDI (Multiple Document Interface), 292, 312-313

member functions, *see* **functions**

member variables, 199-200, 212-214

memory
addresses, 82
device contexts, 234, 338
leaks, MFC class library objects, 109-110

menu items
adding
to CDCTestView class, 344-345, 380
to document classes, 479-481
to menus, 170-173, 188-189
properties, 172
static split views, 332-333
views, 318-319

menu resources, 170-174

menus, 167-176
adding menu items, 170-173, 188-189
creating for views, 317

message boxes, 178-180

message maps, 161

messages (Windows), 144, 148, 155-159
categories, 159
handling, 157-162
menus, 169-170
message maps, 161
MouseTst program, 162-165
queues, 157
receiving, Apply button (property sheet sample project), 419
window procedures, 434
WM_CTLCOLOR message, 366-367
WM_SETCURSOR message, 393-394
see also handling messages (Windows)

methods (OLE controls), 455

MFC (Microsoft Foundation Classes), 5-6, 31-33, 144-149
base classes, 103-111
collections, 125-131
configuring projects, 105

CString class, 70-71
device contexts, 339
diagnostic features, 108
Document/View architecture, 291-299
Dump function, 108-109
memory leaks of objects, 109-110
message routing for menus, 169-170
printing functions, 401-408
projects, creating, 18-19
serialization classes, 467-468

Microsoft Developer Network (MSDN), integrating with Developer Studio, 9

Microsoft FORTRAN Power Station, integrating with Developer Studio, 9

mnemonics (menus), 168

modal dialog boxes, 177, 179

modal property sheets, 413

modeless dialog boxes, 179

Modern font family, 372

monochrome icons, 384

MouseTst program, 162-165

MoveWindow function, 110

multiple document templates, creating, 315-316

multiple views, 311-322

multiple-line edit controls, 205

multiplication operator (*), 29

N

name lookup (variables), 81

Name page (property sheet sample project), creating, 414-415

naming conventions, 41-43

nested menus, 168

New command (File menu), 12, 24-25, 33

new operator, 86-88

New Project Workspace dialog box, 18

New Source File icon (toolbar), 12, 25

not equal to operator (!=), 30

not operator (!), 30

null statements, 28

O

Object Linking and Embedding, *see* **OLE controls**

object-oriented programming, 91-102
classes, 57-60, 93
MFC programs, 31-33

objects, 118-121
collections, 125-131
creating at runtime, 107-108
destroying, exception handling, 139
persistent objects, 465-466
serialization, 465-478

OK button, 199

OLE controls, 6, 453-462

OLE ControlWizard, 5

OnApply function, 412, 419

OnBeginPrinting function, 403-406

OnCancel function, 413

OnCompareItem function, 445

OnDeleteItem function, 445-446, 451-452

OnDraw function, 314-315, 340, 380-381, 402, 481-482

OnDrawItem function, 443-444, 448-450

OnEditUser function, 480

OnEndPrinting function, 403, 405, 407

OnInitialUpdate function, 308, 320-322

OnKillActive function, 412

online help systems, 4, 15-18

OnMeasureItem function, 444-445

OnNewDocument function, 296, 475

OnOK function, 413

OnOpenDocument function, 475-477

OnPrepareDC function, 403, 405, 408
OnPreparePrinting function, 403-404
OnPrint function, 403, 405, 407-408
OnQueryCancel function, 412
OnReset function, 413
OnSetActive function, 413
OnUpdate function, 320-322, 482
OnUpdateTimer function, 270
OnViewMapMode function, 368
Open command (File menu), 14
opening
   menu resources, 170-171
   source files, 14
operators
   address-of operator (&), 83
   assignment operator (=), 29, 43
   bitwise AND operator (&=), 310
   bitwise OR operator (|), 181
   compound assignment operators, 66
   delete operator, 86-88
   dynamic_cast operator, 135-136
   extraction operator (>>), 467-469
   indirection operator (*), 83-85
   insertion operator (<<), 27, 467-469
   inversion operator (~), 310
   mathematical operators, 29-30
   new operator, 86-88
   equality operator (= =), 30, 51
   reference operator (&), 85
   relational operators, 30-31
   sizeof operator, 41, 82-83
orientation (font attributes), 376

output
   device contexts, 337-346
   font attributes, 374-375
   iostream output (<<), 27, 467
overlaid images, 235, 239-240
overloaded functions, 72
overriding Serialize member function, 470-471
owner-drawn controls, 194, 441-452

P

paragraph formatting (rich edit controls), 425-426
parameters
   arrays as function parameters, 66-67
   const function parameters, 86
   templates, 114
parentheses ( ), 30
partial_sort algorithms, 121
Paste command (keyboard shortcuts), 14
pattern brushes, 360
pattern styles (geometric pens), 350
pens, 347-357
persistent classes, 469-470
persistent objects, 465-466
pitch (fonts), 371, 375-376
pointers, 82-88
   base classes, 97-98, 110-111
   casting (RTTI), 134-136
   derived classes, 96
   document pointers, retrieving, 299
polymorphism, 72
pop-up menus, 167-168, 173-176
POSITION variables, 128
precedence, mathematical operators, 30
prefixes for Windows messages, 159
preprocessor directives, 26

preventing resizing of form views, 309-310
printer device contexts, 338
printing, 401-408
private keyword, 58
programs
   building, 10, 22-23
   console mode, 21-27
   CtrlBar sample program, 266, 272-277
   customizing AppWizard programs, 152-153
   DCTest program, 343-346, 354-357, 364-369, 386-388
   editing icons, 386
   exception handling, 136-140
   executing, 26
   execution flow, 49-56
   Hello World program, 25-27, 31-33
   MFC programs, 31-33
   MouseTst program, 162-165
   object-oriented programming, 91-102
   printing, 401-408
   source files, creating, 25-26
   testing, 108
   Windows programs, 143-149, 155-161, 167-189
progress controls, 261-263
Project Workspace command (View menu), 25
projects
   adding
      bitmaps, 232-233
      form views, 303-306
      icons, 385
   compiling via AppWizard, 19-20
   configuring to use MFC class library, 105
   creating, 18-19, 23-25, 147
   dialog box-based projects, 195-203
   executing, 20

property sheet sample project, 414-419

SDI test projects, building, 207

properties
button controls, 198-199
combo boxes, 225
dialog boxes, 184-188
edit controls, 208-209
list boxes, 219-220
list view controls, 280-281
menu items, 172
progress controls, 261-262
slider controls, 260-261
tree view controls, 248-249
up-down controls, 257

property pages/sheets, 409-419

protected keyword, 96

prototypes, declaring functions, 44-45

public keyword, 58

pure virtual functions, 99-100

pushbuttons, *see* **buttons**

Q–R

queues (Windows messages), 157

radio buttons, 193-194
raising exceptions, 137-139
ranges (up-down controls), 258-259
raster fonts, 372
rbegin function, 121
readme.txt, 152
recalculating grid control contents, 462
Redo command (keyboard shortcuts), 14
reference operator (&), 85
references, 85-86
relational operators, 30-31
rend function, 121
report view (list view controls), 283-284
ResetContent function, 222

resizing form views, preventing, 309-310
Resource command (Insert menu), 173, 232, 385
resource editors (Developer Studio), 4
resource strings (document templates), 317
ResourceView tab (Project Workspace window), 19
retrieving
document pointers, 299
icons from image lists, 386
return statements, 27
return values (functions), 47
reverse iterators, 120-121
reversing up-down control ranges, 258-259
rich edit controls, 421-431
Roman font family, 372
rotating text, 380-381
RTF (rich text formatting), 422
RTTI (Run Time Type Information), 133-136

S

sans serif fonts, 372
Save As command (File menu), 13
Save command (File menu), 13
saving
documents (serialization), 475-476
source files, 13
scaleable fonts, 373
schema numbers, 470
scope, 75-79
Script font family, 372
scroll views, 302-303, 325-327
SDI (Single Document Interface), 151-152, 207, 292
Search command (Help menu), 17
searching strings (CString class), 71
selecting
current selection (combo boxes), 227

GDI objects for device contexts, 340-341
selection statements (execution flow), 50-53
self-drawn controls, 442
semicolons (;), 27-28
sequence statements (execution flow), 54-56
sequences, 119
serialization, 465-478
Serialize member function, overriding, 470-471
serif fonts, 372
SetAt function, 71
SetButtons function, 275
SetFont function, 111
SetImageList function, 282
SetModifed function, 418-419
SetOverlayImage function, 239
SetPaneInfo function, 267
SetParaFormat function, 425-426
SetRange function, 258
SetSelectionCharFormat function, 423-424
Settings command (Build menu), 33
setup wizard, 7-8
SetWindowLong function, 284
SetWindowText function, 110, 201-202
shared resources, adding to views, 316-317
short int data type, 40
ShowWindow function, 110, 202-203
simple combo boxes, 224
single-line edit controls, 205
sizeof operator, 41, 82-83
sizing form views to dialog resources, 308-309
slider controls, 259-263
small icons, 384
Smalltalk, compared to Visual C++, 22
smart indenting, 13
solid brushes, 360
sorting algorithms, 121

source files, 12-14, 25-26
spin controls, 255-259
split views, 323-333
stable_sort algorithm, 121
stacks, CStack template class, 114-117
standard cursors, 395-396
standard pushbutton layouts in dialog boxes, 199
Standard Template Library (STL), 6, 9, 118-122
starting
    debugger, 20
    Developer Studio, 9
statement blocks, 27
statements, 26-31, 50-53, 78
static class members, 79
static split views, 323, 329-333
static text control, adding to dialog boxes, 185-186
static variables, 81
status bars, 265-270
stdafx.cpp, 152
stdafx.h, 152
stock brushes, 360
stock pens, 352-353
storage requirements
    data types, 41
    sizeof operator, 82-83
strcpy function, 69-70
strings, 68-71
    adding
        to combo boxes, 225-227
        to list boxes, 221-222
    resource strings, document templates, 317
strlen function, 68-69
structures, 56-57
styles
    defining for status bars, 269
    hatch brushes, 361
    pens, 349-350
    tree view controls, 246-247
subclassing controls, 95, 433-439
subtraction operator (-), 29
superclassing controls, 433, 435

Swiss font family, 372
switch statements, 52-53
switching
    list view control views, 284, 288-289
    to hourglass cursors, 396-397
syntax highlighting, 13

T

tab order (button controls), 203-204
tabbed dialog boxes, 409-419
templates, 113-117
    document templates, 293-295, 315-317
    Standard Template Library (STL), 6, 9
terminate function, 139
test projects, building, 207
testing
    function return values, 137
    programs, 108
text
    adding
        to combo boxes, 225-227
        to list boxes, 221-222
    edit controls, 205-215
    rotating, 380-381
this keyword, 149
throwing exceptions, 137-139
tilde (~), 60, 310
timers (status bars), 269-270
toolbar icons
    Build, 26, 33
    Go, 110
    New Source File, 12, 25
    Open, 14
    Save, 13
toolbars, 265, 274-277
trackbar controls, 259-263
transparent images, 235, 238-239
trapping messages (pop-up menus), 174-176
tree view controls, 243-254
TrueType fonts, 372
try keyword, 138

twips, 405
type safety (variables), 38-39
typedef keyword, 114
typeface names (font attributes), 377

U

unary operators, 83
Undo command (keyboard shortcuts), 14
undocking/docking windows, 16
unsigned variables, 40-41
up-down controls, 255-259
UpdateAllViews function, 296
updating
    multiple views, 319-320
    progress controls via slider controls, 262-263
user input (dialog boxes), 178-179

V

validating data, 211-215
variable pitch fonts, 371
variables, 37-43, 75-88
    Boolean variables, 30
    declaring, 28, 38
    member variables, 199-200, 212-214
    POSITION variables, 128
    structures, 56-57
VBX control specification, 453-454
vector fonts, 372
vectors, 119-120
VERIFY macro, 108
view class, 292
View menu commands (Project Workspace), 25
views, 5
    CTreeView class, 245-247
    form views, 301-310
    list view controls, 279-289
    modifying in documents, 481-482

multiple views, 311-322
retrieving document
  pointers, 299
scroll views, 302-303,
  325-327
split views, 323-333
virtual destructors, 100-102
virtual functions, 98-100
virtual keyword, 98
Visual C++
  advantages, 6
  building programs, 10, 22-23
  compared to BASIC, 22
  compared to Smalltalk, 22
  definition, 3-6
  Developer Studio, 4-5
  documentation, 7
  InfoViewer, 15-18
  installing, 7-9
  InstallShield, 9
  MFC (Microsoft Foundation
    Classes), 5-6
  Standard Template Library
    (STL), 6, 9, 118-122
  Windows programs, 143-144
**Visual Source Safe, integrating
  with Developer Studio, 9**
**Visual Test, integrating with
  Developer Studio, 9**
**vtabl (virtual function
  table), 98**

W–Z

weights (font attributes), 376
while loops, 54
**width/height (font attributes),
  373-374**

**window procedures,
  158-159, 434**
Windows
  creating application
    projects, 147
  messages, *see* messages
    (Windows)
  MFC programs, 31-33
  standard cursors, 395-396
windows
  adding status bars, 268-269
  dockable windows, 16
  split views, 323-333
**Windows 95 Explorer
  icons, 384**
**Windows Open System
  Architecture (WOSA), 6**
Windows programs, 143-144
  device contexts, 148-149
  dialog boxes, 177-189
  menus, 167-176
  message maps, 161
  message queues, 157
  printing, 401-408
  resources, 181-182
wizards
  AppWizard, 5, 18-20, 144,
    149-153
    *creating dialog box-based
      projects, 195-196*
    *Document/View architec-
      ture, 293-295*
  ClassWizard, 5, 144,
    160-164
    *configuring OLE
      controls, 456*
    *Document/View architec-
      ture, 295-296*

device context support,
  339-340
OLE ControlWizard, 5
setup wizard, 7-8
**WM_COMPAREITEM
  message, 445**
**WM_CTLCOLOR message,
  366-367**
**WM_DELETEITEM message,
  445-446**
**WM_DRAWITEM message,
  443-444**
**WM_INITDIALOG message,
  187-188**
**WM_LBUTTONDBLCLK
  message, 162**
**WM_LBUTTONDOWN
  message, 157, 162**
**WM_MEASUREITEM
  message, 444-445**
**WM_MOUSEMOVE
  message, 157**
**WM_NCMOUSEMOVE
  message, 157**
**WM_PAINT message,
  148, 163**
**WM_RBUTTONDBLCLK
  message, 162**
**WM_RBUTTONDOWN
  message, 157, 162**
**WM_SETCURSOR message,
  393-394**

zero-based indexes, 218

Add to Your Sams Library Today with the Best Books for Programming, Operating Systems, and New Technologies

The easiest way to order is to pick up the phone and call
1-800-428-5331
between 9:00 a.m. and 5:00 p.m. EST.
For faster service please have your credit card available.

ISBN	Quantity	Description of Item	Unit Cost	Total Cost
0-672-30602-6		Programming Windows 95 Unleashed (Book/CD)	$49.99	
0-672-30474-0		Windows 95 Unleashed (Book/CD)	$35.00	
0-672-30685-9		Windows NT 3.5 Unleashed	$39.99	
0-672-30462-7		Teach Yourself MFC in 21 Days	$29.99	
0-672-30568-2		Teach Yourself OLE Programming in 21 Days (Book/CD)	$39.99	
0-672-30619-0		Real World Programming with Visual Basic (Book/CD)	$45.00	
0-672-30594-1		Programming WinSock (Book/Disk)	$35.00	
0-672-30655-7		Developing Your Own 32-Bit Operating System (Book/CD)	$49.99	
0-672-30593-3		Develop a Professional Visual C++ Application in 21 Days (Book/CD)	$35.00	
0-672-30737-5		World Wide Web Unleashed, 2E	$39.99	
0-672-30765-0		Navigating the Internet with Windows 95	$25.00	

❏ 3 ½" Disk

❏ 5 ¼" Disk

Shipping and Handling: See information below.		
TOTAL		

Shipping and Handling: $4.00 for the first book, and $1.75 for each additional book. Floppy disk: add $1.75 for shipping and handling. If you need to have it NOW, we can ship product to you in 24 hours for an additional charge of approximately $18.00, and you will receive your item overnight or in two days. Overseas shipping and handling adds $2.00 per book and $8.00 for up to three disks. Prices subject to change. Call for availability and pricing information on latest editions.

201 W. 103rd Street, Indianapolis, Indiana 46290

1-800-428-5331 — Orders   1-800-835-3202 — FAX   1-800-858-7674 — Customer Service

Book ISBN 0-672-30787-1

PLUG YOURSELF INTO...

MACMILLAN INFORMATION SUPERLIBRARY™

que
SAMS PUBLISHING
Hayden Books
que COLLEGE
NRP
alpha books
Brady
ADOBE PRESS

THE MACMILLAN INFORMATION SUPERLIBRARY™

Free information and vast computer resources from the world's leading computer book publisher—online!

FIND THE BOOKS THAT ARE RIGHT FOR YOU!

A complete online catalog, plus sample chapters and tables of contents give you an in-depth look at *all* of our books, including hard-to-find titles. It's the best way to find the books you need!

- **STAY INFORMED** with the latest computer industry news through our online newsletter, press releases, and customized Information SuperLibrary Reports.

- **GET FAST ANSWERS** to your questions about MCP books and software.

- **VISIT** our online bookstore for the latest information and editions!

- **COMMUNICATE** with our expert authors through e-mail and conferences.

- **DOWNLOAD SOFTWARE** from the immense MCP library:
  - Source code and files from MCP books
  - The best shareware, freeware, and demos

- **DISCOVER HOT SPOTS** on other parts of the Internet.

- **WIN BOOKS** in ongoing contests and giveaways!

TO PLUG INTO MCP: →

GOPHER: gopher.mcp.com
FTP: ftp.mcp.com

WORLD WIDE WEB: http://www.mcp.com

Home Page   What's New   Bookstore   Reference Desk   Software Library   Macmillan Overview   Talk to Us